BASIC COMPUTER PROGRAMMING

(Covers BASICA & GW BASIC)

Er. V.K. Jain
B.E. (E), M.Tech. (Applied Electronics)
FIE, FIETE, MISHRAE, Chartered Engineer
Executive Engineer
EXDII CPWD New Delhi-110001

PUSTAK MAHAL®

Administrative office and sale centre

J-3/16 , Daryaganj, New Delhi-110002
☎ 23276539, 23272783, 23272784 • *Fax:* 011-23260518
E-mail: info@pustakmahal.com • *Website:* www.pustakmahal.com

Branches

Bengaluru: ☎ 080-22234025 • *Telefax:* 080-22240209
E-mail: pustakmahalblr@gmail.com
Mumbai: ☎ 022-22010941, 022-22053387
E-mail: unicornbooksmumbai@gmail.com
Patna: ☎ 0612-3294193 • *Telefax:* 0612-2302719
E-mail: rapidexptn@gmail.com

ISBN 978-81-223-0637-8

Edition: 2016

Price : ₹ 165/-

Printed at : AR Emm International, Delhi

Contents

Chapter 1
The Historical Evolution of Computer 7
Introduction 7
1.1 Abacus 7
1.2 Analog Machines & Napier's Bones 7
1.3 Odometer (Speedometer) and Logarithm 8
1.4 Blaise Pascal and his Mechanical Calculator 9
1.5 Charles Babbage: Differential Engine 10
1.6 Herman Hollerith: The Punched Card 11
1.7 Electrical Machines 12
1.8 Howard Aikens and IBM Mark I 12
1.9 Computer Generations 13
1.10 The Ages of Computeronics 18
1.11 Computer Dynasty 18
1.12 Classification Based on Memory Size 20
1.13 Special Purpose Computers 24
1.14 Difference between a Computer and a Calculator 25

Chapter 2
Computer: Its Characteristics, Anatomy and Architecture 30
2.1 What is a Computer? 30
2.2 The Characteristics of a Computer 30
2.3 Capabilities of Computers 31
2.4 Limitations of Computers 33
2.5 Brain versus Computer 33
2.6 Functioning of a Computer 33
2.7 Anatomy of Computer 34
2.8 Stored Program Concept 39
2.9 Types of Memory 40
2.10 Computer Programming 41
2.11 The Management of the Computer 42
2.12 Advantage of Packages 44

Chapter 3
Flow Charts 46
3.1 Flow Charts 46
3.2 Flow Chart Symbols 46
3.3 Rules for Making a Flow Chart 47
3.4 Structured Programming 48
3.5 Development of a Program by Flow Charts 50

Chapter 4
Getting Started With BASIC 51
4.1 Starting BASIC 51
4.2 Direct and Indirect modes 52
4.3 Labels 53
4.4 A Longer Program 53
4.5 Lines and Statements 55

Chapter 5
Basic Arithmetic Statement 57
5.1 Doing Arithmetic 57
5.2 Arithmetic Operator 57
5.3 Use of Parenthesis 57
5.4 Hierarchy of Arithmetic Operators 58
5.5 Integer Division 59
5.6 Assignment Statements 59
5.7 The Variable Counter Technique 61
5.8 Self Replacement Technique 61
5.9 Writing Assignment Statements 61
5.10 Rules for Writing Arithmetic Expressions in BASIC 62

Chapter 6
The Input Statement 68
6.1 Modes of BASIC Operation 68
6.2 The INPUT Statement 68
6.3 Using Input Statement 68
6.4 Printing Prompts for the User 70
6.5 Reading Data from Data Statement 73
6.6 Multiple READ- DATA Statement 75
6.7 Restore Statement 77
6.8 Comparing LET, INPUT, and READ 77

Chapter 7
Putting DATA Out of Computers 88
7.1 Outputting the Data: The PRINT Statement 88
7.2 Print Zones and Commas 89
7.3 Formatting the Output: The Comma Control 90
7.4 Making Tables: The TAB Function 92
7.5 The PRINT USING Statement 95
7.6 LPRINT Statement 99
7.7 The WRITE Statement: 100

Chapter 8
Control Statements 105
8.1 Linear Programming 105
8.2 Structured Programming 105
8.3 The Control Statement 106
8.4 The Unconditional Transfer: The GOTO Statement 106
8.5 Introduction to Loops 110
8.6 Loop Control 111
8.7 Loop Control Variable in Count loop 114
8.8 The FOR/NEXT Loop. 116
8.9 Rules for Constructing FOR/NEXT Loops 117
8.10 Flowcharting the FOR/NEXT Loop 118
8.11 Advantages of Using the FOR/NEXT Loop 118
8.12 Comparison of FOR/NEXT and IF/THEN LOOPS 119
8.13 Nested FOR/NEXT Loops in BASIC 119
8.14 The STOP Statement 126
8.15 The WHILE/WEND Loop 127

Chapter 9
The Conditional Statements 136
9.1 Relational Operators 136

9.2 Single Alternative : IF/THEN (or IF/GOTO) 137
9.3 Double Alternative : IF/THEN/ELSE 140
9.4 Nested IF Statements 141
9.5 Combination of GOTO and IF/THEN 142
9.6 Computed GOTO Statement (ON/GOTO statement): Multiple Branching 143
9.7 Menus 147

Chapter 10
Some Programming Applications 150
Problem 10.1 Temperature Conversion Program 150
Problem 10.2 Calculating Circumference and Area of a Circle 152
Problem 10.3 Computing Average of Three Test Scores 153
Problem 10.4: A wage Computing Program 154
Problem:10.5 Monthly Pay Bills 160
Problem 10.6 Evaluating an Exponential Series 162
Problem 10.7 Evaluation of Cos X 163
Example 10.8 Sun - Sign Evaluator 165

Chapter 11
Arrays 167
11.1 Array 167
11.2 The DIM Statement 168
11.3 One-Dimensional Arrays 169
11.4 Reading Data to an Array 169
11.5 Displaying the Contents of an Array. 170
11.6 Deleting an Array: The ERASE statement 173
11.7 OPTION BASE Statement 175
11.8 Copying an Array in Reverse Order 175
11.9 Two-Dimensional Arrays (Tables) 176
11.10 Reading and Displaying Two-Dimensional Arrays 177
11.11 Transposing the Arrays: 182
11.12 Transposing the Matrix by Nested FOR/NEXT Loops 182
11.13 Sorting Arrays 183
11.14 Sorting Arrays-the Bubble Sort 183
11.15 Some Advantages of Using Arrays 187

Chapter 12
Library and User Defined Functions 196
12.1 Functions and Their Types 196
12.2 Argument of a Function: 196
12.3 Mathematical (or numeric) functions: 197
12.4 The ABS function 198
12.5 DIV Function 198
12.6 MOD Function 198
12.7 The INT function 198
12.8 Trignometric Functions: 199
12.9 Rounding Off Numbers: 200
12.10 String Functions 200
12.11 User Defined Functions 204
12.12 Use of DEF FN in Strings: 206
12.13 Use of DEF FN in Creating New Mathematical Functions 206
12.14 Rules for Writing User-defined Functions: 207

Chapter 13
Subroutines 213
13.1 Structured Programming 213
13.2 The GOSUB Statement 213
13.3 The RETURN Statement 214
13.4 Example of Subroutine Usage 214
13.5 Advantages of Sub-Routines 216
13.6 The ON/GOSUB Statement 216
13.7 Example on Sub-routine Usage 218

Chapter 14
Sequential Files 224
14.1 Data File Types 224
14.2 Creating a Sequential File 224
14.3 OPEN Statement 224
14.4 File Numbers : IF Option 226
14.5 CLOSE Statement 227
14.6 PRINT# Statement 229
14.7 WRITE# Statement 231
14.8 PRINT# USING Statement 232
14.9 INPUT# Statement 233
14.10 INPUT$ Function 234
14.11 EOF Function 235
14.12 LOC Function 235
14.13 LOF Function 236
14.14 Sequential File Processing 236
14.15 Sequential File Maintenance 237
14.16 Deleting a Sequential File 238
14.17 Inserting a Record 240
14.18 Modifying or Upgrading a Record 240

Chapter 15
System Commands 244
15.1 System Command 244
15.2 The command AUTO 244
15.3 The command LOAD 245
15.4. The command SAVE 246
15.5. The command RUN 247
15.6. The command EDIT 248
15.7 The command CLS 248
15.8 The command CONT 248
15.9 The command LIST 249
15.10 The command DELETE 250
15.11 The command KILL 250
15.12 The command NEW 251
15.13 The command SYSTEM 251

Chapter 16
Programming Design and Problem Solving 252
16.1 Characteristics of a Good Program 252
16.2 Program Design 254
16.3 Program Errors 261
16.4 Debugging 262
16.5 Testing 263

The Historical Evolution of Computer

Introduction

The evolution of computer has passed through a number of stages before it reached the present state of development. In fact, the development of the first calculating device named Abacus dates back to 3000 B.C. From the Abacus to the microcomputer, the counting systems have undergone a tremendous change. The efforts are still continuing to make the machine more and more versatile. This chapter describes in brief the historical evolution of the computer, and in detail the modern computers as regards their types, applications, relative merits, and demerits, etc.

1.1 Abacus

The stone age man used pebbles for counting cattle. Later on, when man became more civilized, abacus (Fig. 1.1) came into use. Abacus seems to be the earliest calculating machine, which was developed by Chinese 3000 years ago. Interestingly enough, abacus is still being used in Russia, Japan, Far East and even in India for primary education. It consists of a rectangular wooden frame with horizontal rods which carry round beads. Counting is done by shifting the beads from one side to another. Each of the two beads on the left-hand side of the cross bar has a value of five, and each of the five beads on the right-hand side of the cross bar has a value of one. The topmost line represents the unit's digit, the second line the ten's digit, the third line the hundred's digit, and so on. Numbers are entered in reverse order, starting from top to bottom. In the figure, a decimal number 765,084 has been entered. The abacus is cleared, or set to zero by moving all beads away from the cross bar. Experienced users can calculate very quickly using the abacus. In 1946, a competition took place between a Japanese clerk Matsuzake, an abacus operator, and an American, using an electronic calculator. And surprisingly enough the Japanese won the competition.

1.2 Analog Machines & Napier's Bones

John Napier, the Scottish mathematician, devised a set of rods for use in calculations involving multiplications. These rods were carved from bones and, therefore, called Napier's Bones. Fig. 1.2. shows in the upper half Napier's Bones,

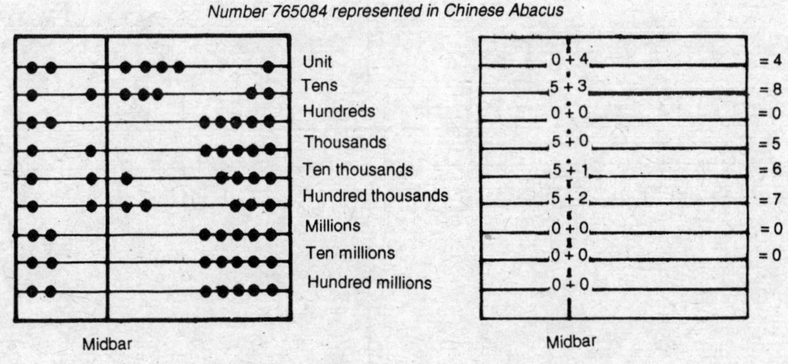

Figure 1.1 Calculations Using Abacus

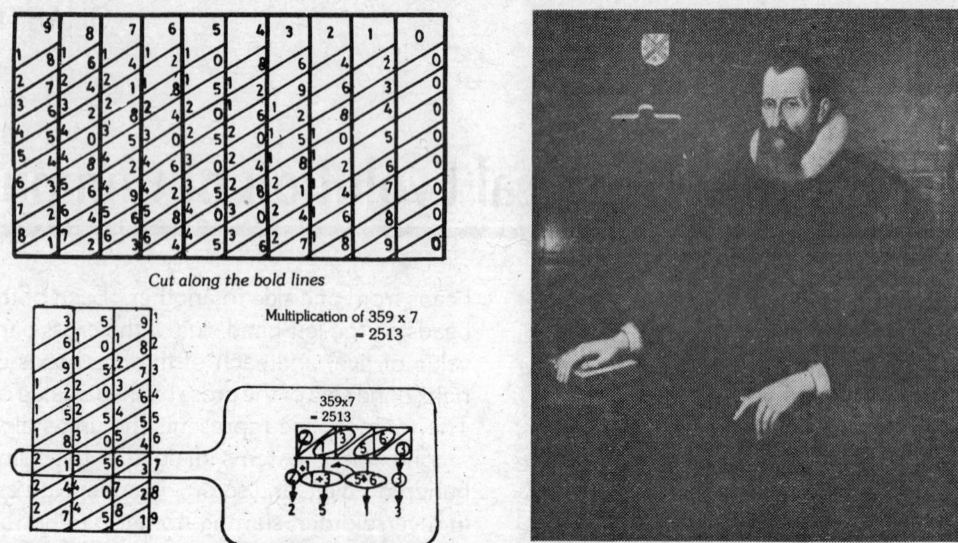

Fig. 1.2 Napier's Bone and Multiplication & John Napier

together with the method of calculation in its lower half.

1.3 Odometer (Speedometer) and Logarithm

Sometime later, the odometer (now called speedometer), was invented perhaps before the birth of Christ, which led to the development of mechanical adders and multipliers. In 1617, John Napier, the distinguished Scottish mathematician, developed the method of logarithm. Logarithmic tables actually represent analog computing technique. In this system, multiplications and divisions can be done by adding and subtracting not the numbers themselves, but with the help of related numbers known as logarithm. Logarithm is nothing but an application of indices. By the use of logarithms, arithmetical calculations regarding multiplications, divisions, square roots, and fractions can be easily simplified by referring to

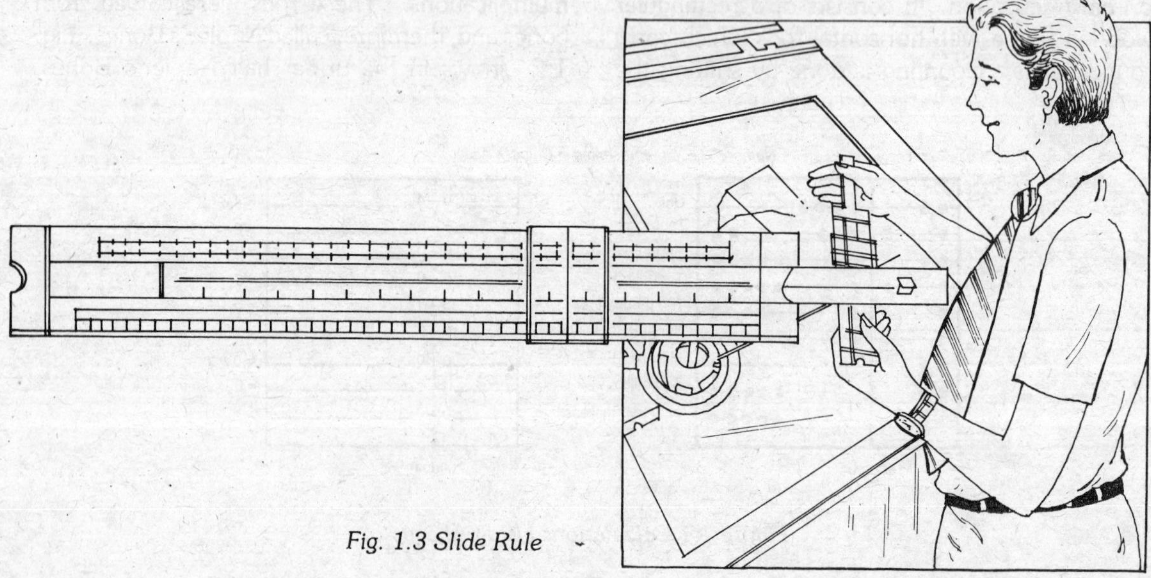

Fig. 1.3 Slide Rule

Figure 1.4 Blaise Pascal

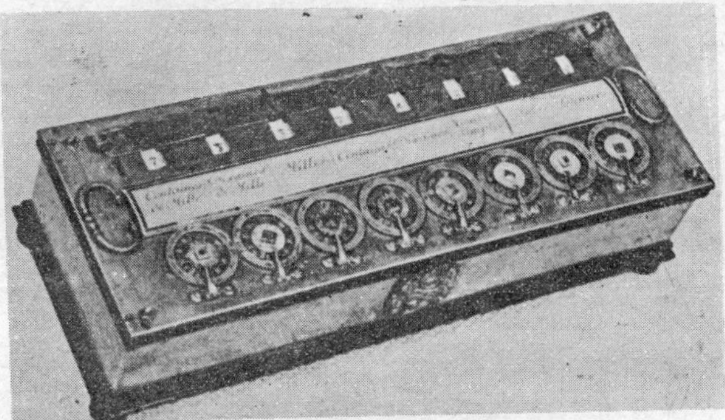

Figure 1.5 Calculating machine built by Blaise Pascal in 1642

the standard tables. If the square of 3 is nine, then 2 is the logarithm of 9 to the base 3. Normally, base 10 logarithm is used, in which case, since the square of 10 is 100, then 2 is the logarithm of 100 to the base 10. Similarly, since the cube of 10 is 1000, then 3 is the logarithm of 1000 to the base 10. In general, if

$b = a^m$ then

$m = \log_a b$

All engineering calculations were being done with the help of logarithm, until a device known as the slide-rule was developed in Germany. The slide-rule was developed in 1620, just three years after the invention of logarithms. William Oughtred invented the slide-rule, which is a calculating device that uses the principles of logarithms (Fig. 1.3). Slide-rule was taken over by pocket calculators of digital design in the start of the 1980s for office use. Another mechano-electrical device known as the FACIT desk calculator was in vogue in the sixties, which not only did the calculations but typed the result also.

1.4 Blaise Pascal and his Mechanical Calculator

The first mechanical calculating machine was made in 1642 by the great French mathematician and philosopher, Blaise Pascal (Fig.1.4). His machine was a simple calculator used for addition and subtraction purposes. Pascal invented the calculator at the age of 18 only to assist his father in tax calculations. His father was appointed as the Tax Superintendent of Royen. His job was back-breaking and he was never able to get to bed before 2 a.m. Blaise was highly motivated to ease his father with respect to endless computations. So he set himself on this task and within two years, he devised a working model which was patented in year 1645.

Figure 1.6 Replica of Mechanical Calculator of Leibnitz in 1671

Figure 1.7 Charles Babbage

Figure 1.8 Differential Engine of Babbage

The machine consisted of gears, wheels, and dials (Fig. 1.5). Each wheel had 10 segments like that of milometers or house energy meters. When one wheel completed a rotation, the next wheel moved by one segment. With this calculator, addition, and subtraction could be performed by dialling these series of wheels bearing the number 0 to 9 around their circumference. The machine was produced on a mass scale and became very popular. Even the Queen of Sweden could not resist ordering one piece for herself. This machine was later on modified by a German, Gottfried Leibnitz, in 1671, who invented a more complex reckoner using toothed wheels. This was the first machine to multiply and divide directly (Fig. 1.6).

1.5 Charles Babbage:

Differential Engine

Charles Babbage (1792-1871, Fig. 1.7), another genius in history of computing, made a machine called Differential Engine (Fig. 1.8) which could evaluate accurately algebraic expressions and mathematical tables correct upto 20 decimal places (20 digit accuracy). Later on, this genius was able to develop the Analytical Machine (Fig. 1.9), which was an automatic computing machine designed to do additions at the rate of 60 per minute and had memory also. Babbage could have designed a better machine during his life-time itself, but the contemporary technology could not assist and match his genius. This machine called analytical engine was never built, although he spent £17,000 on this project at that time. He was determined to add, to the arithmetic capability of the then existing calculators, the ability to store intermediate results for subsequent calculations.

Figure 1.9 Babbage's Analytical Engine

Figure 1.10 Jacquard Loom (French) using punched cards

It thus eliminates the job of copying and re-entering, and most importantly to enter data together with the sequence of operations to be performed on data (now we call it 'a program'), automatically from sets of cards that were compiled together. His idea of using cards was derived from the work of Joseph Jacquard (1752-1834) who in France used punched card (Jacquard's loop cards as shown in Fig. 1.10) to determine the threads to be selected in weaving patterns automatically. A hole in the card permitted a hooked wire containing a thread to enter the pattern, which the absence of a hole would correspondingly prevent. However, humanity had to wait for over a century to realize the significance of the machine which Babbage dreamt of.

1.6 Herman Hollerith: The Punched Card

The next major contribution to the development of computers came from Dr. Herman Hollerith (Figure 1.11) of the United States of America. He was working in USA Census Office during the time the census of 1880 was taken. The data was being compiled and analysed. Tabulation of census manually is a gigantic task for countries like India and the USA. The census is not merely a process of counting people, but also a process of collecting information about various socio-economic aspects which are helpful to the government in planning its priorities. But this data has to be analysed within a very short period so that it remains current and represents a correct cross-section of society. In this case, census analysis could not be completed until 1887, since the analysis process had taken a very long period. The Census Bureau of USA realised the situation in the year 1887 and decided to devise a speedy machine to complete the analysis. The bureau held a competition to find a way of dealing with the census more effectively. Hollerith won this competition by inventing a machine which used punched cards to store and tabulate census data. This machine could sense the punched holes, recognise the number and make the required calculations. This method played a magic role and the census of 1890 could be completed within just six weeks.

Punched card machines were very popular in the first four decades of this century and are even now a common medium for feeding information into a computer. Herman Hollerith then formed his

Figure 1.11 Dr. Herman Hollerith

own company, which later on was incorporated into International Business Machine Corporation (IBM), which is the largest computer manufacturing firm in the world even today. Hollerith's machine dominated the computer scene for the the next four decades but was very slow in action as compared to the first electronic calculator. His machine became obsolete in the fifth decade when electronics came to service of humanity. When the Englishman, Charles Babbage, was developing his differential machine, another Englishman, Lord Kelvin (William Thompson, 1824-1907), was working on analog computers. An analog computer is one in which the signals are analogous to the system under study. The first analog computer was built in the year 1876, but the first working model of analog computer came into the market only as late as in 1936.

1.7 Electrical Machines

During the later thirties and early forties of this century, various types of computers with very unusual names were built in Germany, UK, and USA. The progress in computer technology was abnormally accelerated during the second World War. Computers were used in military operations for breaking codes and for designing of aircraft. In 1936 Conrad Zuse, a young German engineer, started, to make a model mechanical computer Z1, which had a keyboard for putting the numbers into machine. It used the binary system, which enabled him to take advantage of Boole's system of logic. In Z2, he replaced the slow mechanical switches with electrical relays. He also speeded up the input by using 35 mm film with holes punched in it, just in the same manner as paper tapes developed later on. Unfortunately, Adolf Hitler did not take up his suggestions that these computers would be ideal for deciphering coded messages sent by enemy. Conrad Zuse also designed the Z3 and Z4, which got destroyed during bombing and therefore very little is known about them. This was a very unfortunate affair, but Zuse did not give up. He set up his own computer company, which was eventually bought up by Siemens in 1969. The British were not much behind. They built Colossus and used it for breaking the secret code generated by the German code generator known as Enigma. This was later on captured by the Polish secret service.

Figure 1.12 Howard Aikens

1.8 Howard Aikens and IBM Mark I

All the calculating machines invented hitherto were basically mechanical machines. The American multinational company IBM persuaded Howard Aikens (Fig. 1.12) and Grace Hopper of Harvard University, in 1930, to produce an electrically operated computer for general purpose. This computer was very unwieldy and had a monstrous shape, being about 15m long, having wiring of a length equal to the distance from New Delhi to Allahabad (about 800 km). This was called Mark-I and had thousands of electromagnetic relays and multiple number of components. Mark-I could come in actual shape only in 1948 and remained in use till 1959. Mark-I (Fig. 1.13) was the first computer in the real sense of the term i.e. one which could store a program of instructions.

Mark-I could multiply two twenty-digit numbers in about 5 seconds (this speed is much slower than that of a current pocket calculators) and made a lot of noise. It sounded like a room full of ladies knitting and chattering. Although this computer was faster than the machines made earlier but the problem of finding the fault or faulty relay was its main drawback. It actually proved to be very troublesome job for the inventor duo to trace the fault in Mark-I when it refused to function. Finally they caught the fault and the culprit. A moth got entrapped in between the contacts of one of the relays and hence the relay could not close properly. The happening was recorded in the log book like this "The MARK-I was debugged today". The word debugged was later on adopted as a standard

Figure 1.13 Harward University (Manchester) Mark-I (IBM)

term in computeronics. Debugging means to trace the errors in the program and to remove them from the language. In 1950, the Ferranti Mark-I (Fig. 1.14) based on Manchester (Harward) Mark-I was sold commercially in Europe.

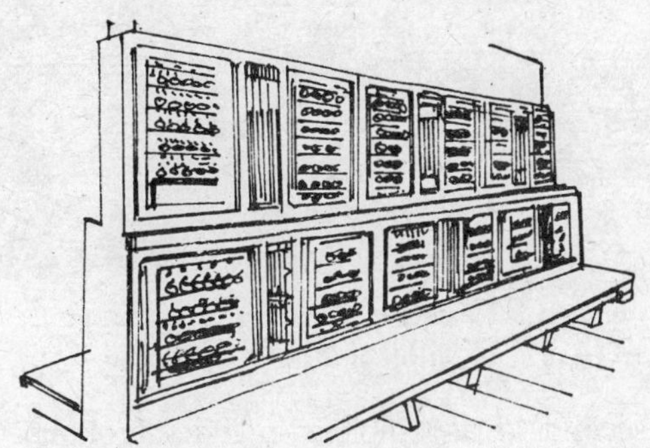

Figure 1.14 The Ferranti Mark-I (1950)

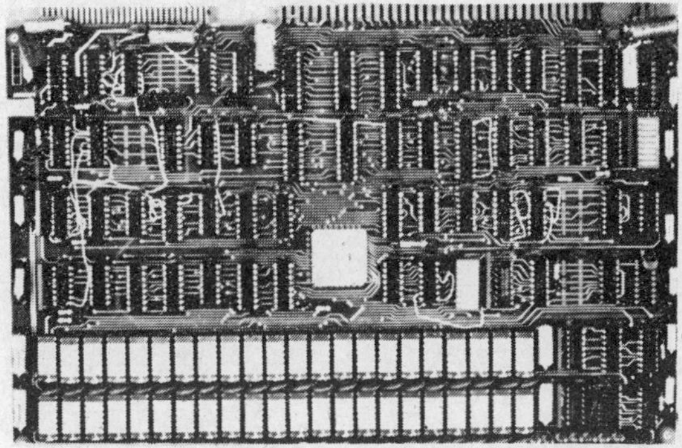

Figure 1.15 Integrated Circuit (3rd generation)

Humanity suffered a lot during the second World War, which resulted in colossal destruction. The reconstruction process could not have been accelerated, if electronic components like valves, rectifiers, etc. would not have been developed.

1.9 Computer Generations

The growth of computer after the end of the World War II was very rapid, but this development took place in five distinct phases known as computer generations. Like human generation gaps (in traditions, thinking and fashions), different computer generations are characterized by their technology of basic computing elements. The different basic elements are shown in Fig 1.15 to 1.17.

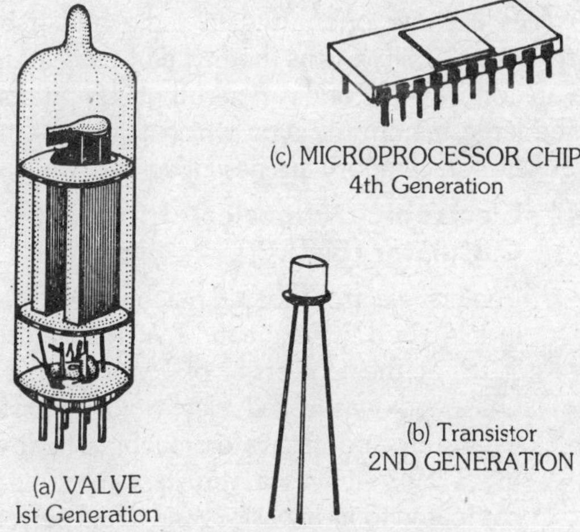

Figure 1.16 Basic Computing Elements

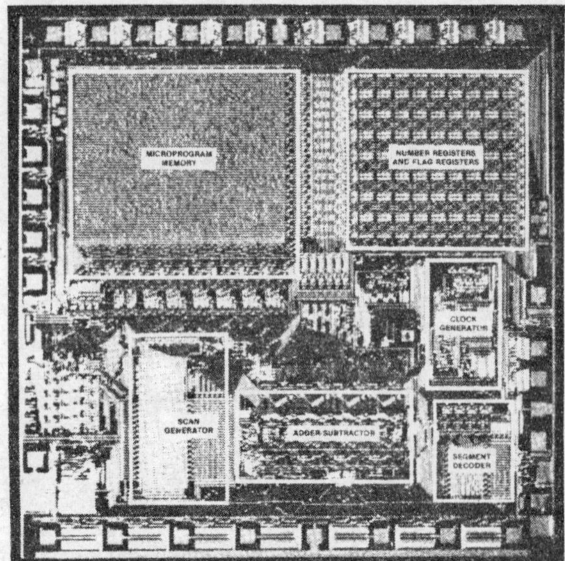

Figure 1.17 Microcomputer on a Chip

1. First generation: Thermionic Valves (1949)
2. Second generation: Transistors (1956)
3. Third generation: Integrated Circuits (1966) (Small and Medium Scale)
4. Fourth generation: Microprocessor Chips (1975)
5. Fifth generation: Large Scale Inference Systems (1980)

1.9.1 First Generation Computers: The first generation computers were the voluminous computers. These computers used electronic valves like the ones used in radio and hybrid television. ENIAC was the first computer of this category. ENIAC and various other computers of the large mainframe type which fall in the first generation category are described here.

(i) Electronic Numerical Integrator & Calculator (ENIAC)

The first electronic based machine was made in 1946 by J.P. Eckert and J.W. Mauchly (Fig 1.18) at the University of Pennsylvania of USA and was called electronic numerical integrator and calculator machine (ENIAC, Fig 1.19). It was a very fast machine as compared to its ancestors and could perform 5000 additions or 350 multiplications in one

Figure 1.18 J.P. Eckert and J.W. Mauchly: The inventor of first computer i.e. ENIAC

Figure 1.19 ENIAC (The first electronic digital computer)

second. It was completed in 1946. It contained 18,000 vacuum tubes, 70,000 resistors, 10,000 capacitors and 60,000 switches and occupied a two-room car garage. It consumed 150 KW of power and had to be water-cooled. It weighed 27 tonnes.

ENIAC was the beginning of the first generation computers. It was 1000 times faster than a machine using relays and could do those numerical calculations in two hours for which 100 engineers would have taken a year. This was based on the decimal system, rather than the binary system being used in all other computers. It did not have any memory system. ENIAC was designed to calculate the ballistic course of shells, a project founded by the US Army.

It was, in fact, more of an electronic calculator

rather than a computer, as understood presently. The computers which were built on the use of binary code and stored program suggested by Dr John Von Neumann in 1945 are illustrated below.

(ii) **Electronic Delay Storage Automatic Computer (EDSAC):** It was built by M.V. Wilkes at Cambridge University in 1949.

(iii) **Electronic Discrete Variable Automatic Computer (EDVAC):** It was built at Pennsylvania University and was completed in 1950.

(iv) **Lyons Electronics Office (LEO):** The first commercial computer was produced by M.V. Wilkes in 1951.

(v) **UNIVAC-I:** It was produced in 1951 by Universal Accounting Company (UNIVAC), set up by Eckert and Mauchly.

(vi) **IBM-701 and IBM-650:** These were introduced in 1953 and 1954 respectively by International Business Machines Corporation (IBM). The IBM-650 was the first modern digital computer produced on a mass scale.

The first generation computers had the following limitations:

1. Slow operating speed and restricted computing capacity.
2. High power consumption and short life-span.
3. Requirement of a very large space.
4. Limited programming capabilities.

1.9.2 Second Generation Computers: The Nobel Prize winners John Burdeen, Walter H. Brattain and William B. Shockley (Fig 1.20), jointly discovered the transistor (short name for transfer resistor) in the laboratories of Bell Telephone, the company that even today runs most of the American telephone systems. The invention of transistor (Fig 1.21) in 1948 led to the development of the second generation computers. Transistors replaced the valves completely as they were far more superior in performance on account of their miniature size, smaller power consumption and heat production rate. Although faster, smaller and more powerful, they were still expensive machines which only large commercial organizations could afford.

In such computers, transistor circuits called flip-flops formed the basis of internal binary operation and storage of binary coded data. The use of transistors reduced the size and manufacturing and running costs, and improved the reliability and processing power. Some of the second generation computers are:

Model	Size	Application
IBM 1620	Small	Scientific
IBM 1401	Small to Medium	Business
IBM 7094	Large	Scientific and Business
CDC 1604	Medium to Large	Scientific
CDC 3600	Large	Scientific
RCA 501	Medium	Business
UNIVAC 1108	Large	Scientific and Business

Leo Mark III, ATLAS, ICL 1901 were also in use.

Figure 1.20 The inventor-trio of Transistor John Burdeen, Walter H. Brattain and William B. Shockley

Figure 1.21 First Transistor

1.9.3 Third Generation Computers (Mini-Computers): In 1964, the third generation computers were introduced. These had integrated transistor circuits (IC) having higher speed, larger storage capacities, and lower prices. These computers were also called mini-computers. Instead of having one transistor of its own, several transistors could be integrated with the other components and sealed up in a small package. The package was called an *integrated circuit*, or, more popularly, a *chip*. The IC was invented by Jack Kilby at Texas Instruments in 1958.

These computers (released in 1964) used integrated circuits (ICs) built on wafer-thin slices of extremely purified silicon crystal called *chip*.

Some of the mainframe computers which belong to this generation are:

1. IBM-360 series
2. ICL-1900 series
3. IBM-370/168
4. ICL-2900
5. Honeywell-6000 series

The IBM-360/370 series is designed to meet the requirements of both scientific computing and business data processing.

The manufacture of mini-computer of the third generation began after the development of large-scale integration (LSI) and very large scale integration (VLSI) and microprocessor chips. The availability of LSI and VLSI chips has led to the production of a variety of mini-computers, some of which can out-perform mainframe computers of the 1960s. These are small-size, low-cost, large-memory, ultra fast computers which are proliferating at a surprising rate. These are mainly used for education and conducting different affairs of local governments, and small business. A few examples are:

1. ICL-2903 - manufactured by International Computers Limited (ICL)
2. CDC-1700 - manaufactured by Control Data Corporation
3. PDP-11/45

Figure 1.22 Clive Sinclair

1.9.4 Fourth Generation Computers: ICs which have the entire computer circuitry on a single silicon chip are called MICROPROCESSORS. The computers using these chips are called microcomputers or, in short, micros. These are, in fact, the scaled down versions of mini-computers.

Due to development of microprocessor chips in 1971 by Intel Corporation of USA, another breed of computers known as microcomputers came into existence in 1974 and became popular as the fourth generation of computers. These computers were introduced by a company known as MITS (Micro Instrumentation and Telemetry) of Albuquerque, New Mexico. *Altair* was the first microcomputer designed by Ed Robert, President of MITS. This was based on a modified version of the Intel 8008 microprocessor chip, known as 8080. A single chip cost was $350 in the year 1975. The Altair had a memory of 1k characters. By the end of 1976, there were about 6 firms making computers of the same kind. Some of them used the more powerful chip Z-80. Over 30,000 micros were sold in the year 1976. It was in early 1970 that an Englishman, Clive Sinclair (Fig 1.22), from Cambridge had designed the smallest and the cheapest calculator available at that time. With slight modifications, the Japanese succeeded in producing the pocket calculators which we use at present. Clive Sinclair later on

Figure 1.23 Sinclair's ZX-81

turned his mind towards designing microcomputers which can be programmed. He produced ZX-80, a tiny computer which could be linked with a television set for visual display. A year later, ZX-81 (Fig 1.23) was developed, using only 4 chips, and sold at a price of Rs 1800.

The first pocket computer (not calculator) was a Japanese one sold in the year 1980. It was called Sharp PC 1211. The Apple series of microcomputers was developed by Steve Wozniak

Figure 1.24 The Apple and Apple Series Inventor Steve Wozniak

(Fig 1.24) and Steve Jobs in 1976. This used 8-bit microprocessor chips. The chip enabled them to put together a complete computer, a keyboard for input, a processor, a few thousand characters in memory and, screen all in a small box. This also helped in reducing the price of computer drastically.

TABLE 1.1 Comparison of the Computers of Various Generations

Parameters	First generation	Second generation	Third generation	Fourth generation	Fifth generation
1. Year	1950	1960	1965	1975	1980
2. Electronic components	Vacuum tubes	Transistors	Small-scale and medium-scale integrated circuits (chips)	Medium-scale and large-scale integrated circuits, microprocessor	Large-scale micro-processor circuits in parallel architecture
3. Programming system	No operating system	No operating system	Operating system including	Improved operating	Highly sophisticated operating systems
4. Quantity in the world (approx.) (general purpose)	1000	5000	35,000	200,000	500,000
5. Computer cost (in Rupees)	...	8×10^7	25×10^7	100×10^7	...
6. Memory cost in rupees (per binary digit)	...	10.00	1.00	0.15	0.03
7. Speed (time for one shift operation)	1000 ns*	30 ns	5 ns	1 ns	0.3 ns

* ns = nano seconds = one thousandth million part of a second

Apple II known as *personal computer* is available for only a few thousand rupees. The personal computer developed by the multinational giant IBM in 1984 uses 16-bit microprocessor and belongs to the fourth generation of computers. A comparative study of computers is given in table 1.1. Computers of this series are:

1. Intel-4004	6. IBM PC
2. Commodore PET	7. ZX-Spectrum
3. Apple Series I & II	8. BBC's Accorn
4. DCM/Tandy's TRS-80	9. Sinclairs ZX-81
5. DCM's Spectrum -7	10. IBM Compatibles

1.9.5 Fifth Generation Computers: The fifth generation is the story of the new super-breed of computers now being planned by the Japanese. These computers will contain bits of information and will be able to think and make decisions—and in certain instances better than human beings. Artificial Intelligence (AI) is thus emerging from the realm of imagination to take its place in the real world. Radically different from the preceding four generations in their construction, capabilities and application, this generation is all set to bring momentous qualitative changes in human lifestyles.

The Japanese call their fifth generation machines, Knowledge Information Processing Systems (KIPS). KIPS will work as amplifier of human thought and intelligence. The entire world is likely to become dependent on these machines for greater efficiency.

The fifth generation will involve major deviations from the know-how used for the first four. New operations of symbolic manipulation and symbolic reasoning will be required for the shift to knowledge processing. The conventional Von Neumann architecture will be discarded in favour of the revolutionary parallel architecture. This will call for new low-level programming language, methods of memory management, processor organization techniques, interfaces and the like. A larger scale of integration will be ushered in. The Japanese visualize chips having the equivalent of tens of millions of transistors on them. These hardware and software innovations will be required to achieve the conceived capacities of 100 million to a billion logical inferences per second (lips). One lips can roughly be translated as 100 to 1000 instructions per second (lips) in traditional Von Neumann architecture. Thus, the Japanese plan calls for performances in the range of 10^{10} to 12^{12} lips.

1.10 The Ages of Computeronics

The computers so far developed i.e. up to the 4th generation do not have any thinking and decision taking ability. But the fifth generation computers being developed by the Japanese will evolve highly expert systems and artificial intelligence. Thus two different ages emerge distinctly: one up to fourth generation in which computer architecture was based purely on what is known as the Von Neumann Report. He set out a summary of the design requirements for the computers. The salient features of this report were:

(a) Binary codes should be used for the representation of data and instructions in a way which would make no distinction between them, and allow them to be stored together and share the storage space within the computer.

(b) The computer should be able to possess both data and instructions. This includes the modification of program by program.

The second age of computeronics is dependent upon KIPS and the parallel non-Von Neumann architecture.

1.11 Computer Dynasty

Computers, in general, are of three types:

(1) Digital computer;
(2) Analog computer; and
(3) Hybrid computer

1.11.1 Digital Computer: In digital computers, mathematical expressions are finally represented as binary digits (0 and 1) and all operations are done using these digits at very high rate. The digital computer basically knows only how to add. Remaining operations like multiplication, division and exponentiation, etc. are first converted into addition and then calculated. A digital computer as shown in Fig. 1.25 operates on inputs that are on-off or incrementally-stepped quantities which are represented by numerical digits.

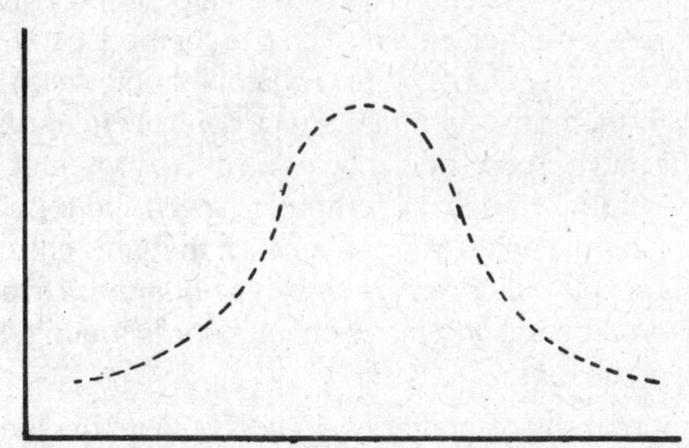

Fig. 1.25 (a) Digital representation

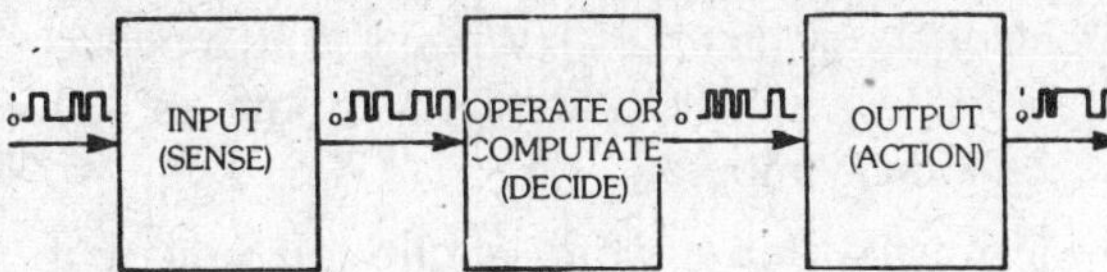

Fig. 1.25 (b) Digital computer

1.11.2 Analog Computer: Analog is a Greek word, which means establishing similarities between two quantities. In analog computer, similarities are established in form of current or voltage signal. Analog computers operate by measuring rather than by counting. In analog computer the variable is an electrical signal which is analogous to the variable of physical system. A cartoon of a man is analogous to his photograph. A stencil is an example of analog device in its easiest form in which you have to move the pencil along the cut-words so as to write words in beautiful form. An example of simple mechanical analog computer is the moving pointer type speedometer of an automobile vehicle. Analog computer refers to gradual type of change rather than changes in the form of steps which can be counted digitally. This difference is represented in Fig 1.26. The figure represents the operation as would be handled by an analog computer. But while dealing with the same figure digitally it may be broken into straight lines (actually dashes) so as to make the information suitable for representation on digital computers (Fig. 1.25a). Similarly while using analog computers, a physical system is first converted into equations, which are then further converted into analogous electrical signals. The arithmetical operations are performed electronically, using small signal amplifier blocks. The answers so obtained are then decoded into the mathematical form or in the form of graphs. Thus, by analog computer method, it is very easy to get graphical results directly.

These are powerful tools to solve differential equations, and we know that all the physical processes can be represented by differential equations. The working of the analog computer is thus based on setting up a mathematical analog of the problem in equation. The speed of a car is measured by the speedometer, which is a good example of analog computation. It receives, as input, the continuously variable rotational speed of the drive shaft and provides as output, the pointer movement in dial, which in turn indicates the speed of the car. The speed of the car is measured by analogous physical quantity, i.e. the rate of rotation of the main drive shaft is converted into the rotation of gears. Linear motion is analogically converted into circular motion and measured by counting the number of revolutions. Mathematically, speed is a derivative of distance travelled with respect to time i.e. $v=ds/dt$ which is a different equation that can be easily represented by an analog computer.

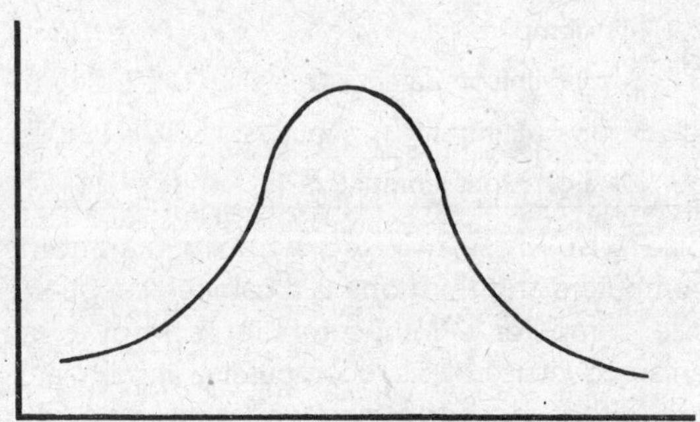

Fig. 1.26 (a) Analog representation

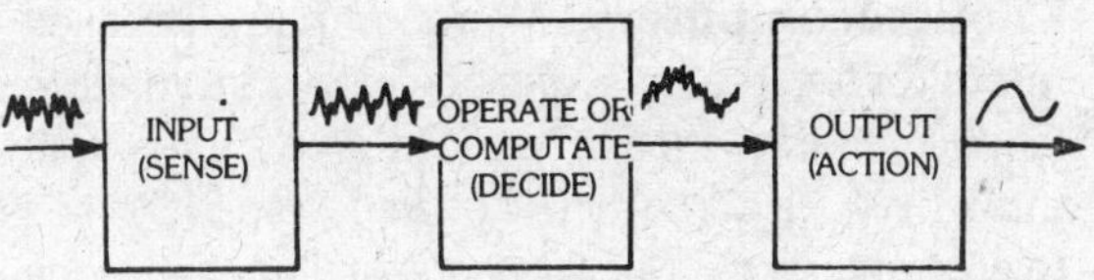

Fig. 1.26 (b) Analog computer

An example of the use of the electronic analog computer is that of controlling a flight simulator for training pilots. The computer responds to the cockpit simulator control movement made by pilot to physically change the altitude of the simulator so that the pilot feels as if he were controlling an actual aeroplane. What's more — this method is very fast. The main advantage of analog computer is that here all the calculations are done in parallel and, hence, it is very fast. But this computer has its limitations. Its accuracy is poor (about 1% deviation).

1.11.3 Hybrid Computer: Hybrid computer is a combination computer using all the good qualities of both the analog and digital computers. In such computers, some calculations are done in the analog portion of the computer and others done on the digital portion of the same computer. Then it utilizes the services of the devices which convert analog signals into digital, and digital signals into analog, wherever necessary.

1.12 Classification Based on Memory Size

Digital computers are also classified in accordance with their memory-size as below:

	Classification	RAM
1.	Microcomputers	(Up to 4 Mb)
2.	Minicomputers	(4Mb-12Mb)
3.	Super Minicomputers	(1 Mb-80 Mb)
4.	Midi or Mainframe Computers	(2Mb-128Mb)
5.	Maxi or Super Computers	(8 Mb-10Gb)

Size wise, first two are actually mainframe computers and third one is a cabinet/cupboard-size computer. Mini-computer system is an enlarged version of microcomputers, and all micros are either desk-top or hand-held type. A comparison of the above stated five computers is shown in Table 1.3.

1. Microcomputers: Microcomputer is called *micro* for two reasons: one because it is miniature in size (micro means millionth part of a unit quantity), and another because it uses microprocessor. Microprocessor is actually the heart-cum-mind of a computer. All computers have essentially five parts namely *input, output, central processing unit, control unit* and *memory*. The entire CPU of microcomputer is contained either in a single chip of thumbnail size, or on a few chips. When equipped (interfaced) with memory and input/ouput control circuitry, the microprocessor is known as a microcomputer. In some of the microcomputers, even the input and output unit is also contained in the same chip. Microcomputers range from single-board size to a system containing many circuit boards mounted in a cabinet.

Entire microcomputer circuitry is built within the typewriter terminal which acts as input unit also. In some systems, this terminal may be interfaced with a visual display unit, In which case it is called a personal computer (PC). When it is attached to a colour television it is known as home and/or educational computer.

Early micros had a word lengths of 8-bits but currently 16 and 32-bits micros are available. The speed of microcomputer is of the order of 100 KIPS. Microcomputers generally have a visual display unit, Keyboard (for data entry and operation), one or two floppy disk drives and printer and may be interfaced with some tools like digitizer, joy stick, tracker ball, light pen, etc. They have memory range of 16 Kb to 4 MB. Mini-Winchester disk drive may be attached with a capacity of 10 Mb, if needed. Micro are generally available in two categories as described below:

1.a Home and Education Computers: Home computers are meant for hobbyists and school-going children rather than for professionals. They have a memory range of 8-64 Kb. They have a keyboard integrated with CPU in one box-like thing and interfaced with an ordinary colour television and audio cassette. They are meant for entertainment, training, and home management purposes. Vendors supply cassette-tapes containing programmes for computer games, like flight simulator, Zork-1, Decathlon Space Oddessey, etc. Besides, built-in lessons on various subjects are available, which can be displayed on television for learning purposes. Built-in programmes are available for home budgeting and accounting purposes. A programme known as Personal Investor guides the owner to

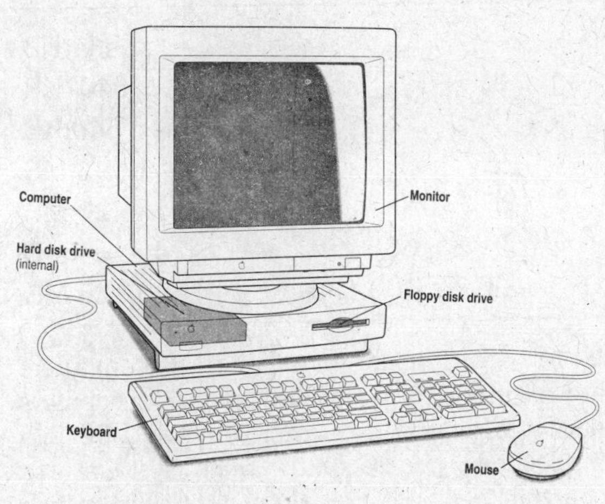

Figure 1.27 An educational computer

computerize his investments like income and other taxes, shares and loans, etc. Most of such computers are available at a price tag of Rs 5,000 to Rs10,000 approximately. Some popular home computers are — ZX-81, Sinclair's Spectrum, Tandy's TRS-80, Atari 400, IBM's PC Junior, Commodore, Apple-II, New Brain, BBC's Acorn, etc. The Semi-conductor Complex Limited (a Government of India enterprise) is producing a computer known as SCL-Unicorn, for mass computer literacy project for Indian schools. This project was known as CLASS (Computer Literacy and Studies in Schools). One educational computer is shown in Fig 1.27.

1.b Personal Computers (Fig. 1.28)**:** Personal computers are called so because they are designed for personal use of individual or individual small business. They are meant for professionals, small business units and office automation systems. Such computers are now available at extremely low cost within Rs 20,000 in India.

PCs can be used for a variety of applications like: computer literacy, Basic programming, fun and games, home and school applications, business and professional applications, electronic spread sheets, telecommunications, data base management, accounting, word processing. PC can also be played like a musical instrument which generates a range of several octaves.

IBM, the foremost computer manufacturing firm in the world, introduced a computer called **Personal Computer** (IBM-PC) on 12.8.1981.

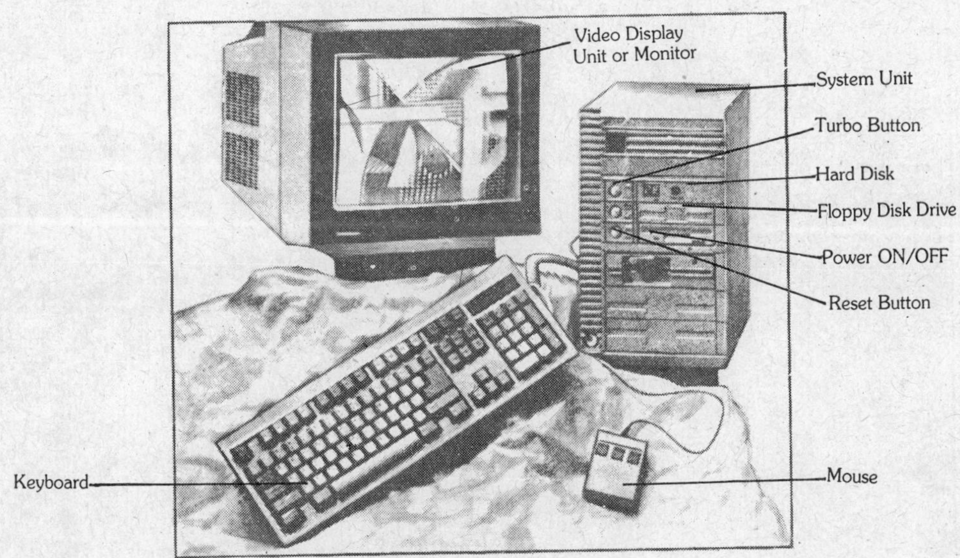

Figure 1.28 Personal Computer System

Table 1.2: Models of Personal Computer (IBM-PC)

Name	Chip	Cycle MHZ	Memory
IBMPC Junior	—	—	64 KB
IBMPC	Intel 8088	8	640 KB
IBMPC XT	Intel 8088	18	640 KB
IBMPC AT	Intel 80286	25	1 to 4 MB
IBM PC AT/386	Intel 80386	25, 30,40	1 to 20 MB
IBM PC AT/486	Intel 80486	25, 33, 66	4 to 64 MB
IBM PC Pentium	Pentium	33, 66, 100,135	4 to 120 MB

It had several models as detailed in the table 1.2.

An IBMPC compatible system is at present costing Rs 20,000 to Rs 1,00,000. Over 100 different brands have been introduced in India which are said to be IBMPC compatibles. By compatible, we mean those computers which will have the similar memory, cycle time, and chips as used by IBM and they will be able to support all softwares developed by IBM. The total number of softwares developed by IBM was more than 5000 in the year 1984 itself.

2. Minicomputers (Fig. 129): Minicomputers are at least five times faster than microcomputers having CPU speed of approximately 500 kilo instructions per second. Such systems are characterized by their main memory size, which may be 256 Kb to 12 Mb and word length of 16/32-bits and are designed for 4 to 8 users in time sharing modes. They use Winchester hard disks drives of 80 Mb each, 1 or 2 floppy drives, 7 to 8 printers, 9 on-line printers digitizers, plotters and fixed storage of 160 Mb, and magnetic tapes. The

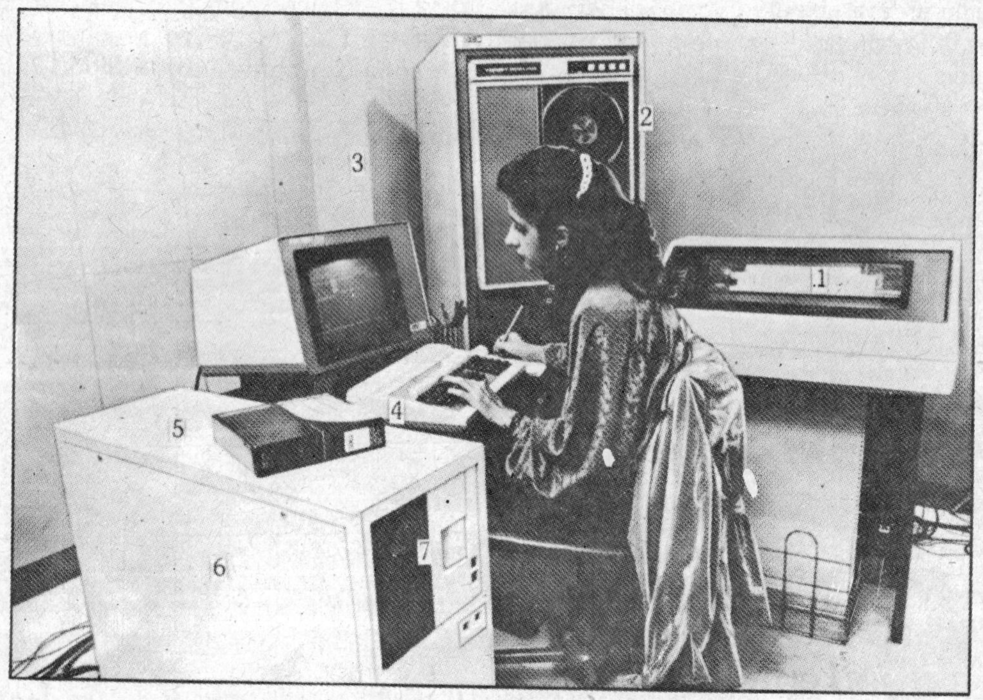

Figure 1.29 Mini Computer (Micro Galaxy DCM)

DEC is the major minicomputers manufacturer. DEC's Vax-Series 8200 and 8300 are two major series. Other popular minicomputers include ICL's series 39 level 20, 50 and 60, Honeywell XPS-100, IBM's system/36 and system/38 with their upgraded models of 5360 series and model 100 to 700 of series 38, TDC 316 SN-23, PDP 11/70, Nordsk. IBM introduced a minicomputer series 9370 which uses the same architecture, as IBM's 370 mainframe series.

3. Super Minicomputers: These computers have recently come into existence, possessing the memory-range of mainframe computer installed in the size of minicomputer. These machines have 32-bit word length and support memory sizes in the range of 1 to 80 Mb, and are getting good support in research, on-line production control technique, and data processing. VAX-II, 780/8600, TDC 332, Wipro's Pyramid 90x, Blue Star's Series 930, etc. are good examples of these computers.

4. Mainframe Computers: These are the large-size computers (Fig 1.30) which occupy a large air-conditioned roomful space and main memory size up to 128 megabyte. Since all its peripherals are mounted in large cabinet type of frames, these computers are also known as main frame computers. Such a computer system can be used by 128 users simultaneously in time sharing mode and employing mini computers as a front-end processor. All the first to third generation computers, which work with the speed of 5 to 100 million instructions per second, fall under this group. IBM's 308x-580 series, IBM-3090, 4300, 4381, DEC 1090, 10, 20, Cyber's 170, ICL's Series 9, Honeywell's DPS 88/860, etc., Burrough 7800, UNIVAC 1100/60, ACOS 100 are the popular midi or mainframe computers.

5. Super Computers: By definition super computer means a computer having main memory of 256 megabytes (compare this with your computer's memory of only 32 kilobytes, exactly 8,000 times). This computer is 5 million times faster than the first computer i.e. ENIAC.

Conventional computers solve problems by a series of sequential steps in much the same way as an individual mathematician would solve the same. In a parallel processor of a super computer, however, many computations can be performed simultaneously. On the first super computer ILLIAC-IV, 64 different calculations could be made at a time, i.e. it was equivalent to 64 different mainframe computers. It was the first large scale array computer which became operational in November 1975. The ILLIAC consists of a single control unit that broadcasts instructions to 64 processing elements operating simultaneously. Each of these processing elements has a working memory of 2K, sixty-four-bit words. The main memory of ILLIAC is contained in disk, with a

Figure 1.30 A Mainframe computer (ICL System 4 Computer)

capacity of eight million words, at a transfer rate of 500 megabyte. Arithmetic can be performed in 8, 32, or 64-bits mode. The ILLIAC can execute instructions at a rate of 300 millions per second.

Large classes of problems concerning ballistic missile, reactor design, climate modelling, large linear programming, seismic data processing, etc. could not be solved, because neither all the third-generation nor most of the fourth-generation computers could operate at the speed required for such calculations. The speed needed was practically not possible. This is the limitation of speed at which a signal can be propagated through an electric conductor. Electronic signal travels at the speed of light, which is approximately 300,000 km per second. At this speed, the signal travels at less then 30 cm in a nano second. Although through miniaturization, the length of the interconnecting conductors had already been reduced substantially, lengths of more than 30 cm may be encountered, delaying the travel of signal, and thus making calculations impossible. This problem can be circumvented by parallel architecture. Super computers of the fourth and fifth generation use this architecture.

In 1972, Control Data Corporation (CDC) deviced a super-computer, by name Star, which worked at the rate of 50 megaflops. In 1976 Semour Cray designed a super computer performing at the rate of 180 megaflops, based on emitter-coupled-logic, much different from its ancestors, which were all based on MOSFET technology. This super computer known as Cray-1 had 2.5 million transistor equivalents in it, but occupied only 6 sq. meter of space, but required super-cooling by Freon gas. This opened up a pathway for similar super computer Cyber-205 from CDC in 1980, having performance speed of 400 megaflops. Cray quickly took over this speed by marketing Cray-2 series XMP computers having 2 to 4 multiprocessors.

Japanese company NEC marketed SX-2, in competition to which ETA-10 emerged as most desirable computer for supercomputing. India also procured one Cray-XMP-14 Supercomputer for its weather computation needs and installed it at Mausam Bhawan in New Delhi.

1.13 Special Purpose Computers

Several special-purpose computers are being used which are tailor-made for specific uses in several fields.

1. Hidden Computers: Such computers are designed to control a particular process or job and, as such, are installed inside the machine being automized. These are digital computers with hybrid applications.

Their hardware is designed for very rugged application and tough duty schedule. Computers so installed activate the machine in a very faithful manner, eliminating any chances of human error, favouritism, nuisance, handling, and sabotage. They have limited memory and speech, which is suited only for that particular machine. LAN (Local Area Network) and WAN (Wide Area Network), using the electronic message switching systems, employ such computer robots in intensive care units and other hospital instruments. Automatic washing machines, digital clocks, Hot-Shot cameras, all use hidden computers for their accurate and automatic operation.

2. User Friendly: Any computer having software or hardware which is easy to operate by non-technical and untrained operator is said to be user friendly. They utilize special softwares which guide the user in handling the computer software further through built-in menus, display instructions, commands and directory. They provide codes for easy remembrance and pictures instead of descriptions. Their hardware uses devices like electronic mice, light pens, graphics pads, touch tablets, tracker ball, and joy stick, etc.

3. Knowledge Information Processing Systems (KIPS): A series of computers being developed by the Japanese as the fifth-generation machines shall incorporate the ability of reasoning, thinking, and decision-making. In such computers, all hardwares and softwares of a computer will work in parallel memory operations having capabilities of 100 million to a billion lips (logical inferences per second). One lip itself is equivalent to 100 to 1000 instructions per second.

4. Optical Computers: These computers are

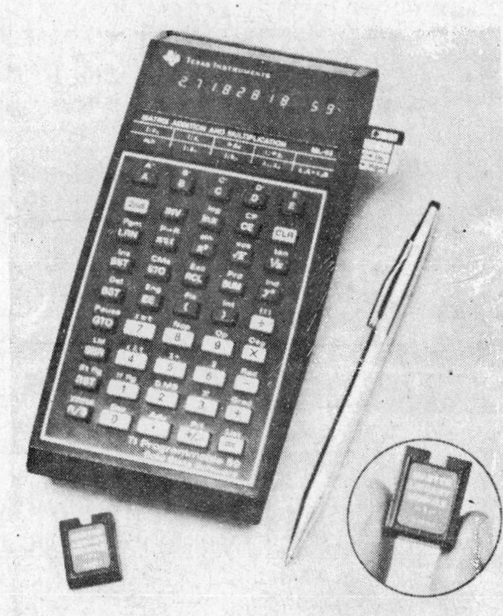

Figure 1.31 Programmable Hand-held Computers

under the process of design and may emerge on commercial scale only after 4 to 10 years. If the speed of operation of a computer is to be increased beyond some point, the travel of signal through metallic conductor poses problem. This problem is solved by using optical fibre technology and using quadral logic instead of binary logic, on which the present day computers are based.

5. **Hand-Held and Pocket Computers:** These are small pocket-size computers having memory size of 4 to 16 Kb and small in-built, alphanumeric display which can be used for all scale personal and scientific computing. Besides, they provide facility for playing games. Computer programming in BASIC is possible through a small cartridge which is to be inserted in the computer. One such computer is shown in Fig 1.31 which shows a small cartridge containing games and languages in its memory.

1.14 Difference between a Computer and a Calculator

This is a question often asked, as a calculator costs only Rs 130 due to difference in the Rs 100 to 300 whereas even the smallest computer would require handsome money running into several thousands of rupees. The difference lies in their method of working. Three major differences are:

1. The calculator can process only numerals, that is, the digits 0,1,2,3,.....9 but not alphabets (i.e. words). To put it differently, a calculator works on numeric data whereas a computer works with alphanumeric data.
2. With a calculator, the operator (that is, you) has to work manually with his own hands for inputting the data. One has to push the button on the face of the calculator to feed in or type in the data. Also, for lengthy calculations the operator has to take up the calculations one by one, i.e. he can take up the second calculation only when the result of the first calculation is known. The microcomputer has got the option of typing the data manually or feeding the data according to an automatic method known as programming. Once the program has been given to the computer, it does the calculations automatically.

   It may be noted that nowadays programmable calculators of limited capacity are also available.
3. A calculator cannot store instructions or informations whereas a computer can store instructions or informations.
4. The input to calculator is in the form of pressing or touching the push buttons but in case of computer it may be in several forms like punched cards, audio cassette, magnetic tapes, joy stick, light pen and floppy disk etc. Similarly output may come in several forms.

Advantages of Using Minicomputer Over Microcomputer

1. They are more versatile, and have a better addressing scheme with longer word lengths.
2. They are faster than micros in operating speeds.
3. Addressing modes are more efficient and have wider applications.
4. The internal registers are larger in number and, therefore, the necessity of frequent memory referencing during the execution of programs can be minimized. The execution time is thus reduced.

5. The interrupt schemes available on minicomputers are more sophisticated than in microprocessors.
6. Since a variety of bit microprocessors are available, standard programming facilities, in terms of a common machine language, are just not available. This poses problems in training and of intercompatibility.

Reasons for the wider use of Microprocessors:

1. They are much more cost-effective than minicomputers.
2. The variety of applications, including real-time process control, are sufficiently large enough, and this advantage is obtained at almost equivalent speed and lower costs.
3. The utilization factor of microprocessors is much higher than that of minicomputers.
4. Since the component count is lower for microprocessors, reliability is proportionately much higher, they, therefore, require minimum maintenance.
5. Mean time to repair (MTTR) is also very much reduced.
6. Because of its compact structure, it is easy for design production and testing. Indeed, the turn round time for systems design has been very effectively and considerably reduced.

It appears that microprocessors have not only come to stay but would almost completely displace the minicomputers from any potential applications.

TABLE 1.3: Comparison of Characteristics of Computers

Computer Type	Main Memory Size	CPU Speed	Cost Range	Word Length/ & No. of Users	Most Popular Series
1. Micro					
(a) Home	8 to 64 Kb	100 Kips	\$400 to \$1000	8 bits, only one user,	BBC Acorn, Commodore & Atari, Sinclair's Spectrum, ZX-81 Apple-II, IBMPC Jr.
(b) Personal	64 Kb to 120 Mb	1000 Kips	\$800 to \$10000	8 to 16 bits, only one user	IBMPC & PS/2, HCL, PCL MAC, WIPRO, DCM, Power PC
2. Mini	16 Mb to 256 Mb	500 Kips to 5 Mips	\$10000 to \$20000	16 or 32 bits, 4 to 8 user	DEC, VAX PDP, IBM, ICL Honeywell
3. Super Mini	4 Mb to 256 Mb	1 to 5 Mips	\$50000 to \$500000	32 bits, 16 to 32 users	VAX-8600, Wipro's 90X, ICI 39, 2904, Wipro's Pyramid, TDC-332
4. Midi, Main Frame	10 Mb to 256 Mb	5 to 100 Mips	\$500000 to \$5 million	32 to 64 bits 32 to 128 users	IBM 308, 580, 3090, 4381, DEC-10, 20-XMP, ICL-9, Honeywells Burrough Univac
5. Super or Maxi	256 Mb to 10 Gb	500 M-Flops	\$ 5 M to \$ 50 M	64 to 96 bits, Unlimited users	CRAY's, XMP, CRAY-3, CYBER 205(CDC), NEC SX-11, ETA-10, Fujitsu, Hitachi

Note: (i) At present (1995) 1\$ = 32 Rs. (ii) Mb = Megabyte, Kb = Kilobyte, Kips = kilo instructions/second, Mips - million instructions/sec (iii) The above is only a tentative guide which is changing at a fast rate (iv) M-flops means million floating point operations per second. (v) Gb means gigabyte, which is equal to 1000 megabyte or one million Kb.

EXCERCISE

1. What is the Von Neumann Report and what are its contents?
2. What is meant by the different generations of computers and how do they differ in usage?
3. What is the difference between the analog and digital computers?
4. Classify the computers based on their configuration and size.
5. What is parallel Von Neumann architecture?
6. Write a brief note on various calculating machines in use before the advent of the electronic computer.
7. What is the difference between a calculator and a computer?
8. Mention the names of 10 different calculating machines.
9. Write the names of various basic computing elements of different generations of computers.
10. Distinguish between
    - (a) Chip and integrated circuit
    - (b) Integrated circuit and microprocessor
    - (c) Microprocessor and microcomputer
    - (d) Analog and digital computer
    - (e) Valve and transistor
    - (f) Mainframe, mini and microcomputer
    - (g) Computer and calculator
11. Fill in the blanks with appropriate words:
    - (a) The speed of the third generation computer is............. nanoseconds.
    - (b) You can have............. insight in Analog and Hybrid computers.
    - (c) The accuracy of............. computers is superhigh.
    - (d) The accuracy of calculation in............. computer is 99%.
    - (e) The microcomputer has got a word processing capacity of............. words to............. words.
    - (f) The memory capacity in a minicomputer is of............. Kb.
    - (g) ENIAC was the............. of the first-generation computer.
    - (h) A common computer in office is for............. processing.
12. What are the advantages and disadvantages of microcomputers over minicomputers?
13. Put the correct word in the blanks:
    - (a) There are historical evidences to prove that abacus was first used in............. (India, Japan, China, Indonesia)
    - (b) The first mechanical calculator was made by............. (Blaise Pascal, Napier, Charles Babbage)
    - (c) Z1, Z2 were the............. computers. (Electrical, Mechanical, Electronical)
    - (d) The first relay operated computer was developed by............. (IBM, Conrad Zuse, Howard Aikens)
    - (e) .... was the first successful electrical computer. (Manchester Mark I, Ferranti Mark I, Z3)
    - (f) ENIAC belonged to............. generation of computers. (Second, Primitive, First)
    - (g) Computers are mostly used in offices for............. processing. (Data, Word)
14. State True or False:
    - (a) ENIAC was the first programmable computer.
    - (b) Second generation computers were faster than first generation computers but bulkier than them.
    - (c) Herman Hollerith was a great mathematician.
    - (d) Computers are programmable calculators.
    - (e) The pocket calculator currently being used in India (Japanese Sharp, Nelco) is a computer.
    - (f) The basic computing unit in a microcomputer is transistor flip-flop.
    - (g) Computer does not have more intelligence than a cockroach.

(h) The battery operated pocket calculator may be considered as a limited purpose digital computer.

(i) The first electronic computer used transistor.

(g) The abacus is still useful for adding numbers.

15. A modern fast mainframe digital computer can perform up to.............. operations per second.
    (a) 1000
    (b) 100,000
    (c) 1000,000
    (d) 1,000,000,000

16. A modern electronic computer is a machine that is meant for
    (a) doing quick mathematical calculation:
    (b) input, storage, manipulation and outputting of data.
    (c) electronic data processing.
    (d) performing repetitive tasks accurately.

17. The operation of a digital computer is based on the.............. principle.
    (a) counting
    (b) measuring
    (c) electronic
    (d) logical

18. The proper definition of a modern digital computer is
    (a) an electronically automated machine that can solve problems involving words and numbers.
    (b) a more sophisticated and modified electronic pocket calculator.
    (c) any machine that can perform mathematical operations.
    (d) a machine that works on the binary code.

19. A modern digital computer has
    (a) extremely high speed.
    (b) large memory.
    (c) almost unlimited accuracy.
    (d) all of the above.

20. The very small and cheap computer built into many home devices is called.............. computer.
    (a) mainframe
    (b) mini
    (c) micro
    (d) analog

21. Mark the WRONG Statement

    A digital computer scores over an analog computer in terms of
    (a) speed.
    (b) accuracy.
    (c) cost.
    (d) memory.

22. The main distinguishing feature of the fifth generation digital computers will be
    (a) liberal use of microprocessors.
    (b) artificial intelligence.
    (c) extremely low cost.
    (d) versatility.

23. IBM 7000 digital computer.
    (a) belongs to second generation.
    (b) uses VLSI.
    (c) employs semi-conductor memory.
    (d) has modular construction.

24. Match the following:

(a) Hollerith's	(1) IBM-Mark I
(b) Babbage	(2) Microprocessor
(c) Aikens	(3) Differential Engine
(d) Von Neumann	(4) Architecture of computer
(e) Eckert	(5) Punched card
(f) Sinclair	(6) KIPS systems
(g) Fifth Generation	(7) Very large scale IC
(h) 8085	(8) Analog + 1 Digital
(i) VLSI	(9) ZX-81
(j) Hybrid	(10) ENIAC

25. Match the column A with column B:

Column A	*Column B*
(a) First generation computers used	(1) will be possible with fifth generation
(b) Second generation	(2) belong to fourth generation
(c) Third generation	(3) are mainframe computers working on parallel architectutre
(d) Microcomputers	(4) is a super computer
(e) Artificial intelligence	(5) computers used transistors
(f) Supercomputers	(6) valves as basic element
(g) ILLIAC	(7) began with development of ICs
(h) ENIAC	(8) belongs to first generation

ANSWERS

11. (a) 5
    (b) Direct
    (c) Digital
    (d) Analog
    (e) 512W-8 kilowords
    (f) 256 kilobytes
    (g) First (h) Word

13. (a) China
    (b) Blaise Pascal
    (c) Mechanical
    (d) Howard Aikens
    (e) Manchester Mark 1
    (f) First
    (g) Word

14. (a) False (b) False
    (c) False (d) True
    (e) False (f) False
    (g) True (h) Yes, but not programmable
    (i) False (j) True

15. (d) 20. (c)

16. (b) 21. (b)

17. (a) 22. (b)

18. (a) 23. (d)

19. (d)

24. (a) – (5), (b) – (3), (c) – (1), (d) – (4), (e) – (10), (f) – (9), (g) – (6), (h) – (2)

25. (a)-(6), (b)-(5), (c)-(7), (d)-(2), (e)-(1), (f)-(3), (g)-(4), (h)-(8)

From the giant size of ENIAC, computers have constantly reduced their bulk to become as dwarfish as possible, even then experts say that computers are growing their shape and size.

CHAPTER 2

Computer: Its Characteristics, Anatomy and Architecture

2.1 What is a Computer?

Computer literally means a tool or equipment or machine which computes or does calculations. The definition covers all sorts of computing equipments like abacus counting tables, slide-rule, Napier's bones, and decimal logarithm, pocket and desk calculators, mainframe, mini and microcomputers. Computers of yesteryears were devices capable of only accepting data, solving problems and supplying the results. Nowadays computer practically is a device which can process, store and retrieve automatically (i.e. it can call back any data from its memory) miscellaneous information , which may be of audio, visual or linguistic type.

Computers perform only three basic functions:

(i) Do arithmetic calculations i.e. addition, subtraction, multiplication and its reciprocal (i.e. division);

(ii) Compare values;

(iii) Store, search, and retrieve.

It should be very clearly understood that although computer essentially does all above functions automatically, it does not possess any intelligence of its own. Its intelligence quotient or IQ is zero i.e. it does not have any thinking, arguing or decision-making power of its own. This power is intelligently conferred to it by proper programming methods by persons handling it. Let us see where computer stands in comparison to human brain.

2.2 The Characteristics of a Computer

Computers display following characteristics to a greater or lesser extent depending on their type and application. Computers are not merely calculators but are programmable calculators which help reduce the burden on human memory and burden of mechanical processing. Computers have assumed their importance due to following qualities:

(1) Speed: Computers make calculations at a very fast rate. But how fast? Let us multiply 369 with 514. It takes about 50 to 60 seconds for an expert calculator to do this job with the help of pencil, his wisdom and memory. Similarly, think how long it would take you to count up to one million (10 lakhs)? Try! If you are exceptionally fast, even then it will take about a minute in counting up to 100 numbers. With this speed, it will take 3.5 days of your continuous counting. But a modern computer can do 30,000,000 (thirty million or 3 crore) such calculations in one minute and that too, without any mistake. Currently, a medium-sized computer executes over a million instructions per second over and over without any mistake.

How much is a quantum of one million instructions? It means roughly all the arithmetical operations an average intelligent human being can afford to do in an entire year. This could be properly understood in another way like this. A computer deals with that amount of arithmetic jugglery in a minute which will take the entire life of a man expected to live long up to 100 years. In 1968, the author himself worked on digital computer IBM-7044 at IIT, Kanpur under the able guidance of the first man of computers in India, Dr Raja Ramanna, the then head of the Department of Mathematics at IIT, Kanpur. Perhaps, the computer itself was the very first digital computer in India and the fastest in India during that period. This computer was so fast that it could do all calculations in one hour what would normally take an expert engineer at least ten years of manual labour. Computers at least 10,000 times faster than this have been already built. A low-cost computer at the rental of Rs 30,000 per month can update an inventory file of 25,000 items with 5,000 different types of transactions within 15 minutes.

(2) Superhigh Accuracy and Degree of Reliability: Computers are designed in such a way that their individual components have a very high life and degree of reliability. All mechanical parts have superhigh endurance capacity so that a computer works without getting tired. It works on the basis of electric pulses, due to which there is no chance of its making mistakes. It can repeat the same job for a number of times in exactly the same way.

(3) Storage Capacity or Memory: The computers have got superb inbuilt and auxiliary memory systems. A computer system can store a great amount of information in it. The success of computers lies not only in storing the information but in the great speed of utilizing the memory storage. Any item of data or any instruction stored in the memory can be retrieved by the computer at lightning speeds. A modern computer can call back any data out of its stored memory in a few nanoseconds. One nanosecond is 1 millionth of 1000th part of a second (i.e. 1 nanosecond = 0.000000001 second). The idea of a computer having memory was incapsulated by the great scientist John Von Neumann in 1946, while he was working on an atomic bomb project.

(4) Integrity: It is the ability to take in and store a sequence of instructions for obeying. Such a sequence of instructions is called a program and must be written in the language of computer. It is also the ability to obey a sequence of program instructions, provided the instructions are stored within the computer. The program instructions will be obeyed in sequence automatically, without the need for manual intervention at each step. This is very different from the operation of a typical pocket calculator, which needs buttons to be pressed for each operation, and where the person using the calculator controls the sequence of operations.

(5) Power of Making Logics: The ability to use simple logical rules to make for their own internal control, or for the control of some external activity, e.g. to take over the role of the calculator operator.

(6) Versatility: The ability to communicate with other systems and adopt several modes like audio-visual, graphics, user-friendly, etc.

(7) Superiority of Manufacture: Computer hardware is manufactured with the best materials by the most sophisticated process. So the chances of failure are rare.

2.3 Capabilities of Computers

- Computers offer unmatched speed, performing computations faster than humans.
- Computers undertake boring and repetitive tasks, relieving us for more critical, creative activities.
- Computers perform tasks repeatedly without error, avoiding the fatigue that affects humans.
- Computers can do critical and dangerous tasks that may be hazardous to humans.
- Computers provide information we can use in decision-making.
- Computers offer services in medicine and science that previously did not exist.
- Computers are an existing entertainment medium, as well as educational tools.
- Computers allow society to undertake new activities in various fields and to function more efficiently.
- Computers are impartial. They offer a means of data processing unaffected by racial, religious, or cultural bias. They can handle large quantities of data uniformly and randomly, without prejudice. The computer will not make exceptions for favours owed, political alliances, or family ties. These are done by human beings only.

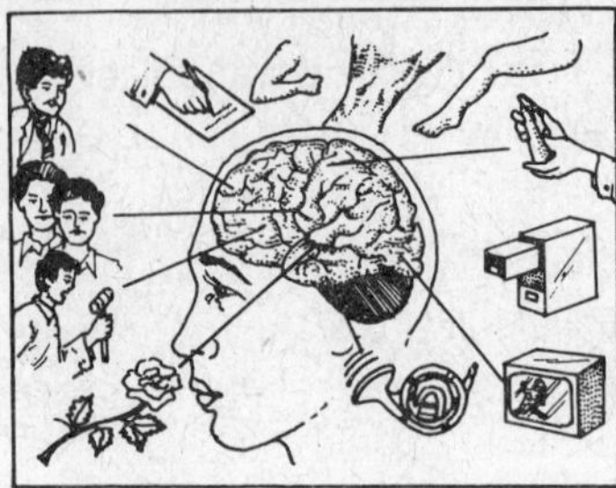

The Human Brain

The Human Brain:

1. Weighs about 1.5 kg.
2. Energy source is blood glucose.
3. Needs a steady temperature.
4. Number of basic computing elements is estimated at about a hundred billion ($1x10^{11}$ or put 11 zeros after 1). These nerve cells are known as *neurons*.
5. The various parts of the brain must stay in one place.
6. Rapid memory recall, apparently unlimited because of the way the brain stores ideas. Limited memory. Memory affected by physical fitness. The cerebrus system cannot be relieved of its memory storage at will.
7. Averagé intelligence rated at an IQ level of about 100. Maximum is 160. In-built intelligence, wisdom and negotiation power available.
8. Damages are not reparable at present. But the brain has got self-repairing capability.
9. The brain's memory is divided in two portions — LTM and STM, i.e. long-term and short-term memory. Memory stays in mind or goes off depending upon the psychology. Memory cannot be washed off at the will of human being.
10. Signal transmission speed is only 60m/sec or 0.04 million instructions per second.
11. Pulse duration = 1/10 sec.
12. Primary storage capacity is ultra high, 10,000,000 million bits — but not dependable. Storing capacity is arbitrary and emotionally controlled.
13. The human brain is about ten thousand times more densely packed with information but its rate of transmission of binary pulses is ten billionth to that of a computer.

Computer:

1. Weighs from a few grammes to many tonnes.
2. Energy source is electricity. (The amount of power a computer needs is getting less each year). Microcomputers need less power than consumed by a television set.
3. Less sensitive to heat and cold.
4. At best, about a thousand million basic computing elements, but increasing all the time.
5. The various parts can be in different places and linked by wires, satellites, laser beams, etc.
6. Access speed to memory store limited by present technology. Almost unlimited memory can be created for human purposes. Memory can be relaxed or modified at will.
7. General intelligence about that of a very stupid worm. Intelligence created by logic. However, fifth generation computers may possess artificial intelligence.
8. Repair, replacement and alterations easily possible.
9. The local memory of a computer is of two types — ROM and RAM. ROM is the permanent store in computer for its operation and stays even if the computer is switched off. RAM is the short-term memory storage which gets washed away immediately after its use or when computer is put off.
10. Signal speed is tremendously high at 22,000,000 m/sec or 140,000 MI/sec.
11. Pulse duration = 1 μs
12. Primary storage capacity is 1 million bits at present but increasing every day. The super computers of the fifth generation will have even more capacity than the brain.
13. Information dealing capacity of the KIPS series of computers shall be far superior than the human brain.

The human brain resembles a digital computer in that it processes discrete electrical pulses in binary format.

2.4 Limitations of Computers

- **Non-Affordability:** Initial cost of installing computers is very high, which puts limitation over its use.
- **Compatibility:** Programs and softwares prepared for one type of computer (based on microprocessor type) are not usable on other types of computers.
- **Need of being Expert Programmer:** A number of computer languages and uses of software is required to be learnt for using a computer effectively.
- **Non-standardization:** Each manufacturer develops a software and hardware that requires a lot of practice and customization before it could be used. A number of versions, said to be nearly 250, of the most popular computer language (-) BASIC, are available. No sincere efforts have so far been made to standardize the various softwares and hardwares.
- **General:** The computer does what it is programmed to do and nothing else, this does not mean that it must be stupid. A clever program can be written to direct the computer to store the results of previous decisions. Then, by using the program's branching ability, the computer may be able to modify its behaviour according to the success or failure of past decisions.

2.5 Brain versus Computer

Some people think that it is only a question of time when a computer would be programmed to function like a human brain, while others believe it is a fantasy of science fiction stories. Here are some of the features of a human brain compared with a present-day computer.

The human brain is made up of a hundred billion nerve cells, which are basic information gathering centres called 'Neurons'. Thousands of fibres extend out of the neurons and these fibres, known as dendrites, link the neurons with each other. The length of these dendrites in a single mind itself is in the range of 1 lakh kilometres or so. The dendrites do not actually connect with each other but there is a small gap between them known as synapse. It is through these gaps that the nerve cell acts and transfers the signal to other human systems. Through this incredible network of nerve cells, electrical and chemical impulses are generated day and night to constitute the processes of thinking and psychology.

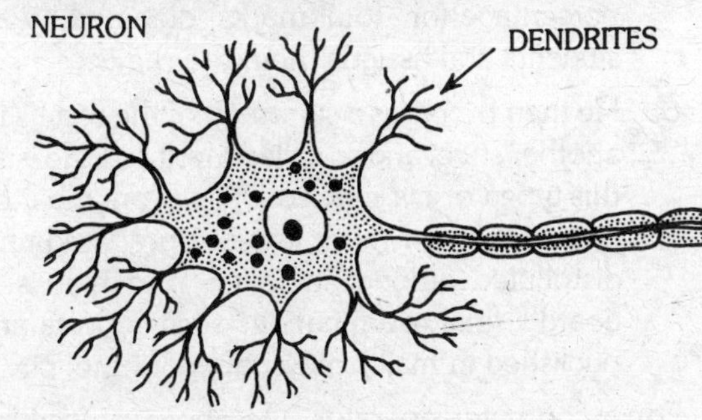

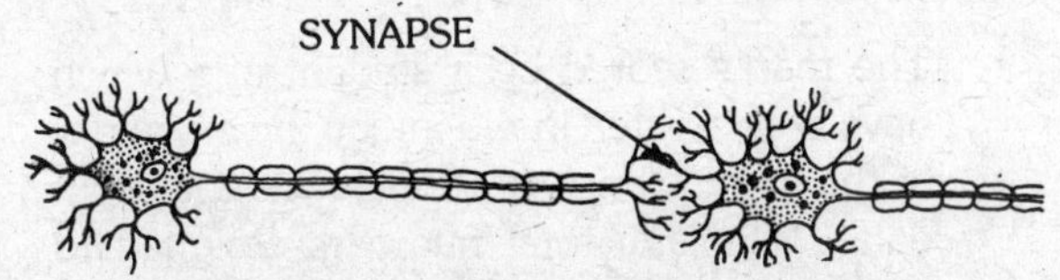

Figure 2.1 The tissues of Human Brain.

2.6 Functioning of a Computer

The working of a computer can be compared with the operations undertaken by a teacher in the preparation of final report book or result sheet, i.e. in tabulation of the class result.

1. The class teacher collects all the answer-sheets of different subjects which have been examined by individual subject-teachers and then enters the marks obtained by a student in different subjects, in a sheet which also contains the name, roll number, class and section of the student.
2. He (or she) also enters the full marks assigned to individual subjects.
3. Teacher tabulates the marks obtained by the student in the projects, assignments (home work), and unit tests in the different terms, i.e. 1st term, 2nd term and 3rd term. This, he does on the basis of student's report book. He also enters the marks obtained in the half-yearly examination.

4. Now, he calculates the weightage for promotion and works out the total percentage in individual subject. Then, he adds up the total marks obtained and gets the final percentage.
5. He prepares the similar report cards for all students in the class. He then compares the percentage (or total marks) obtained by all students and assigns them the ranks.
6. He then prepares a summary of the results in another sheet and so called merit list. He gets this typed or cyclostyled. Thus, a number of result sheets or merit lists are prepared and distributed among students. And if it is a board's final examination, such reports are published in major newspapers of the city.

For a computer operator, the above procedure means following:

1. The marks scored by a student and which have been written in red ink by the examiner at the top of answer-sheet forms the input data. Similarly total numbers assigned to each subject also form an *input data*.
2. The report card and merit list forms the *output data*.
3. The process of tabulation is called data processing.
4. The teacher is working on a definite task i.e. preparation of report sheet and merit list in a set procedure which is called program. The program is prepared on the basis of certain instructions given by the principal or board of secondary education. These instructions are that — (i) minimum percentage for student's promotion to next class is 35% in aggregate (total) and 30% in each of the subjects; (ii) weightage of unit test, assignment, project work, half-yearly, and annual examination shall be 20, 10, 10, 20 and 40%; (iii) minimum attendance should be 75%.
5. The teacher fills the marks of previous tests, assignments based on previous sections of the report books, which forms a stored secondary (but permanent) memory or *backing storage*. Similarly, while tabulating the various percentage marks, the teacher does not refer back to all the instructions. He bears in mind certain amount of instructions and information. This memory is called primary (temporary) memory or *Immediate Access Storage* (IAS).
6. While preparing the report book, the teacher uses the printed result sheet in which he fills the marks obtained by the student. The sheet is once again examined by a clerk or another teacher and may be finally seen by the principal. These two features combined together mean a *control unit* or monitoring.
7. For calculating the percentage of individual subjects and for summing up the total marks obtained by a student, the teacher may use a pocket or desk calculator or standard table, which is called the *Arithmetic Logic Unit* (ALU).
8. The last three functions put together are known as *central processing*.
9. The printed mark-sheet and merit list used by the teacher can be taken as software; teacher, clerk, principal, and typist are collectively known as humanware; and the pocket calculator and typewriter are termed as hardware. The format of printed mark-sheet can be taken as *firmware*.

2.7 Anatomy of Computer

In principle, a computer of any kind works in much the same way as a teacher. It is concerned with accepting data as input, storing all the information, which is relevant to it, processing the data in a predetermined way that conforms with a program of instructions and then communicating the results as ouput. Thus, a computer essentially consists of three elements (Fig 2.2 & 2.3)

1. Input device
2. Central Processing Unit (CPU)
3. Output device.

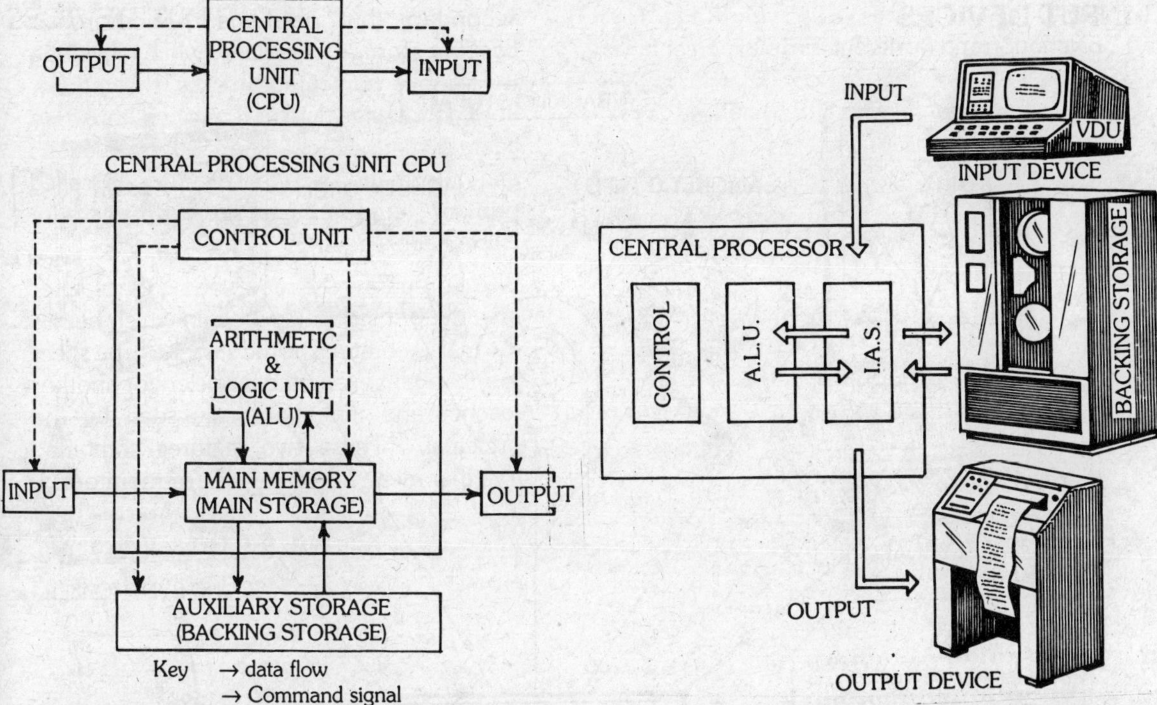

Figure 2.2 Digital Computer's Anatomy

Figure 2.3 Computer System

Input and output devices provide man-to-machine and machine-to-man communication, and since they surround CPU, they are also called *peripheral devices*.

2.7.1 Input devices

Input devices are of many types, but basically they are meant for presenting the information to the computer in machine readable form. A computer system may have one or more of following input devices, depending upon its type, size and use.

a. Punch card reader
b. Punched paper tape reader
c. Magnetic tape
c. Magnetic disk
e. Floppy disk
f. Teleprocessing terminal (teletypewriter terminal)
g. Optical scanners
   (i) Optical Mark Reader
   (ii) Optical Character Reader (OCR)
h. Magnetic Ink Character Reader (MICR)
i. Visual Display Unit (VDU)
j. Voice Data Entry terminal (VDE)

2.7.2 Central Processing Unit (CPU)

It is the mind and heart combined with the central nervous system of a computer. So the CPU performs functions similar to the cerebrus, cardiac, and command functions of a human body. It consists of three components, all of which are electronic based:

a. Arithmetic Logic Unit (ALU)
b. Storage devices (memory)
   (i) Main memory storage or Immediate Access Store (IAS)
   (ii) Auxiliary memory
c. Control Unit (Monitor)

The functions of CPU are to:

a. Store data as well as instructions,
b. Control the sequence of operations as per the stored instructions,

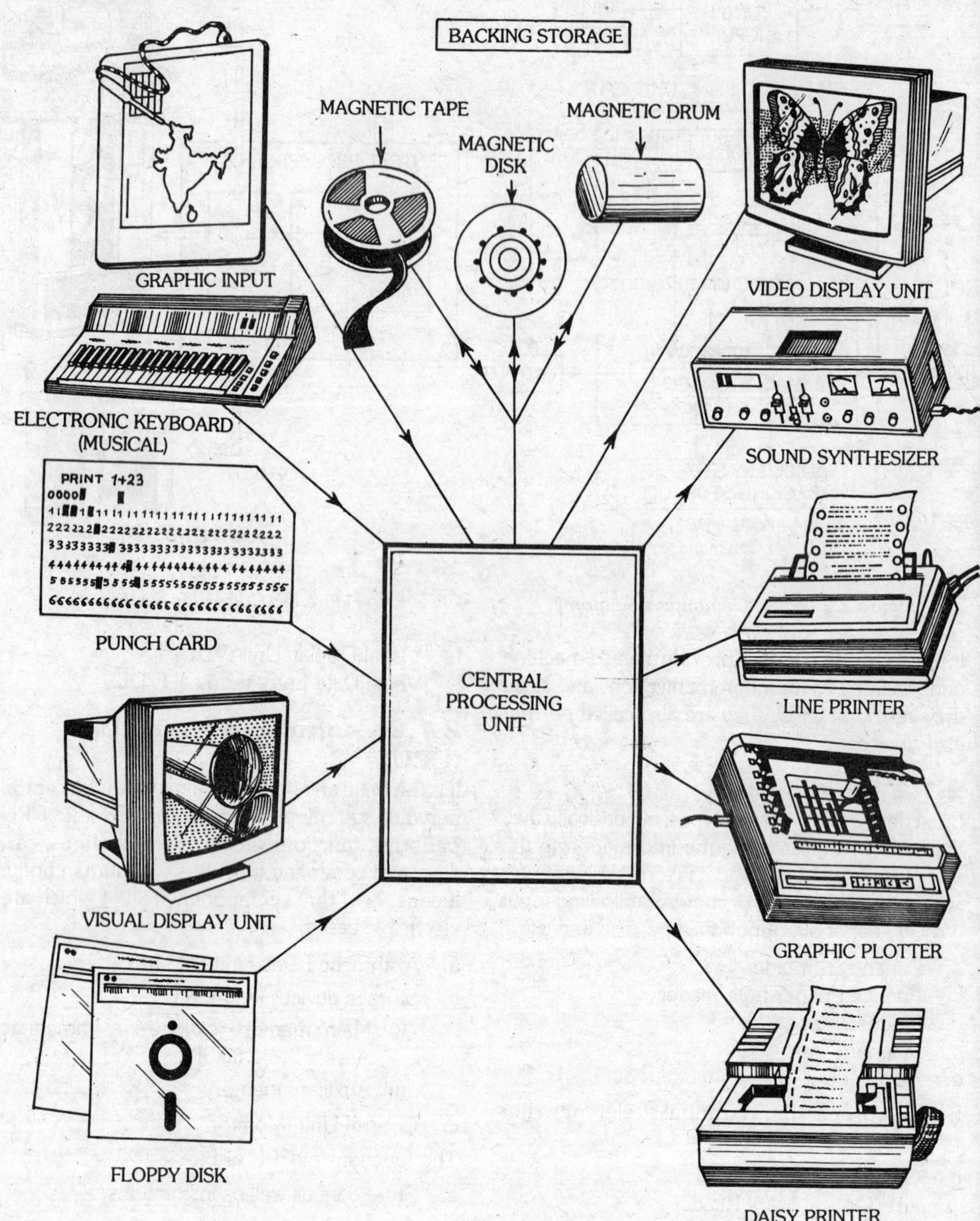

Figure 2.4 Central Processing Unit and Input/Output Devices

c. Issue commands to all parts of the computer system and
d. Carry out data processing and to send results to output.

2.7.3 Output Devices

The results of any computer processing has to be communicated to the users.

Outlet devices translate the computer's output into a form understandable by human beings. Similar to input devices, these also involve the presentation of information in a variety of forms. Output devices include:

1. Card puncher (obsolete now)
2. Printers
3. Tape puncher
4. Magnetic tape
5. Magnetic disk
6. Floppy disk
7. Plotter
8. Visual display terminal (VDU)

2. 7.4 Arithmetic and Logic Unit (ALU)

It operates on the data available in the main memory (IAS) and sends them back after processing, once again to the main memory. ALU performs two functions:

1. It carries out arithmetical operations like addition, subtraction, multiplication and division, and
2. It performs certain logical actions based on AND and OR functions.

ALU comprises a number of accumulators and registers. It derives all the data from the main memory as directed by the control unit, based on program given to it. This data gets loaded into accumulators in the ALU. For example, if two numbers A and B are to be added, the control unit selects number A from its address in the memory and loads it into arithmetic unit. Then, the value of B is selected and added to A in the arithmetic unit. The results are placed in the main storage (again under the direction of control unit), or may be retained in the accumulators themselves for further calculations. Some logical operations of the ALU enable the computer to have decision-making quality.

2. 7.5 Storage Devices

Storage devices are of two types:

1. Main storage or Immediate Access Storage (IAS), which is a part of central processing unit .
2. Auxiliary memory storage or backing storage, which is external to the central processing unit.

2.7.6 Memory Storage or Immediate Access Device Storage (IAS)

It is also called the computer's main or primary memory, because like the human memory, it is able to store information, which can be recalled or accessed, when required. The program of instructions has to be stored in the main memory in order to make it work automatically. This memory forms an integral part of ALU and is synthesized wholly by electronic components, due to which its operation is extremely fast. Any item of data or any instruction stored in memory can be retrieved by the computer at lightning speed. Modern computers do this in a few nanoseconds. The main high speed memory is limited in size and is very costly to buy; as such, only limited memory is provided, which is optimally necessary for immediate purposes. The rest of the programs and data are kept in secondary storage devices also known as backing storage devices.

Main memory storage is used by:

1. Instructions waiting to be obeyed by other components of the CPU.
2. Instructions currently being obeyed.
3. Data awaiting processing.
4. Data currently being processed.
5. Processed data awaiting output.

2.7.7 Auxiliary Memory Storage Devices

These are devices that hold the mass of information,

which may be transferred for use during processing as and when required and for record purposes. As compared to primary or main storage, it has much larger capacity, but is not as fast. Computer thus takes slightly more time to retrieve data from secondary storage. While retrieval from the main memory needs just a few nanoseconds, it may take milliseconds (.001 second) in case of secondary storage. But secondary storage is virtually unlimited in size and is much cheaper than main memory. For example, in our report card, the information like names, roll numbers, class and section, name of school, etc. shall be kept in secondary storage. It can be stored in the form of holes in the punched cards, paper tapes, but mostly it is in form of magnetic hardware as given below:

(a) Floppy disks or diskettes

(b) Hard disk

   (i) Fixed disk which cannot be removed from disk-drive

   (ii) Fixed head disk – a fixed disk having one read/write head for each track

   (iii) Exchangeable disk

   (iv) Winchester disk fixed in airtight units intended for use in dusty or humid environments.

Magnetic tape provides serial access to the data whereas magnetic disk provide both serial and direct access. Two types of secondary memories which provide large capacity and have no moving parts are:

a. Magnetic bubble memory and

b. Charged-coupled devices (CCDs)

The first one is non-volatile (i.e. memory does not wash away whenever the computer is put off) and second is volatile but both are serially accessible. They are very reliable and faster than disk memory.

2.7.8 Storage Hierarchy

The data and programs are stored in the computer at three different levels:

- Cache memory
- Main (internal) memory
- Auxiliary (external) memory

Internal memory is otherwise known as main memory, or Immediate Access Storage (IAS). It is known as Immediate Access Storage, as this is the portion of the computer's central processing unit where current data and/or program remain resident for execution in the computer. So when the computer is to process a program, the program instructions and associated data should be immediately available. Computers require internal memory not only for storing instruction and data awaiting execution of a program, but also for storing the results, which can thereafter be transferred to the output unit.

The CPU executes a sequence of instructions, which we call a program, in order to fulfil some processing goal. Since the CPU can deal with only one instruction at any given time, there must be a place to store all of the instructions of the program, and to fetch them, one at a time, for execution. This is the primary use of memory by the computer to store the program instructions. Programs and data need to be in the main storage in order to be executed or referenced. Programs or data not needed immediately may be kept on secondary storage until needed and then brought into the main storage for execution or reference. Secondary storage media such as tape or disk are generally less costly than the main storage and have much greater capacity. The main storage may generally be accessed much faster than secondary storage. In systems with several levels of storage, a great deal of shuttling goes on in which programs and data are moved back and forth between the various levels. This shuttling consumes system resources such as CPU time, that could otherwise be put to productive use.

In the 1960s, it became clear that the storage hierarchy could be extended by one more level with dramatic improvements in performance and utilization. This additional level, the cache, is a high-speed storage that is much faster than the main storage. Cache storage is extremely expensive compared with the main storage and, therefore, only relatively small caches are used.

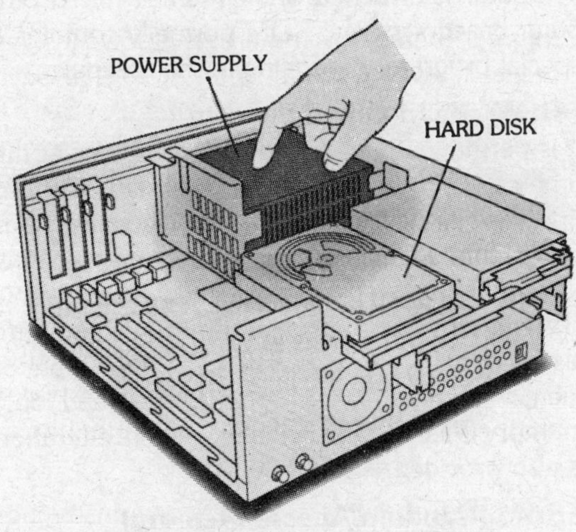

Figure 2.5 The Microcomputer

Cache storage imposes one more level of shuttling on the system. Programs in the main storage are shuttled to the very high-speed cache before being executed. In the cache, they may be executed much faster than in the main storage. The hope of designers using the cache concept is that the time involved in shuttling programs back and forth will be much smaller hence the performance increase would result due to the faster execution possible by this method.

In fact, cache memory is a part of the computer's main memory.

For comparison, we move from external to cache memories.

- Storage access time decreases
- Storage access speed increases
- Storage cost per bit increases
- Storage capacity decreases

2.7.9 Control Unit

The control unit directs all operations inside the computer. It is known as nerve centre of the computer because it controls and co-ordinates all hardware operations i.e. those of the CPU and input - output devices. Its actions are given below:

I. It gives command to transfer data from the input device to the memory (IAS) and from there to arithmetic logic unit.

II. It also transfers the results from ALU to the memory and on to the output device for printing.

III. It stores the program in the memory, takes instructions one by one, understands them, and issues appropriate commands to the other units.

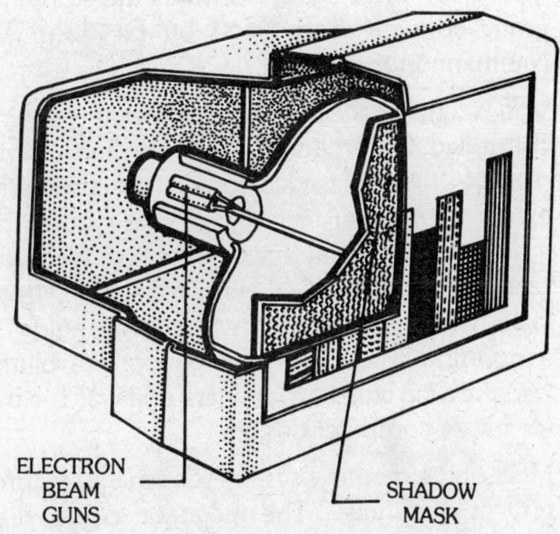

Figure 2.6 Cathode Ray Tube (CRT) (Screen of Computer)

4. It fetches the required instructions from the main storage via memory data register (MDR) and places it in the control instruction register (CIR). Then it interprets the instructions in CIR and gets it executed by sending a command signal to the concerned hardware device. Memory data register is a special register which holds all data instructions temporarily as they pass in and out of the main memory. Control instruction register is also a special register which holds machine instructions currently being interpreted by control units.

2.8 Stored Program Concept

In the year 1833, Lord Babbage envisaged an automatic calculating machine. This machine was designed to store one thousand, 50-digit numbers for calculations and make decisions depending on the results. This is a feature that distinguishes a computer from a calculator, i.e. a computer can make decisions. He thought of designing a machine for solving the problem and also those problems which are generated during course of calculation and are likely to be used in further calculation. This concept for immediate access is known as stored program concept.

Any program being processed must remain in primary storage during its execution. This requirement once again illustrates the stored program concept introduced by Dr John Von Neumann in the 1940s.

Von Neumann theorized that computers could be controlled by programs held in their primary storage units. This idea conflicted with the then existing computer technology. The stored program concept meant that computers could handle many tasks when asked by a program. Different tasks could be handled without changing the supporting hardware. This concept revolutionized the then existing hardware and was the basis for future computer design.

Most of the memory systems use magnetic property of materials. The magnetic cores, disks, drums and tapes are examples of this category. Another type of memory system uses transistorized flip-flop circuits which are very costly, occupy a large space, and are very fast in action. Due to this reason, their use is limited as compared to register or buffer memories for storage of intermediate result. Nowadays, with the development of IC technology, large scale integrated circuits (LSI chips) and microprocessors are being used as semiconductor memories, which are completely replacing valve technology. Other devices for memory storage are punched holes in tapes and cards, plated wires, thin films, delay lines, tunnel diodes, twister, ferrites transfluxers, and cryogenics. The most recent development is of using magnetic bubbles, charged couple devices, and holography (laser technology).

2.9 Types of Memory

The main memory storage is divided into two portions ROM and RAM, the latter is of more than double the size of the former. Programs held in ROM are called firmware. They are stored permanently in the ROM and are ready for use when computer is switched on. On small microcomputer based systems, ROM normally contains a special program for logging in the computer.

• ROM (Read Only Memory)

It is permanently in-built in the computer at the time of its production. ROM is otherwise called firmware also. It stores a set of instructions permanently which instructs the computer how to work. In ROM, permanent data and programs like trignometric and logarithmic functions are also stored. In one variation of this type of memory, known as programmable read only memory (PROM), the flexibility of data alteration is also provided.

• RAM (Random Access Memory)

This is also a part of computer's local memory, where the computer stores all the data and instructions it receives from input and the results as it works through its calculations. RAM is short-term memory or volatile memory, i.e. when the computer is switched off, all the information disappears, whereas ROM is permanent memory. The random access memory requires some time for access to each data and is considered to be the fastest memory. Generally, magnetic core memories and semiconductor memory systems fall in this category.

Each bit in a RAM stores information by means of electric charge, where the presence of an electric charge indicates a '1' and the absence a '0'. One variety of RAM is the so-called Dynamic RAM (such as the Intel 2116), where this electric charge tends to leak out in a few milliseconds, so that the information present in the RAM is lost (like a leaky tin which can hold water only for a short while). Consequently, the sets of information stored in such RAMs need be refreshed periodically, before all the charge has leaked out. For this purpose, special refresh circuitry has to be provided.

As against this, we have Static RAMs (such as the Intel 2114), which are not leaky and therefore do not require any refreshing. They also tend to be faster — a typical Static RAM today has an access time of 80 nsec which means that it would take 80 nsec to read from or write into any location. The corresponding figure for a Dynamic RAM is 120 to 200 nsec. However, Static RAMs tend to be more expensive than their Dynamic counterparts and are not used for large memories.

• Difference Between ROM and RAM

The basic difference between a Read Only Memory (ROM) and a RAM is that the former is permanent memory. Programs or data once placed in ROM, remain there even if the power supply is switched off. This feature makes it very convenient for storing programs for dedicated applications where the microprocessor computer will always be executing the same program.

• PROM

A commonly used version is the Programmable ROM or PROM, which is supplied in blank form by the manufacturer. The user must write the desired program into it once, by a special process. Subsequently, the contents cannot be changed. The procedure is analogous to buying a blank stencil, and typing.

• EPROM

PROM has a defect. Nobody writes a correct working program in one shot. Every program needs to be written, tested, and rewritten for a number of times, before it works satisfactorily (a process known as debugging). And if we were to use a PROM to store and test every intermediate version, we would be wasting a large number of PROMs.

This led to the concept of Erasable PROM or EPROM. Simply shine ultraviolet light on an EPROM for 20 minutes, and the EPROM is erased. These are the most commonly used ROMs today.

• EEPROMs

But manufacturers are trying to make the chips smarter. Instead of ROM, many devices now incorporate EEPROMs (electrically erasable PROM) which can be easily reprogrammed by the application of a small voltage. Such microcontrollers are very useful in prolonging the use of machine tools. The device can sense the wear and automatically compensate by reprogramming its EEPROM so that frequent adjustments of the machine are not required.

2.10 Computer Programming

Computer programming means giving instruction to a computer in the language which it understands. Such instructions can be written in three different languages as given below:

(1) Machine language
(2) Assembly language
(3) High level language

2.10.1 Machine Language

A computer is an electronic machine which can understand any instruction given to it in a coded form. Since its memory can store only '0's and '1's, hence the instructions must be given to computer in binary code. A computer program means a sequence of the instructions written logically in such a manner that it consists of minimum instructions so that the typing of a program into computer (or feeding the computer program) takes minimum time. A program written in binary coded form (or any other coded forms like Hex or Octal) which can be directly fed to computer for execution is known as *machine language* and represents the lowest level of programming. It is worth indicating here that machine languages are different for different microprocessors. Instructions are given to the computer's mechanism with the help of the binary system. In binary system, '0' represents the absence of a pulse and '1' its presence, a sequence such as 01010100 has some specific meaning for the computer. Such a binary representation was used in early computers and the programs based on these binary numbers were said to be written in machine language. Writing a program in machine language is a very difficult and cumbersome process. For example, a series of numbers 0011, 1000, 1001 in the machine language means "Add a number stored in location 8 to another number stored in location 9 and store the above result in the location 8". (The code number 0011 stands for the 'addition' operation.) For each instruction, different codes are used. Also, the rules of the machine language differ from one computer to the other.

Instructions in a form which can be used directly by the control unit are called machine instructions and programs written in the form of machine instructions are said to be written in machine language. We have already seen that it is very cumbersome to prepare a computer program in machine language as it contains instructions written in very long numerical chains and it is very difficult to remember the code of machine language.

2.10.2 Assembly Language

The assembly language is a compromise between a high-level language and a machine language. To reduce the programmer's burden, symbolic languages or addresses were developed in 1950. These languages permit the use of alphanumeric symbols (numbers and letters) instead of numeric operation codes and addresses. The computer operating system automatically translates these symbols with the help of a symbol equivalence table in order to obtain the numeric code that it needs to execute the program.

Because the correspondence is one-on-one between the symbolic and numeric operation codes, this language retains a high level of flexibility for the programmer. Symbolic languages are also machine-oriented and their coding is time consuming. Assembly language is not as cumbersome to use as the machine language, nor is it as complicated as a high-level language like BASIC and FORTRAN. This is also called symbolic machine language and it allows a precise specification of the details of a particular microprocessor while retaining some symbolic and mnemonic information. A mnemonic is a means by which information can be memorized easily and is generally in the form of abbreviations of the name of operations to be carried out. Thus, LDA is a mnemonic representation for LoaD Accumulator and STA might stand for STore Accumulator.

2.10.3 High-Level Language

A set of languages have been devised which are very close to our native language. Because of their strict grammer such a set of languages is called high-level language. A program expressed in a high-level language has to be translated into machine language before the computer's microprocessor can perform all operations specified by these languages. BASIC, FORTRAN, PASCAL, COBOL and C are some of the popular high level languages.

2.11 The Management of the Computer

The computer is not a single machine or apparatus and a computing system is not something that just does calculations. The word computer means a group of various machines which are utilized for processing a set of information. The systems involved during computer programming and for computer upkeeping are:

1. Hardware
2. Software

2.11.1 Hardware

It is a general term used to represent the physical and tangible components of the computer itself, i.e. those components which can be touched and seen. It includes:

a. Input devices
b. Output devices
c. Central Processing Unit
d. Backing storage or auxiliary memory devices*

N.B * (All of these have been explained above in the chapter)

The electronic circuits consisting of Resistors, Capacitors, ICs, etc. inside a computer are all examples of *Computer Hardware.*

2.11.2 Software

It is a general term to describe all the forms of programs associated with the computer. Without software, a computer is like a car without petrol, or a TV without a film. Softwares can be of following two basic types:

a. System software
b. Application software

(a) System Software

By system, we mean computer system. The user of a computer has at his disposal a large amount of software provided by the manufacturer. Much of this software will be programs which contribute to the control and performance of the computer system. Such programs are given the collective name *system software. System software can be sub-divided as follows:*

I. Operating systems and control programs
II. Translators
III. Utilities and service programs
IV. Data Base Management Systems (DBMS)

Compilers, assemblers, DOS, UNIX, Interpreter and DBMS are systems programs.

(b) Application Software

Applications programs may be provided by the computer manufacturer or supplier but in many cases the user produces his own applications programs called *user programs*. (e.g. payroll programs, stock control programs, etc.). A single applications program is often called a *job*. Sometimes, a job may be divided into smaller units called *tasks*. A job may comprise program + data. Most applications programs can only work if used in conjunction with the appropriate systems programs. further sub-division of application software is following:

I. User applications programs
II. Applications packages
III. Pre-packaged software

A more detailed sub-division of different softwares is as follows:

(c) Operating Systems and Control Programs

These are the programs usually written by computer manufacturers. These programs are inbuilt into the computer and are used to govern the control of the computer hardware components, such as processors, memory devices and input/output devices. They, in fact, act as an interface between the user's programs and the computer components and facilitate the execution of his programs. Operating systems can handle several programs at a time in the time-sharing mode and can optimize the use of computer hardware. The operating system of a computer is one of the main factors which contribute to its capabilities.

(d) Translators

They are also known as language processors. This software is used to translate the programmer-written instructions into machine code instructions. This is a machine-dependent software and is popularly known as *assembler/compiler*.

(e) Utilities and Service Programs

These are also pre-written programs, usually by the manufacturers, and supplied with the system. These are increasingly used in data-base management systems to manipulate data and print out results. A good range of such utility programs can make the task much simpler for the user. Other examples of utility programs are:

1. Program to load a program into memory, and
2. Program to duplicate magnetic tapes.

(f) User Application Programs

Application programs are user-written programs to perform certain specific jobs. They are unique in their construction and can be used only for identical jobs. Recently, many such application programs have been made commercially available under the name *program package*. These can be changed marginally to fit individual needs and to meet the system requirements. Standard packages for application areas such as payroll, billing, PERT/CPM, inventory control, and linear programming are available.

(g) Application Packages

These are similar in concept to utility (service) programs except that application packages are generalized programs for solving business problems as opposed to programs for carrying out computer systems tasks.

Many users have the same type of problem to put onto a computer and thus manufacturers and specialist software writers have written standard programs to solve these problems and sell them to the many users who want them. Examples are Stock Control, Sales Invoicing, Network Analysis.

(h) Prepackaged Software

The personal computer brought computing power to the individual user. Using their personal computers, users could now fulfil their own informational needs and perform analysis previously not possible.

Users, generally programmers and professionals, could now focus on information useful to them, thus increasing their effectiveness on the job. Although this was a positive step, in many cases it created some problems. Users had to learn how to master their personal computers. This took extra time and efforts before they learned to perform the desired analysis. Also, the need to develop these analytic programs put extra pressure on an already overburdened DP staff.

Many personal computer users know what they want to do, but they do not have the skills to write the necessary software.

Naturally, they turned to their DP staff for help. Due to this, many private software development concerns became aware of these conditions and wrote programs to satisfy these needs. This prepackaged, or canned software is designed to be used by professionals from all levels and is marketed for all types of microcomputers. These prepackaged, prewritten programs became very useful. Users did not have to write their own programs; all they had to do was learn to use them.

Most prepackaged software today is user-friendly and can be purchased in diskette form. It is designed for interactive usage and is accompanied by documentation which explains its purpose. These prepackaged programs prompt the user by asking questions to which she or he must reply. Generally, within a short time, users become acquainted with their canned software and begin to be productive.

Prepackaged software is generally classified into four categories to help users identify commercially sold products. The four categories represent software written for the areas of games, home, education, and business.

2.12 Advantage of Packages

- The main advantage is the saving of programming effort and expenses on the part of the user. Development costs are effectively shared between the users.
- The user gets a well-tried-and-tested program which he is able to use with confidence.
- Relatively quick implementation results from the use of packages.

EXERCISE

Objective-Type Questions

1. The basic components of a modern digital computer are:
   (a) central processor.
   (b) input device.
   (c) output device.
   (d) all of the above.
2. The Arithmetic and Logic Unit (ALU) is called the ....of a computer.
   (a) heart
   (b) master despatcher
   (c) primary memory
   (d) all of the above
3. A typical modern computer uses
   (a) magnetic cores for secondary storage.
   (b) LSI chips.
   (c) magnetic tapes for primary memory.
   (d) more than 10,000 vacuum tubes.
4. A VDU is used as
   (a) input device.
   (b) output device.
   (c) voice data entry device.
   (d) both (a) and (b).
5. Computer memory
   (a) performs all calculations.
   (b) receives input data.
   (c) is extremely limited.
   (d) is better than human memory.
6. The central processor of a modern digital computer consists of
   (a) control unit.
   (b) primary memory.
   (c) all of the above.

7. The control unit is often called the .... of a digital computer.
   (a) nerve centre
   (b) master despatcher
   (c) clock
   (d) all of the above
8. Mark the wrong statement. Programmable Read Only Memory (PROM) of a digital computer
   (a) is permanent.
   (b) contains program instructions.
   (c) is programmed during manufacture.
   (d) is volatile.
9. As compared to the secondary memory, the primary memory of a computer is
   (a) large.
   (b) cheap.
   (c) fast.
   (d) slow.
10. Computer memory consists of .... microchips.
   (a) RAM
   (b) ROM
   (c) PROM
   (d) all of the above
11. Backing storage is so named because it
   (a) lags behind the main memory.
   (b) is slow and backward.
   (c) backs up the computer's main memory.
   (d) is always kept at the back of the CPU.
12. In a computer, RAM is used as a short memory because it
   (a) is volatile.
   (b) has small capacity.
   (c) is very expensive.
   (d) is programmable.
13. Fill in the blanks with most appropriate word(s) or numerical values:
   (a) The three functional elements of a digital computer are: input device,................ and output device.
   (b) The central processing unit of a computer consists of................., Control Unit and Arithmetic and Logic Unit (ALU)
   (c) Winchester disks are ideal for use in ....and humid environments.
   (d) The central processing unit (CPU) is called ....of a computer.
   (e) The control unit (CU) is called the......................centre of digital computer.
   (f) Locations in the main memory of a computer are called..............
   (g) The main storage is also called main ....
   (h) The control unit of a CPU is also called the master despatcher and............of the computer.
   (i) The controlling program computer is held in ROM because it is a............ memory.
   (j) The primary memory of a computer is quite ....
   (k) In the main memory of a computer, RAM is used as a short-term memory because it is..........
14. What are the various characteristics of computers which have made them so versatile and popular?
15. What are the three basic ingredients of a computer?

ANSWERS

1. (d), 2. (c), 3. (b), 4. (d), 5. (b), 6. (d), 7. (d), 8. (d), 9. (c), 10. (d), 11. (c), 12. (a)

13. (a) central processor, (b) memory, (c) dusty, (d) heart, (e) nerve, (f) words, (g) memory, (h) clock, (i) non-volatile/ permanent, (j) expensive, (k) volatile

CHAPTER 3

Flow Charts

3.1 Flow Charts

The computer is a brainless superservant of humanity, but wisdom is imparted to it by human beings by giving proper instructions to get a proper service from it. The set of instructions given to it is called *program*. Before writing any program, it is necessary that a flow chart is drawn up. A *flow chart* is a step-by-step diagramatic representation of the logic paths contained within a computer program and *flow charting* is the technique of drawing the flow chart. In other words, a flow chart is a diagrammatic representation of the procedure for solving the problem. Flow charts are drawn up as a pictorial guide by programmers for planning the procedure for the solution of a problem. It helps a person to understand at a glance the sequence of steps necessary to solve a given problem. A flow chart indicates the direction of flow of a process, relevant operations and computations, points of decisions, and other information which is a part of the solution. Once developed and properly checked, the flow chart provides an excellent guide for writing the program.

Flow charts also facilitate communication among the programmer and the authorities which do not understand programming exactly. They also help in debugging the program, i.e. in finding out the mistakes in the programs.

3.2 Flow Chart Symbols

For easy visual recognition, a standard convention is used in drawing flow charts. The symbols as given below are as per conventions followed by International Standards Organisation (ISO).

Terminater: Rectangle with rounded sides (oval ◯) is used to indicate either START (or BEGIN) and END of a progrm.

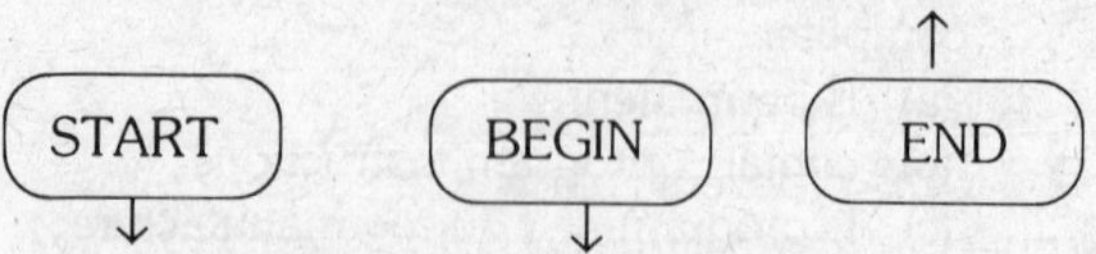

Process Indicators: Rectangle ▭ is used to indicate set of processing operations such as for storage arithmetic operations. Normally, LET statement is used for such operations.

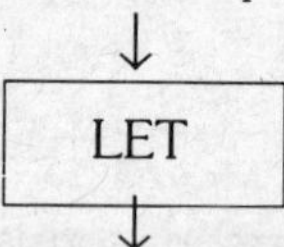

INPUT and OUTPUT Indicators: Parallelograms ▱ are used to represent input and output operations. Statements like INPUT, READ and PRINT are represented in parallelograms.

Decision Makers: The diamond ◇ is used for indicating the step of decision making and therefore known as *decision box*. It is used to indicate the process of logic in a program which may be of getting an answer to a question, or may be of testing any condition. The further flow path is selected by computer based on the answer. Thus, a decision box, which is normally entered from top, represents a point at which different process paths may be selected. In other words, it represents the occurrence of a question, the answer to which will determine the path to be taken. The decision box (as shown above) must have at least two exits, although a third may be added sometimes if desired.

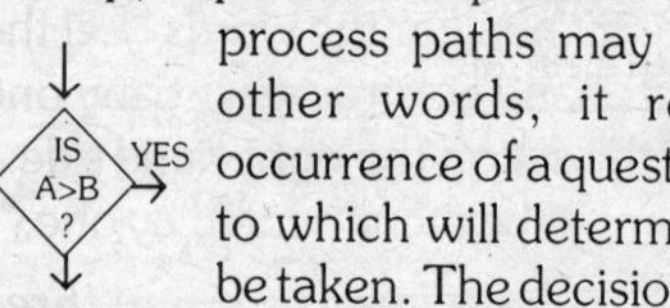

A decision box may contain a single question, of which the answer may be Yes or No, depending upon the answer computer will follow the further path. Sometimes, the decision box may be used to test a condition which may be True or False. In a

BASIC program, the Yes (True) path is always the THEN path and NO (False) path is always to the statement that immediately follows the IF.

Arrow: An arrow (←↑→ ↓) is used to indicate the direction of flow of information. Every line in a flow chart must have an arrow on it.

Connector: A circle ○ is used to join different parts of a flow chart as a connector. The use of connectors gives a neat appearance to a flow chart. If the flow chart extends over more than one page, the different parts are joined with a connector. The fact that two joints are to be joined is indicated by enclosing them in circles and by writing the same identifying letter or digit inside both the circles. The connector symbol may also be used to eliminate the crossing lines between one part of the flow chart to another.

3.3 Rules for Making a Flow Chart

The following rules may be remembered while making a flow chart:

1. The symbols as given in Fig. 3.1 should be used;
2. The arrows in the flow chart represent the direction of flow of control in the problem;
3. The usual direction of the flow of a procedure or system is from left to right or top to bottom. If this convention is followed, then arrows are not necessary;
4. Flow lines should not cross each other normally; and
5. Horizontal arrow indicates that the terms on both sides of the arrows are synonymous. It can be taken as symbol for the words "Let the term on the left-hand side represent any one of the term of the set on the right-hand side." Or, Let the number be incremented by one.".

Example 3.1: *To pick up largest of any three given numbers.*

First of all, the three numbers A, B and C are read. Then A is compared with B. If A is larger than B, in that case A is compared with C. If A turns out to be the larger number again, then it is declared the largest number; else C is declared the largest

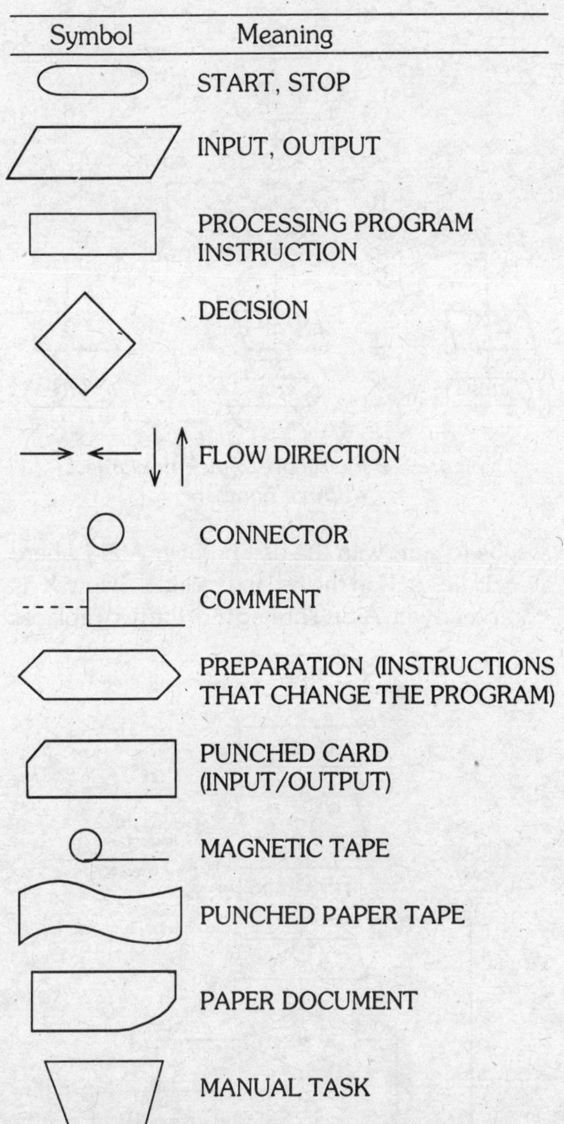

Fig. 3.1 Symbols for Making a Flow Chart

number. If in the first top itself, A is found less than or equal to B then B is compared with C. If B is larger, then it is the largest number, otherwise C is the largest number. This procedure is represented in the flow chart shown in Fig. 3.2.

Example 3.2: *To find out the largest of a set of 100 integer numbers.*

For solving this problem, the method used in Example 1 cannot be applied since it will involve a large amount of subroutes. The proper method

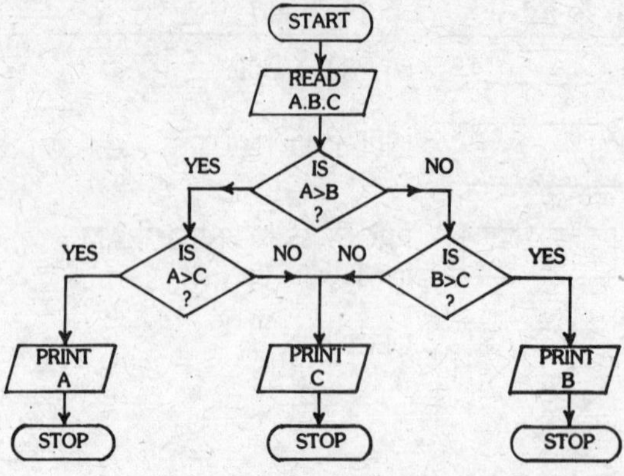

Figure 3.2 Flowchart to pick the largest of three numbers

will be to start with the first number A(*N*) where *N* = 1, i.e. A(1) in the list and call it *X*. Now *X* is compared with A(2). The larger of the two replaces

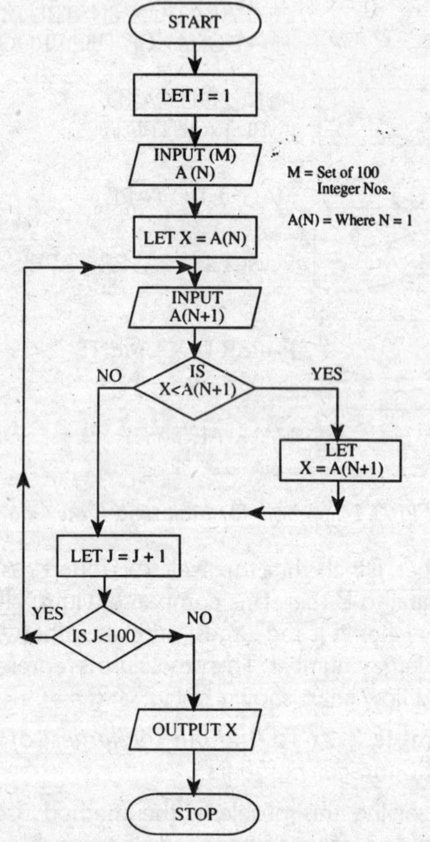

Figure 3.3 Flow chart to Pick the Largest of 100 Numbers.

X. In the next step, X is compared with A(3) and the procedure is repeated. Thus, X will contain at all times the current largest number. After all the numbers have been scanned, X will contain the largest number in the list as shown in Fig. 3.3. In this example A(*N*) represents a set of 100 numbers such that *N* = 1 to 100 integer numbers. This set of numbers can be fed to computer as input data through punched cards which remains in memory and any one of the numbers can be called back whenever needed.

3.4 Structured Programming

The flow chart for any program procedure can be built from a combination of just the following three basic kinds of flow charts:

3.4.1 Simple sequence: This consists of a set of independent instructions which are to be followed one after another from beginning to end. Let us take an example of making of tea. First, we have to put the stove on, take utensil and put it on the stove. Then fill it with a cup of water which is

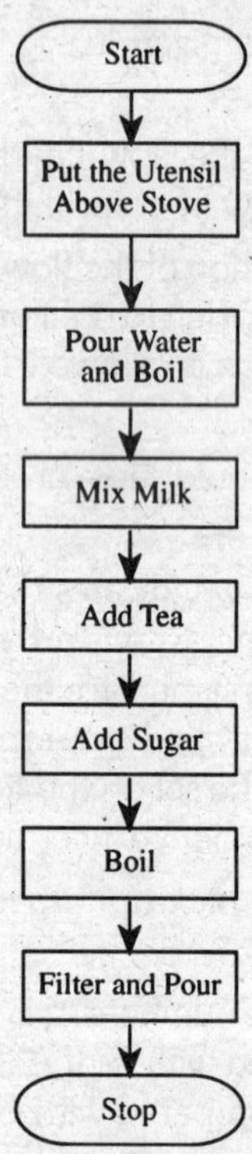

Figure 3.4 Flow chart of a Simple Sequence

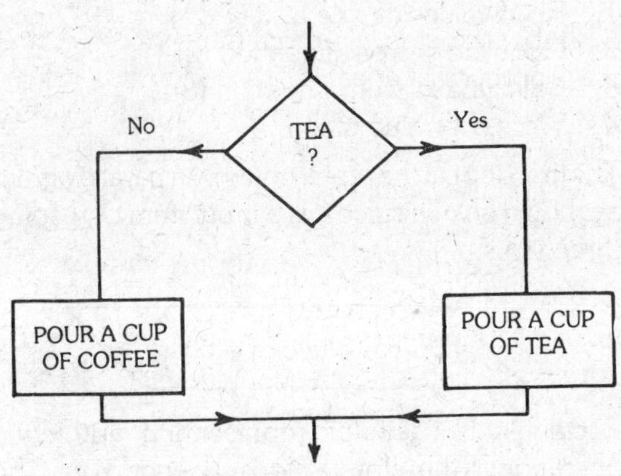

Figure 3.5 Flow chart of simple selection

further mixed with milk, sugar and tea. Then it is boiled, filtered and poured in various cups. The stove is then turned off. This procedure can be represented graphically by a set of instructions as shown in Fig. 3.4.

3.4.2 Simple Logical Selection (Decision making): This can be illustrated by an example of a party where both tea and coffee are available to series of guests. If you like tea you have to pour a cup of tea, else pour a cup of coffee **(Fig. 3.4).**

A procedure can be accomplished either by a single decision box or by several selections as is illustrated by flow chart (Fig.3.6) of selecting a drink and process of sugar mixing, etc. First, we can write the steps which are necessary in pouring a drink of one's choice in a party.

1. Decide which drink
2. Pour milk into cup
3. Fill the cup with tea or coffee as per decision
4. Decide whether you need sugar or not
5. Add spoonful of sugar
6. Stir the drink and drink

3.4.3 Simple Repetition: The beauty of using computer is that it can perform millions of calculations repeatedly without tiring. It evolves an expression for various values of a variable by increasing its value in specified steps. It does the same calculations a number of times by increasing the values of the variables in necessary steps and repeating the procedure. This is shown in a flow chart with the help of loops Fig. 3.7. Let us see how loops are used to show the repetitive process by an example of knocking a nail in.

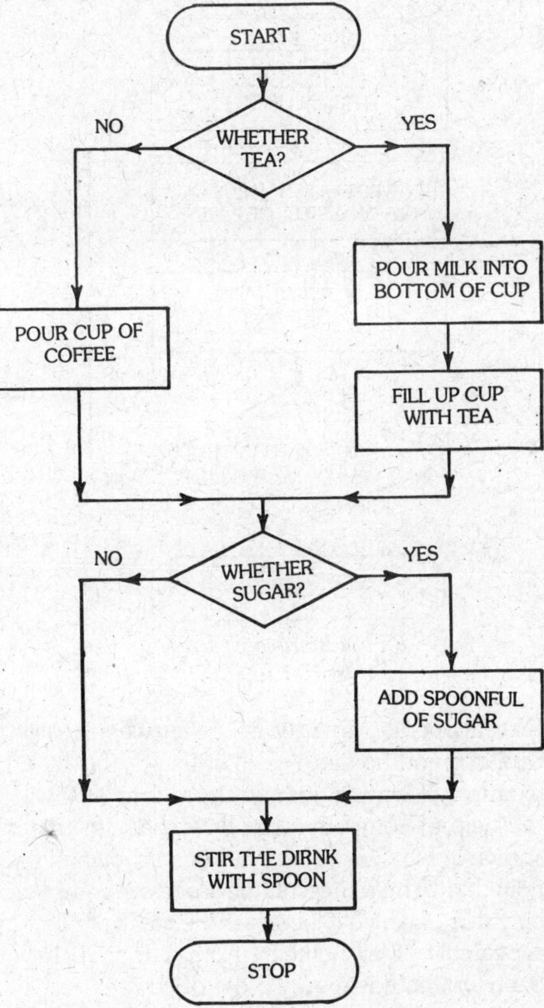

Figure 3.6 Flow chart of decision making

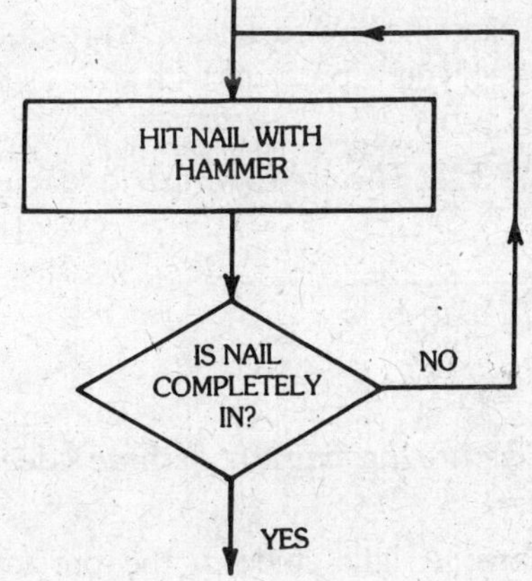

Fig. 3.7 Repeatition or looping

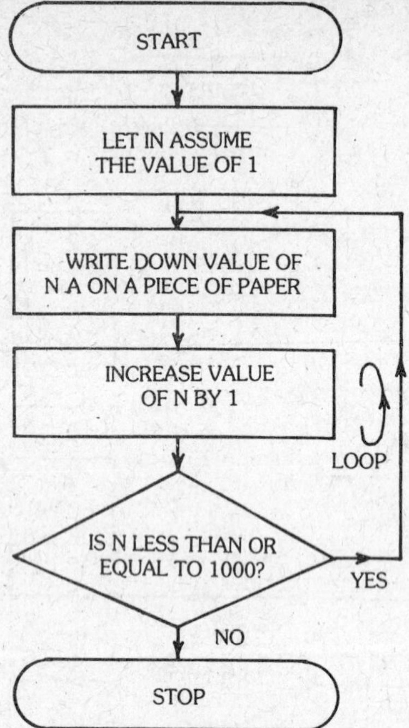

Fig. 3.8 Flowchart of writing numbers from 1 to 1000

Repeat operation may be necessary when answer to a decision box is 'Yes'. Let us see this by an example of writing numbers from 1 to 100 with the help of computer. The flow chart for this is shown in Fig. 3.8. A loop has been shown in the flow chart. This represents the process in computer by virtue of which it increases the value of *N* by 1 repeatedly till all numbers from 1 to 100 have been written down on a piece of paper.

3.5 Development of a Program by Flow Charts

We shall examine how to develop a program flow chart for solving a problem with the help of an example.

Example 3.4: *The area of any triangle is given by*

$$x = \sqrt{s(s-a)(s-b)(s-c)} \qquad (1)$$

where $s = (a + b + c)/2$ *(2)*

and a, b & c are the measure of three sides of the triangle.

Algorithm: A little study of the problem will reveal following steps:

1. Read values of side a, b & c
2. Calculate *s* from Equation (2)
3. Calculate *x* from Equation (3)
4. Write the value of *x*

The first step can be represented by a parallelogram as shown below, since it is a input item of reading three sides:

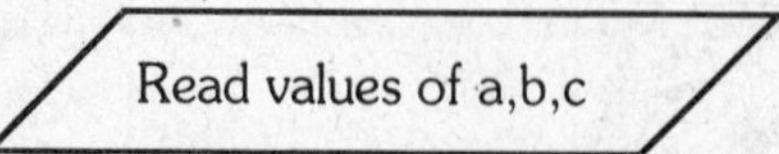

Rectangle is used for representing arithmetic operations, therefore, Steps 2 and 3 can be represented by rectangles as

$S = (a+b+c)/2$ or $S \leftarrow (a+b+c)/2$

$X \leftarrow \sqrt{S(s\text{-}a)\ (s\text{-}b)\ (s\text{-}c)}$

After the calculations have been made, the value stored in x is written out. The symbol to denote this is (being output operation)

Write X

The start and stop of the program is always indicated by the oval-shaped symbol, so at the top we have to add START and at the bottom of flow chart STOP. The complete flow chart is shown below

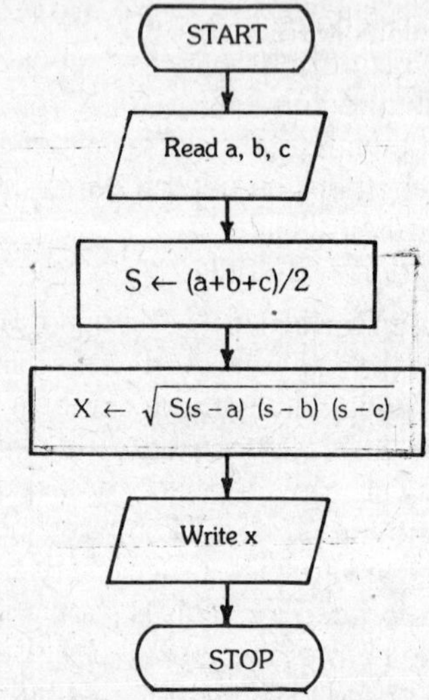

Fig. 3.9 Flow Chart of the Example Given

CHAPTER 4

Getting Started With BASIC

4.1 Starting BASIC

Type GWBASIC and press ↵ to load the BASIC interpreter. The screen will look similar to this:

```
The IBM Personal Computer Basic
Version D2.10Copyright +
IBM Corp. 1981,1982,1983
61327 Bytes free
Ok
```

Notice the word "**Ok**" on the screen. It is the BASIC prompt, which tells you that the computer is ready to accept BASIC commands and statements.

We will now issue our first BASIC instruction to the computer. Type the following (exactly as it appears here):

```
PRINT "HELLO"
```

and press Enter (↵) key.

Watch that following appears on screen.

```
PRINT "HELLO"
```

The _ on the left is the prompt telling you that the BASIC interpreter is waiting for an instruction. The characters on the right have just been typed by you. Nothing has happened as yet. Do you remember why?

This is because you must hit the return key to enter your instruction. Now press return. Your screen should look like this:

```
PRINT "HELLO"
HELLO
Ok
_
```

The interpreter has received your instruction and has immediately executed it by displaying **HELLO** as requested. Next, the interpreter displays a new prompt (_), telling you that it is ready for a new instruction.

Let's examine our first BASIC instruction more closely:

```
PRINT "HELLO"↵
```

This instruction has two parts **PRINT** and **"HELLO"**. **PRINT** is a reserved word that has a specific meaning to the BASIC interpreter. **"HELLO"** is the message to be printed. It must be enclosed within the quotes. You can use any message within the quotes. Let's try another Type:

```
PRINT "HOW ARE YOU?"↵
```

The symbol ↵ denotes that you have to press Enter key after entering the program line, for getting the instruction executed.

The following should appear on your screen:

```
PRINT "HOW ARE YOU?"
Ok
_
```

Try again. Display your own message, but remember: if you forget one of the quotes or if you misspell PRINT, it will not work, and you will get an error message. Go ahead; try it. You won't damage anything.

You may now be wondering why this instruction is called **PRINT** when in fact it merely displays and does not print the information on your screen. Even if you have a printer connected to your computer, nothing will be printed. You have probably guessed the reason. The early terminals were typewriter-like, and in fact, did print (not display) the information. And, although the technology has changed, the BASIC instruction has not. Another BASIC instruction is now used to send information to the printer, rather than to the display. This instruction is called **LPRINT**, because its main use is to list programs on paper.

Before we proceed, make sure that the BASIC prompt appears on your screen, i.e., that the BASIC interpreter is ready to accept another command. If the prompt does not appear, you cannot execute a BASIC command. Try pressing return or **Ctrl-Break**, or if that doesn't work, try restarting your system.

We will now write our first BASIC program, rather than just execute a single instruction or "statement." Type the following:

```
10 PRINT "HELLO"
20 PRINT "WHAT IS YOUR NAME?"
30 END
```

Your screen should look like this:

```
10 PRINT "HELLO"
20 PRINT "WHAT IS YOUR NAME?"
30 END
_
```

You may be surprised that nothing has happened. The computer merely responds with a _. These three lines are more than just three BASIC statements. They constitute a short BASIC program. Note that each line begins with a number; this number is called a line number or label. It tells the computer that we want to write a complete program, and not execute each instruction immediately. Now, type:

```
RUN
HELLO
WHAT IS YOUR NAME?
Ok
_
```

How does this work? First we created a three-line program and stored it in memory, a line at a time, by pressing return. Then we executed the program by typing **RUN**. This is the normal way of writing and executing a program. We shall follow this procedure from now on. All lines will be preceded by a numerical label, and the program will be executed automatically in the order of the labels.

4.2 Direct and Indirect modes

If at any time you type an unlabeled BASIC statement in response to a _ , the statement will be executed immediately; it will not be memorized. This is called the *direct* mode in IBM PC BASIC.

If at any time you type a labeled BASIC statement in response to a _ , the statement will be memorized when you hit return, but not executed until you type **RUN**. This is called the *indirect* mode. Let's demonstrate how this works.

Our three-line program has been stored in memory. It can be executed for any number of times, expanded or modified. So, type:

```
RUN↵
```

again, and you should see:

```
HELLO
WHAT IS YOUR NAME?
Ok
_
```

Let's now examine the computer's memory and display its contents. To do this, type:

```
LIST↵
```

and you should see the following displayed on your screen:

```
10 PRINT "HELLO"
20 PRINT "WHAT IS YOUR NAME?"
30 END
_
```

RUN:	Command used to excute a program in in-direct mode
LIST:	Command used to list program on screen
SAVE:	Command to save program on diskette SAVE d:filename

Your program is listed on the screen as it is stored in the computer's memory.

You can even save this first program on a diskette. To do this, the command SAVE d:file name where d is the drive and filename is the name you wish to give to your program. You can then read it back later by typing:

LOAD: Command to retrieve program from disk to memory

```
LOAD a:file name↵
```

To demonstrate differences between the immediate and deferred instructions, type:

```
PRINT "GOODBYE"↵
```

You see on the screen:

```
PRINT "GOODBYE"
GOODBYE
Ok
_
```

Warning: Saving with the old name will overwrite the previous program from diskette.

Loading a new program from disk overwrite the program in the memory.

Now type:

```
LIST↵
```

again, and you should see on your screen:

```
10 PRINT "HELLO"
20 PRINT "WHAT IS YOUR NAME"?
30 END
Ok
_
```

The new direct instruction: PRINT "GOODBYE" is no where to be seen. It has not been memorized.

In summary, a direct statement is executed as soon as you type it. It is not stored in the computer's memory, and you will need to type it every time you want to execute it. This facility is called the direct mode. (In practice, this mode is used infrequently ,generally when you want to verify some values after a program has stopped.) Feel free to experiment by typing BASIC instructions and see what happens.

When a line is preceded by a label, the mode is called the indirect mode. In this mode, each line of the program is stored away in the computer's memory. When a complete program has been typed in, you simply issue the RUN command, and the entire program will be executed. Remember that when you turn the computer off, the contents of the RAM memory disappear, including any program you may have typed. If you wish to keep your program for later use, you must **SAVE** it on a diskette.

4.3 Labels

Labels are positive integers type at the beginning of each statement to

- set the sequence of commands to be processed by the computer
- provide a convenient way to delete or add more statements inbetween, before, or after the existing commands

Each line of a BASIC program must start with a label. The label specifies the order in which the line will be executed. Thus, line 10 will be executed before line 20.

The **END** statement, line 30 in our example, is optional with IBM PC BASIC. The **END** statement tells the interpreter that it has reached the legitimate **END**, rather than an accidental one, during execution.

As a final detail, note that the digit O must look different from the letter O. The traditional way to avoid confusion has been to show the digit O as ø,an O over-stricken with a slash. The digit O appears this way on the IBM PC screen.

4.4 A Longer Program

RUN, **LIST**, and **SAVE** are called commands. They are reserved words used by themselves to specify special actions carried out by the computer system, or more exactly by the interpreter. These commands are also part of BASIC. We will progressively learn more statements and commands as we continue through this book.

Let's now write a more complete program, using the **PRINT** statement and the **NEW** command. Type the following:

```
NEW↵
```

Then:

```
LIST↵
```

Nothing happens. There is no longer any program in the memory. The NEW command clears the computer's memory. Now type:

```
NEW
10 PRINT "THIS"↵
20 PRINT "IS"↵
30 PRINT "ANOTHER"↵
40 PRINT "EXAMPLE"↵
50 END↵
```

> **NEW**: Erases away program from computer memory

Let's find out what this program does. Type:

```
RUN↵
```

You should now see on your screen:

```
THIS
IS
ANOTHER
EXAMPLE
Ok
_
```

Our program displays the text as expected. Let's verify that the program has been stored correctly in memory by typing:

```
LIST↵
```

The program on should now see on your screen:

```
10 PRINT "THIS"
20 PRINT "IS"
30 PRINT "ANOTHER"
40 PRINT "EXAMPLE"
50 END
Ok
_
```

The **NEW** command has been used to clear the memory of the computer, i.e. to erase it, to make a room for the new program. If the **NEW** command is not used, the new statements would erase and replace any older statement with identical labels previously typed into memory. This could lead to errors since old statements might be "leftover" in a new program. If you do not use **NEW**, then every time you type a statement with the label 10, the new version will automatically erase any older version of that statement. But, beware, if you had previously written a statement with the label 15, then type in the above program without a NEW, the statement "15" would remain in the computer's memory and would automatically be incorporated into your new program in sequence (since the label 15 is not used in the new program). Let us demonstrate this. Type:

```
15 PRINT "* * * * *"↵
```

Then:

```
RUN
```

Your screen should look like this:

```
THIS
* * * * *
IS
ANOTHER
EXAMPLE
Ok
_
```

As you can see, the new **PRINT** statement, labeled 15, has been automatically inserted in the older program after statement 10.

Let's list program. Type:

```
LIST↵
```

The program on screen should look like this:

```
10 PRINT "THIS"
15 PRINT "* * * * * "
20 PRINT "IS"
30 PRINT "ANOTHER"
40 PRINT "EXAMPLE"
50 END
Ok
_
```

You can verify that statement 15 is now a part of your program. Remember that every time you type a program statement with a label, it is automatically inserted in the memory of the computer in the proper sequence.

We will now demonstrate that when you use a label number that already exists, your new statement will automatically erase the previous one. Let's now use this feature to erase statement 15. Type:

```
15 PRINT "........"↵
```

Then:

```
RUN
```

Your screen should look like this:

```
THIS
........
IS
ANOTHER
EXAMPLE
Ok
_
```

As you can see, your new PRINT statement with

the label 15 has superseded the previous one. Verify it by typing:

```
LIST↵
```

Your screen should look like this:

```
10 PRINT "THIS"
15 PRINT "........"
20 PRINT "IS"
30 PRINT "ANOTHER"
40 PRINT "EXAMPLE"
50 END
Ok
_
```

To avoid accidents, whenever you write a new program, you should use the NEW statement to clear your computer's memory and avoid interference by "leftover" statements from previous use.

Let's now erase statement 15. There are many ways to do this. Here we will type:

```
15↵
```

This statement merely consists of a label. This is called an empty statement.The statement 15 does nothing, except erase any previous version. Now type RUN. You should see the following on your screen:

```
THIS
IS
ANOTHER
EXAMPLE
Ok
_
```

Be careful. This feature can be dangerous. If you type:

```
20
```

by accident, you will erase the previous version of statement 20, and replace it with an "empty" statement that does nothing. To avoid surprises, always verify your program listing prior to execution.

To delete a complete statement use

```
Delete linenumber
```

4.5 Lines and Statements

Although you may not recognize the fact at this time, you have already entered and executed your first BASIC program. Every BASIC program consists of one or more line numbers. In turn, each line number contains one or more BASIC statements, such as the PRINT statements.

A BASIC program line always begins with a line number and is terminated by the Enter key. Valid line numbers range between **0** and **65,529** and may contain a maximum of 255 characters, including the enter character. When this logical line exceeds 80 characters in length, it will "wrap" itself onto the next physical line as you continue to enter data.

If the logical line exceeds 255 characters in length, the extra characters will be truncated when the Enter key is pressed. Although the extra characters will appear on your display, they will not be processed by BASIC.

EXERCISE

1. Write a program that prints the following:
   "HAVE A NICE DAY."
2. Write a program that prints:

```
E
DD
CCC
BBBB
AAAAA
```

3. Write a program that prints:

```
* * * * * * *
* T I T L E *
* * * * * * *
```

4. Define the following terms:
   (a) label
   (b) indirect mode
   (c) direct mode
   (d) empty statement
   (e) cursor
   (f) control key
   (g) key pad
   (h) reserved word
   (i) prompt
5. What is the difference between **PRINT** and **LPRINT**?
6. Can you execute a whole program by typing statements one at a time in the immediate mode?
7. Why use **NEW** before typing a new program?
8. Can you type labeled program statements out of sequence?
9. Give examples of some IBM PC BASIC commands.
10. Is the following statement a valid way to display the word example?
    PRINT EXAMPLE
11. What is the use of the return key?
12. Explain how to erase statement 20 in a program.
13. If you have already typed statement 30 and wish to substitute a new statement 30, do you have to erase the old one first?
14. Write a program that displays the following:

```
TTTTTTTTTTTT  HH          HH  EEEEEEEEEEEE
     TT       HH          HH  E
     TT       HH          HH  E
     TT       HHHHHHHHHHHHHH  EEEEEEEEEEEE
     TT       HH          HH  E
     TT       HH          HH  E
     TT       HH          HH  EEEEEEEEEEEE
```

15. When is the **NEW** command used?
16. What is the syntax of the instruction to execute a program that has been saved on a diskette?
17. The **LOAD** command erases anything currently present in the computer's main memory. True or false?
18. What is the command to list a program through Line printer?
19. When is the programmer ready to enter a new program?
20. Name the seven BASIC commands presented in this chapter.
21. Give the explanation of list in the chapter or specify the chapter number explaining the command.
22. What does the **SAVE** command do?
23. When is the **NEW** command used? What does it do ?
24. The following program lines are not written correctly. Correct the errors in each one.

```
(a) 160 "PRINT" HELLO
(b) 150 PRINT "HELLO"
(c) 120 PRING "HELLO"
(d) 130 "HELLO" PRINT
```

CHAPTER 5

Basic Arithmetic Statement

5.1 Doing Arithmetic

Let's perform simple arithmetic calculations. Type:

```
PRINT 5 + 5↵
```

The PRINT statement prints or displays the results of processing. It can be used to print the values of variables, literals, arithmetic expressions, or a combination of these.

Remember : After entering a statement Enter key must be pressed each time. Hereafter the symbol ↵ will not be shown on the text; but it is implied. As such do not forget to press the ENTER. The result appearing on your screen should be:

```
10
```

We have just performed our first arithmetic computation. The addition symbol, +, is called an operator. An operator is a symbol that represents an operation to be performed on one or more operands.

5.2 Arithmetic Operator

BASIC provides these five built-in arithmetic operators:

- \- (minus)
- \+ (plus)
- * (multiplication)
- / (division)
- ^ (exponentiation or power)

Remember: Some versions of BASIC use double asterisks ** instead of caret symbol ^.

Now try this example. Type:

```
PRINT 2*5
```

The result should be **10**. The * symbol is the symbol for multiplication. The usual multiplication symbol, X, could be confused with the letter **x**, so BASIC and other programming languages use the * symbol instead.

Here are other examples of valid arithmetic statements:

```
PRINT 2+3*4
```

The result is **14**

```
PRINT 6-7
```

The result is **-1**

```
PRINT 10/2
```

The result is **5**

```
PRINT 1+2+3+4
```

The result is **10**

5.3 Use of Parenthesis

Since BASIC allows decimal numbers, the following statement is also legal:

```
PRINT (12/6+12/4)/2
```

The result is 2.5

Note that parentheses have been used in this example to clarify the grouping of operations. Let's try another example. Type:

```
PRINT 3+4+10/2
```

The result is 12.

The division (/) was performed first on the 10. This is due to the fact that in BASIC, if given a choice (i.e., if parentheses are not used), the division (/) or the multiplication (*) will take place before the addition (+) or the subtration (-). If you had intended to divide the group 3 + 4 + 10 by 2, then it would have been necessary to type:

```
PRINT (3+4+10)/2
```

The result would then be **8.5.**

The division would then have been performed on the group **(3+4+10)**. It is a good practice to use parentheses freely, to avoid any confusion. For example, the following expression (or group of values and operators)

$$\frac{2 + 3 + 4}{5 + 7} \times 3$$

could be translated into the following BASIC expression:

```
[(2 + 3 + 4)/(5 + 7)]*3
```

or

```
[(2 + 3 + 4)*3]/(5 + 7)
```

because execution proceeds from left to right when operators have the same precedence (standing), i.e., the division occurs here before the multiplication. If you were to write the following in BASIC:

$$\frac{2+3+4}{(3+7)\times 7}$$

it would be written as:

```
(2 + 3 + 4)/(5 + 7) *3
```

Use parentheses to denote groups. Be sure that there is always a matching right parenthesis for each left one.

Explain the concept of variables before its use?

5.4 Hierarchy of Arithmetic Operators

Table 5.1 lists the BASIC arithmetic operators according to their hierarchy of operations. The hierarchy of operation is important, since, together with the order of execution, it defines how a formula is evaluated. BASIC formulae are evaluated equivalent to mathematical expressions, in that operations are conducted from left to right with a given hierarchical group. As an example, consider the following formula expressed using BASIC operators.

```
A + B/C +D²
```

Proceeding from left to right, the value of the variable **A** is added to the value of the variable **B** divided by the value of variable **C**. Next, the previously computed value is added to **D** squared. Suppose the mathematical formula you wished to evaluate was

$$\frac{(A+B)}{C} + D^2$$

then, the initial formula you expressed would be incorrect.

You can alter the way operations are conducted in BASIC through the insertion of pairs of parentheses into formulas. When parentheses are inserted into formulas, the operations within the parentheses are performed as separate entities. If several pairs of parentheses are nested within a formula, the operations within the innermost pairs of parentheses are performed first, followed by the operations within the second innermost pair and so on. Within each pair of parentheses, the hierarchy of operations as shown in Table 5.1 will apply unless they are altered by other pairs of parentheses that are embedded inside the outer pair. To properly express the required mathematical formula in BASIC, you could use parentheses to modify the initial BASIC expression as follows:

```
((A + B) / C) + D ^2
```

Now, the value of variable **A** will be added to the

Table 5.1 Arithmetic Operators

Operator Symbol	Operation	Hierarchy Precedence	Sample Expression Using Operator
^	Exponentiation	**1**	**A^B**
-	Negation	**2**	**- A**
*	Multiplication,	**3**	**A*B**
/	Floating Point Division	**3**	**A / B**
\	Integer Division	**4**	**A\B**
MOD	Modulo Arithmetic	**5**	**A MOD B**
+,-	Addition, Subtraction	**6**	**A + B**

value of variable **B** and the sum will then be divided by the value of variable **C** summed up with square of **D**.

5.5 Integer Division

An integer division operation is denoted by the backslash **( ][ )** character. When integer division is specified, the operands are first rounded to integers if they are not integer values ,then integer division is performed. The operators must lie in the valid range of numbers between **-32768** and **32767**, and, after division is performed, the quotient is truncated to an integer. Several examples of the results obtained from the use of integer division are illustrated by the program shown below.

```
10 LET A = 10\4
20 LET B = 11\4
30 LET C = 12\4
40 LET D = 13\4
50 PRINT A,B,C,D
60 LET E = 40.25\5
70 LET F = 36.49\5
80 LET G = 36.51\6
90 PRINT E,F,G
RUN
2   2   3   3
8   6   6
Ok
```

Note that in integer division no rounding occurs. Only the "whole" or integer portion of the division is assigned to the appropriate variable and the remainder is discarded.

Example 5.1 Solve **10 + 12/4 -2**

Since division has higher order or priority than addition, or subtraction, in the above calculations, the term **12/4** shall first be solved, and then addition and subtraction operations shall be taken up. The answer shall be **11**. It may be noted that since + and - have equal priority, plus operation is performed first as it appears first in the calculation.

Example 5.2 In the expression from left to right:

X=3^5+20*10+5*2-6/2-(65+35)/(60-10)

The execution takes place in the following order:

1. (65+35)=100 Parentheses left most
2. (60-10)=50 Next parentheses
3. 3^5=245 Exponentiation
4. 20*10=200 Multiplication (left most)
5. 5*2=10 Next multiplication
6. 6/2=3 Divsion (left most)
7. 100/50=2 Division
8. 243+200=443 Addition
9. 443+10=453 Addition
10. 453-3=450 Subtraction of left most two terms
11. 450-2=448 Subtraction

The final answer shall be **X = 448.**

5.6 Assignment Statements

In BASIC, there are several methods to assign a numerical or a string value to a variable. One of the most popular methods employed is through the use of the assignment statement whose format is shown below.

5.6.1 The Syntax of an Assignment

The rules (or syntax) for writing an assignment statement are simple. The general form of an assignment statement is:

```
LET<Type of variable>=expression>
```

The purpose of the **LET** statement is to assign values to variables. The computer evaluates the expression on the right side of the equal sign and stores its value in the variable on the left side of the equal sign.

The keyword **LET** is optional in BASIC. There must always be a variable on the left and an expression on the right. More precisely, an expression is:

- a number or a variable, or
- a number or a variable followed by an operator (such as + , – , /), and another expression.

The asignment is from right to left i.e., the value of right expression is stored in variable towards left of equal to sign.

Here are a few sample expressions:

5	(a number)
x	(a variable)
5 + 3	(number, operator, number)
y + 2	(variable, operator, number)

```
z + B * 3   (variable, operator, expression)
```

Note: On the left hand side of equal to mark, it is strictly necessary to have one and only one variable.

Expressions may be enclosed in parentheses, for example:

```
5 + (8+5)/2
x + ((Z*2) + (D/2))/4
```

Here are examples of valid assignment statements:

```
A = -7 +9   (-7 is a negative integer)
Z = A + 1
C = (3 *5) + (A/B)
AVERAGE = SUM/NUMBER
SQUARE = A * * 2
X = B * * 2 - (4 * A* C)
SUM = B + C
```

The following assignments, however, are not valid:

`X + Y = SUM`	(only one variable, not an expression on the left of the = sign)
`5 =A`	(there must be a variable, not a value on the left), this could be **A=5**.
`SUM = B + C(D/3)`	(Missing operator after **C**. Remember (is not an operator.
`(AVERAGE) = (B+C)/2`	(no parentheses allowed on the left), because **AVERAGE** here is being taken as Variable.
`A =`	(missing value on the right)

Finally, note that at the time an assignment is executed, all variables on the right of the = sign must have received a value. If you write

```
10 B = 5
20 SUM = B + C
30 Let C = 5
```

the program will fail at line **20**, since **C** does not have a value.We shall learn about **INPUT** in the next chapter. You probably meant to write:

```
10 B = 2
20 INPUT C
30 SUM = B + C
```

In some versions of BASIC, the word **LET** is not optional. However, in most versions of BASIC on the PC, it is optional. Here, the equal sign is sufficient when assigning an expression, numeric, or a string value to a variable. Some examples of the use of the assignment statement are shown below.

```
10 LET X = 10
20 LET NAME$ = "INDIA"
30 A = X + Y + Z
40 PRODUCT = A * X * Y * Z
```

In line **10**, the numeric variable **X** is assigned the value **10**. Since the keyword **LET** is optional, this statement could have been written as:

```
10 X = 10
```

In line **20**, the string variable **NAME$** is assigned the string value **"INDIA"**

In line **30**, the sum of the values associated with the variables **X, Y,** and **Z** are assigned to the variable named **A**. If, at the point of assignment, the variables in a statement are undefined, BASIC will assign a value of zero to such variables. While forgetting to assign values to variables prior to their use can cause incorrect results, it can also cause an overflow error if the unassigned variable is used as a divisor in an equation. In such instances, this will cause a **"Division by zero"** error message to occur.

From the preceding examples, note that the variable to the left of the equal sign and the term to the right must be of the same type, numeric or string. If you attempt to assign a numeric value to a string variable or a string value to a numeric variable, you will obtain a "Type mismatch" error as shown below.

```
10 NAMES = 420
RUN
Type mismatch in 10
Ok
```

Although there are many assignment terms that look like algebraic equations, there are certain assignment terms that make little sense if you view them as an algebraic equation. One example of this is

```
50 LET X = X + 1
```

The assignment term `X = X + 1` does not correspond to an algebraic equation, since the equation `X=X+1` has no meaning in algebra. When written in BASIC, you are increasing the value of the numeric variable X by one unit. Here, the assignment term becomes logical when you interpret it to mean you wish to add 1 to the value represented by the variable **X** and then assign this new value to **X** . This new value of **X** will then replace the old value. Later, you will see that this type of assignment statement is frequently used as a counter in BASIC. Although some BASICs allow multiple assignments of the form,

```
70 A = B = C = 0
```

such assignments are not permitted in any version of PC BASIC. Instead, you must use several statements, although you can include multiple assignment statements on a single line as long as each statement is separated from the preceding statement by a colon (:). An example of this is:

```
70 A = 0 : B = 0 : C = 0
```

* : the colon is used to write many statements within a single label.

5.7 The Variable Counter Technique

Remember that a variable is simply a name given to a memory location. A value can be stored in a memory location by using an INPUT statement or an assignment statement (=). In this example, we want to change the value of a variable repeatedly, in order to count events. The technique we will use to do this is called the **Variable Counter Technique.**

Let's now demonstrate how successive assignments can change the value of the variable **N**. Type the following in the direct mode:

```
N = 1
```

The value is automatically stored in **N**. Let's verify it. Type: **PRINT N**

The value 1 appears. Now type: **N = 2**

N now contains **2**. Type: **PRINT N**

The response is: **2**

This value **2** has been substituted for the value **1** in **N**. Type:**N = 3**

Now type: **PRINT N**

and verify that the value 3 has been stored in N. This mechanism works.In other words, a variable can be used as an event counter.

5.8 Self Replacement Technique

Type

```
100 LET Z = 3
110 LET Z = Z + 10
```

In this expression, Z is previously defined as being equal to 3 in statement 100. So when statement 110 is taken up, its value is increased by 10 as per expression Z + 10 on R.H.S. Then this new value of 13 is placed in L.H.S. and stored in the memory accordingly.

The above example illustrates a very important application of **LET** statement which is known as **Self-Replacement Technique**. Such a technique is extensively used in counting the number of repetitive operations performed by the computer. It can also be used to generate a new value of a variable based on its previous value. For example:

```
30 LET Y = Y + 1
50 LET B = B * B
120 LET A = A * B + (N/M)*Q
```

5.9 Writing Assignment Statements

(1) Whenever any **LET** statement is encountered, the expression on the right hand side is evaluated first and the result is either assigned to the variable or it replaces the previous value on the left hand side. Some examples of **LET** statement are given below:

```
120 LET P = 11.1
130 LET A = A + 3.9
```

Line **120** sets the variable **P** equal to **11.1.** Line **130** increases the previous value of **A** by **3.9** and this increased value is placed on LHS of the expression. Here the = sign does not mean the same as in algebraic equations. It actually means to evaluate what is on the right and assign it to the variable named on the left. So the expression **130 LET A = A + 3.9** instructs the computer to get the number stored in location **A**, add **3.9** to this number, and put the result back in storage location named A. Likewise, the statement

```
140 C = P + Q
```

instructs the computer to get the number stored in locations named P and Q, add them together and put the result in the storage location named C. Thus, equal sign means to evaluate what is on right hand side and assign it to the variable named on the left.

(2) It is necessary that variables of any expression must be properly defined in the program before they are used for calculation in a statement.

(3) LET statement can be used with string constants and variables. It is to be noted that all the items on both sides of equal sign should be of one type i.e. either numeric or string type. They cannot be mixed. Examples are:

```
10 LET M$ = "CAPTION" (Valid)
10 LET M = "CAPTION"   (Invalid)
10 LET N$ = CAPTION    (Invalid)
```

The last example is invalid since CAPTION is not enclosed in inverted commas and as such is not taken by BASIC as string whereas the variable N$ on LHS is of string type.

(4) LET statement must have a variable on L.H.S. Any LET statement containing only the constant on L.H.S. is invalid virtually. A Statement like 90 LET 3 is invalid since 3 is not a valid variable.

(5) The LET statement, can have only one variable on the L.H.S. and only one expression on the right hand side. Statements like:

```
50 LET A,B = C + N
60 LET X, Y = A+B, X*Y
```

are not valid.

(6) In a LET statement, Variable is equal to Value and not the Value = Variable

5.10 Rules for Writing Arithmetic Expressions in BASIC

1. A multiplication operator is never implied or assumed but is actually applied. In ordinary algebra, when we write A=BC, we assume that the multiplication sign is there in between B and C, but in BASIC the operator for multiplication i.e. * is always applied. So we write A=B*C. Similarly, A=B(C + D) is always written as A = B*(C + D).
2. Two operators should never appear together, i.e. adjacent operators are not permitted e.g. expressions like. A/-B or A^-B are wrong. To write such expressions, bracket may be used in BASIC i.e. correct way of writting A/-B is A/(-B) and of A-B; is A^ (-B). Here it should be remembered that brackets are not operators.
3. No attempt should be made to raise zero to a negative power. Also division by zero is not allowed. For example; in AB, A should not be zero while B is negative. When M = 0,N= P/M is invalid.
4. A negative value should not be raised to a real number e.g. (-3)^3.5 is not valid.
5. Brackets should be used to avoid any ambiguity, say expressions like Q=P/R-S are ambiguous unless written as (P/R)-S or P/(R-S). So is A = B/C*D which can be either A =B/(C*D) or (B/C)*D.
6. When in doubt, we can always add extra brackets just to make sure that the priority assumed is just what we want. However while unnecessary brackets do not harm, they waste space. While using brackets, operator * must be explicitly used i.e. 6(2+1) should always be written as 6*(2+1).
7. String constants or string variables are not allowed in expressions, e.g.

```
A + "D" * C          Y * 3.8 - "7 + 2"
     P$ * A ^N
```

etc. are invalid expressions. While addition is only allowed with string variables and such additions is called concatenation.

```
X$ = "M" + "D"
Print X$ will print MD
```

8. We must make sure that while using variables in an expression, they have been assigned values, before attempting to evaluate the expression.
9. Every left bracket must be matched by a right bracket.

EXERCISE

1. What is the output of following program segments ?

(a)
```
100 PRINT "WELCOME TO THIS
PROGRAM"
110 PRINT "IT DOES NOTHING"
120 REM WELL, ALMOST NOTHING
130 END
```
(b)
```
100 LET X = 14
110 PRINT X
120 LET X = X - 5
130 PRINT X; X - 5
140 LET y = 3
150 LET X = Y
160 PRINT "X"; X
170 END
```
(c)
```
100 REM THIS PROGRAM
    PRINTS A MESSAGE
110 PRINT "THIS PROGRAM
    PRINTS A MESSAGE"
120 REM THE MESSAGE:
130 PRINT "FOUR SCORES AND
    SEVEN YEARS";
140 PRINT " IS 87 YEARS."
150 END
```

2. Write a **LET** statement for each of the following situations.
   (a) Assign a value of **2.54** to the variable **C**.
   (b) Assign a value of **12** to the variable **X**.
   (c) Assign the value represented by the variable **N** to the variable **N1**.
   (d) Assign the string **JANUARY 31** to the variable **A$**.
   (e) Assign the string represented by the variables **S$** to the variable **T$**.
   (f) Assign the value represented by the formula **(A ^ 2+ B^ 2 + C^2)** to the variable **F**.
   (g) Increase the value assigned to the variable **C7** by **0.01**.
   (h) Assign the value represented by the formula **(I + J)** to the variable **I**.

3. Write a multiple **LET** statement for each of the following situations in one line.
   (a) Assign a value of **-37.5** to the variables **C1, C2** and **C3**.
   (b) Assign the string **"**ERROR**"** to the variables **P5$** and **P7$**.
   (c) Assign the value represented by the formula **(I +J)/K** to the variables **M** and **N**.

4. Write a **LET** statement that corresponds to each of the following algebraic equations.
   (a) **x/ y + 3** (b) **x / (y + 3)** (c) **(u + v) / (s + t)**

5. Write a program to assign four numbers in the program and display the total, the average, and the product of the four numbers.

6. The following program segment contains syntax and logic errors. Find and correct them.

```
100 REM THIS PROGRAM COMPUTES
    AND PRINTS THE
110 REM AVERAGE OF THREE
    NUMBERS.
120 LET A = 14.2, LET B = 121,
    LET C = 7
130 LET X = A + B + C/3
140 PRINT "X"
150 END
```

7. Are the following assignments valid?
   (a) `A + 1 = A`
   (b) `A = A + A + A`
   (c) `A = B + C`
   (d) `B + C = A`
   (e) `3 = 2 + 1`
   (f) `NUMBER = FIRST + LAST * 2`

8. Point out the mistakes in the following expressions if any:
   (1) `(P+) - Q`
   (2) `X + (-3) ^0.5`
   (3) `5M + N`
   (4) `A*"Q"/R`
   (5) `AB + 7`
   (6) `(A + B ) * (C - D)`
   (7) `(A + B ) ^ (C - D)`

9. Write down the BASIC equivalents of following algebraic equations.

(a) $\frac{p.q}{r.s} + m.n$

(b) $\sqrt{a^2 + b^2}$

(c) $\frac{x + y}{z} - \frac{x - y}{z - x}$

(d) $M\ (1 + \frac{r}{100})^n$

(e) $\frac{d^e}{f-b}$

10. Find the error in the following statements:

(a) `100 LET X, Y = A`
(b) `60 LET P = X*B$-Y`
(c) `180 LET K = 16*-10`
(d) `80 LET E = (-33.7^2.5)^2`
(e) `110 LET M-X = J-A*B`
(f) `100 LET M = 7 + 10, 5*3`
(g) `40 LET X = Y/0.0+Z`
(h) `30 LET X = Y & C`
(i) `60 LET X = B + SQR (-36)`
(j) `70 LET C = (A + B)/ (D-D*1.0)`

11. Write assignment statements to evaluate the following:

(a) $C = \frac{F - 32}{1.8}$

(b) $A^2 = B^2 + C^2$

(c) $A = \sqrt{S\ (S-a)\ (s-b)\ (s-c)}$

(d) $A = \frac{\pi}{4} d^2$

(e) $V = \frac{4}{3} \pi R^3$

(f) $P = \frac{V^2}{RT}$

(g) P = WRT/V

12. Write down the results of following:

(a) `A = 12/6/2`
(b) `B = 12/6*2`
(c) `C = 8/2*2/2`
(d) `D = 12/2+2/2`
(e) `E = 8/2*(2+2)`
(f) `F = 12/2-2^2`
(g) `G = 2^3^2 73`

13. A program uses the following variables:

P = price of a dish.
V = value added tax
S = service charge
T = total charge of the meal in a restaurant.

Write a program that gives **P** the value of **7.5** and then calculates **V** (which is **15 %** of the meal price) and S (which is 10% of the meal price). After calculating the total charge, the program should print out the values of **P, V, S,** and **T** on one line of the screen. (Multiply by **0.15** to find **15%** Multiply by **0.10** to find **10 %**).

14. What is the result of printing following program.

(a)
```
10 LET M = 6
20 PRINT M*9
30 LET M = 7
40 PRINT M*3
```
(b)
```
5 LET N1 = 35
10 LET N2 = 30
15 LET N3 = 40
20 LET N = N1 + N2 + N3
25 PRINT N/3
```
(c)
```
10 LET A = 8
20 LET B = 2
30 PRINT A, B, A * B, A ^ B
```

15. Write a statement that calculates distance travelled (use variable **D**) when intitial mileage (use variable **M1**) and final mileage (use variable **M2**) are given.

16. Write a program to calculate the interest when principal **P** (i.e amount borrowed) and interest rate **R** is given. Amount borrowed is Rs. 500/- and interest rate is 10%. The amount of interest should be printed.

17. Find out which of the following is not a valid numeric variable

(a) **2Z** (b) **AB**
(c) **A 20** (d) **N$**
(e) **TO** (f) **CARSPEED**
(g) **DEL.BOMBSY(h) A2**

18. Write the statement to

(a) Add the contents of **A, B** and **C3** and store the result in **D**.
(b) Subtract **9** from **Q2**

(c) Put the cube of **A** in **G2**

(d) Divide **A1** by **A2** squared and place the result in **A3**.

(e) Divide **A** by sum of **B** and put the result in **X**.

19. Whether a **PRINT** statement prints a result only or makes arithmetic calculations also.

20. What shall be the result of following program?

```
10 PRINT 12 + 2
20 PRINT 12 - 2
30 PRINT 12 * 2
40 PRINT 12/2
50 PRINT 12 ^ 2
60 PRIT 12.2
```

21. Write a program that will print out the results of adding Rs. 5.0, Rs. 67 and Rs. 0.75

22. Write a program that will print the results of the multiplying 9 by 2.5 and the result of dividing 10 by 3. What will appear on the screen?

23. Write a program that will print out 30% of 70 and 70% of 30. (Hint. The 30% in decimal fraction is equal to 0.3. So multiply it with 70 to give you 30% of 70)

24. Identify any error in the following program

(a)
```
10 PRINT $100-$3
```

(b)
```
20 PRINT 100/30
30 PRINT 75-25
40 PRIN 30-20
```

(c)
```
10 PRINT 2/4
20 PRINT 2 +4
   PRINT 2 ^ 4
40 PRINT 7 -3
```

25. Write a program that will print out the value of 4 dollars in Rupees. At present 1 dollar equals to Rs. **31.30**.

26. A(n) .... is an expression consisting of any combination letters, numbers, or special characters.

27. The following program segment is supposed to find the area of a rectangle with sides L and W, but it contains errors. Find and correct them.

```
200 LET L = 16.3
210 LET W = 21,8
220 LET A = (L + W) / 2
230 PRINT THE AREA IS; A
```

28. The following program segment is supposed to print the name & age of a person but, it contains errors. Find and correct them.

(a)
```
10 REM THIS PROGRAM PRINTS
20 A NAME AND AGE OF A PERSON.
30 REM
40 LET A = 21
50 LET N$ = STAR
60 PRINT N$, A
99 END
```

(b)
```
10 REM ***THIS PROGRAM
   CALCULATES***
20 REM ***THE AVERAGE OF TWO
   NUMBERS***
30 LET A + 1 = 10
40 LET B = 15
50 LET X = A + B/2
60 PRINT X
99 END
```

29. Write a BASIC formula that corresponds to each of the following algebraic expressions.

(a) $3x + 5$

(b) $i + j - 2$

(c) $x^2 + y^2$

(d) $(x + y)^2$

(e) $a/b + c/d$

(f) $(u + v)^{k-1}$

(g) $(4t)^{1/6}$

30. Which of the following relational expressions are true?

(a) **"ED" <"DAVID"**

(b) **"EDWARD" >"ED"**

(c) **"OHIO" = "OHIO"**

31. LET X = 1 and Y = 2, determine whether each of the following relational expressions is true or false.

(a) **2 * X + Y ^ 2 > Y + 3**

(b) **X > Y OR X > 0 AND Y > 0**

(c) **NOT (NOT (X = 0) AND NOT (Y = 0))**

ANSWERS

1. (a) **WELCOME TO THIS PROGRAM.**
   IT DOES NOTHING.
   (b) **14**
   9 4
   X 3
   (c) **THIS PROGRAM PRINTS A MESSAGE FOUR SCORES AND SEVEN YEARS IS 87 YEARS.**
2. (a) `10 LET C = 2.54`
   (b) `20 LET X = 12`
   (c) `30 LET N1 = N`
   (d) `40 LET A$ = "JANUARY 31"`
   (e) `50 LET T$ = S$`
   (f) `60 LET F = A^2 + B^2 + C^2`
   (g) `70 LET C7 = C7 + .01`
   (h) `80 LET I = I + J`
3. (a) `C1 = C2 = C3 = -37.5`
   (b) `P7$ = "**ERROR**" : P5$ = P7$`
   (c) `N = (I + J)/K : M = N`
4. (a) `10 LET Z = X/Y+3`
   (b) `20 LET Z = X/(Y+3)`
   (c) `30 LET W = (U+V)/(S+T)`
5.
```
10 INPUT A, B, C, D
20 SUM = A + B + C + D
30 AVG = SUM/4
40 PROD = A * B * C * D
50 PRINT SUM, AVG, PROD
60 END
```
6.
```
120 LET A = 14.2
122 LET B = 121
124 LET C = 7
130 LET X = (A + B + C) / 3
140 PRINT X
150 END
```
7. **b, c, f** are valid.
8. (1) Brackets placed incorrectly. It should be **P + (-Q)**
   (2) Negative number raised to the power of decimal number.
   (3) The multiplication operator is missing in between **5** and **M**.
   (4) String constants like **"Q"** are not permitted in numeric expression.
   (5) **AB** cannot be a BASIC numeric variable. Either it should be **A* B** or simply **A**.
   (6) The first opening bracket is not matched. It should be **(A + B) * (C - D)**
   (7) No mistake
9. (a) `P*Q/(R*S) + M*N`
   (b) `(A*A + B*B) ^0.5`
   (c) `(X + Y)/Z -(X - Y)/(Z-X)`
   (d) `M*(1+R/100)^N` or `M*(1+R/100)**N`
   (e) `D^E/(F-G)`
10. (a) Two variables (on **LHS**) are not allowed in one statement.
    (b) Mixed variables are not allowed.
    (c) Two operators (i.e. * and - in this case) are not allowed.
    (d) Negative value should not be raised to the power of real number.
    (e) Expressions are not allowed on L.H.S.
    (f) Two expressions or constants are not allowed on R.H.S.
    (g) Division by zero is not allowed.
    (h) The sign '**&**' is not a valid operator nor the sign '**x**' can assume two variable values.
    (i) You can't have the square root of a minus real number.
    (j) Denominator is actually zero, which is not allowed.
11. (a) `C = (F-32)/1.8`
    (b) `A^2 = B^2 + c^2`
    (c) `A= (S* (S-A)* (S-B)* (S-C)^0.5` or `(S* (S-A)* (S-B)* (S-C)^ (1/2)`
    (d) `PIE = 3.14`
    `A = (PIE/4)* d^2`
    (e) `PIE = 3.14`
    `V = (4/3)* PIE* R^3`
    (f) `P = V^2/(R*T)`
    (g) `P = W*R*T/V`
12. (a) **1** (b) **4** (c) **4** (d) **7** (e) **16** (f) **2** (g) **64.**
13.
```
10 LET P = 7.5
20 LET V = P * 0.15
30 LET S = P * 0. 10
40 LET T = P + V + S
```

```
50 PRINT P, V, S, T
60 END
```

14. (a) **54,   21**
    (b) **35**
    (c) **8,   2,   16,   64**

15. **10 LET D = M2-M1**

16. (Interest rate is 10% which in fractions is equal to 0.1). Also let I be the interest

```
10 LET P = 500
20 LET R = 0.1
30 LET I = R * P
40 PRINT I
```

We can write above program in another way

```
10 LET P = 500
20 LET R = 0.1
30 PRINT R * P
```

17. (a) No number should be used as starting character in alphanumeric variable.
    (b) In some computers two alphabets are not allowed in alphanumeric variable.
    (c) In some computers more than one character are not allowed.
    (d) This is a string variable as **$** is written after **N**.
    (e) **TO** is a command
    (f) No gaps are allowed in a numeric variable name.
    (g) Dots are not allowed.
    (h) No space is allowed in between.

18. (a) **LET D = A + B + C3**
    (b) **LET Q9 = Q2 - 9**
    (c) **LET G2 = A ^ 3**
    (d) **LET A3 = A1/A2 ^2**
    (e) **LET X = A/ (B +C)**

19. It does both.

20. **14**
    10
    24
    -6
    144

In case of line 60 computers will give error message because spelling of PRINT is incorrectly typed as PRIT

21. **10 PRINT 5 + 67 + 0.75.** It is better that 0 is omitted prior to 75.

22.

```
10 PRINT 9 * 2. 5
20 PRINT 10 / 3
```

The following will appear on the screen

```
RUN
22.5
3.3333333
```

22.

```
10 PRINT .03 * 70
   20 PRINT .07 * 30
```

24. (a) Symbols like $, and & should not be used
    (b) Spelling of **PRINT** wrongly written in line number **40**
    (c) Line number missing in third statement.

25.

```
10 PRINT 4 * 31.3
20 END.
```

Writing END statement is optional.

26. Literal

27.

```
210 LET W = 21.8
220 LET A = L * W
230 PRINT "THE AREA IS "; A
```

28. (a) Line No. 20 does not contain key word **REM** prior to putting up the remarks and line No. 30 is unnecessary as it is without any remark.
    (b) Line number 30 contains a numerical expression on left hand side. It should be **LET A = 10-1 or A = 9**. Line No. 50 will calculate the sum of **A** and **B** / 2 and not the average of **A** and **B**. It should be replaced by statement

    50 LET X = (A+B)/2

29. (a) **3 * X + 5**
    (b) **I + J - 2**
    (c) **X ^ 2 + Y ^ 2**
    (d) **(X + Y) ^ 2**
    (e) **A/B + C/D or (A/B) + (C/D)**
    (f) **(U + V) ^ (K -1)**
    (g) **(4 * T) ^ .16666667 or (4 * T) ^ (1/6)**

30. (a) false   (b) true   (c) true

31. (a) true   (b) false   (c) false

CHAPTER 6

The Input Statement

6.1 Modes of BASIC Operation

There are two modes of feeding program and data to computer, known as

- Direct mode
- Interactive mode.

Direct mode uses the **READ** and Data statements and interactive method uses **INPUT** statement. Interactive mode is used in situations when the data changes each time the program is executed. For example, think of a program that calculates the petrol required for your car. Each time you run this program, you need to enter new values for the number of miles travelled and amount of gas used. If such a program used assignment statements to assign these values to variables, the statements would have to be rewritten every time you wanted to calculate your petrol average. A more practical approach to this programming problem is to use the INPUT statement.

6.2 The INPUT Statement

The INPUT statement enables the user to enter data at the keyboard while executing the programs. The format of the I**NPUT** statement is as follows:

Format

line # INPUT *variable* 1 [*variable2*,.....]

Brackets ([ ]) indicate that the item enclosed is optional. In this statement, for example, it is not necessary to specify more than one variable.

The following are all valid **INPUT** statements:

```
110 INPUT STUDENT$, RN, YR
120 INPUT ADDRESS$
130 INPUT PAY, TAX, GPF, NETPAY
```

The following are examples of invalid INPUT statements:

`180 INPUT CITY$ ST$`	(No comma separating variables)
`INPUT BEANS,CARROTS, CELERY`	(No line number)
`240 TABLE, DATA, CHAIR`	(Reserved word DATA in wrong place)

6.3 Using Input Statement

The `INPUT` statement is used to supply data. Rules for writing input Statements are given in box. By putting certain variables of the program into the `INPUT` statement, they can be given values. Consider, for example

```
200 INPUT X,Y,Z,
```

During execution when such statement is encountered, BASIC understands, that is after getting values for variables `X,Y,Z`, from the terminal, it has to proceed further. Instantly a questionmark (?) appears on the screen. It means that the BASIC is waiting for the data values to be supplied. When the typing in of the three values separated by commas is finished, the corresponding variables get those values and the next statement is taken up for execution.

Rules of Writing Input Statement

1. The data items must correspond in number and in type to the variables listed in the **INPUT** statement (i.e., numbers must be supplied for numeric variables, strings for string variables).
2. The data items must be separated by commas.
3. The data items must consist of numbers and strings. Formulas are not permitted.
4. Strings containing commas or beginning with blank spaces must be enclosed within the quotation marks. Other strings may be enclosed within the quotation marks if desired.
5. No record of values supplied to **INPUT** is kept.
6. INPUT waits a question mark **(?)** to supply values.
7. In **INPUT** the program is interrupted and an operator must be sitting at the desk of the computer to feed values.
8. In **INPUT** data cannot be reused. It has to be resupplied.

In this way, by **INPUT** statement one can develop a program which can be executed for any data value. Without modification of the program, one can give different data, whenever the program is to run.

Any type of the variables can be used in the **INPUT** statement. The only precaution required is that the values one types should match in number and types with the variables in the INPUT statement. Numeric variable should be given a string value and a string variable should be given a string value and in all cases values must be separated by commas. If one does not put commas, BASIC is sure to give an error message. Expressions are not accepted. There are a lot of chances of mistakes if the string values are not enclosed within the quotes (" "). So make it a practice to use quotes.

As soon as an **INPUT** statement is encountered, BASIC types a question mark (?) on the screen. Its position on the screen will depend on how a previous **PRINT** statement had ended. It may be on a new line or in continuation. Try to have a few **PRINT** statements preceding **INPUT** statement while supplying values.

A sample program with its results:

```
10 PRINT "ENTER RATE AND PRINCIPAL"
20 INPUT R, P
30 LET I = R * P / 100
40 PRINT "INTEREST EARNED = ",I
50 END
```

When run computer will prompt the user by displaying:

```
RUN
ENTER RATE AND PRINCIPAL
?
```

Here the user has to type the values of RATE and Principal after which the computer will display the entered values at the side of above sentence as:

```
ENTER RATE AND PRINCIPAL ? 10,2000
```

The computer answers to this as

```
INTEREST EARNED =             200
```

Notice that computer has printed the result after a gap of 12 spaces after the = symbol.This is because computer prints the results in zones of 14 characters including the characters of the result.One addition space is left by computer due to one space left by us in the string **"INTEREST EARNED = "**after the equal to symbol.If you once again run the same program the computer responds by showing

```
RUN
ENTER RATE AND PRINCIPAL ? 5, 1600
INTEREST EARNED =             80
```

Same way once again

```
RUN
ENTER RATE AND PRINCIPAL ? 8, 4000
INTEREST EARNED =            320
```

The program was executed thrice with different **INPUT** values, in all the three cases **PRINT** statement outputs a prompting message.

The following program uses **INPUT** statements to enter the data needed to calculate the Petrol Average.

```
10 REM * * * COMPUTE PETROL AVERAGE * * *
20 REM
30 INPUT DISTANCE
40 INPUT PETROL
50 LET AVERAGE = DISTANCE / PETROL
60 PRINT
70 PRINT "DISTANCE", "PETROL USED", "AVERAGE"
80 PRINT
90 PRINT DISTANCE, PETROL, AVERAGE
99 END
RUN
? 420
? 20
DISTANCE     PETROL USED     AVERAGE
 420            20              21
```

When this program is run, the computer encounters the **INPUT** statements in line 30, prints a question mark, and waits for the user to enter the distance traveled. Once the user has entered this value and pressed the **ENTER** key, the computer continues executing the program.

This process is repeated when the **INPUT** statement in line 40 is encountered. After the user has entered the amount of petrol used and pressed the **ENTER** key, the program continues execution, calculates the average, and prints the results.

Now **INPUT** statements request that a numeric value be entered by the user. If the user enters a character string instead, an error message is printed and program execution stops prematurely. If an **INPUT** statement requests a character string, the input need not be surrounded by quotation marks.

If an **INPUT** statement contains more than one variable, only one question mark appears on the screen when the program is run. In this case, the user needs to enter the correct number of data items and must separate them with commas. For example:

```
20 INPUT CITY$, ADD$, PIN
```

When this statement is executed, only one question mark appears on the monitor screen, but three data items must be entered by the user:

```
NEW DELHI, C-142, 110001
```

The user must enter the exact number of data items needed by **INPUT** statement and must include the commas. If fewer data items are entered, an error message is printed.

```
? Redo from start
```

6.4 Printing Prompts for the User

In the previous example, when the **INPUT** statement was executed, only a question mark (?) appeared on the monitor screen when it was time for the user to enter data. The user was not told what type of data or how many data items were to be entered. Therefore, the programmer should also have included a prompt to tell the user what to enter.

A prompt can consist of a **PRINT** statement placed before the **INPUT** statement in the programs, or it can be contained within the **INPUT** statement itself. Following program shows the modification of program shown previously with prompts using **PRINT** statements preceding the **INPUT** statements.

```
10 REM * * COMPUTE PETROL AVERAGE
20 REM
30 PRINT "ENTER THE DISTANCE TRAVELLED"
40 INPUT DISTANCE
50 PRINT "ENTER THE PETROL USED"
60 INPUT PETROL
70 LET MILEAGE = DISTANCE / PETROL
80 PRINT
90 PRINT "DISTANCE" , "PETROL", "MILEAGE"
100 PRINT
110 PRINT DISTANCE, PETROL, MILEAGE
999 END
RUN
ENTER THE DISTANCE TRAVELLED
? 420
ENTER THE PETROL USED
? 20
DISTANCE     PETROL USED     MILEAGE
  420            20              21
```

Line 30 of the program prints the prompt.Line **40** is the **INPUT** statement:

```
40 INPUT DISTANCE
```

After line 40 is executed, the computer stops and waits for the user to enter the distance travelled. Then execution continues until the second **INPUT** statement is encountered. Again, the program waits for the user to enter the requested data and then continues its execution.

The prompt can be included within the **INPUT** statement, using the following syntax:

line # INPUT *prompt; variable1* [*,variable 2,....*]

There, lines 30 and 40 of the program could be replaced with the following single statement.

```
30 INPUT "ENTER THE DISTANCE TRAVELLED", DISTANCE
```

When the program is run with this modification, the question mark and the prompt appear on the same LINE as shown in program below. Using this format simplifies the writing of the program and makes the logic easy to follow.

```
10 REM * * * COMPUTE PETROL AVERAGE * * *
20 REM
30 INPUT "ENTER THE DISTANCE TRAVELLED " ; DISTANCE
40 INPUT "ENTER THE PETROL USED " ; PETROL
50 LET AVERAGE = DISTANCE / PETROL
60 PRINT
70 PRINT "DISTANCE", "PETROL" ,"AVERAGE"
80 PRINT
90 PRINT DISTANCE, PETROL, AVERAGE
99 END
RUN
ENTER THE DISTANCE TRAVELLED ?  420
ENTER THE PETROL USED ?  20
```

```
DISTANCE      PETROL USED    AVERAGE
  420            20             21
```

Example 6.1: Program to find out geometric properties of a triangle.

The following program enables the user to find out areas of a triangle if the measurements of its all the three sides are known.Moreover it finds out the areas of largest inscribing circle and smallest circumscribing circle using following formulae:

- Area Ao = $\sqrt{s(s-a)\ (s-b)\ (s-c)}$
- Area of largest inscribing circle A1 = $3.14159 \left(\frac{Ao}{s}\right)^2$
- Area of smallest circumscribing circle A2 = $3.14159 \times \left(\frac{a.b.c}{4.Ao}\right)^2$
- Angle between two sides A and B given by Cos C $=[(a^2+b^2-c^2)/2ab]$

To find out the included angle **C**,since BASIC does not have **COS** inverse **(ARCCOS)** function, the program first finds out the tangent of the angle from its cosine and then computes the arc of tangent by **ATN** function.

```
10  REM GEOMETRIC PROPERTIES OF A TRIANGLE
20  PRINT "LENGTH OF FIRST SIDE = ";
30  INPUT A
40  PRINT "LENGTH OF SECOND SIDE = ";
50  INPUT B
60  PRINT "LENGTH OF THIRD SIDE = ";
70  INPUT C
80  S=(A+B+C)/2
90  A0=(S*(S-A)*(S-B)*(S-C))^.5
100 R1 = A0/S
110 A1=3.14159*R1^2
120 R2 = A*B*C/(4*A0)
130 A2 = 3.14159*R2^2
140 C1 =(A^2+B^2-C^2)/(2*A*B)
150 PRINT "AREA OF TRIANGLE = ";A0
160 PRINT "AREA OF LARGEST INSCRIBED CIRCLE = ";A1
170 PRINT "AREA OF SMALLEST CIRCUMSCRIBED CIRCLE IS = ";A2
180 PRINT "THE ANGLE BETWEEN SIDES A AND B IS =" ;ATN(((1/((C1))^2)-
    1)^.5)*(180/3.14159)
190 PRINT
200 PRINT "PRESS Y IF YOU WANT MORE COMPUTATION, OTHERWISE PRESS ANY KEY."
210 INPUT Y$
220 IF Y$ = "Y" GOTO 20 ELSE 230
230 END
```

When the above program is run, following will be displayed.

```
RUN
LENGTH OF FIRST SIDE = ? 5
LENGTH OF SECOND SIDE = ? 5
LENGTH OF THIRD SIDE = ? 5
AREA OF TRIANGLE = 10.82532
AREA OF LARGEST INSCRIBED CIRCLE = 6.54498
AREA OF SMALLEST CIRCUMSCRIBING CIRCLE IS = 26.17992
THE ANGLE BETWEEN SIDES A AND B IS = 60.00005
PRESS Y IF YOU WANT MORE COMPUTATION ,OTHERWISE PRESS ANY KEY.
? N
Ok
```

Since, after typing the execution is stopped, correctness of program is tested.The line number 182 directs the program to go to line 20 and restart asking for the length of sides of the triangle in case you type **Y** in response to computer's asking for any more computation.Pressing any other key stops the program by virtue of **ELSE** part of the **IF-THEN -ELSE** statement.

6.5 Reading Data from Data Statement

BASIC provides another way of storing data with its **READ** and **DATA** instructions. You may wonder why yet another way to store data is needed. That is needed to store the permanent type of data.

Various items of data can be made available to the computer when it is running a program by placing them in a **DATA** statement in the program. A **DATA** statement consists of the word **DATA** followed by the items, which are themselves separated by commas. Thus, we can place the four words **'HAPPY'**, **'BIRTHDAY'**, **'TO,'** and **'YOU'** as four items of data in a single **DATA** statement in this way.

```
DATA "HAPPY", "BIRTHDAY", "TO", "YOU"
```

The order of the items is important, for the first **READ** statement to be obeyed by the computer in a program reads the first item of data from the **DATA** statement, the second **READ** instruction that is obeyed reads the second, item, and so on. If we cannot fit all the items of data into one **DATA** statement, or if we choose not to, then we may use several **DATA** statements and the line numbers of **DATA** statements indicate the order of the data items in a quite natural way. The following program will read the words from a **DATA** statement and print them in the order in which they appear:

```
10 READ A$
20 PRINT A$
30 READ B$
40 PRINT B$
50 READ C$
60 PRINT C$
70 READ D$
80 PRINT D$
90 DATA "HAPPY", "BIRTHDAY", "TO", "YOU"
```

The words would equally well have been given in four separate **DATA** statements as:

```
90 DATA "HAPPY"
100 DATA "BIRTHDAY"
110 DATA "TO"
120 DATA "YOU"
```

This presents the items in exactly the same order as in the single **DATA** statement in the original program.

Many BASIC programs require that a large number of variables be initialized or changed to certain values within a program. While you can use many assignment statements to accomplish this, it may be cumbersome to do so. Instead, you may use one or more pairs of **READ** and **DATA** statements. When used in **BASIC**, a **READ** statement must always be used in conjunction with one or more **DATA** statement. **DATA** statements contain the values of constants that **READ** statements will assign to the variables in **READ** statement. **READ** statement variables may be numeric or string; however, the values read from the **DATA** statement must correspond to the types of constants in the **DATA** statements. That is, a variable in a **READ** statement must correspond to a numeric constant in **DATA** statement. The formats of the **READ** and **DATA** statements are:

Format READ *var* **[**, *var* . . .**]**
DATA constant **[**, *constant* . . .**]**

6.5.1 Rules for Writing READ-DATA Statements:

1. When executed, the **READ** instruction reads the 'data item' form the **DATA** statement and stores it under 'name'.
2. A **DATA** statement may contain a list of data items separated by commas, or a program may contain several **DATA** statements.
3. The order of the data items is from left to right in a single **DATA** statement or, if there is more than one **DATA** statement, it starts with the left-hand item in the statement with the lowest line number, continues to the right, starts again at the left of the statement with the next highest number, and so on.
4. When more than one **READ** statement is obeyed by a program, the first one reads the first data item, the second one the second, and so on.
5. Normally strings should be enclosed within the quote's marks, but it is not essential.
6. A program can contain any number of **READ** and **DATA** statements.
7. **DATA** statements are non executable,and therefore can be placed anywhere in the program.
8. The computer collects the values from all the **DATA** statements in a program and places them in single list, referred to as the data list. The values in this list are arranged in order, from the lowest to the highest line number and from left to right within a single **DATA** statement
9. When two or more data values are placed in a single **DATA** statement, the values are separated by commas. Character strings require quotation marks only if they contain leading or trailing blanks, commas, or semicolons.
10. When the program encounters a **READ** statement, it goes to the data list and assigns the next value in that list to the corresponding variable in the **READ** statement. If the variable is numeric, the data value also must be numeric. If it is a character string variable, however, the computer allows a numeric value to be assigned to it. No computation can be performed with numbers that have been assigned to character string variables.
11. If there is inadequate data for a **READ** statement (that is, if there are no more data values in the data list), an **OUT OF DATA** error message appears and program stops execution.
12. If there are more data values than variables, these extra data values remain unread. This condition does not result in an error message.

Let us examine following program segment that contains **READ** and **DATA** statements. When the computer executes this segment., it first encounters the **READ**

```
100 READ NAM$,S1,S2,S3
105 PRINT NAM$,S1,S2,S3
110 READ NAM$
120 READ S1,S2
130 READ S3
140 DATA JYOTSNA
150 DATA 60,53,12,DEEPA
160 DATA 62,58
170 DATA 54
180 PRINT NAM$,S1,S2,S3
RUN
JYOTSNA        60          53          12
DEEPA          62          58          54
```

Statement in line **100** instructs computer to read four data values from the data list, and to assign these values to the variables **NAM$**, **S1**, **S2**, and **S3** respectively. After this task is completed, program execution continues at line **110**, where the next value in the data list, **DEEPA**, is assigned to the variable

NAM$. This new value of **NAMs** replaces **JYOTSNA**, the previous value.

Note that computer "remembers" where it is the data list. Whenever it encounters another **READ** statement, it assigns the next value in the list to that variable.

In above example one important point is noteworthy. The statement in line **100** specifies that you should read the values for five variables from one or more **DATA** statements. The first three variables are numeric and must be expressed as numeric constants in the associated **DATA** statement or statements. The fourth variable is a string variable and the value in the associated **DATA** statement must be a string. The fifth variable in the **READ** statement is a numeric variable, and the value of the associated **DATA** statement must be a numeric constant.

If there are more variables in the **READ** statement or statements than there are constants in one or more **DATA** statements, when the pointer is shifted to the right and encounters no data, the error message **"Out of DATA"** will occur and the program will terminate. This is shown by the following example where you attempt to read these elements from a data pool that only contains two data items.

```
50 READ X,Y,Z
75 DATA 1,2
RUN
Out of DATA in 50
Ok
```

6.6 Multiple READ- DATA Statement

You can have multiple **READ** statements within a program. When this occurs, the second and subsequent **READ** statements will continue to take values from the data pool in sequence, with each value assigned to the variable in each **READ** statement in their order of occurrence. This is shown by the following example.

```
10 DATA 1,3,5,9, "LAXMI", "FRIDAY"
50 READ A , B , C
75 READ D, GOD$
100 READ DAY$, X$
150 DATA "BASIC", "PRICE"
```

The two **DATA** statements generate the values assigned to the data pool as follows:

```
"LAXMI", "FRIDAY", "BASIC", "PRICE"
```

With the pointer at the beginning of the data pool, the **READ** statement in line 500 can be thought of as causing the following pointer actions to occur .

```
1       3       5       9           "LAXMI" "FRIDAY" "BASIC" "PRICE"
```

When **A** was **READ**, the pointer moved to the first value and assigned the contents of the first position in the data pool to that variable. Thus, **A** was given the value **1**. Next, **B** was assigned the value **3** and **C** was assigned the value **5**. Note that the pointer is now at the position where the value **5** was held in the pool. Upon encountering the **READ** statement in line **75**, the pointer would again move to the right one position for each variable in the **READ** statements. Here, the variable **D** would be assigned the value **9** and the string variable **GOD$** would be assigned the string value **LAXMI**. The movement of the pointer in response to the second read statement is shown below.

```
1     3     5     9     "LAXMI"     "FRIDAY"     "BASIC"     "PRICE"
```

Since there are two variable names contained as part of the **READ** statement in line 100, the execution of this statement will cause the pointer to move two positions to the right through the data pool. As the pointer moves over the string **"FRIDAY"**, this string will be assigned to the string variable **DAY$**, that in this short program example, the number of data constants in the data pool exceeds the number of string variables in **READ** statements. This is perfectly valid as something you may branch around one or more **READ** statement and forgo assigning constants to variables based on certain program conditions. In such cases, the extra data (like PRICE) will be ignored. The opposite of this situation, however, is not permitted. That is, you cannot read more variables in **READ** statements than there are constants in data statements, unless you reread the constants. The mechanism to reread constants is obtained through the **RESTORE** statement, which will be covered shortly.

Two final notes on **READ** and **DATA** statements: You can obtain an idea of the rationale for using these statements instead of multiple assignment statements by comparing the previous example using **READ** and **DATA** statements to a program segment performing the same variable assignment using assignment statements as shown below.

```
100 A = 1
110 B = 3
120 C = 5
130 D = 9
140 GOD$ =  "LAXMI"
150 DAY$ =  "FRIDAY"
160 X$ =  "BASIC"
```

From the above, it is apparent that **READ** and **DATA** statements are labour saving devices for the assignment of constant values to variables.

Although the preceding examples showed quotation marks around string constants contained in **DATA** statements, there are occasions where we can safely do without such string specifiers. If a string does not have commas, semicolons, or significant leading or trailing blanks, you can place that string in a **DATA** statement without surrounding quotation marks. This is *illustrated by the following example.

```
10 PRINT "SURNAME", "FIRST NAME", "CODE"
20 READ LAST$, FIRST$, CODE$
30 DATA JOSHI, INDU ,000456
40 PRINT LAST$, FIRST$, CODE$
RUN
      SURNAME        FIRST NAME        CODE
       JOSHI           INDU             000456
Ok
```

Example below shows the sample petrol average program, rewritten using **READ** and **DATA** statements. Line 30 tells the computer to take the first value in the data list and put it in the storage location named **DISTANCE**. The statement also says to take the next value in the data list and assign it to the variable **PETROL**. The program then goes on to calculate and print the gas mileage. To run this program again with different data, we could need to change line 100, the **DATA** line.

```
10 REM * * * COMPUTE PETROL AVERAGE
20 REM
30 READ DISTANCE , PETROL
40 LET AVERAGE = DISTANCE / PETROL
50 PRINT
60 PRINT "DISTANCE", "PETROL", "AVERAGE"
70 PRINT
80 PRINT DISTANCE, PETROL, AVERAGE
90 REM * * * DATA STATEMENTS * * *
100 DATA 420, 20
110 END
RUN
DISTANCE     PETROL          AVERAGE
420           20               21
```

6.7 Restore Statement

There are many programming situations in which you should like to read the data more than once. To do this requires a mechanism to move the position of the pointer in the data pool back to its initial position at the beginning of the first data element. This repositioning of the data pool pointer is accomplished by the **RESTORE** statement whose format is:

Format: `RESTORE [LINE]`

When a **RESTORE** statement is executed, the first variable in the next **READ** statement in the program will be assigned the value of the first item in the first **DATA** statement in the program. If a line number is specified in the **RESTORE** statement, first variable in the next **READ** statement will be assigned the value of the first item **DATA** statement specified by the line number of the **RESTORE** statement. Thus, specifying a line number within a **RESTORE** statement permits us to selectively move the data pool pointer through the data pool. This is shown by the following example.

```
10 READ P,Q,R,S
20 DATA 1,3,5,7,11,13
30 PRINT P,Q,R,S
40 DATA 17,19,23,29
60 READ X,Y,Z
70 PRINT X,Y,Z
80 RESTORE 40
90 READ X,Y,Z
100 PRINT X,Y,Z
RUN
 1              3               5               7
 11             13              17
 17             19              23
Ok
```

In the preceding example, the data pool contains **10** constants, formed by data in lines **20** and **40**. The **READ** statement in line **10** results in the assignment of **1** to **P**, **3** to **Q**, **5** to **R**, and **7** to **S**. The **PRINT** statement in line **30** outputs the values of the four variables. Here, the comma (,) between each variable is a print control mechanism that permits data to be placed in fixed positions on a line when used as a separator in the **PRINT** statement. The use of print separators will be covered in detail later in this chapter when the **PRINT** statement is examined.

The **RESTORE** statement in line **50** moves the pointer back to the beginning of the data pool, since no line number was specified. The execution of line **60** will cause the values of **1,3** and **5** to be assigned to the variables **X,Y** and **Z**. The result of the **PRINT** statement in line **70** confirms the assignment of these values. In line **80**, the line number appended to the **RESTORE** statement causes the pointer in the data pool to be repositioned to the first element in the referenced **DATA** statement. Now, the **READ** statement in line **90** will result in the assignment of the values **17,19,23** to the variables **X,Y**, and **Z**. This is confirmed by the execution of the **PRINT** statement in line **100**.

6.8 Comparing LET, INPUT, and READ

We now have three ways of supplying input data to a program: **LET, INPUT** and **READ** statements. The **INPUT** statement is fundamentally different from the other two. It allows for the interactive use of the computer; the others do not. With **INPUT**, data can be entered by the user during program execution; with **LET** and **READ**, input data are part of the program and must be known prior to execution.

The **INPUT** statement is ideal when data values change frequently, because it allows the data to be entered at the keyboard during program execution.

The **READ** and **DATA** statements are well suited to programs that use large quantities of data, because the user does not have to enter a long list of data values during program execution, as would be necessary with the **INPUT** statement.

The **READ** and **DATA** statements are most useful when data values are the same for each program execution. When the data values change, however, the program itself must be altered.

The following guidelines govern the use of these statements in a very general way.

1. Use **LET** for calculations and to initialize a relatively small number of variables.
   200 let pay = rate * HOURS [calculation]
   300 LET COUNT = 0 [initialization]
2. Use **READ** to supply input data when
   (a) the desired data are known at the time the program is written; and
   (b) there is a relatively large amount of data to input. A large amount of data could also be input using external data files as we'll see in corresponding chapter.)
3. Use **INPUT** whenever you want to allow the user to enter data during execution. You should use **INPUT** if the data to be entered are likely to vary from run to run.

The following program will illustrate the use of three types of input methods.

1. Using the **LET** statement

```
10 LET A = 1
20 LET B = 2
30 LET C = 3
40 PRINT
50 PRINT A ; B ; C
60 PRINT A^2 ; B^2 ; C^2
99 END
RUN
  1  2  3
  1  4  9
```

2. Using the **INPUT** statement

```
10 PRINT
20 PRINT "VALUES FOR A,B,C"
30 INPUT A, B, C
40 PRINT A^2; B^2; C^2
99 END
RUN
VALUES FOR A, B, C
?  1, 2, 3
1  4  9
```

3. Using the **READ / DATA** statements

```
10 READ A,B, C
20 DATA 1,2,3
30 PRINT A;B;C
40 PRINT A^2; B^2; C^2
99 END
RUN
  1  2  3
  1  4  9
```

Note: **READ** statement is non-executing and does not interfere if no **DATA** statement is there in the program.

Items listed in a **DATA** statement may be re-read by means of a **RESTORE** statement. The program shown below assigns values **1, 2,** and **3** to variables **A, B,** and **C,** and then reassigns these values to variables **L, M,** and **N.**

```
10 READ A, B, C
20 DATA 1, 2, 3
30 PRINT
40 PRINT "A = " ; A, "B = " ;B, "C = " ; C
50 RESTORE
60 READ L, M, N
70 PRINT "L = ";L, "M = " ;M, "N = " ; N
99 END
RUN
A = 1      B = 2      C = 3
  L = 1      M = 2      N = 3
```

Example 6.2 Conversion of rectangular co-ordinate into polar co- ordinates.

```
10 REM * CONVERTING FROM RECTANGULAR TO POLAR *
15 PRINT "INPUT THE MAGNITUDE  OF X AND Y  COORDINATES  SEPARATED BY
COMMAS";
20 INPUT X, Y
30 R = SQR(X*X + Y*Y)
40 T = 57.29578 * ATN(Y/X)
50 PRINT "THE MAGNITUDE OF POLAR COORDINATE IS = "; R
55 PRINT "THE ANGLE OF THE POLAR VECTOR IS ";T;" DEGREES"
60 END
```

When the above program is run, following will be displayed.

```
RUN
INPUT THE MAGNITUDE OF X AND Y COORDINATES SEPARATED BY COMMAS? 40
Redo from start
? 40,40
THE MAGNITUDE OF POLAR COORDINATE IS = 56.56854
THE ANGLE OF THE POLAR VECTOR IS 45.00001 DEGREES
Ok
```

Notice that since the user has entered a part of data to the querry about inputting the magnitude of **X** and **Y** coordinates,the computer has directed the user for redoing the entry from start.This is done by computer automatically by virtue of **INPUT** statement.When the user has correctly entered the data, computer has responded with the answer to the querry.Let us once again make mistake in entering the data and see what happens.

```
RUN
INPUT  THE  MAGNITUDE  OF  X  AND Y COORDINATES SEPARATED BY COMMA? 0,40
Division by zero
THE MAGNITUDE OF POLAR COORDINATE IS = 40
THE ANGLE OF THE POLAR VECTOR IS 90 DEGREES
Ok
RUN
INPUT THE MAGNITUDE OF X AND Y COORDINATES SEPARATED BY COMMA ? 40,0
THE MAGNITUDE OF THE POLAR COORDINATE IS = 40
THE ANGLE OF THE POLAR VECTOR IS 0 DEGREES
Ok
```

Example 6.3

```
10 REM * CALCULATION OF THE FUTURE VALUE OF AN INVESTMENT *
20 CLS
30 DEFDBL F, D, E, B, C, A
40 INPUT "ENTER THE CONSUMER PRICE INDEX FOR PREVIOUS YEAR = " , F
```

```
50 INPUT "ENTER THE CONSUMER PRICE INDEX FOR CURRENT YEAR = ", E
60 INPUT "ENTER THE PRESENT  VALUE OF THE INVESTMENT (OR PRODUCT/SALARY)=
RS.", C
70 INPUT "ENTER THE NUMBER OF PERIODS TO BE CALCULATED = ", B
80 A = (100 * (E - F ) / F ) / 100
90 D = INT ((C * (A + 1) ^ B) * 100 + .5) / 100
100 PRINT
110 PRINT "THE FUTURE VALUE IS: RS. " ; D
120 END
```

When above program is run, following will appear on screen:

```
RUN
ENTER THE CONSUMER PRICE INDEX FOR PREVIOUS YEAR = 1234
ENTER THE CONSUMER PRICE INDEX FOR CURRENT YEAR =1980
ENTER THE PRESENT VALUE  OF THE INVESTMENT (OR PRODUCT/SALARY) = RS.100
ENTER THE NUMBER OF PERIODS TO BE CALCULATED = 4

THE FUTURE VALUE IS: RS. 662.83
```

Example 6.4 Solving quadratic equation inter-actively.

```
10 REM * PROGRAM TO CALCULATE THE ROOTS OF A QUADRATIC EQUATION *
20 PRINT "ENTER VALUES FOR A, B AND C SEPARATED BY COMMAS"
30 INPUT A,B,C
40 LET R =(B ^ 2 - 4 * A * C )^.5
50 LET X1 = (- B + R) / ( 2 * A )
60 LET X2 = (- B - R) / ( 2 * A )
70 PRINT
80 PRINT "A = "; A, "B = ";B, "C = "; C
90 PRINT "X1 = "; X1, "X2 = "; X2
100 PRINT
110 GOTO 20
120 END
```

EXERCISE

PART I : Objective Type Questions

A1.Multiple Choice Questions

Choose the best possible alternatives from the following:

1. If a program contains one **READ** statement with three variables listed, and there is no **RESTORE** statement in the program, then the data block (choose one);
   (a) must contain exactly three items.
   (b) must contain more than three items.
   (c) cannot contain more than three items.
   (d) none of the above.
2. Which of the following does not occur when an **INPUT** statement is executed?
   (a) Execution pauses.
   (b) A symbol, usually a question mark, is displayed.
   (c) The computer checks that number
   (d) Execution resumes when the **ENTER** key is pressed.

B1.Fill in the Blanks

(1) When data must be entered to a program while it is executing, a(n) .... statement is used.
(2) A .... is used to tell the user what kind of data to enter to program.
(3) .... statements contain the data values that will be assigned to the variables listed in a READ statement.
(4) The .... statement causes the next **READ** statement encountered to start at the beginning of the data list.

C1 True or False

(a) A string must contain at least two characters.
(b) When a character string is **INPUT**, user must type it enclosed in quotation marks.

ANSWERS

A1 1.- b. 2- c. does not occur.

B1 (1) INPUT

(2) Prompt

(3) DATA

(4) RESTORE

(5) Variable

(6) DATA.

C1 (a) T (b) T

EXERCISE

PART - II

1. Write the statement to prepare a data list with the values **28, 429,6.3.14159** and your name.
2. Write the statements to start again at the head of the data list and put the name in **N$**.
3. Write the statement to assign your name to **N$** from the user terminal.
4. What will be the result of typing **84,5** in response to the statement:

   INPUT A,C,R
5. What is wrong with these statements?

```
742 DATA 8,12,"ONE"
744 READ A,C,R
```

6. What will be the output of the following programs:

(a)
```
10 REM * AREA OF RIGHT TRIANGLE
20 INPUT BASE
30 INPUT HEIGHT
40 LET AREA =(HEIGHT* BASE)/2
50 PRINT AREA
60 END
```

Your response may be **5** and **10**.

(b)
```
10 INPUT N$
20 INPUT M$
30 PRINT "NAME,CAST", N$; M$
```

Your response may be **AMIT, JAIN.**

(c)
```
10 INPUT B,C
20 INPUT D
30 Q = (B-C)/D
40 PRINT B,C,D,Q
50 END
```

Your response may be **5,7** and **3**.

(d)
```
10 INPUT X1,X2, X3,
20 P = (X3*X3) + (X1 * X2)
30 PRINT R,X3,X1,X2
40 END
```

Your response may be ?.6,4,5.

(e)
```
10 INPUT N$,A
20 INPUT M$,B,C
30 PRINT N$,A*B, M$,(A*B)*C
40 END
```

Your response may be

```
? ASHOk,5
? PLOT,7,8
```

7. Write an appropriate statement, or set of statements, for each situation described below.

(a) Enter numerical values for **X,Y,** and **Z** and string values for **A$** and **B$**. All of the data are to be typed on one line of a typewriter terminal.

(b) Enter the values for **A, N$** and **B** on one line, and the values for **M$** and **C** on the next line.

(c) Enter numerical values for **A,B** and **C** and string values for **M$** and **N$**. Each value is to be typed at the start of a new line.

(d) Print a message saying

PUT IN VALUES OF X,Y,Z,A$ AND B$

and then enter the requested data on the same line as the printed message.

(e) Print the message described in part (d) then enter the requested data on the next line.

(f) Print the values of **A,B,C, M$** and **N$** on one line with normal spacing between each item.

(g) Print the values of **A,B,C,M$** and **N$** on one line spacing the items as closely as possible.

(h) Print the values of **A,B** and **C** on one line spacing the items as closely as possible. Allow for subsequent output to begin on the same line immediately after the value for **C**.

(i) Print the values of **A,B,C, (A+B+C) ^ (1/3)** and **(A ^ 2+B, ^ 2+C)^.5** all in one line. Follow this with a blank line, then a third line with the value of **M$** printed near the left margin and the value of **N$** printed near the right.

(j) Print the numerical values of **A, B** and **C** all in one line. Precede each number with an appropriated descriptive label.

(k) Print the values of **M$** and **N$** on separate lines, with a blank line between them. Precede the value of **M$** with the label **NAME**: and precede **N$** with the label **CODE NUMBER** : Central the output as closely as possible.

8. Show how the input data will appear in each of the following situations

(a) **15 INPUT A,B,C**
20 INPUT M$,N$
where **A = 0.0000045 M$ = REKHA**
B = 83.5 x 10^{-10} N$ = RAJESH
C = -9000

(b) **20 INPUT P1,P2,T$**
where **P1 = -743.08 T$ = SARITA**
P2 = 0.00987

(c) **25 INPUT A$,B$,C$**
where **A$ = BOMBAY**
B$ = CALCUTTA C$ = NEW DELHI

(d) **15 INPUT P,P$,Q,Q$**
where **P =2,770, 543 Q = 48.8x10^9**
P$ = MARCH 24, 1943 Q$ = SEVEN O'CLOCK

9. Show how the input data will have to be fed in each of the following situations?

(a) **10 INPUT X1,X2,X3,X$**
where **X1 = 5.29 X 10^{-3} = 345.43**
X2 = 623 X$ = GITA

(a) **10 INPUT X$,X1'**
20 INPUT X2,X3

where the variables have the same values as in part (a).

(a) **30 INPUT A, A$,A!**
where **A = 620**
A$ = MARCH 24, 1943
A1 = -3.17

10. Write a program that will convert pounds sterling to dollars, given an exchange rate of $2.15 to the pound. The user should be able to type in the number of pounds (P). After the corresponding number of dollars is printed out, the computer should request further input from the user.

11. A person hires a car form a firm, which bases its charges on miles driven. A program to calculate the charges uses the following variables:

R = rate per mile

M1 = initial mileage

M2 = final mileage

M = miles driven

12. Write a program to calculate taxi fare payable to a taxi driver. The hire charges are Rs. 200 per day of 8 hours and drive of 80 km. Any thing over is payable at the rate of 10 Rs. per hour **(H)** and Rs. 2 per km **(KM)**.

13. Write a program that will convert kilograms to pounds weight, given that one kilogram equals 2.2 pounds. The user should be able to type in repeatedly a number of kilograms **(K)** to be converted.

14. A gas bill consists of a standing charge **(S)** plus a rate per unit consumed **(R)**. Write a program that will print out the total cost when the number of units consumed **(U)** is typed in. It should be possible to type in the number of units repeatedly, but the standing charge and the rate need be typed in once only.

15. Write a program that will convert hours **(H)** and minutes **(M)** into minutes. Assume the user will type in the hours and minutes on the same line on the screen.

16. Write a program that will print out the value of 15% of each of these four numbers: 14, 23, 100 and 17. Use one **READ** statement and four **DATA** statements. (To find 25% multiply by 0.25)

17. What numbers will be printed out when the above program is run?

18. Write a program that will print out the result of the following three expressions. Use variables **P, Q** and **R**.

6 x 9 x 2
8 x 4 x 1.5
21 x 6.2 x 124

19. When the program given below is run, what ages will appear on the screen ?

```
10 READ A
20 IF A > 45 THEN 40
30 GOTO 10
40 PRINT A
50 GOTO 10
60 DATA 24, 39, 49, 45, 30, 65, 21,
35, 46, 21, 25, 31
70 DATA 60,20,44
80 END
```

20. Amend the program given in question No. 19 so that it will print out all ages equal to or under 30.

21. The following table gives data for electricity bills:

Name **(N$)**	Units used **(U)**	Rate per unit **(R)**
RS GUPTA	**102**	**27**
NP SHARMA	**56**	**27**
AK YADAV	**63**	**50**

22. Write a program that will search the following list of salaries (S) and print out those at 7000 or more:

4200, 6100, 7350, 9000, 6000, 2140, 6100, 10400, 12000, 4000, 5000

23. The following table gives marks gained by candidates in three tests:

Candidate's number (C)	Physics (P)	Chemistry (C)	Maths (M)
1020	21	20	15
1021	16	25	10
1025	15	15	15
1027	15	15	20

Adding the marks together from three tests gives the total marks **(T)**. Assuming the pass mark is 50. Write a program that will print a list containing the number of each successful candidate.

24. In the following program, **H** represents a person's height (in inches):

```
10 INPUT H1
20 READ H
30 IF H < H1 THEN 20
40 PRINT H
50 GOTO 20
60 DATA 66,67,68,70,64,68,65,73,70
70 DATA 69,65,67
80 END
```

Indicate what shall be the result if following is input 75,100. Also indicate what shall be printed if you change < symbol of line 30 to > and type 60 when the program is run.

25. The following is the type of data on clients used by a computer dating agency or marriage bureau:

Name(N$)	Age(A)	Height(H)
JYOTSNA BAJAJ	25	64
SARLA SETH	21	66
NIRA JOSHI	31	62
DIVYA JAIN	17	68

Write a program that will ask the user to type in minimum acceptable age **(A1)** and maximum acceptable height **(H9)** in response to appropriate questions displayed on the screen. The program should then print out the names of all suitable clients.

26. The following program calculates commission **(C)** on the value of sales made **(S)**. The commission rate **(R)** is typed in when the program is run. **N$** represents a salesman's name.

```
10 PRINT "TYPE COMMISSION RATE IN
FRACTION"
20 INPUT R
30 READ N$,S
40 LET C = S*R
50 PRINT N$, "COMMISION" ,C
60 GOTO 30
70 DATA "ASHA"
80 DATA 1234.5
90 DATA "KAVITA",2345.6
100 END
```

If the commision rate typed in is 0.1, what will be displayed on the screen after this program is run? (Note that the program assumes the rate typed in as a decimal. Here 0.1 represents 10%)

27 When sales **(S)** are below Rs. 1000. the bonus **(B)** is Rs. 15. In other cases the bonus is Rs. 45. Write a program that will print out sales followed by the bonus on the same line of the screen. The user should be able to type in the value of sales at the time the program is run.

28. Write a program that will allow the user to type in repeatedly the marks gained by

candidates in three tests (use variables **M1, M2,** and **M3**). The program should add the marks together to obtain the total marks **(M)** for a candidate. The pass mark is 45. The program should print out only those totals that are equal to or exceed the pass mark.

29. Write a program that will calculate hotel costs, given the number of nights stayed **(N)** and the rate for the night **(R)**. For 2 nights or less the rate is Rs. 240 per night. For up to 6 nights the rate is Rs. 260 per night. For more than 6 nights the rate is Rs. 160 per night.

30. Suppose the program is running on a computer and the invitation to type sign is being displayed, what results will be printed out if the user types (a) 11 and (b) 6 in response to the invitation to type sign?

31. Detect the syntax errors in the following BASIC statements.
   (a) `IMPUT M`
   (b) `OUTPUT A`
   (c) `PRINT N8`
   (d) `IF A ( ) B THEN 40`
   (e) `LET ( ) 2 + y ( ) 2 = Z`
   (f) `LET H = 1 = J`
   (g) `LET X ( ) = 36 + Y/Z`
   (h) `IF A ( ) B ( ) THEN END`
   (i) `EXIT`
   (j) `IF P ( ) Q THEN 510`

32. Using the input as indicated, give the output of each program segment.
   (a)
```
490 INPUT X, Y, Z
500 INPUT P$
510 PRINT P$
520 PRINT X, Y, Z
Input: ? 7, 5, 3
? JAI KAPOOR
```
   (b)
```
90 INPUT P2$, P3$
100 PRINT "THE IS:"
110 PRINT P3$
120 PRINT P2$
Input: ? MOTHER, INDIA
```

33. Write following program lines as a single INPUT statement.
```
70 PRINT "WHAT ARE THE HEIGHT AND
WEIGHT?"
71 INPUT ht, wt
```

34. What is displayed when each of the following segments of code is executed?
```
200 READ A, B
210 READ C
220 PRINT A; B; C
230 REM
240 DATA 1
250 DATA 2, 3, 4
```

35. List the output of following program
```
200 READ X$, Y$ , A
210 READ Z$, B
220 PRINT Y$, B
230 PRINT Z$; B
240 REM
250 DATA SARITA, JAIN,30
260 DATA "' ' ", 10
```

36. What will be the output of following program.
```
200 READ A, B
210 RESTORE
220 READ A, C, D
230 PRINT A; B; C; D
240 REM
250 DATA 1, 2, 3, 4
```

37. Correct the syntax errors, if any, in the following statements:
   (a) `300 REAX, X, Y, N$`
   (b) `350 READ A, B.`
   (c) `400 1; 2; 3`
   (d) `450 DATA 8.7. _4. "" JAYA""`

38. Rewrite the following program using INPUT statements for the input data instead of LET statements.
```
15 LET X = 5.34
25 LET Y = 14.2
35 LET A = (X + Y) / 2
40 PRINT A
45 END
```

39. Find the logic and syntax errors in the following program:
```
10 REM THIS PROGRAM INPUTS TWO
NUMBERS AND COMPUTES AND
11 REM PRINTS THE SUM OF THEIR
SQUARES
12 INPUT, X
13 LET Y = X
14 LET S = X ^ 2 + Y ^ 2
15 END
```

40. What is the advantage of using **INPUT** rather than **LET** to supply input data to a program?

ANSWERS

1. **112 DATA 28,429.6,3,14159,"V.K JAIN"**
2. **114 RESTORE**
   115 READ A,B,C dummy
   117 READ N$
3. **119 INPUT "YOUR NAME", N$**
4. A request for more data (second?). **REDO FROM START?**
5. The variable R does not match the **DATA** entry **"ONE"** (which is a string).
6. (a) **25**
   (b) **RUN**
   ```
   ? Amit
   ? Jain
   NAME,CAST          Amit Jain
   ```
   (c) **RUN**
   ```
   ?   5,   7
   ?   3
       5    7    3    -.6666667
   ```
   (d) **RUN**
   ```
   ?   4,   5,   6
       56   6    4    5
   ```
   (e) **RUN**
   ```
   ASHOK   35   PLOT   280
   ```
7. (A)
   (a) **10 INPUT X,Y,Z,A$,B$**
   (b) **10 INPUT A,N$,B**
   15 INPUT M$,C
   (c) **10 INPUT A**
   12 INPUT B
   14 INPUT C
   16 INPUT M$
   18 INPUT N$
   (d) **10 PRINT "ENTER VALUES FOR A,B,C,M$ AND NS",**
   20 INPUT A,B,C,M$,N$
   (e) **10 PRINT "PUT IN VALUES OF X,Y,Z,A$, AND B$"**
   20 INPUT A,B,C,M$; N$
   (f) **100 PRINT A,B,C,M$,N$**
   (g) **100 PRINT A;B;C; M$;N$**
   (h) **120 PRINT A;B;C;**
   (i) **200 PRINT A;B;C; (A+B+C)/3;(A*B*C)^(1/3);(A^2+B^2)^.5**
   210 PRINT
   220 PRINT M$,,,,N$
   (j) **300 PRINT "A ="; A,"B=,",B, "C=",C**
   or
   300 PRINT "A ="; A; "B=",B,"C=",C
   or
   300 PRINT "A =", A;"B" =, B, "C =",C
   (k) **500 PRINT,, "NAME:" M$**
   510 PRINT
   520 PRINT,, "CODE NUMBER:" N$
8. (a) **9.3 E-6,83.5E-10,7000**
   ? SHEKHAR,RAJESH
   The first line of data can also be typed as
   ?.0000093,.835E-10, -7000
   (b) **?-743.08,.00987, SARITA**
   or
   ?-.74308E + 3,.987E-2,SARITA
   (c) **?"BOMBAY","CALCUTTA","NEW DELHI"**

   (The quotation marks are required around NEW DELHI because of the inclusion of blank space. In the case of CALCUTTA and BOMBAY, the quotation marks are optional.)

   (d) **?2770543,"MARCH 24,1943" ,48.8E+9,"SEVEN O' CLOCK"**

   (The strings must be enclosed within the quotation marks because of the blank spaces and the comma.)
9. (a) **? 5.29E-3, -633, 345.43, GITA**
   or
   ? .00529, -633, 345.43, GITA
   (b) **? GITA, J.29 E-3**
   ?-633, 345.43
   (c) **? 620, "MARCH 24, 1943',-3.17**
10.
```
10 R = 2.15
20 INPUT Enter number of pounds ";P
30 PRINT P * R
40 GOTO 20
50 END
```
11.
```
10 INPUT R
20 INPUT M1,M2
30 LET M = M2 - M1
40 PRINT M1,M2,M,R,M *R
50 GOTO 20
60 END
```

12.
```
1 INPUT H
2 INPUT KM
3 LET OT = 10 * H + 2 KM
4 LET TF = 200 + OT
5 PRINT TF
```

13.
```
10 INPUT K
20 PRINT K * 2.2
30 GOTO 10
40 END
14. 10 INPUT S
20 INPUT R
30 INPUT U
40 PRINT S + (R * U)
50 GOTO 30
60 END
or
10 INPUT S. R
20 INPUT U
30 PRINT S + (R * U)
40 GOTO 20
50 END
```

14.
```
10 INPUT H.M
20 PRINT (H * 60 ) +M
30 END
```
The brackets are optional.

15.
```
10 READ N
20 PRINT N * 0.15
30 GOTO 10
40 DATA 14
50 DATA 23
60 DATA 100
70 DATA 17
80 END
```

16.
```
20
9.2
18. 10 READ P, Q, R
20 PRINT P * Q * R
30 GOTO 10
40 DATA 6, 9, 2
50 DATA 8, 4, 1.5
60 DATA 21, 6.2, 124
70 END
```

19.
```
RUN
49
65
46
60
Out of DATA in 10
```

20. **Change line 20 as 20 IF A >= 30 THEN 40**

21.
```
10 READ N$, U,R
20 LET C = U * R
30 PRINT N$ , U, R, C
40 GOTO 10
50 DATA "RS GUPTA" 102, .27
60 DATA "NP SHARMA 56, . 27
70 DATA "AK YADAV" 63, .50
9999 END
```

22.
```
10 READ S
20 IF S > = 7000 THEN 40
30 GOTO 10
40 PRINT S
50 GOTO 10
60 DATA 4200, 6100, 7350, 9000,
6000, 2140, 6100, 10400
70 DATA 1200, 4000, 5000
80 END
```

23.
```
10 READ C,
20 LET T = P + C + M
30 IF T > = 50 THEN 50
40 GOTO 10
50 PRINT C
60 GOTO 10
70 DATA 1020, 21,20,15
80 DATA 1021, 16, 25, 10
90 DATA 1025, 15, 15, 15
100 DATA 1027, 15, 15, 20
110 END
```

24. H1 represents minimum height. The following is printed in response to your entries as 70 and 100.
```
? 70
70
73
70
Out of DATA in 20
? 100
Out of DATA in 20
```

26. TYPE COMMISSION RATE IN FRACTION
```
? .1
ASHA COMMISSION 123.45
KAVITA COMMISSION 234.56
```

27.
```
10 INPUT S
20 IF S < 1000 THEN 50
30 LET B = 45
40 GOTO 60
50 LET B = 15
60 PRINT S, B
70 END
```

28.
```
10 INPUT M1,M2,M3
20 LET M = M1 + M2 + M3
30 IF M < 45 THEN 10
40 PRINT M
```

```
50 GOTO 10
60 END
```

The INPUT statement (in line 10) could be replaced by three separate INPUT statements.

29.
```
10 INPUT N
20 IF N > 2 THEN 50
30 LET R = 240
40 GOTO 90
50 IF N > 6 THEN 80
60 LET R = 200
70 GOTO 90
80 LET R = 160
90 PRINT N, R, N * R
100 GOTO 10
110 END
```

30.
```
1 night
up to 7 nights
up to 28 nights
over 28 nights
```

31. (a) `INPUT H`
(b) `PRINT A`
(c) `PRINT N8`
(d) `IF A <> B THEN 40`
(e) `LET Z = X ( ) 2 + y ( ) 2`
(f) `LET H = 1`
(g) `LET X = 36 + Y / Z`
`LET J = 1`
(h) `IF A <> B THEN STOP` note: this is not a syntax error but a matter of style.
(i) `EXIT` is not a legal verb
(j) `IF P <> Q THEN 510` note: mixed data type in condition as well as negative line number in statement.

32. (a) `7    5    3`
(b)
```
THE    IS;
INDIA
MOTHER
```

33. `INPUT  "WHAT ARE THE HEIGHT"; HT, WT`

34.
```
RUN
1  2  3
```

35.
```
RUN
JAIN  10
' ''10
```

36. `1 2 2 3`

37. (a) `300 READ X, Y, N$`
(b) `350 READ A, B`
(c) `400 DATA 1, 2, 3`
(d) `450 8.7, = 4., "JAYA,"`

38.
```
5 REM ** INPUT EXERCISE **
10 PRINT "THIS PROGRAM FINDS THE AVERAGE OF THE TWO"
15 PRINT " NUMBERS THAT YOU INPUT"
20 PRINTER "ENTER THE NUMBERS : "
25 INPUT X
30 INPUT Y
35 REM
40 LET AVG = (X + Y) / 2
45 REM
50 PRINT "THE AVERAGE OF "; X; "AND "; Y' "I S "; AVG
55 REM
60 END
```

39. The INPUT statement allows the input data to be easily changed from run to run. The program's user does not need to change the code, which would be the case using LET.

EXERCISE

PART III

1. What is a data list, and how is it created?
2. Which statement should be used when there is an enquiry/response situation in a program?
3. What does the computer do when it comes to an INPUT statement?
4. What symbol separates the variables in an INPUT statement?
5. A ...... explains to the user what values are to be entered. It can be used either in an INPUT statement or in a PRINT statement that precedes an INPUT statement.
6. How does the RESTORE statement work?
7. What is the effect of a comma in a PRINT statement?
8. What is the difference between the TAB function and the SPC function?
9. What happens if a program asks for a string value and the user enters a numeric value instead?

CHAPTER 7

Putting DATA Out of Computers

7.1 Outputting the Data: The PRINT Statement

Just as there are a number of statements that can be used to input data values into a program, similarly a variety of methods exist to transmit numerical or string output data from the computer. Two of the most commonly used statements are PRINT and LPRINT statements.

The PRINT statement provides you with the mechanism to display data on your screen. The LPRINT statement functions very similar to the PRINT statement, with the exception that data will be printed on the attached printer instead of the display.

The PRINT statement consists of a line number, the keyword PRINT, and an optional list of expressions that can consist of numbers, formulae, or strings. The two formats of this statement are shown below:

By itself, the keyword PRINT (or the question mark character) will cause a blank line to be displayed. This is equivalent to generating a carriage return and line feed character. Thus, you can use the PRINT statement to control horizontal spacing when you desire to display a heading and skip one or more lines prior to printing the body of a report.

Concerning vertical spacing within a PRINT statement,the position of each printed item will be determined by the punctuation character employed to separate the items in the list of expressions. Successive items in the list of expressions must be separated by either a comma(,) or a semicolon;

Format

PRINT [*list of expressions*]

The expression can be either separated by a comma (,) or semicolon (;). The word PRINT can be substituted by the symbol? also

Examples

```
PRINT X
```

displays the value of variable X.

```
PRINT A$
```

displays the character(s) stored in A$.

```
PRINT "I AM YOUR COMPUTER"
```

displays `I AM YOUR COMPUTER.`

```
PRINT A+B
```

displays the numeric sum of the values stored in variables A and B.

```
PRINT A$ + B$
```

displays the contents of strings **A$** and **B$**, one after the other. This is known as **concatenation**.

When numbers are displayed by a PRINT, most BASICs insert a leading blank before positive numbers and a minus sign before negative numbers.

7.2 Print Zones and Commas

The IBM screen consists of 2,000 print positions: 80 columns across and 25 rows down. The 80 columns are divided into five print zones, each containing 14 print positions (columns). The zones are divided as follows:

Zone 1	Zone 2	Zone 3	Zone 4	Zone 5
(1-14)	(15-28)	(20-43)	(43-56)	(57-80)

Each print zone contains either 10 or14 print positions. A logical line containing more than one physical line will have the second, and subsequent print lines contain a contracted first zone.

First line	1 14	15 28	29 42	43 56	57 70	71 80
Succeeding lines	5 14	15 28	29 42	43 56	57 70	71 80

If more than five items are in the list of expression and you are using commas as separators, the 6 through 10 items will be printed on a second line with their positions on the line corresponding to the persons of the zones for succeeding lines. Similarly, item 13 through 18 would be printed on a third line and so on. An example of a printout being "wrapped" around from line to line is shown by the following example. Note that BASIC always prints positive numbers preceded by a space if you wish to verify the zone positions in this example.

```
10 PRINT 1,2,3,4,5,6,7,8,9,10,11,12,13,14,15
RUN
 1            2            3            4            5
 6            7            8            9            10
 11           12           13           14           15
 Ok
```

If you type the PRINT statement with numbers separated by semicolons as below the numbers are printed with two gaps, the second gap, reserved for the sign of the number.In case of negative numbers - sign will appear instead.

```
20 PRINT 1;2;3;4;5;6;7;8;9;10;11;12;13;14;15
RUN
1 2 3 4 5 6 7 8 9 10 11 12 13 14 15
```

Thus, The **PRINT** statement is used, as its name implies, to print information on the user's terminal. It can be used in a variety of ways to print string or numeric information and, with formatting control, can produce tabulations.

The simplest form of the **PRINT** statement uses the work **PRINT** and single constant or variable:

```
10 PRINT "TEST PRINTING"
20 PRINT P
30 PRINT P$
40 PRINT
50 PRINT R*3
```

Execution of line **10** will cause the words **TEST PRINTING** to appear on the user's terminal; line **20** will print the current value of the numeric variable **P**; line **30** prints the current value of the string variable **P$** and line **50** computes the three times the current value of the numeric variable **R** and prints the answer.In all cases printing will be done if variables have been correctly defined,and this shall be printed on screen of computer and not by printer. For getting results printed by printer on piece of paper, you have to use **LPRINT** statement. In each of these cases the **PRINT** statement is terminated with a carriage return and life feed so that only a single value is printed per line. Line 40 has caused a blank line to be printed (or left) in the display.

If you wish to print more than one value on a line then you should separate the items either with semi-colons or with commas. When separated with semicolon the items in a **PRINT** statement will appear without intervening spaces:

```
100 LET L$ = "LEFT "
110 LET R$ = "RIGHT "
120 PRINT "SEE "; L$;"OR "; R$
```

These statements will cause the following to be printed.

```
SEE LEFT OR RIGHT
```

(Note the spaces within the string constants.)

When the last item in the list is followed by a space as in line 120 above, the PRINT statement will terminate with a carriage return and line feed. If, however, a semicolon follows the last item then the terminal print head remains in the current print position until the next PRINT statement is fed. Thus the following statements will achieve the same result as line 120 above:

```
200 PRINT "SEE";
210 PRINT " LEFT"; " OR";
220 PRINT " RIGHT"
```

The following illustrates how the output will be listed with comma and semicolon control.

```
10 PRINT "GITA"
20 PRINT "SITA";"SARITA";
30 PRINT "NITA","RITA"
40 PRINT "NITA","RITA"
50 PRINT "RAM",
60 PRINT "SYAM"
```

This will generate following output

```
RUN
GITA
SITASARITANITA RITA
NITA RITA
RAM SYAM
```

7.3 Formatting the Output: The Comma Control

Separation of the PRINT statement items with commas causes BASIC to print in zones. For this width of the page is divided by BASIC into 5 zones each of 14 characters. Thus zone 1 begins in print position 1, zone 2 in print position 15, zone 3 in prints position 29, zone 4 in point position 43 and zone 5 in print position 57 and ends at 70th. Remaining spaces are left blank. But second or subsequent lines start from fifth space only.

Commas not only separate items within a **PRINT** statement, but also control the format of those items. A comma indicates that next item to be printed will start at the beginning of the next empty print zone. The following example shows how this works:

```
10 READ NAM$,DATE,YEAR
20 PRINT NAM$, DATE,YEAR
30 DATA "GITA", 07, 1990
```

The first item in the **PRINT** statement is printed at the beginning of the first print zone. The comma between **NAM$** and **DATA** causes the computer to space over to the next unused print zone; then the value in **DATA** is printed. The second comma directs the computer to space over to the next zone (Zone 3) and prints the value in **YEAR**. Thus the output is as follows:

```
RUN
GITA                07                  1990
```

If the more items are listed in a PRINT statement than, there are more print zones in a line, the print zones of the next line are also used, starting with the first zone. Notice the output of the following example:

```
10 READ SEX$, AGE, NAM$, BAS, HRA, GPF, GPA
20 PRINT SEX$,AGE, NAM$, BAS, HRA, GPF, GPA
```

```
30 DATA M,25, SUSHMA, 1500,350,90, 1760
RUN
M               25              SUSHMA              1500              350
90              1760
```

Note that we have not selected the variable for name as **NAME$** as **NAME** is a reserved word in BASIC.

If the value of strings to be printed exceeds the width of the print zone, the entire value is printed, regardless of how many zones it occupies. The comma causes printing to continue in the next unused print zone, as shown in the following example:

```
10 LET SPOT$ = "NAGALAND"
20 PRINT "YOUR NEXT CHANGE WILL BE", SPOT$
```

← ZONE 1 →	← ZONE 2 →	← ZONE 3→
YOUR NEXT CHANGE WILL BE		NAGALAND

1 14 15 28 29 42

A print zone can be skipped by enclosing a space (the character blank) in quotation marks. This technique causes the entire zone to appear empty:

```
60 PRINT "NAME", " " , " ROLL NUMBER"
```

It is also possible to skip a zone by typing consecutive commas:

```
60 PRINT "NAME", , "ROLL NUMBER"
```

Both techniques cause the literal NAME to be printed in the first zone, the second zone to be blank, and the literal ROLL NUMBER to be printed in the third zone:

← ZONE 1 →	← ZONE 2 →	← ZONE 3 →
NAME		ROLL NUMBER

If a comma appears after the last item in a PRINT statement, the output of the next PRINT statement encountered will begin at the next available print zone, as shown by the following statements and output:

```
10 READ NAM$, SEX$, CASTE$
20 PRINT NAM$,
30 PRINT SEX$,CASTE$
40 DATA "JYOTSNA", "F", "JAIN"
99 END
```

When above program is RUN, following message will be printed:

```
RUN
JYOTSNA          F               JAIN
```

Each comma in PRINT statement is regarded as an instruction to move to the first print position of the next available zone before commencing printing. If the print head is currently somewhere in zone 5 then the next comma will move it to zone 1 of the next line. The use of zones for tabulation is illustrated in the following coding showing part of a print-out of salesman's expenses l

```
10 READ J(1),J(2),J(3),F(1),F(2),F(3)
20 PRINT , "MONTH", "AMITABH", "JYOTSNA", "ANURAG"
30 PRINT, , "(MANAGER)"
40 PRINT "JAN", J(1),J(2),J(3)
50 PRINT "FEB", F(1),F(2),F(3)
60 DATA 16,18,20,22,24,26
```

The resultant print-out is as shown:

```
RUN
                MONTH           AMITABH         JYOTSNA         ANURAG
                                (MANAGER)
JAN             16              18              20
FEB             22              24              26
```

Note the use in line 20 of a comma as the first item to step the **PRINT** statement on to zone 2.

A semicolon appearing after the last item in a **PRINT** statement prevents the output of the next **PRINT** statement from starting on a new line. Instead, the next item printed appears on the same line, at the next available print position:

```
10 PRINT "DIVYA BHATNAGAR"
20 PRINT 142; "C-BLOCK NEW DELHI."
RUN
DIVYA BHATNAGAR
142 C-BLOCK NEW DELHI
```

PRINT statements can contain both semi-colons and commas. When a semi-colon is encountered, the next constant or variables is printed immediately; when a comma is encountered the print position moves to the beginning of the next zone. As an example, suppose that the letters "RS" are to be added to the expense program above; lines 40 and 50 can be amended as follows:

```
20 PRINT "MONTH", "AMITABH", "JYOTSNA", "ANURAG"
40 PRINT "JAN", "RS";J(1), "RS"; J(2), "RS"; J(3)
50 PRINT "FEB", "RS",;F(1), "RS"; F(2), "RS", F(3)
```

The resultant print-out now as follows:

```
MONTH         AMITABH             JYOTSNA          ANURAG
              (MANAGER)
JAN           RS 16               RS 18            RS 14
FEB           RS 22               RS 24            RS 26
```

7.4 Making Tables: The TAB Function

Tab used with PRINT or LPRINT, behave similarly to the TAB key on a type writer. TAB inserts a specified number of spaces before PRINTING. The comma and semicolon are easy to use, and many reports can be formatted in this fashion. There are times, however, when a report should be structured differently. The TAB function allows output to be printed in any column in an output line, thus providing the programmer greater flexibility in formatting printed output.

As with the comma and semicolon, one or more TAB functions are used within a PRINT statement. The general format of the TAB function is as follows:

Format: `TAB (expression)`

The *expression* can be a numeric constant, a variable, or an arithmetic expression. Its final arithmetic value must be between 1 to 225. However, if the **TAB** value is less than 1, 0 is assumed. *An n value* having the greater line length wraps the remaining spaces back to the *start of the line.*

When **TAB** function is encountered in a **PRINT** statement, the computer spaces over to the column number indicated in the expression. The next variable value or literal found in the **PRINT** statement is printed starting in that column. The **TAB** prints blank spaces as it moves to the specified column, thereby erasing anything that was on the screen previously. The TAB function is separated from the items to be printed by semicolons. For example, the following statement causes the literal **HELLO** to be printed starting in column 10:

```
50 PRINT TAB(10) ; "HELLO" ; TAB(25); "HEMA"
```

Then, starting in column 25, the literal HEMA is printed .

TAB always measures from the first character position on the line, not from the cursor position. If more than one TAB is used on a line, n must become progressively larger, otherwise, PRINTing may "overrun" the TABs.

Sample Program

```
10 REM 'TAB' FUNCTION PROGRAM
20 PRINT TAB(5) ; "RAM"
30 X = 10
40 PRINT TAB(X) ; " SYAM"
```

```
50 PRINT TAB(6 * X/5+8) ; "GHANSYAM"
RUN    RAM
              SYAM
                        GHANSYAM
```

Note: The : (semicolon) after **TAB (n)** is optional.

Example 7.1 :Computation of compound interest (Inter-active Method).

```
10 REM * COMPOUND INTEREST *
20 PRINT "BORROWED AMOUNT";
30 INPUT P
40 PRINT "ANNUAL INTEREST RATE";
50 INPUT R
60 PRINT "NUMBER OF YEARS";
70 INPUT N
80 R1 = R/100
90 A = P* (1+R1) ^ N
100 I = A - P
110 PRINT TAB(5)"AMOUNT PAYABLE" ;
120 PRINT TAB(25) "INTEREST" .
130 PRINT TAB(5) A;
140 PRINT TAB(25) I
150 END
```

When the above program is run, following will be displayed.

```
RUN
BORROWED AMOUNT? 100
ANNUAL INTEREST RATE? 10
NUMBER OF YEARS? 5
    AMOUNT PAYABLE          INTEREST
    161.051                 61.05101
```

The **TAB** function can be used only to advance the print position from left to right; backspacing is not possible. Therefore,if more than one **TAB** function appears in a single **PRINT** statement, the column numbers specified should increase from left to right. When a **TAB** function specifies a column to the left of the current print position, the computer leaves space to that column on the next line, as shown in the previous example. Another example will illustrate this point:

Example 7.2 Making a RIGHT-ANGLED TRIANGLE

```
5 REM *PRINT A RIGHT TRIANGLE*
15 PRINT TAB(15);"X"
25 PRINT TAB(15);"X";TAB(18);"X"
35 PRINT TAB(15);"X";TAB(21);"X"
45 PRINT TAB(15);"X";TAB(24);"X"
55 PRINT
TAB(15); "X";TAB(18); "X";TAB(21); "X";TAB(24); "X";TAB(27);"X"
65 END
```

Following diagram will be drawn by the program:

```
X
X  X
X     X
X        X
X  X  X  X  X
```

The above method is very simple but lengthy.One can make use of **IF-THEN-ELSE** statement in making such diagrams which reduces the burden on programmer but requires higher skills in making the program.The following example uses this technique.You shall learn about **IF-THEN-ELSE** statement in unit 8 of this book in detail.

Example 7.3 Making an equilateral triangle.

```
10 REM *TRIANGLE*
20 A=0
30 X=20
35 Y=0
40 PRINT TAB(20); "*"
45 A=A+1
46 Y=Y+1
50 PRINT TAB(X-Y);"*";TAB(X+Y);"*"
70 IF A=4 THEN 75 ELSE 45
75 PRINT TAB(15); "************"
90 END
```

The above program prints following triangle on screen.If you change the word **PRINT** to **LPRINT** in lines **40,50** and **75**, then you can get the diagram on the piece of paper by the printer.

```
        *
      *   *
    *       *
   *          *
 *               *
****************
```

You can analyze it like this,Line 40 prints a star symbol * in column 20 by virtue of its TAB statement.Line 46 increments the value of Y by 1 every time the loop 45-70 is executed by computer.The loop is executed by virtue of line 45 which increments the value of A that acts like a counter and prints rows 2nd to 5th of the diagram.Line 50 prints the star,a position ahead and after the star of first row of the diagram in the second row.Similarly in the third row of diagram, a star is printed two positions ahead and after the star of the first row and so on.Line 70 counts the number of the rows of star to be printed and then prints the last line of the diagram.

Example 7.4 Making a diamond

```
10 REM *MAKING A DIAMOND*
20 A = 0 : B = 0
30 X = 20
40 Y = 0
50 PRINT TAB(20); "*"
60 A =A + 1
70 Y =Y + 1
80 PRINT TAB(X-Y); "*"; TAB(X+Y) ; "*"
90 IF A < 4 THEN 60
100 Y = 4
110 B = B + 1
120 PRINT TAB(X-Y) ; "*" ; TAB(X+Y) ; "*"
130 Y = Y - 1
140 IF B < 4 THEN 110
150 PRINT TAB(20); "*"
160 END
```

```
    *
   * *
  *   *
 *     *
*       *
 *     *
  *   *
   * *
    *
```

7.5 The PRINT USING Statement

Another convenient feature for controlling output is **PRINT USING** statement. This feature is especially useful while printing table headings or aligning columns of numbers. The general format of the **PRINT USING** statement is as follows:

Format `PRINT USING "format control characters"; DATA`

PRINT USING is the most powerful **PRINT** statement and is used to format printed output precisely.

Here **DATA** is the data to be displayed. It can be a variable,a mathematical equation,or characters enclosed in quotes.

Format control character or characters (also known as format string) can be any one or a combination of the symbols shown in Table 7.1

Table 7.1 : Format Control Characters

#	A "place holder" to format and justify right numbers,represents each digit positions.
+	Activates a leading plus or minus sign.
-	Activates a trailing minus sign after negative numbers only.
,	Activates a comma after every third digit of the number.
**	Fills leading spaces with asterisks.
$	Places a dollar sign in the output.
$$	Places a "floating" dollar sign in front of **DATA**.
**$	Fills leading spaces with asterisks and places a dollar sign immediately in front of the number.
^^^	Displays output in exponential notation,when placed after the digit position character.
,.	Causes a comma to be printed to the left of every third digit to the left of the decimal number.
_	Underscore causes the next character to be displayed as a string (literal) character.
!	Displays the first character of string data.
\n\	Displays n+2 string characters starting from the left side of the string.
&	Displays string **DATA** exactly as it appears.

Note: (1) Any characters other than those above of string literals are displayed by PRINT USING as they appear in the format string.

(2) After format string we have to always put a semicolon and not a comma.

Examples

(a) **Use of "#"**

```
PRINT USING "#";7
PRINT USING "##";28
PRINT USING "###";115
PRINT USING "###.##;235.15
```

displays 7,28,115,235.15 in a row.

Sample Program

```
10 REM * PRINT USING PROGRAM *
20 N=1
30 PRINT USING "####";N
40 N=N * 10
50 IF N<1001 THEN 30
```

```
RUN
      1
     10
    100
   1000
```

(b) **Use of "." (The period)**

A period is placed in the format string to indicate the desired decimal position. For example:

PRINT USING "##.##";12.5

displays **12.50**. A # to the right of the decimal point acts as a place holder inserting a trailing 0 if necessary.

PRINT USING "##.##";64

displays **64.00**.

When a number contains a decimal, and no decimal is indicated in PRINT USING's format, that number is rounded to an integer:

PRINT USING "####"; 12.5

displays **13**, whereas **12.49** would get displayed as **12**.

If **PRINT USING's** format does not allow enough places to display the entire number properly,the number is displayed, but its position on the page is out of line. A leading percent sign (%) is used to indicate the problem. For example:

PRINT USING "##"; 256

displays %256.

(c) **Use of "," (comma) sign:**

When a comma is placed anywhere in a PRINT USING string (except in the front), a comma is displayed after every third digit in the printout:

PRINT USING "######,#"; 12345

displays 12,345.

(d) **Use of + (plus) Sign :**

A plus sign in the first position displays the output with a leading plus or minus sign, according to the sign of the number.

Examples

PRINT USING "+###"; 123

displays +123.

PRINT USING "+###";-123

displays -123.

(e) **Use of - (minus) sign :**

A minus in the last position display negative numbers with a trailing minus sign. (Positive numbers are displayed with a trailing blank-space.)

Examples

PRINT USING "####-";-23

displays 23- (with two leading blanks).

PRINT USING "####-" ;154

displays 154 (with a leading and trailing space).

(f) **Use of ** (Double asterisks):**

Two asterisks (**) cause all leading blanks to be filled with asterisks.

Examples

```
PRINT USING "**####.##"; 123.45
```

displays ***123.45.

```
PRINT USING "+**####.##"; 124.5
```

displays ***+124.50.

(g) **Use of $ (dollar) sign and - (minus) sign**

TO add a dollar sign in any financial documents etc, place a $ after the two asterisks.For example

```
PRINT USING "**$####.##"; 123.45
```

displays ***$123.45.

Example

```
10 REM "PRINT USING" PROGRAM
20 FOR X=1 TO 6
30 READ N
40 PRINT USING "**$####.##-";N
50 NEXT X
60 DATA 67772,-203.678
70 DATA 799.03,-0.62
80 DATA 73295.3, 1234567890.36
RUN
*$67772.00
***$203.68-
***$799.03
*****$0.62-
*$73295.30
%$12345678000.00
```

In first case, since in statement 40 we have placed sign prior to two asterisks from right, computer has automaticlly introduced two zeros after decimal. In second, data after decimal sign has been rounded off and trailing minus sign is introduced. In last case, since the data contains more digits than the asterisks in the given format, % sign has been printed by computer to show the mistake done by operator (overflow of data).

To display the $ without the leading asterisks, simply remove the double asterisks. For example:

```
PRINT USING "$###.##"; 673.75
```

displays **$673.75**

Notice here that there is no gap between the $ sign and the amount. To place the $ sign immediately before the number, use double $s with a gap. For example:

```
PRINT USING "$$###.##"; 777.77 displays $ 777.77
```

(h) **Use of ^ (caret) sign**

Four caret signs `(^^^^)` at the end are used to display numbers in exponential notation. For example.

```
PRINT USING "####^^^^"; 679
```

displays **-679E+00**. However if you type:

```
PRINT USING "####^^^^"; 679567
```

the result will be displayed as 690E+00. Note that computer has rounded off the number.

```
PRINT USING "####^^^^"; 111779
```

then the answer will be **112E+03**. Notice that computer has rounded off the number in mantissa portion of the exponential notation.

(i) **Text manipulation**

Text can be included in **PRINT USING** (except for the above delimiters).

Examples:

```
10 REM "PRINT USING" PROGRAM
20 FOR Z=1 TO 5
30 PRINT USING "STUDENT NO,##";Z
40 NEXT Z
RUN
STUDENT NO, 1
STUDENT NO, 2
STUDENT NO, 3
STUDENT NO, 4
STUDENT NO, 5
```

(j) **Use of ! (exclamation) sign**

PRINT USING may also display and format strings. Use of an exclamation sign causes PRINT USING to display only the left-most character in a string or string variable.

Examples

```
PRINT USING "!"; "ZEBRA"
```

displays the letter Z.But if you type :

```
PRINT USING "!,"; "ZEBRA"
```

the computer will print **Z,**.

```
10 G$=ALPHA
20 PRINT USING "!"; G$
```

displays the first characters of G$ the same as LEFT$(G$,1)

(k) **Use of \ \ back slashes**

Back slashes **(\ \)** are used to display a specific number of characters. The number of characters displayed is equal to the number of spaces between the two back slashes, plus two.

Note: The number indicated below in the statement are not to be actually typed between the back slashes, but indicate the number of blank spaces.Also remember that in such cases only back-slashes are to be used and not forward slash **(/)**.

Examples:

```
A$= "SUNITA"
PRINT USING "\ 2\"; A$
```

displays **SUNI** i.e. the four left-most characters in A$.

```
PRINT USING "\ 3 \"; "abcdefg"
```

displays abcde.

Examples:

```
10 A$= "BOOKEEPER"
20 PRINT "LEARN BASICA HAND"
30 PRINT USING "\ 2\"; A$
RUN
LEARN BASICA HANDBOOK
```

If the back slashes are typed with no spaces,two characters are printed; (if the back slashes are typed with one space between them,three characters are printed, and so on). If the string is longer than the field,the extra characters are ignored.If the field is longer then the string,the string is left-justified in the field and padded with spaces on the right. For example

```
10 A$= "GOOD"
20 B$= "BYE"
30 PRINT USING "\  \";A$; B$
40 PRINT USING "\   \"; A$; B$
50 PRINT USING "\ \";A$; B$
RUN
GOODBYE
GOOD BYE
GOOBYE
```

Line 30 creates a print field of four characters (the two back slashes plus the two spaces between).The string **"GOOD"** is four characters long, so it is printed in the field as it is. However the string **"BYE"** is only three characters long, so it is left-justified in the format field.

Line 40 creates a print field of five characters.Both strings are left-justified in the print field, but with this example you can see the padding at the end of the field.The string **"GOOD"** used only four characters, even though five characters were allotted in the format; thus it was left-justified and a blank was added at the right. This blank separates the string **"BYE"** from the string **"GOOD"** in the output.

The last example, line 50,allows only the first three letters of **GOOD** to be printed.

(l) **Use of {_} (underscore or underline symbol)**

An `underline`causes the next character in a string to be treated as a "literal" and displayed in the output.

Examples:

```
10 REM "PRINT USING" UNDERSCORE PROGRAM
20 A=100000!
30 PRINT "NOBEL PRIZE IS WORTH ";
40 PRINT USING "_!$####,###.##_!";A
RUN
NOBEL PRIZE IS WORTH !$ 100,000.00!
```

By virtue of introduction of underscore symbol _ prior to and after the symbol ! in the string,the output is printed with ! sign as it was in the string.

(m) **Use of { & } (ampersand symbol)**

An ampersand displays a string exactly as it appears. For example:

```
PRINT USING "&"; "MAHATMA GANDHI"
```

displays **MAHATMA GANDHI**.

7.6 LPRINT Statement

While the **PRINT** statement caused data to be displayed on the screen, the **LPRINT** statement causes computer to print information on and the printer as per a giver format. While you can always output data to the screen and use the shift +PrtSC keys to obtain a printed copy of the display,many times you will prefer to use the BASIC **LPRINT** statement to automatically generate printed information.While the distinction between using Shift + PrtSC keys and the **LPRINT** statement may not appear very meaningful when you are printing a few lines of data, consider the case in which you have to output a report consisting of hundred lines of data. Obviously, you would prefer not to hit the shift + PrtSC key every time 24 lines of data are displayed.Thus,you will have a tendency to use the **LPRINT** statement to generate reports of substantial data output, whereas you may prefer to use the PRINT statement when you need the results of some computation, and hard copy may not be necessary or can easily be obtained by the shift +PrtSC keys.

Format: `LPRINT (list of expressions)`

In comparison to the **PRINT** statement,the only difference in formats is the prefix of **L** in the keyword, this indicates that the expressions in the list will be printed.This statement functions similar to the **PRINT** statement, including the use of the **SPC** and **TAB** functions within the statement. This is the key difference on the screen, while the **LPRINT** statement causes the output to be listed on the printer.

The **LPRINT** statement assumes a default value of an 80-character width in the printer. This width can be changed if your printer capable of recognizing special control characters to perform condensed printing, has switched for changing print width,or has a platen greater than 80 character in width. We can also change the width of the printer through the use of the **WIDTH** statement. When BASIC is initialized, the value of the width of the printer is set to 80 characters. Some printers, like the IBM 80 cps graphics printer,are capable of printing up to 132 characters per line in a condensed print operating mode. Other printers have extended carriages and can normally print up to 132 characters per line in their normal print mode.

If your printer is capable of changing its settings by receiving special codes, you can change its operation under program control.Table given in the manual contains a list of special print functions and their control codes for the Epson, Citizen or IBM 80 cps graphics printer. Since this printer was manufactured by Epson, the control codes used by that printer are also known as Epson printer control codes.Many other printer including IBM'S Proprinter as well as printers manufactured by other vendors,are designed to respond to these control codes. This means that those printers can usually operate with software designed for the use with an Epson printer. We say usually because there is little difference between the control codes used in different models of Epson printers as well as between Epson printers and IBM printers.As an example,some printers have a Near Letter Quality (NLQ) print feature which, when enabled,results in a higher density of dots used to form each printed character. Unfortunately,some printers without this feature "hang-up" when an NLQ print code is sent to them and they must then be manually turned off and on to reset the printer.Therefore,it is recommended that you consult your printer manual to ascertain the appropriate control codes to perform the printing functions available if you have a non-IBM printer attached to your system.

7.7 The WRITE Statement:

The operational result of the execution of the **WRITE** statement is very similar to the **PRINT** statement. The difference between these two statements is that the **WRITE** statements insert commas automatically between items to be displayed and delimits strings with quotation marks. The format of this statement:

Format `WRITE (list of expressions)`

Like the **PRINT** statement,if the list of expressions is omitted,a blank line will-be generated by the **WRITE** statement.Although you will normally display data without commas between items and quotation marks surrounding strings,on occasions you may wish to use this statement to facilitate displaying examples of how data should be entered into a program. The following example illustrates one possible use of this statement:

```
20 PRINT "RESULT OF EXAM 90"
21 X=93
22 Y$="FIRST GRADE,2nd POSITION"
23 NOTE$ = "PROMOTED"
24 WRITE X, Y$, NOTE$
RUN
RESULT OF EXAM 90
93, "FIRST GRADE,2nd POSITION", "PROMOTED"
Ok
```

Note: Generally used in data files to store the data for future use.

EXERCISE

1. The.......function causes output be printed in a column specified by the programmer.
2. A semicolon between items in a PRINT statement tells the computer to skip to the next available........ to print the next item.
3. What output will the following statement produce?

```
110 PRINT "HOME"; "WORK"
```

4. When a PRINT statement ends with a comma or semicolon,the next value output begins
   (a) on the next line.
   (b) on the next page.
   (c) on the same line, if there is room.
5. What could be the format used for printing a five-digit number with a decimal point two positions to the left and with a dollar sign in front?
6. Write the statement to print your name on the terminal.
7. Write the statement to print the values of the variables A,B,C each multiplied by 3(print the answer in zones).
8. Rewrite the answer to number 7, printing the values without space in between.
9. Write the statement (s) to produce two blank lines.
10. Choose one answer.The **PRINT USING** statement does not
    (a) allow numbers to be rounded easily.
    (b) provide a means of displaying a column of numbers with the decimal points aligned.
    (c) display positive numbers with a leading blank.
    (d) allow large numbers to be displayed with commas every three digits.
11. Fill in the blanks
    (a)

```
10 REM*FINDING AVERAGE AGE*
20 READ A1,A2,A3
30 DATA 20,30,40,
40 LET AVE =.......
50 PRINT ........
```

    (b)

```
10 REM *READING AND PRINTING 3
    NAMES & THEIR MARKS*
20 REM *PRINT STARTING 5TH AND
    30TH COLUMN*
30 N=0
40 N=N + 1
50 READ N$ , M
60 PRINT........,........
70 IF C < 5 THEN ..........
80 DATA ..........
90 END ..........
```

    (c)

```
10 REM*PRINT A RIGHT TRIANGLE*
20 PRINT TAB(15);"*"
30 PRINT TAB(15);"*";TAB
    (18);"*"
40 PRINT.......
50 ............
60 ............
70 END
```

    (d)

```
10 REM*DRAW X DIAGRAM
20 A=0: B=0
30 N=6: M=12
40 A=A+1
50 PRINT TAB(N);"x"; TAB (M)
    ;......
60 M=M-1: N=N-1
70 A<3 THEN .........
80 B=.........
90 PRINT TAB(_);"x"; TAB(M);"x"
95 N=N-1: M=M+1
100 IF B<4 THEN ......
110 END
```

12. Determine whether each of the following statements is *true* or *false*:
    (a) An **INPUT** statement may contain constants in the input list.
    (b) A **READ** statement allows the user to enter data during program execution.
    (c) If a **PRINT** statement ends with a comma,the carriage return is suppressed.
13. Complete the following statements:
    (a) An input .... tells the user what kind of data to input.
    (b) The .... statement allows us to reuse items in the block during a program run.
    (c) To skip a line in program output,use a statement that contains just the keyword ....
14. Find out the errors and write corrected program.

(a)
```
10 LET 20 = A
20 LET B = A
30 LET C = A * ( B + 9)
40 PRINT A, B, "C = " ;C
```
(b)
```
10 REM *PERIMETER OF TRIANGLE*
20 READ A;B;C
30 10, 20, 30
40 LET T=A+B+C
50 PRINT T
60 END
```
(c)
```
10 SUM=A+B+C
20 A=5
30 B=6
40 C=7
50 PRINT SUM
60 END
```

15. What will be the out put of the following programs

(a)
```
10 READ A,B,C,D,E
11 DATA 16,4,10,20,40
12 N=5
13 X=(A+B+C+D+E)/N
14 PRINT A,B,C
15 PRINT D;E;
16 PRINT X
17 STOP
```
(b) Take input value of temp. as 32 to test the program.
```
10 PRINT "INPUT DESIRED
   TEMPERATURE IN DEGREES
   FAHRENHEIT"
20 INPUT F1
30 C1 = ( F1 - 32 ) / 1.8
40 K1 = C1 + 273
50 R1 = F1 + 460
60 PRINT "GIVEN VALUE OF
   F1 = ";F1
70 PRINT "VALUE OF F1 IN
   CELSIUS & KELVIN
   IS = ";C1;K1
80 PRINT "TEMP. IN RANKINE
   = ";R1
90 END
```
(c)
```
10 REM *TEMPERATURE PROGRAM*
15 READ F1
20 DATA 32
25 C1=(F-32)/1.8
30 K1=C1+273
35 R1=F1+460
40 PRINT "GIVEN VALUE OF
   F1 = ";TAB(90);
50 PRINT
55 PRINT "VALUE OF F1 IN
   CELSIUS & KELVIN IS =
   ";C1;K1
60 PRINT "TEMP IN RANKINE =
   ";R1
99 END
```
(d)
```
12 PRINT "HELLO"; TAB(30);
   "SANJAY"; TAB(90);
17 PRINT "HOW ARE YOU";
22 PRINT TAB(40) "OK"
27 PRINT "THANK YOU MY DEAR"
```

16. Comment upon the syntax errors in the following BASIC statements.

(a) `INPUT A;B;C`
(b) `INPUT A,B,C!`
(c) `READ X;Y,Z`
(d) `DATA -6: 14,32;`
(e) `RESTORE DATA`
(f) `PRINT"FLIGHT NUMBER;`
(g) `PRINT"NAME OF ACCOUNT"N$`
(h) `PRINT TAB (32);X;TAB(16);Y`
(i) `PRINT;PRINT;PRINT`
(j) `PRINT X/TAB (18);Y;TAB(36):Z`

17. Dry-run the following program segment with the data provided.
```
10 READ A,B,C
20 DATA 8, 16, 32,"EIGHT", "SIX-
   TEEN", "THIRTY-TWO"
30 READ D$,E$,F$
40 RESTORE
50 READ X,Y,Z
```

18. Give the following program segment a dry-run and comment upon the errors.
```
10 READ A,B
20 DATA "SALARY","TAX"
30 RESTORE
40 READ X$,Y$,Z$
```

19. Comment upon the figure that will be output when the following program segment is run.
```
10 LET R=1
20 PRINT TAB(20);"I"
30 LET R=R+1
40 IF R<4 THEN 20
50 LET C=17
60 PRINT TAB(C);"-" ;
70 LET C=C+1
80 IF C<24 THEN 60
90 PRINT ""
```

```
100 PRINT TAB(20);"I"
110 LET R=R+1
120 IF R<7 THEN 100
140 END
```

20. What is displayed when each of the following code segment is executed?

```
20 LET X = 3
21 PRINT "123456789 123456789"
22 PRINT TAB(3);"**";TAB(2*X);X
23 PRINT "**";TAB(5)
24 PRINT"X"
```

21. Write the soft copy output of following.

```
31 LET Y=4
32 PRINT "123456789 123456789
   123456789"
33 PRINT
34 PRINT "GOOD',"" "BYE"
35 PRINT Y,
36 PRINT 4*Y
```

22. Write a single **PRINT USING** statement to display the given numbers in the indicated format.
    (a) Print 19.5 and -75.61 with three places before the decimal point and two places after it.
    (b) Print 1234567 in the usual dollars and cents notation with a dollar sign immediately preceding the number.

ANSWERS

1. **TAB**
2. position
3. **HOMEWORK**
4. **c**
5. **PRINT USING$$##.##**
6. **112 PRINT "V.K JAIN"**
7. **114 PRINT A*3,B*3,C*3**
8.
```
114 LET A$="$$##+#### ####.##"
116 PRINT USING "L$#######
####.##;" A*3;B83;C*3
```
9.
```
214 PRINT
216 PRINT
```
10. (b)
11. (a)
```
40 LET AVE=(20+30+40)/3
50 PRINT AVE
```
(b)
```
60 PRINT TAB(5);N$;TAB (30);M
70 IF C<5 THEN 40
80 DATA RAMESH, SURESH,
   KAMELESH, DEVESH, NARESH,
   75, 60, 30, 0, 45, 99
```
(c)
```
40 PRINT TAB(15);'*";
   TAB(21);"*"
50 PRINT TAB (15); "*";
   TAB(24); "*"
60 PRINT TAB(15);"*";T
   AB(18) ;"*" TAB(21);
   "*"TAB(28);"*";
   TAB(27);"*"
70 PRINT TAB(N);"x";TAB(M);"x"
```
(d)
```
70 IF A<3 THEN 40
80 B=B+1
90 PRINT TAB(N);"x";
   TAB(m); "x"
100IF B<4 THEN 80
```
12. (a) **-T** (b) **-F** (c) **-T**
13. (a) **PROMPT** (b) **RESTORE** (c) **PRINT**
14. (a)
```
10 LET A = 20
20 LET B=A
30 LET C=A*(B+9)
40 PRINT A,B,"C = ";C
```
The answer will be

```
20 20 C = 580
```

(b) LINE 20 commas to be used in place of semicolons. The command DATA is missing from line 30.

(c)
```
10 A=5
20 B=6
30 C=7
40 SUM=A+B+C
50 PRINT SUM
60 END
```
15. (a)
```
16 4 10
20 40 18
Break in line 170
```
The break message has come due to programmer's using STOP at the end instead of END statement.

(b) **GIVEN VALUE OF F1 = 14**
VALUE OF F1 IN CELSIUS & KELVIN
IS = 0.273
EMP IN RANKINE = 492

(c) **Same as for 15(b)**

(d) **HELLOW SANJAY**
HOW ARE YOU OK
THANK YOU MY DEAR.

16. (a) Variables names should not be separated by semicolons. INPUT A,B,C is legal.

(b) Exclamation mark at the end of statement illegal.

(c) Semicolon is not a legal separators in a READ statement. READ X,Y,Z is legal.

(d) Colon and semicolon are not legal separators in a DATA statement and put. DATA -6,14,32 is legal.

(e) The BASIC statement should be **RESTORE**.

(f) String delimiter is missing.

(g) Semicolon or comma are the separators missing between string literal and variable.

(h) This is not a syntax error but back tabulation is not common to many BASIC dialects.

(i) Multiple PRINT must appear on separate lines.

(j) /and; are illegal separators.

17.
```
RUN
8            16             32
EIGHT        SIXTEEN        THIRTY-TWO
```

18.
```
Line A    B      X$     Y$     Z$
Number
10       Error Data       Type Mismatch
40       SALARY TAX       Out of data
```

19.
```
                                   I
Col.20

                                   I
                                   I
Column 17 - - - - - - - -
                                   I
                                   I
                                   I
```

20.
```
123456789 123456789
  ** 3
   * *  X
```

21.
```
123456789  123456789  123456789

GOOD                BYE
 4                  16
```

22. (a) **PRINT USING "###.##";19.5**

(b) **PRINT USING "$$#######;##"; 1234567**

CHAPTER 8

Control Statements

8.1 Linear Programming

In Units up to 7, we have learnt how to write statements for linear and straightforward programming in a sequential manner. This type of programming does not involve any decision making. We view these programs as simple not so because of their limited length, but because of their structure: they are what we term straight-line programs. That is, they reflect operations that are simply sequential in nature. The general model of these straight-line programs is:

- Read a data value.
- Compute an intermediate result.
- Use the intermediate result to compute the desired answer.
- Print the answer.
- Stop.

Although we might occasionally need to solve a real problem of this kind, more often than not, you may find that such a simple structure is not appropriate for your problem.

8.2 Structured Programming

The remarkable versatility of the digital computer lies not in its ability to carry out a specific sequence of calculations in a short period of time, but in its ability to make logical decisions and repetition of a given set of instructions automatically without any mistake, and most often in carrying out an appropriate set of orders based on the outcome of certain logical decisions.

In most of the cases, programs require that a group of consecutive instructions be executed repeatedly until some logical condition has been satisfied. Generally the required number of repetitions will not be known in advance. This type of repetition is known as conditional looping. A related operation is unconditional looping (or just plain looping), in which the execution of a group of consecutive instructions is repeated for some specified number of times.

Another situation that arises frequently is the need to carry out a logical test and then take some particular action which depends upon the outcome of that test. This is known as conditional execution. And finally, there is a special kind of conditional execution in which a particular group of statement is chosen from several available groups. This is sometimes referred to as selection.

Most of the time decision making process is so complicated that it requires choosing one of the several paths or branches available. The computer then chooses the required branch. Consider following situations:

(a) **IF** the person is under 18 years
THEN, do not allow the person to vote.

(b) **IF** tea is hot;
THEN drink it;
ELSE (otherwise) order cold drink,

There are also times when it is desirable for a program to "loop back" over a set of statements a number of times. We shall also discuss procedures which allow such looping in this chapter.

If branching and looping can be used, then much more complex algorithms can be written which, in turn, result in more complex programs. There are procedures that can be used for writing these complex programs that make them much less error-prone and much easier to debug. The techniques for writing such programs are referred to as structured programming.

8.3 The Control Statement

The control statement is a powerful programming tool that will be used in all program. From this point of view control statement can be divided into following categories:

(a) Transfer operations
  (i) Unconditional Transfer
  (ii) Conditional Transfer
(b) Looping
(c) Sub-routines
(d) Functions.

Control statements enable the programmer to control the order in which program statements are executed. The **GOTO, IF THEN/ELSE,** and **ON/GOTO** statements are control statements introduced in this unit.

8.4 The Unconditional Transfer: The GOTO Statement

All of the programs we have written so far, have been executed in a simple sequential manner, that is, they were executed from the lowest-numbered line to the highest numbered line.To solve many programming problems, however, it is necessary to use control statements to alter the sequence in which statements are executed. One type of control statement is the GOTO statement that breaks this sequence and the program branches to a specified line number. For example:

```
50 GOTO 140
```

would cause a program to branch to line 140.

Some versions of BASIC allow a space between **GO** and **TO**, while others do not.BASIC does not allow this difference. You can type either **GOTO** or **GO TO** but while listing the program, computer will list if of **GOTO** only. In this book we will use **GOTO** without space.

Now program (but do not run it on a computer until you have read the paragraph below on stoping a program):

```
5 LET A = 3
10 LET B = 1
15 PRINT A + B
20 GOTO 15
25 END
```

In this program the **END** statement is never reached. The program will loop continuously between lines 15 20, printing out an endless series of 4s.

To break into the loop and stop the program the user must press a key marked **ESCAPE or BREAK** or something similar on the computer keyboard Ctrl + Break

This program was used simply to illustrate the **GOTO** statement.

The general format of **GOTO** statement is :

Format `GOTO transfer line #`

The transfer line number tells the computer the line number of the next statement to be executed and control transfers to that program line regardless of its location in the program.

When a **GOTO** statement is executed, any of three possible actions may be taken:

1. If the statement indicated by the transfer line number is executable, it is executed, and program

execution continues from that point.

2. If the statement indicated by the transfer line number is non executable (such as a **REM** or **DATA** statement), control passes to the next executable statement after it.
3. If transfer line number does not correspond to any statement in the program,an error message **"illegal function call"** is displayed and execution is terminated.

Because control of the execution path always changes when the **GOTO** statement is encountered, such a statement is known as an unconditional transfer. The following program segment shows how execution paths are controlled with **GOTO** statements. The **GOTO** statement in line 30 causes control to pass to line 50. Therefore, only the value of **B** is printed skipping the line number 40 line .

```
10 X = 20
20 Y = 10
30 GOTO 50
40 PRINT A
50 PRINT B
120 END
```

Although the **GOTO** statement gives the programmer increased control over the logical flow of a program, unconditional transfer can produce an execution path so complex that the logic is virtually impossible to follow, and debugging becomes a nightmare. Later in this chapter and in the next chapter, you will be introduced to control statements that are preferable to the **GOTO** statement. The **GOTO** statement should be used only when it is not feasible to use another control statement.

One Principal use of the **GO TO** is to instruct the computer to repeat a series of statement. In our sample program above, if we had wanted to evaluate **Y** for a number of values of **X**, we could accomplish this with the **GO TO** statement. Then program would become

```
10 READ A,B
20 READ X
30 LET Y = A * X + B
40 PRINT "X = "X, "Y = "Y
50 GO TO 20
60 DATA 3,5
70 DATA 1,2,3,4,5
80 END
```

Line 50 sends the computer back to line 20 to read another value of **X**. The computer then proceeds through lines 30 and 40 . Line 50 returns the computer to line 20. This "loop" continues until the data list has been exhausted.

A RUN command would generate the following output

```
RUN
X = 1 Y = 8
X = 2 Y = 11
X = 3 Y = 14
X = 4 Y = 17
X = 5 Y = 20
Out of data in line 20
```

The message **"OUT OF DATA IN LINE 20"** indicates that the computer tried to read another value of **X** in line **20** but found no more numbers .

After this, program goes to line number 60 where the **GOTO** statement directs the program to **GOTO** line number 120 and then the program ENDS.

Example 8.1: Use of GOTO statement.

The following small program illustrates the use of **GO TO** (which may also be written **GOTO**) to create a continuous loop:

```
20 PRINT "INPUT THE RADIUS"
30 INPUT R
40 PRINT "AREA IS " ; R ^ 2 * 3.142
50 GO TO 20.
```

Let us RUN the program and watch the screen:

```
RUN
INPUT THE RADIUS
? 6
AREA IS  113.112
INPUT THE RADIUS
? 5
AREA IS  78.55
INPUT THE RADIUS
?
```

Like this the program will repeatedly request a value for the radius of a circle, then compute and print out the area of the circle. To stop program execution, the **CONTROL** and **BREAK** keys should be pressed.

Using **IF/THEN** statement, the program to calculate circle areas can be improved. Now the coding will stop only when a zero is entered:

```
20 PRINT "INPUT THE RADIUS"
30 INPUT R
40 IF R < > 0 THEN 60
50 STOP
60 PRINT "AREA IS" ; R ^ 2 * 3. 142
70 GO TO 20
```

By running the program and entering two values of radius as 5 and 0 we can test the program as below:

```
RUN
INPUT THE RADIUS
? 5
AREA IS  78.55
INPUT THE RADIUS
? 0
Break in 50
Ok
```

Note the use of the STOP statement in line 50 . This has the effect of reverting control to the system, having terminated program execution.

Remember that

(1) It is a good programing practice to avoid having a **GOTO** branch to another **GOTO**.

(2) Although **GOTO** may be written as two words (**GOTO**), after a program is LISTed or SAVEd, **GOTO** is changed to **GOTO**.

(3) BASIC ignores any statements or data, appearing on the same line after **GOTO** linenum except for a statement separator (the colon).

Example 8.2: Finding square of given numbers.

A program segment illustrating the use of a **GOTO** statement and its execution with sample data is shown below. Note that as constructed, this program contains an infinite loop by repeatedly branching back to line number 10.

```
5 REM * FIND SQUARE *
10 INPUT "ENTER A NUMBER " ; N
11 SQ = N * N
12 PRINT "THE SQUARE OF" ; N ; " IS" ; SQ
13 GOTO 10
OK
RUN
ENTER A NUMBER?6
THE SQUARE OF 6 IS 36
ENTER A NUMBER?36
THE SQUARE OF 36 IS 1296
ENTER A NUMBER?-1
THE SQUARE OF-1 IS  1
```

To terminate the execution of this program, you could enter the multi key combination Ctrl + BREAK. Later, you will examine a conditional branch that can be used to automatically terminate a program under predefined conditions. Remember that this is not a complete program.If you happen to enter a negative value, it will produce error message.

Example 8.4: Computing the value of SIN X.

Solution:The value of Sine for any given value of **X** can be computed by following formula

$$\sin X = X - \frac{X^3}{3!} + \frac{X^5}{5!} - \frac{X^7}{7!} + \text{---------}$$

where **X** is in radians and ! represents factorial of the number following it.

```
10 PRINT "INPUT ANGLE IN DEGREES"
20 REM * SUMMING SINE SERIES *
30 INPUT X
40 Y = X*3.14159/180
50 S = 0
60 N = 1
70 T = Y
80 S = S + T
90 IF ABS(T/S) < .0000001 THEN 130
100 N = N + 2
110 T=-T*Y^2/(N*(N-1))
120 GOTO 80
130 PRINT "SIN (" ; X ; ") = " ; S
140 GOTO 20
150 END
```

When the above program is run, following will be displayed.

```
RUN
INPUT ANGLE IN DEGREES
? 90
SIN ( 90 ) = 1
? 45
SIN ( 45 ) = .7071063
? 30
SIN ( 30 ) = .4999997
? 0
DIVISION BY ZERO
DIVISION BY ZERO
```

The computer keeps on printing above message unless it is stopped by pressing of the keys CTRL+BREAK.Statement 40 converts the value of angle in radians automatically (remember pie radians=180 degrees),as value of x should be in radians only.Statement 120 repeats the computation,term by term of the series and statement 120 terminates the program for very low values of the terms.

8.5 Introduction to Loops

One of the many powers of computers is their ability to be repetitive; that is, to do the same thing over and over again without becoming bored or tired. Such repetitions are done by making LOOPS round and round repeating the the same process. A simple diagram will illustrate the idea.

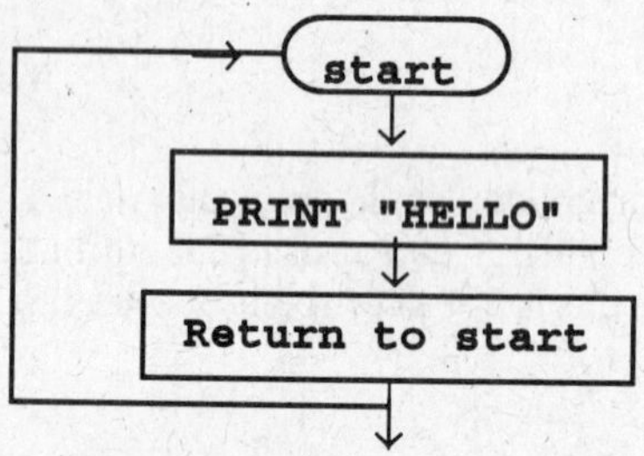

Fig. 8.1 : Flow Chart for Looping

A program to make the computer loop like this will print the word **"HELLO"** over and over again without stopping.

```
10  PRINT "HELLO"
20  GOTO 10
```

Often a situation arises in which a single task must be performed several times. For example, a teacher may need a program to find the average test score of all the students in a given class. The job of processing a single student's data is simple enough.

```
Read name. score
Print name, score
```

Now consider the problem of repeating these steps for a class of thirty students:

```
Read name,score
Add score to total
Print name,score
Read name,score
Add score to total
Print name, score

Read name, score
Add score to total
Print name,score
Divide total by 30
Print class average
```

The same three statements to process a single student's data would have type written thirty times, or they could be written once in a subroutine which the main program would call thirty times. The problem could be simplified greatly by writing the processing statements (or the subroutine call) just once, then executing those statements as many time as needed. This procedure, called looping, is flowcharted in Fig. 8.2.

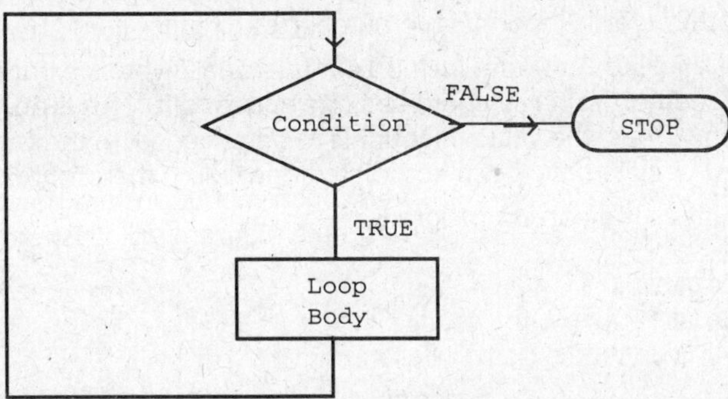

Fig. 8.2 Flow Chart for Known Number of Repetitions

One of the most important uses of control statements is the creation of loops. Control statements can determine which actions are to be repeated and the number of repetitions to be made. Some techniques for loop control include the use of trailer values, counters, and such looping statements as the **FOR/ NEXT** statement.

There are number of ways of making loops,

1. Using **GOTO**
2. Using **FOR/NEXT**
3. Using **WHILE/WEND**
4. Using **REPEAT/UNTIL**

BASIC does not have the facility of **REPEAT/UNTIL**

8.6 Loop Control

8.6.1 Types of Loops

There are two different ways of knowing when a loop has been repeated for enough number of times.

- When you know exactly how many loops you want to make. An example of this would be if you wished this program to print the word Hello exactly 7 times. We will call a loop of this kind a **COUNT -LOOP**.
- When some condition has been fulfilled. This condition might be that a set of numbers should be written by the computer on the screen, one after another until the number 99 is reached. Then the looping should stop. We will call this a **CONDITION- LOOP**.

Let us use the word **GOTO** to produce a program which will repeatedly print **HELLO**. We start with this way of doing it because it is the easiest to understand. First type in **NEW** to remove any program in the memory and then type in this short two-line program.

```
20 PRINT "HELLO"
80 GOTO 20
```

Now type in RUN and press **ENTER**. The computer will display an unending column of the word Hello on the screen. This program does not tell the machine when to stop, and for this reason it is a bad program. The only way it can be stopped is for you to intervene and press the Ctrl - loop & Ctrl + Break.

Let us modify the above two-line program so that it prints the word Hello exactly 10 times. This can be done by setting a COUNT-LOOP for which the following new lines need to be added to the program.

```
10 COUNT = 0
14 COUNT = COUNT + 1
15 PRINT "HELLO"
16 IF COUNT = 10 THEN GOTO 20
20 END
```

Now **RUN** this program and check if it does in fact print Hello 10 times. **LIST** the program now and look at it. The word 'count' is actually a variable used to stand for the number of times the computer circuits the loop. In other words it counts the number of circuits.

In line 10 count is put equal to zero, and in line 14 it is increased by one during each circuit, that is, the number in the unit of memory labelled count has one added to it. This is an unusual use of the equality sign. We could read line 14 as: the value of count is to be put equal to the value of count plus one. Line 16 checks to see if 10 circuits have been completed and, if so, the program ends at line 20.

To print HELLO 10 times the correct program is

```
10 COUNT = 0
14 COUNT = COUNT + 1
15 PRINT "HELLO"
16 IF COUNT < 10 THEN GOTO 14
20 END
```

8.6.2 The CONDITION LOOP

Suppose we wished to input some numbers, square them, and print the result on the screen. In this case we do not know how many of these numbers there are. We will first produce a program to handle the input and calculation process, and we will then consider the need for a stopping routine which will have to take the form of a CONDITION-LOOP. First type in NEW to remove the program in memory, then type in this program and the RUN it.

```
100 INPUT NUM
140 PRINT NUM , NUM * NUM
160 GOTO 100
```

A question mark will appear on the screen in response to line 100. That is, the machine is expecting the input of a number from you. Type in 7 and press ENTER. The computer will make the variable called NUM equal to 7 as a result of line 100. In line 140 , this number i.e. 7 and its square 49, are printed on the screen. Then line 160 sends the program back to line 100 to wait for another input.

Now press the Cntrl + Break key to return to COMMAND MODE so that some new lines can be added to the program. These will allow you to escape from the program at any time. To do this we use a dummy number, and we must choose one that we are unlikely to wish to find the square of. In this case we have used 999 as the dummy number. Type in the lines:

```
120 IF NUM = 999 THEN 180
180 END
```

Line 120 is the CONDITIONAL line which is used to end the program's run whenever we wish. To test this type in RUN and press ENTER. As before a question mark will appear on the screen. This time type in 999 and the program will end.

8.6.3 Using GOTO and IF/THEN in Count-loop

A computer loop can be defined as a repeating sequence of program statements. Using the GOTO and **IF/THEN** statements, you can construct a program loop as illustrated by the following example, which results in a table of squares for the numbers 1 to 5.

Example 8.4: Table of squares

```
5 PRINT "NUMBER", "SQUARE"
10 I = 1
20 IF I > 5 THEN 60
30 PRINT I , I ^ 2
40 I = I + 1
50 GOTO 20
60 END
OK
RUN
```

```
NUMBER             SQUARE
1                  1
2                  4
3                  9
4                  16
5                  25
Ok
```

In this example, a loop control variable was initialized to 1 in line 10. In line 20, the value of the loop control variable was tested against the value you wanted to exit from the loop when reached. In this example, you wished to exit the loop and branch to line 60 when the value of 1 exceeded 5. In line 30, the **PRINT** statement will cause the value of 1 and its square to be displayed.

While this loop shows only the repeated use of a **PRINT** statement, you could construct a loop to repeatedly obtain a set number of input data items or to perform a series of computations a desired number of times. In line 40, your loop control variable is incremented by 1 and line 5 causes the program to unconditionally branch back to line 20 where the program again tests the value of loop control variable against 5. Once you circle through the loop 5 times, you will have the value 6 and the statement in line 20 will cause the program to branch to line 60, terminating the loop.

Where the basic idea is to execute statements between 20 to 40, 5 times which can be done any way from 1 to 5 or 50 to 10 or even by 100 to 500 with the jump of +100.

```
5 PRINT "NUMBER", "SQUARE"
10 I = 50
20 IF I < 10 THEN 60
30 PRINT I, I ^ 2
40 I = I - 10
50 GOTO 20
60 END
Ok
RUN
NUMBER              SQUARE
 50                  2500
 40                  1600
 30                  900
 20                  400
 10                  100
Ok
```

8.6.4 The IF/GOTO Technique

We will begin by examining a program that automates a loop, using the **IF/GOTO** technique. As we examine this program we will point out certain features common to all loops. For example, we will examine the use of a counter variable, incrementation, initialization, and test before exit.

Example 8.5: Computing sum of first ten integers

Following program segment computes the sum of the first ten integers. Examine the program for computing sum of first 10 integers.

```
1  REM * * * SUM OF FIRST 10 INTEGERS * * *
10 SUM = 0
20 I = 1
30 SUM = SUM + I
40 I = I + 1
50 IF I = 11 THEN 70
60 GOTO 30
```

```
70 PRINT "THE SUM OF THE FIRST 10 INTEGERS IS: " SUM
80 END
```

When run, this program types following

```
THE SUM OF THE FIRST 10 INTEGERS IS: 55
```

Two variables are used in this program and type viz. **SUM** and I. The variable **SUM** accumulated the sum of the first 10 integers as we kept on adding them, it is the equivalent of a subtotal on a calculator. I is the integer that is being added to **SUM**.

Recall that a variable must have a value when it is used for the first time. Thus, before we use **SUM** and I in a formula, we must set their values to an initial value (0 and 1, respectively). This is accomplished by statements 10 and 20. These statements are called initialization statements.

The basic function of variable I is to set the starting point of the loop to 1 and with the constant imcrement of 1 every time, take it to the final limit of 10. This variable is mainly contrary to the number of iterations and hence called *Counter* and sum is used.

The next statement is:

```
30 SUM = SUM + I
```

This statement adds the value of the current integer I to the current **SUM**. When this statement is executed for the first time, the value of **SUM** is 0 and the value of I is 1. As a result this statement assigns the value 0 + 1 = 1 to SUM. Following execution of that statement, **SUM** contains the value 1.

The next statement is:

```
40 I = I + 1
```

The current value of I is 1. The result of this statement is to give I the new value, 2. This is the counter technique: I is incremented by one in order to generate the next integer. At the same time, the value of I indicated how many integers have been added so far. In other words, I is used as the current integer and as a *Counter*. Counter is a variable used to check the begining and all the consecutive values of the loop.

One method of controlling a loop is to create a special variable to keep track of the number of times the loop has been executed. Such a variable is called a *Counter*. The counter is increased by a fixed amount (usually 1) each time the loop is executed. When the programmer knows in advance how many times the loop should be repeated, the counter can be tested by an **IF/THEN** statement after each loop execution to see if the proper number has been reached. To set up a counter for loop control, you should perform the following steps:

1. Initialize the counter (before entering the loop) by setting it to a beginning value.
2. Increment the counter each time the loop is executed.
3. Text the counter each time the loop is executed to see if the loop has been performed for the desired number of times.

8.7 Loop Control Variable in COUNT Loop

The loop is an extremely powerful and vital programming tool. Many looping methods exist in various programming languages, but all these methods share some basic components. A loop control variable, for example, is a variable whose value is used to determine the number of times a loop is repeated. The counter variable is an example of a loop control variable. This is mostly designated by either I, J or K or N & M. All loops contain some action that may be performed repeatedly; the statements that perform such an action make up the loop body. Execution of the basic loop structure consists of the following five steps:

1. The loop variable is initialized to a particular value before loop execution begins.
2. The program tests the loop control variable to determine whether it should execute the loop body or exit the loop.

3. The loop body, which can consist of any number of statements, is executed.
4. At some point during loop execution, the value of the loop control variable must be modified to allow exit from the loop.
5. Conduction of loop-control variable.

The control variable is a conduction loop which may or may not be the counter variable of the loop. Any variable whose value is taken as a decisive value to exit out of the loop is called Control Variable ect.

As an example of this concept, consider the following loop:

```
10 READ AGE
20 IF AGE > 18 THEN 99
30 PRINT AGE
40 GOTO 10
60 DATA 17,1,12,15
99 END
```

This loop begins with a READ statement, because the GOTO statement at the end of the loop always branches to line 10. The READ statement initializes and modifies the value of the variable AGE, but does not test it.So when the program is run you will see:

```
RUN
17
1
12
15
Out of DATA in 10
```

The same loop is better designed as follows:

```
10 READ AGE
20 IF AGE > 18 THEN 99
30 PRINT AGE
40 READ AGE
50 GOTO 20
60 DATA 17,1,12,15,20
99 END
```

When run this program will produce following result::

```
RUN
 17
 1
 12
 15
Ok
```

Notice that the program has not printed the last of the data i.e. 20.The extra **READ** statement within the loop makes line 20 the first statement of the loop, a good programming principle. Remember this when setting up a loop.

In this program, no counter is defused as the number of repetitions are not fixed but Age is a control variable.

The basic steps in loop execution are as follows:

1. The loop control variable is initialized to a particular value before loop execution begins.
2. The loop control variable is tested to determine whether the loop body should be executed or the loop should be exited.
3. The loop body, consisting of any number of statements, is executed.

4. At some point during loop execution, the value of the loop control variable must be modified to allow exit from the loop.
5. The loop is exited when the stated condition determines that the right number of loop repetitions has been performed.

8.8 The FOR/NEXT Loop.

FOR/NEXT statement are used together to form a loop that is repeated for a stated number of times.Following program contains a single program that uses a **FOR/NEXT** loop to add ten numbers together. In this program, the value of SUM is initially set to zero. The **FOR/NEXT** loop is then entered.

Example 8.6: Program to add given 10 numbers.

```
10 SUM = 0
20 FOR I = 1 TO 10          ┐
30 READ NUMBER              │  Loop I
40 SUM = SUM + NUMBER       │
50 NEXT I              ←────┘
60 PRINT SUM
70 DATA 4,15,72,80,6,29,34,42,96,9
99 END
RUN
 387
```

As already stated the variable I is referred to as a loop control variable; it is the variable that determines if the loop will be executed. When the FOR statement is executed, the loop control variable is set to an initial value (in this case 1). This value is tested against the terminal value. As long as the value of I is less than or equal to the terminal value, the loop is executed.

The statements in line 30 and 40 constitute the body of this loop, constrain the actions that the loop performs. In each execution of the loop, the next number is read from the DATA statement and added to SUM. Notice that the loop body is indented. Indenting control statements make no difference to the computer, but make the program more readable for humans.

When the **NEXT** statement in line 50 is reached, the value of I is incremented by one and program control is transferred to the top of the loop. If the current value of I is less than or equal to the terminal value, the body of the loop is executed again; if I is greater than the terminal value, program control is transferred to the first statement following the next statement. In this example, after the loop has been executed ten times, control is transferred to line 60 and the sum of the ten numbers is printed.

Since the value of control variable is not being incremented by a seperate statement but rather being incremented automatically in statement, hence this loop is also called self-increment type loop.

In the loop of above program both the initial and terminal values are numeric constants. These value could be numeric expressions or variables instead.

In next example, the initial value is numeric expression and the terminal value is a numeric variable.

```
30 A = 8
40 FOR I = 6 TO A
50 PRINT I
60 NEXT I
```

This loop executes three times, and the output appears as follows:

```
6
7
8
```

It is possible to alter the value by which the loop control variable is incremented. This is done by placing a step value at the end of the FOR statement. The FOR statement in the first program given below has a step value of 2.

If a FOR statement contains no step value, a step value of + 1 is assumed. The following FOR statements are equivalent, because the default step value is +1:

```
FOR I = 10 TO 20 FOR I = 10 TO 20 STEP 1
```

The **FOR/NEXT** loop in above program executes 10 times, and the even numbers from 2 through 20 are printed. It is also possible to have a negative step value, as shown in the first portion of program given above. When a negative step value is used, the loop control variable is decremented each time through thee loop. This program prints the even numbers from 20 through 2, but the initial value has to be greater than final value in the for statement.

(a) **Program using positive step value**: Ascending order

```
10 REM *** PRINT THE EVEN NUMBERS FROM ***
20 REM *** 2 TO 20 IN ASCENDING ORDER ***
30 FOR EVEN = 2 TO 20 STEP 2
40 PRINT EVEN;
50 NEXT EVEN
99 END
RUN
2  4  6  8  10  12  14  16  18  20
```

(b) **Program using negative step value**: Descending order

```
10 REM *** PRINT THE EVEN NUMBERS FROM ***
20 REM *** 20 TO 2 IN DESCENDING ORDER ***
30 FOR EVEN = 20 TO 2 STEP -2
40 PRINT EVEN;
50 NEXT EVEN
99 END
RUN
 20  18  16  14  12  10  8  6  4  2
```

8.9 Rules for Constructing FOR/NEXT Loops

Several rules must be kept in mind when constructing a **FOR/NEXT** loop. These rules are summarized below.

1. The running variable can appear in a statement inside the loop, but its value cannot be altered. i.e the variable should not appear as the left side of assignment operation.
2. If the initial and final values of the running variable are equal and the step size is non zero, then the loop will be executed once.
3. The loop will not be executed at all under the following three special conditions.
   (a) The initial and final values of the running variable are equal and step size is zero.
   (b) The final value of the running variable is less than the original value, and the step size is positive.
   (c) The final value of the running variable is greater than the original value, and the step size is negative.

   (Usually the conditions described in rules 2 and 3 occur only by accident.)
4. Control can be transferred out of a loop but not in, (the transfer out can be accomplished by a **GO TO, IF/THEN** or **ON-GO TO STATEMENT).**

For example, a loop containing either of the following statements would not be executed at all.

```
10 FOR x = 10 TO 5 STEP 2
20 FOR COUNT = 4 TO 6 STEP - 1
```

The initial terminal, and step values cannot be modified in the loop body. It is possible to modify the loop control variable in the loop body, but this should never be done. Note how unpredictable the execution of the following loop would be, because the value of 1 is depended on the integer entered by the user.

```
30 FOR I = 1 TO 10
40 INPUT " ENTER AN INTEGER";X
50 I = X
60 NEXT I
```

If the step value is zero, an infinite loop is created:

```
10 FOR X = 10 TO 20 STEP O
```

This loop could be rewritten so that it would execute ten times, as follows:

```
10 FOR X = 10 TO 20 STEP 1
```

Each **FOR** statement must have a corresponding **NEXT** statement.

8.10 Flowcharting the FOR/NEXT Loop

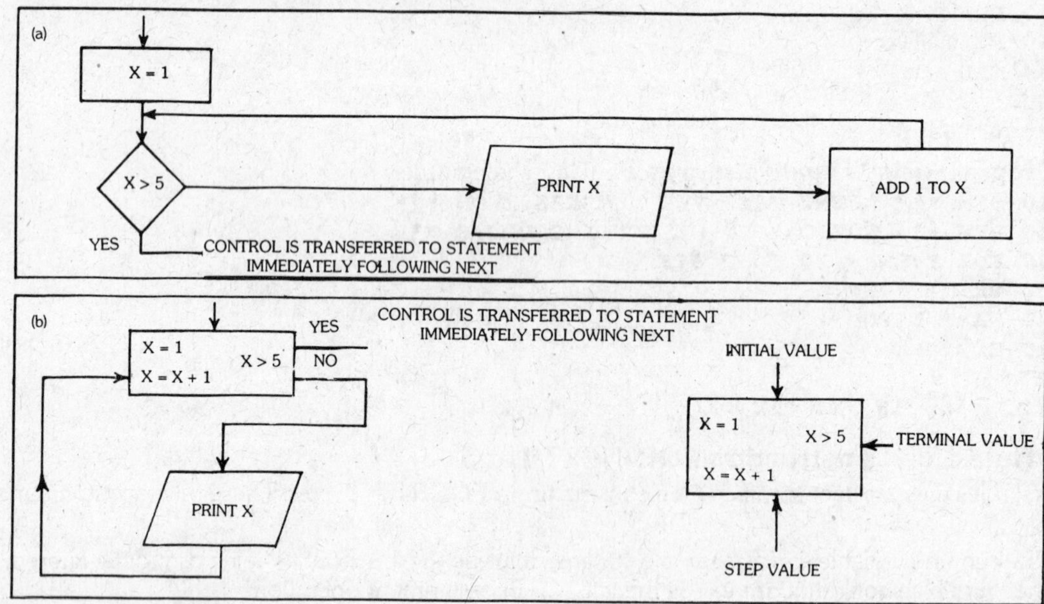

Fig 8.3 (a) & (b) Flowcharting the FOR/NEXT Statements.

Fig.8.3 (a) shows the common flowcharting of a **FOR/NEXT** loop. An alternate method, shown in fig. 8.3 (b) shows a convenient shorthand symbol that we have developed. This symbol provides a concise way to indicate the initial, terminal, and step values. The symbol represents the actions of both the **FOR** and **NEXT** statements. As long as the terminal condition indicated on the right portion of the symbol is false, the execution path containing the loop body is followed. The arrow from the last loop body action to the step value portion of the symbol indicates the action of the **NEXT** statement. When the terminal condition is true, the path containing the actions following the loop, is taken.

8.11 Advantages of Using the FOR/NEXT Loop

The **FOR/NEXT** loop often is used in programs because it performs many tasks automatically. Also, the condition that controls loop repetition is checked automatically each time the FOR statement is executed. Therefore, the programmer does not need perform these tasks.

Note: The **FOR/NEXT** loop is very useful while writing programs that use counting loops, in which the exact number of loop repetitions is known before the loop is executed for the first time.

8.12 Comparison of FOR/NEXT and IF/THEN LOOPS

The **FOR/NEXT** loop should be used whenever possible since it is much easier to interpret. All of the information about which variable is changing, over what limits it is changing, and step size are all clearly displayed in the **FOR** statement. The end of the loop is identified by the **NEXT** statement.

There is one important case where **IF/THEN** loop should be used. In a **FOR/NEXT** loop, you must know (or be able to compute) the limits (the beginning value and final value) and *step size* for the changing variable. In some problems this is not possible, e.g. the decision to exit the loop may be based on some condition being satisfied. For these cases, **IF/THEN** loops are necessary.

For example, if you wish to write a program which flips a coin 100 times then you should use a **FOR/NEXT** loop. On the other hand if the program is to flip the coin until 100 "heads" are produced, you should use an **IF/THEN** loop. The **IF/THEN** loop should be used since you do not know, in advance, how many times the coin must be flipped to get 100 "heads".

8.13 Nested FOR/NEXT Loops in BASIC

It is possible to nest two or more **FOR/NEXT** loops. This means that a **FOR/NEXT** loop can be placed within another **FOR/NEXT** loop, as shown in the following example.

```
FOR I = X TO Y STEP 2
    FOR J = 1 TO 2
    .
    .
    .
    NEXT J
NEXT I
```

Each time the outer loop (loop I) is executed once, the inner loop (loop J) is executed twice because I varies from 1 to 2. When the inner loop has terminated, control passes to the first statement after the **NEXT J**, which in this case is the statement **NEXT I**. This statement causes I to be increased by I and tested against the terminal value of 4. If I still is less than or equal to 4, the body of loop I is executed again. The loop J is again encountered, the value of J is reset to I, and the inner loop is executed until J is greater than 2. Altogether, the other loop is executed I times (4 times in this case) and the inner loop is executed I x J times (4 x 2 = 8 times)

The following rules should be remembered when using nested **FOR/NEXT** loops:

Each loop must have a unique loop control variable. The following example is invalid, because execution of the inner loop modifies the value of the outer loop control variable.

```
FOR I = X TO Y STEP 2
   FOR I = Q TO R
   .
   .
   .
   NEXT I
NEXT I
```

These nested loops should be rewritten so that each uses a unique loop control variable:

```
FOR I = X TO Y STEP 2
   FOR J = Q TO R
   .
   .
   .
   NEXT J
NEXT I
```

The NEXT statements for an inner loop must appear within the body of the outer loop,so that one loop is entirely contained within another.

Invalid

```
FOR I = 1 TO 5
    FOR J = 1 TO
    .
    .
    .
    NEXT I
NEXT J
```

valid

```
FOR I = 1 TO 5
    10   FOR J = 1 TO 10
    .
    .
    .
    NEXT J
NEXT I
```

In the invalid example, the J loop is not entirely inside the I loop, but extends beyond the NEXT I statement.

It is possible to nest many loops within one another as shown in following multiple nested loops.

Example of multiple nested FOR/NEXT loops

```
10 FOR I = 1 TO 3
20      PRINT I
30      FOR J = 1 TO 4
40      PRINT J
50      FOR K = 1 TO 2
60      PRINT K
70      NEXT K
80      NEXT J
90 NEXT I
```

Loop 1 is executed 3 times, loop 2 is executed 3 x 4 = 12 times, and loop 3 is executed 3 x 4 x 2 = 24 times. Each loop is completely contained within its outer loop.

Program given below shows an application of nested **FOR/NEXT** loops. The program prints the multiplication tables for the numbers 1, 2 and with each table in a single column. The inner loop **S** controls the printing of rows. The first time the outer loop is executed, the first row prints the inner loop then prints three statements on that row. The first time the S loop is executed, **R = 1** and **S = I**, so the printed statement is **1x1=1**. The comma at the end of line 80 causes a space to appear before the next output.

Example 8.7: Multiplication table

```
10 REM *** PRINT MULTIPLICATION TABLES OF 1,2,3 ***
20 CLS
30 REM * R = OUTER LOOP INDEX *
40 REM * S = INNER LOOP INDEX *
50 REM
60 FOR R = 1 TO 10
70 FOR S = 1 TO 3
80 PRINT S; " X " ; R ; " = " ; S * R,
90 NEXT S
100 PRINT
110 NEXT R
999 END
```

When the S loop has been completed (when three statements have been printed on the first 2 rows), the **PRINT** statement in line 100 causes the remainder of the line to remain blank; the next output starts at the left margin on the next line. As line 120 increments **R** and passes control back to the top of the **R** loop, this loop begins a second execution during which a second row is printed. The program ends when the **R** loop has been executed ten times rows have been printed.The printout shall be :

```
1 X 1 = 1        2 X 1 = 2        3 X 1 = 3
1 X 2 = 2        2 X 2 = 4        3 X 2 = 6
1 X 3 = 3        2 X 3 = 6        3 X 3 = 9
1 X 4 = 4        2 X 4 = 8        3 X 4 = 12
1 X 5 = 5        2 X 5 = 10       3 X 5 = 15
1 X 6 = 6        2 X 6 = 12       3 X 6 = 18
1 X 7 = 7        2 X 7 = 14       3 X 7 = 21
1 X 8 = 8        2 X 8 = 16       3 X 8 = 24
1 X 9 = 9        2 X 9 = 18       3 X 9 = 27
1 X 10 = 10      2 X 10 = 20      3 X 10 = 30
```

In nested loops, **NEXT** can take more than one format. Each loop can be closed with a separate **NEXT** Loop as in the Sample Program below.

```
10 REM 'NEXT' NESTED LOOP PROGRAM
20 FOR A = 1 TO 4
30 FOR B = 1 TO 3
40 PRINT A;B,
50 NEXT B
60 NEXT A
```

Sample Run

```
1  1        1  2   1  3
2  1        2  2   2  3
3  1        3  2   3  3
4  1        4  2   4  3
```

A single **NEXT** followed by several variables can replace several complete **NEXT** statements. When more than one variable is used in this manner, they are separated by commas. **NEXT X,Y,Z**, for example, matches earlier **FOR** loops stated with variables **X, Y,** and **Z**.

To demonstrate **NEXT** with multiple variables, delete line 60 in sample Program # 2 and changes line 50 to:

```
50 NEXT B, A
```

The variables must be "nested" backwards, i.e., in the opposite order in which the program encounters them. Although program output is the same, using NEXT with multiple variables (NEXT B,A) executes faster than using a separate NEXT for each variable. As with "non-nested" loops, NEXTs without variables can be used .

```
50 NEXT : NEXT
```

When one loop is nested within another, the body of the inner loop should be indented from the body of the outer loop.

Consider the following code:

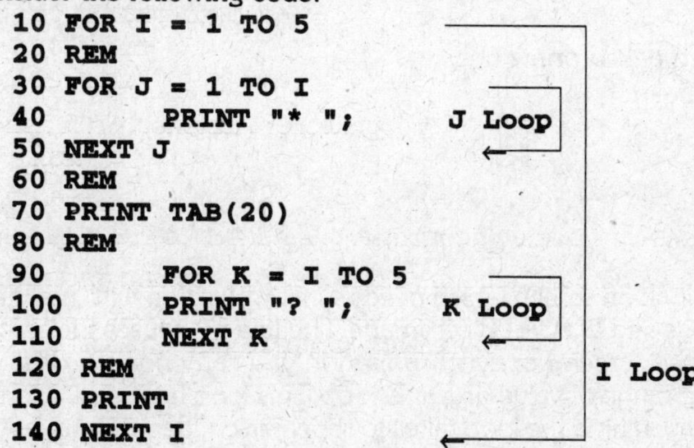


```
10 FOR I = 1 TO 5
20 REM
30 FOR J = 1 TO I
40         PRINT "* ";
50 NEXT J
60 REM
70 PRINT TAB(20)
80 REM
90         FOR K = I TO 5
100        PRINT "? ";
110        NEXT K
120 REM
130 PRINT
140 NEXT I
```

There are two inner loops here: a J loop and a K loop. Let's examine, or walk through, a couple of iterations of the outer loop.

With I = 1, the J loop goes through one iteration (J runs from 1 to 1) and so only prints a single asterisk. We then tab over to column 20 and enter the K loop. It goes through five iterations (K runs from 1 to 5) and prints five question marks. Then statement 130 advances the cursor to the next line and is incremented by 1.

The second time through the outer loop, J runs from 1 to 2, printing two asterisks and K runs from 2 to 5 printing four question marks. In this manner, two triangular patterns are created.

```
*                    ? ? ? ? ?
* *                  ? ? ? ?
* * *                ? ? ?
* * * *              ? ?
* * * * *            ?
```

The above program can be broken into two different program segments.

First Segment

```
10  FOR I = 1 TO 5
20  REM
30  FOR J = 1 TO I
40  PRINT "* ";
50  NEXT J
130 PRINT
140 NEXT I
```

The first portion of the program as given above prints only

```
*
* *
* * *
* * * *
* * * * *
```

Second Segment

```
10 FOR I = 1 TO 5
20 REM
30 FOR K = I TO 5
40 PRINT "? ";
50 NEXT K
60 REM
70 PRINT
80 NEXT I
```

and the second part of the program as given below prints only

```
? ? ? ? ?
? ? ? ?
? ? ?
? ?
?
```

Example 8.8: Making a Digital clock

The following program generates a digital clock on screen which needs synchronisation with real time clock.This is a good example of nested loops and **LOCATE** command.The line 50 causes the screen to be cleared before the clock appears on the screen.For synchronisation you can enhance or slow-down speed of the clock by manipulating the range of value of **Z** in **Z**-loop.This loop has been inserted into program simply for this purpose.How much time the loop takes to repeat itself, depends upon the clock speed of the computer's processor chip.If this clock is working slow you increase the value of loop's operation from 6000 to any value which suits to your computer's speed.So go-on seeing the second's hand of your wrist watch and set the speed of your computer's digital watch by increasing or decreasing the number in statement 44.

```
4 KEY OFF
10 M = 0 :S = 0
20 FOR M = 0 TO 59
30 FOR S = 0 TO 59
31 LOCATE 13,58:PRINT "- - - - - - - - - - - - -"
32 LOCATE 15,58:PRINT "- - - - - - - - - - - - -"
33 LOCATE 12,59:PRINT "M":LOCATE 12,66:PRINT "S"
35 LOCATE 14,60
40 PRINT M; ":" ; S
44 FOR Z = 1 TO 6000
45 NEXT Z
50 CLS
60 NEXT S
70 NEXT M
99 END
```

When the above program is run, following will be displayed on a new page of screen.Also notice that due to KEY OFF command the last line of the screen containing the key menu has disappeared from screen.The locate command locates the cursor at the desired point.In many versions of basic, TAB function also provides the facility of locating the cursor at a particular place.

```
         M         S
- - - - - - - - - - - - -
           0  :  8
- - - - - - - - - - - - -
```

Example 8.9: Generating Armstrong numbers

The following program is designed to find out the Armstrong numbers i.e. a three digit numbers such that the cubes of its digit are equal to the number itself.The program takes the advantage of place value of the digit of a number.

```
10 REM *THREE DIGIT ARMSTRONG NUMBERS *
20 PRINT "THREE DIGIT ARMSTRONG NUMBERS ARE;"
30 FOR N=100 TO 999
40 X =INT (N/100)
50 Y =INT (N/10) -10 * X
60 Z =N -100 * X -10 * Y
70 IF N < > X^3 + Y^3 + Z^3 THEN 90
80 PRINT N;
90 NEXT N
99 END
```

When run it generates following

```
RUN
 153        370        371        407
```

Example 8.10: Generating Armstrong numbers by another method

Armstrong number can be found by another method as illustrated by following program example.See one more such program in example 10.

```
10 REM * ARMSTRONG NUMBER *
20  FOR I = 1 TO 9
30  S1 = I * I * I
40  FOR J = 0 TO 9
```

```
50   S2 = J * J * J
60   FOR K = 0 TO 9
70   S3 = K * K * K
80   M = K + J * 10 + I * 100
90   ARM = S1 + S2 + S3
100 IF ARM <> M THEN 120
110 PRINT TAB(5); M
120 NEXT K
130 NEXT J
140 NEXT I
150 END
```

Notice in above program that statement has been staggered (indented) in respect of FOR/NEXT loops so that the programmer clearly visualizes as to which loop is inside another loop and mistake of loop crossing does not occur.When the above program is run, following will be displayed.

```
RUN
153
370
371
407
```

Example 8.11: Prime number generator

This program Utilizes the FOR/NEXT and IF/THEN statements for finding out the prime numbers out of first 200 natural numbers.

```
10 REM * PRIME NO. GENERATOR *
20 FOR X=3 TO 200
30 FOR I=2 TO X-1
40 IF X/I = INT(X/I) THEN 70
50 NEXT I
60 PRINT X;
70 NEXT X
80 END
```

When the above program is run, following will be displayed.

```
RUN
  3   5   7   11  13  17  19  23  29  31  37  41  43  47  53  59  61  67  71  73
  79  83  89  97  101 103 107 109 113 127 131 137 139  149 151 157
  163 167 173 179 181 191 193 197 199
```

Example 8.12: Generation of Fibonacci numbers and listing for prime numbers

Fibonacci series consists of a sequence of numbers in which each number is equal to the sum of previous 2 numbers.In other words

$$F_i = F_{i-1} + F_{i-2}$$

where F_i is the ith Fibonacci number the first two numbers are defined to be 1 and 1 and then you can find out remaining by above equations.Since all the numbers of this series are positive and odd integers, some of them are bound to be prime numbers.

A prime number is that positive integer that is divisible, without a remainder,only by one or by itself.For example ,7 is a prime number because it is divisible fully by either 7 or 1 but 9 is not a prime number since it is divisible by 3.It is easy to calculate Fibonacci number, but the calculation of prime numbers requires some explanation.

Suppose we want to determine if a given integer whose value is greater than 2 can be divided evenly by a small integer.Let us call the given integer **F** and the divisor **J**.The procedure is to calculate quotient,**Q**,as

```
Q=F/J
```

We then calculate a truncated quotient,Q1,as

```
Q1=INT(Q)
```

The letters **INT** refer to a BASIC library function that will determine the largest integer that does not exceed **Q**.(We will learn more about BASIC library functions in unit 1.1).Thus if **Q** has a value of 3.7,then **Q1** will have a value of 3.

If **Q** and **Q1** have the same value,then **F** is evenly divisible by **J**.Furthermore,if **F** is evenly divisible by any value of **J**,from **J=2** to **J=INT(/F)**,then **F** cannot be prime.Hence **F** will be prime number only if **Q** and **Q1** are not equal for **J=2,3,...,INT (/F)**.

Algorithm

Let us refer to F as a given Fibonacci number (i.e.,Fi),F1 as the previous Fibonacci number (Fi-2).We can now write an outline of our program as follows:

1. Read **N**.
2. Set **F1** and **F2** equal to **1**.
3. Print **F1** and **F2**,identifying each as a prime.
4. Do the following calculations for **I=3,4,.......N**.
   (a) Calculate a value for F using the formula **F=F1+F2**
   (b) Do the following for **J=2, 3,..., R**, where **R** is the largest integer that does not **/F**. (test for a prime number.)
      (1) Calculate values for **Q** and **Q1**,and test to see if they are equal.
      (2) If **Q** and **Q1** are equal for any values of **J**,then **F** must be prime number.Hence print **I** and **F**,and proceed directly to step 4(c) below.
      (3) If **Q** and **Q1** are unequal for all values of **J**,then **F** must be a prime number.Hence print I and **F**,identifying **F** as a prime,and proceed to step 4(c) below.
   (c) Update **F1** and **F2** (i.e.,assign the current value of **F1** to **F2**,then assign the current value of **F** to **F1**),in preparation for calculating a new Fibonacci number(i.e.,a new value for **F**).
5. Stop.

A complete BASIC program corresponding to the above outline is shown below.Notice that the program contains a nest of loops.The purpose of the inner loop (statement 120-160) is to determine whether or not each Fibonacci number is a prime,whereas the outer loop (statement 100-210) causes the desired sequence of Fibonacci numbers to be generated.Notice the use of the library function **SQR** (in line 120) which is used to obtain the square root of F.Also,note the conditional transfer of control out of the inner loop when **Q = Q1** (statement 150).

```
10 REM GENERATION OF FIBONACCI NUMBERS AND SEARCH FOR PRIMES
20 PRINT "N = ";
30 INPUT N
40 PRINT
50 PRINT "GENERATION OF FIBONACCI NUMBERS AND FINDING PRIMES OUT OF THEM"
60 PRINT
70 F1 = 1 : F2 = 1
90 PRINT "I = "; 1, "F = " ; 1 ; " (PRIME)"
100 PRINT "I = "; 2, "F = " ; 1 ; " (PRIME)"
110 FOR I = 3 TO N
```

```
120 F = F1 + F2
130 FOR J = 2 TO INT(SQR (F))
140 Q = F / J
150 Q1 = INT(Q)
160 IF Q = Q1 THEN 200
170 NEXT J
180 PRINT "I = " ; I, "F = "; F ; " (PRIME)"
190 GOTO 210
200 PRINT "I = " ; I, "F = "; F
210 F2 = F1 :F1 = F
230 NEXT I
240 END
```

When the above program is run following will be displayed.

```
RUN
N = ? 15
GENERATION OF FIBONACCI NUMBERS AND FINDING PRIMES OUT OF THEM
I = 1        F = 1        (PRIME)
I = 2        F = 1        (PRIME)
I = 3        F = 2        (PRIME)
I = 4        F = 3        (PRIME)
I = 5        F = 5        (PRIME)
I = 6        F = 8
I = 7        F = 13       (PRIME)
I = 8        F = 21
I = 9        F = 34
I = 10       F = 55
I = 11       F = 89       (PRIME)
I = 12       F = 144
I = 13       F = 233      (PRIME)
I = 14       F = 377
I = 15       F = 610
```

8.14 The STOP Statement

When the **STOP** statement is executed, it causes the program to end. Sometimes a STOP statement is placed immediately before the subroutines of program so that the subroutines are not executed after the last line of the main program is reached. The general format of the **STOP** statement is as follows:

```
line # STOP
```

When a **STOP** statement is encountered, the program will terminate execution and return to command level. Prior to generating the command level prompt **"Ok"** this statement will display the message:

```
Break in nnnn
```

Here, nnnn is the line number where the **STOP** statement was executed. Unlike the **END** statement, this statement will not close any open files. The use of this statement is illustrated by the following program segment:

```
100 INPUT "ENTER LENGTH AND WIDTH ";L,W
110 A = L * W
120 IF A > 0 THEN 140
130 STOP
140 PRINT "AREA = " ; A
150 END
RUN
ENTER LENGTH AND WIDTH ? - 2 , 4
BREAK IN 130
Ok
```

Here the **STOP** statement is used to halt program execution when an apparent illogical computation had occurred.**STOP** is the software equivalent of the **BREAK** key. Program execution may usually be continued by the CONTinue command.

8.15 The WHILE/WEND Loop

Another type of loop available in BASIC is the **WHILE/WEND**. Unlike the **FOR/NEXT**, which executed for a specified number of times, the **WHILE/WEND** continues to execute as long as a stated condition is true. **WHILE** starts a loop which is executed repeatedly till a condition is true. The loop is closed by with a **WEND** statement. The format of the **WHILE/WEND** loop is as follows:

Format **WHILE** *expression*
Other Statements
WEND

It is a numeric or logical expression or a variable that **WHILE** evaluates. If *expression* is true (a non-zero value), program executes loops between the **WHILE** and **WEND** statments. When *expression* becomes false (or zero), **WHILE** fails the test, and program execution passes through the **WEND** statement.

In contrast to the **FOR/NEXT** loop, the **WHILE/WEND** involves no automatic initialization or incrementing of the loop control variable. A statement before the **WHILE** statement must initialize the loop control variable, and another statement within the loop body must change the value of the loop control variable so that the expression of the **WHILE** statement can become false and loop could be ended. Otherwise an infinite loop results, as shown here:

```
200 WHILE COUNT < 50
210 PRINT COUNT
220 WEND
```

This loop could be written correctly as follows:

```
190 COUNT = 50
200 WHILE COUNT < 50
210 PRINT COUNT
220 COUNT = COUNT + 1
230 WEND
```

The loop is more or less same as loop created by **IF/THEN** with an exception of go to statement in between.

The loop executes according to the following steps:

1. The expression, which can be a numeric expression or a numeric variable,is evaluated as true or false. If the expression is a variable, it is true if it is not equal to zero.
2. If the expression is true, the statements in the loop body are executed until the **WEND** statement is encountered. If the expression is false, control passes to the first statement after the **WEND**.
3. When the **WEND** is encountered, control passes back to the **WHILE** statement and the expression is evaluated again.
4. If the condition is still true, the loop body is executed again; if false, the loop is exited to the statement following the **WEND**.

Examples

```
WHILE X <> 0
```

(program statements..)

```
WEND
```

executes the program statements between **WHILE** and **WEND** until the value of X becomes zero

```
WHILE A = B
```

(program statements....)

```
WEND
```

executes the program statements between **WHILE** and **WEND** until the value of A is no longer equal to the value of B.

```
WHILE A$ <> "FINISHED"
INPUT A$
WEND
```

Continues to ask for string input until the work FINISHED is entered. When A$ = FINISHED, WHILE fails the <> condition test, and program execution drops through the **WEND** statement.

Program

```
10 REM 'WHILE ' PROGRAM
20 WHILE L$ <> "LAST"
30 READ X,Y,L$
40 PRINT X; Y; L$
50 WEND
55 PRINT "EXECUTION FINISHED"
60 DATA 1, 10, FIRST
70 DATA 2, 20, NEXT
80 DATA 3, 30, LAST
RUN
 1 10 FIRST
 2 20 NEXT
 3 30 LAST
 EXECUTION FINISHED
```

Like **FOR/NEXT** statement loops, **WHILE/WEND** loops may be nested. **WEND** always continues the most recent **WHILE** loop until the **WHILE** statement's condition becomes false.

Sample Program

```
10 REM 'WEND' PROGRAM
20 X = 10
30 WHILE X > 0
40 PRINT X ;
50 X = X-2
60 WEND
RUN
10  8  6  4  2
```

As long as **X** is a positive number, the program loops between the **WHILE** and **WEND** statements. When **X** becomes zero, indicating "false" to the computer, the **WHILE** test fails, and program execution passes through the **WEND** statement.

EXERCISE

PART I

(A) OBJECTIVE TYPE QUESTIONS

A. Multiple Choice Questions: Choose the best possible answer.

1. The FOR statement serves to ....
   (a) initialize and test the loop control variable.
   (b) increment the loop control variable by the step value.
   (c) pass control to the **NEXT** statement.

B1. Fill in the blanks

(a) A statement that always alters the execution path when it is encountered is a (n)

.... transfers statement.

(b) A control statement that makes a decision based on the value of an expression is called a (n).......... transfer statement.

(c) Must the condition of the **IF/THEN** statement be evaluated only as true or false?

(d) The .... clause indicated that both conditions must be true for the **THEN/GOTO** clause to be executed.

(e) When the terminal value is exceeded in a **FOR/NEXT** loop (using a positive step value), control passes to first statement following the ......statement.

(f) When no step value is specified in a **FOR** statement, it is assumed to be........

(g) A loop is completely enclosed by another loop is called (n) - .... loop.

C1. Determine whether each of the following statements is true or false.

(a) Do UNTIL loops never used in basic programming.

(b) Control structures should have one entry and one exit point.

(c) Unrestricted use of GOTO statements can lead to programs that are difficult to read.

(d) Two or more nested loops can have the same loop control variable name. True or false?

EXERCISE

1. When the following program is run, what will be the first five lines printed out?

```
10 LET A = 9
20 LET B = 3
30 PRINT A + B
40 PRINT A - B
50 PRINT A * B
70 END
```

2. The income tax rate on the first Rs. 18000 of Income is zero. All income above Rs 18000 is taxed at 20%. Write **A** sequence of five statements that first calculates taxable income **(P1)**, then calculates income tax **(T)**, and then prints out pay and tax on the small line of the screen.

Assume the sequence forms part of a program, starting at line 50. (Multiply by 0.2 to find 20 %).

3. When the following program is run, What will be the first three lines printed out? (Assume the computer can print up to five results per line.)

```
10 PRINT 1, 2, 3, 4, 5,
20 GOTO 10
30 END
```

4. What will be the result of following program?

```
20 PRINT 11, 22
30 PRINT 33, 44
40 PRINT 55, 66
50 GOTO 20
60 END
```

5. What will be the first five lines printed, when the following program is run:

```
10 LET A = 9
20 LET B = 3
30 PRINT A +B
40 PRINT A - B
50 PRINT A *B
60 GOTO 40
70 END
```

6. Identify the errors, if any, in the program segments shown below. Make the necessary corrections.

(a)
```
10 NEXT I 20 ..........
30 FOR I = 1 TO 10
```

(b)
```
10 FOR J = 1 TO 3   TO 50
20 READ K
30 DATA 10, 20, 30
40 ..............
50 NEXT K
```

(c)
```
10 LET 1 = 0
20 FOR J = 1 TO 3
30 LET K = 1 + J
40 ..............
50 NEXT J
```

(d)
```
10 FOR L = 1 TO 5
20 -
30 NEXT L
40 GO TO 20
```

(e)
```
10 FOR M > 10
20 ..........
30 NEXT M
```

(f)
```
10 FOR N = STEP 1
20 ..............
30 NEXT M
```

7. Identify the errors, if any, in the FOR statements shown below. Assume that the loop is to be executed more than once. Make the necessary corrections.

(a) `10 FOR 1 = 3 TO 6 STEP - 1`

(b)
```
10 LET A = 5
20 FOR J = A TO B STEP 2
```

(c) `10 FOR K = 5 TO 25`

(d) `10 FOR L = 10 TO STEP 3`

(e)
```
10 LET A = 4
20 LET B = 16
30 FOR M = A TO M STEP 2
```

(f)
```
10 LET A = - 6
20 LET B = -12
30 FOR N = A TO B
```

(g) `10 FOR P = + 1 TO 10 STEP + 1`

(h) `10 FOR Q = Q TO 10 STEP 5`

(i)
```
10 LET A = -1
20 LET B = -20
30 FOR R = A TO B - 1 STEP - 1
```

(j)
```
10 LET A = 36
20 FOR S = A / 3 TO A/6
```

8. Identify the errors, if any, in the program segments shown below. Make the necessary corrections.

(a)
```
10 FOR 1 = 5 TO 14 STEP 3
20 FOR J = 1 TO K STEP 1
...
60 NEXT J
70 NEXT 1
```

(b)
```
10 FOR I = 3 TO 7 STEP 2
20 FOR J = 1 TO 4
...
60 NEXT I
70 NEXT J
```

(c)
```
10 FOR I = 3 TO 12 STEP 3
20 FOR J = 5 TO 20 STEP 5
...
50 NEXT J
60 FOR K = 1 TO 6
...
90 NEXT K
100 NEXT I
```

(d)
```
10 FOR I = 1 TO 4
20 FOR J = 1 TO 5
30 ...
40 NEXT J
50 GO TO 30
60 NEXT I
```

(e)
```
10 FOR I = 1 TO 10
20 FOR J = 1 TO 14
...
60 LET K = J + 1
70 IF K > 20 THEN 140
80 NEXT J
90 ...
...
130 NEXT I
140 ...
```

(f)
```
10 FOR I = + 02 TO + 08 STEP +02
20 FOR J = + 01 TO + 04 STEP +
01
...
60 IF J < = + 04 THEN 20
70 NEXT I
```

9. What values will the index take on in each of the following FOR statements. Do not include the value that terminates the loop.

(a)
```
10 FOR A = 3 TO 13 STEP 2
...
60 NEXT A
```

(b)
```
10 FOR B = 15 TO 29 STEP 3
...
60 NEXT B
```

(c)
```
10 FOR C = 32 TO 16 STEP -4
...
60 NEXT C
```

(d)
```
10 FOR D = 10 TO - 20 STEP -5
...
60 NEXT D
```

(e)
```
10 FOR E = - 21 TO 9 STEP 6
...
60 NEXT E
```

(f)
```
10 FOR F = + 2 TO +9 STEP +2
...
60 NEXT F
```

10. Fill in the blanks in the following programs.

(a)
```
10 PRINT
20 FOR I = .. TO .. STEP ..
30 PRINT I;
40 NEXT I
99 END
RUN
12  17  22  27
```

(b)
```
10 PRINT
20 FOR J = .. To .. STEP ..
30 PRINT K ;
40 NEXT J
99 END
RUN
6  3  0  -3
```

(c)
```
10 PRINT
20 FOR K = .. TO .. STEP ..
30 PRINT K ;
40 NEXT K
99 END
RUN
3  7  11  15
```

11. How many times is the inner loop executed in the following program segment ?

```
10 FOR I = 1 TO 3
20 FOR J = 1 TO 13 STEP 3
 - -
60 NEXT J
70 NEXT 1
```

12. What is the output of each of the following programs?

(a)
```
10 FOR 1 = 1 TO 3
20 PRINT
30 PRINT * 1 = * ; 1
40 FOR J = 2 TO 6 STEP 2
50 PRINT * J = * ; J,
60 NEXT J
70 PRINT
80 NEXT 1
99 END
```

(b)
```
10 PRINT
20 LET N = 12
30 FOR I = N TO 1 STEP - 1
40 FOR J=1 TO 1 STEP 1
50 PRINT * ** ;
60 NEXT I
70 PRINT
80 NEXT I
99 END
```

13. How many times is each of the following loops executed?

```
FOR I = 50 TO 10 STEP -5
FOR J = 1 TO 6 STEP 2
FOR K = 5 TO 5
NEXT K
NEXT J
NEXT I
```

14. Find out the mistakes in following programs.

(a)
```
10 REM *** READ AND PRINT TEN
NAMES.          ***
20 FOR 1 = 1 TO 5
30 READ NAME
40 NEXT
50 PRINT NAME
60  DATA, RITA, NITA, GITA,
SITA, MITA,
```

(b)
```
10 FOR X = 1 TO 5
20 FOR Y = 1 TO 10
30 FOR Z = 1 TO 20
40 PRINT X, Y, Z
50 PRINT "*", "*", "*"
60 SUM = X + Y + Z
70 PRINT SUM
80 NEXT Y
90 PRINT "Z = "Z
100 NEXT Z
110 PRINT "X = ";X
120 NEXT X
```

15. Write each of the following program segments as a control structure with only one entry and one exit point:

(a)
```
200 READ X, Y
210 REM
220 FOR I = 1 TO X
230 IF I > Y THEN 260
240 PRINT X, Y
250 NEXT I
260 REM
```

(b)
```
300 READ X, Y
310 REM
320 IF X > Y THEN 350
330 IF X * Y = 0 THEN 380
340 PRINT X
350 PRINT Y
360 READ X, Y
370 GOTO 320
380 REM
```

16. Rewrite the following code so that it performs the same function as it does now, but with a minimum of GOTOs

```
400 READ X, Y
410 IF X > Y THEN 440
420 PRINT "Y IS LARGER"
430 GOTO 460
440 PRINT "X IS LARGER"
450 GOTO 460
460 PRINT "GOODBYE"
```

17. What will be the output produced by each of the following segments of code?

(a)
```
200 LET N = 3
210 FOR I = N TO N + 2
220 PRINT I / 10
230 NEXT I
240 PRINT I
```

(b)
```
200 FOR K = 10 TO 7 STEP - 2
210 PRINT K
220 NEXT K
230 PRINT K
```

(c)
```
200 LET X = 6
210 FOR I = X TO 4
220 PRINT X
230 NEXT I
240 PRINT " BYE"
```
(d)
```
200 FOR J = 1 TO 5 STEP 2
210 PRINT TAB(J); " *** "
220 PRINT "!" ;
230 NEXT J
```

18. Write a program segment containing the **FOR** statement **FOR I = 1 TO 3** that will produce the output:
```
20
30
40
```

19. Rewrite the following code using **FOR** and **NEXT** statements to construct the counter controlled loop.
```
30 LET N = 1
31 REM
32 IF N > 10 THEN 37
33 INPUT XS
34 PRINT XS
35 LET N = N + 1
36 GOTO 32
37 REM
```

20. What shall be the output of following program segments?

(a)
```
200 FOR I = 2 TO 4
210 FOR J = 5 TO 6
220 PRINT I; J;
230 NEXT J
240 NEXT I
```
(b)
```
200 FOR I = 1 TO 5 STEP 2
210 PRINT 1;
220 FOR J = I TO I + 1
230 PRINT I * J
240 NEXT J
250 NEXT I
```
(c)
```
200 FOR A = 4 TO 2 STEP -1
210 PRINT " GOOD ";
220 FOR B = 4 TO 2
230 PRINT B;
240 NEXT B
250 PRINT "BYE"
260 NEXT A
```
(d)
```
210 FOR N = 1 TO 5
220 LET S = 0
230 LET C = 0
240 LET S = S + C
250 LET C = C + 1
260 IF C < N THEN 240
270 PRINT N ; S
280 NEXT N
```

21. Correct the errors in each segment of code.

(a)
```
5 FOR K = 1 TO 5
10 FOR J = 1 TO K
20 PRINT K + J
30 NEXT K
40 NEXT J
```
(b)
```
10 LET S = 0
20 FOR X = 1 TO 10
30 LET S = S + X
40 PRINT S
```

22. What is the output of following program segment?
```
20 FOR 1 = 7 TO 10 STEP 2
21 PRINT I ;
22 NEXT I
23 PRINT I
```

23. The following program is supposed to print out a square of 16 squares (4 x 4),but it does not work. Find out the mistake(s).
```
40 FOR I = 1 TO 4
50 FOR J = 1 TO 4
60 PRINT "*"
70 NEXT I
80 PRINT
90 NEXT J
```

24. Correct the mistakes in following program segments

(a)
```
10 FOR P = 1 TO 10 STEP 1
20 - - -
30 NEXT P
```
(b)
```
10 FOR Q = 4 TO 26 STEP 2
20 - - -
30 NEXT P
```
(c)
```
10 FOR R = 3 TO 21 STOP 4
20 - - -
30 NEXT R
```
(d)
```
10 FOR S = 10 TO 2 STEP 2
20 - - -
30 NEXT S
```
(e)
```
10 FOR I = -9 TO 9 STEP 3
20 - - -
30 NEXT T
```
(f)
```
10 FOR U = + 5 TO STEP +5
20 - - -
30 NEXT U
```

EXERCISE

PART - II

1. When should a loop structure be used in a program?
2. What are the five elements of a controlled loop?
3. What is a control statement?
4. Why is the **GOTO** statement an unconditional transfer statement?
5. Why is the **IF** statement a conditional transfer statement?
6. What tasks are performed automatically by the **FOR/NEXT** loop?
7. Which of the following are valid **FOR** statements?
   (a) `20 FOR I =8 TO 12 STEP 3`
   (b) `100 FOR K = 20 TO 25 STEP -4`
   (c) `80 for N$ = 3 TO 5 STEP .5`
   (d) `400 FOR X = -2 TO -1`
   (e) `FOR I = 1 TO 100 STEP 20`
8. When the step value in the **FOR/NEXT** loop is negative, does a loop stop executing when the loop control variable is grater than or less than the terminal value?
9. What happens when the step value of a **FOR** statement is zero?
10. What is counting loop?
11. What happens if no step value is specified in a **FOR** statement?
12. What are the three fundamental control structures?
13. State three basic principles of structured coding?

ANSWERS

1.
```
12
6
27
6
27
```

3. It prints out following repetitively:
```
1        2        3        4        5
```

4. It prints following pattern endlessly
```
11       22
33       44
55       66
11       22
```

5. First five lines are
```
12
12
6
27
6
```

6. (a) Exchange line No. 30 with 10.
   (b) No mistake.
   (c) Line 10 should read **K=0**
   (d) Line 10 should be **40 GOTO 10**
   (e) Greater than symbol is used instead of=
   (f) To clause is missing from statement 10.

7. (a) After **FOR** some variable should be there and not **1**,correct **1** as **I**.
   (b) B is not defined prior to use in **FOR** statement.
   (c) Alright.
   (d) Second value is missing after **TO**.
   (e) Line 30 should read
   `30 FOR M = A TO B STEP 2`
   (f) Line 30 should be either
   `30 FOR N = B TO A or`
   `30 FOR N = A TO B step -1`
   (g) No mistake,however no + sign is necessary.
   (h) After = sign,same variable cannot be used,also if any other variable is used it must be defined prior to use.
   (i) In line number 30 there is no gap between TO and variable.
   (j) No mistake.

8. (a) Line 10 and 70 1 written instead I.
   (b) Exchange lines 60 and 70.
   (c) No mistake.
   (d) Line 50 should be **50 GO TO 20** or not

at all there.

(e) Line 70 is either unnecessary or clear as **K** will be never more than 20.

(f) Case of loop crossing and missing **NEXT** for **J** loop.

9. (a) 6 (b) 5 (c) 5 (d) 7 (e) 6 (f) 4

10. (a) 12,27,5 (b) 6,-3,-3 (c) 3,15,4

11. 5 Times

12. (a) Following is printed:

```
I = 1
J = 2      J = 4      J = 6
I = 2
J = 2      J = 4      J = 6
I = 3
J = 2      J = 4      J = 6
```

(b) Following pattern is generated:

13. **I** loop 9 times, **J** loop 3 times, and **K** loop only one time.

14. (a) Following mistakes are there:

(1) In first line **M** is missing from the word **NAME**.

(2) Since **NAME** is a reserved word in BASIC it can not be used as a variable name. Also for names to be read in by **READ/DATA** statement this variable has to be string type. There you should use any variable for this as such **NAM$**, **NME$**, or **N$**.

(3) **NEXT** statement in line 40 should appear after **PRINT** statement.

(4) No comma to be put up after **DATA** statement.

(5) In line 20 probably the letter (in fact the variable) I has been typed as 1. The correct program will be something like this

```
10 REM *** READ AND PRINT
TEN NAMES. ***
20 FOR I = 1 TO 5
30 READ NAM$
40 PRINT NAM$
50 NEXT
60 DATA RITA, NITA, GITA,
SITA, MITA,
```

(b)
```
10 FOR X = 1 TO 5
20 FOR Y = 1 TO 10
30 FOR Z = 1 TO 20
40 PRINT X, Y, Z
50 PRINT "*", "*", "*"
60 SUM = X + Y + Z
70 PRINT SUM
80 NEXT Y
90 PRINT "Y = ";Y
100 NEXT Z
110 PRINT "X = ";X
120 NEXT X
```

(1) In line 90 probably the variable Z had been typed instead of Y. Also semicolon is missing before the variable.

(2) Line number 100 has been typed as line 10.

15. (a)
```
200 READ X, Y
210 LET I = 1
220 REM
230 WHILE I <= X AND I <= Y
240 PRINT X, Y
250 LET I - I + 1
260 WEND
270 REM
```

(b)
```
300 READ X, Y
310 REM
320 IF X <= Y AND X * Y = 0 THEN
370
330 IF X <= Y THEN PRINT X
340 PRINT Y
350 READ X, Y
360 GOTO 320
370 REM
```

16. Replace the line number 410 to 450 by **410 IF X > Y THEN PRINT "X IS LARGER"**

420 IF X<= Y THEN PRINT "Y IS LARGER"

17. (a)
```
.3
.4
.5
1
```
(b)
```
10
8
6
```
(c) **BYE as go to is missing.**

(d) ***

```
! ***
!   ***
!
```

18.
```
10 FOR I = 1 TO 3
20 PRINT 10 * I + 10
30 NEXT I
```

19.
```
30 FOR N = 1 TO 10
40 INPUT X$
50 PRINT X$
60 NEXT N
```

20. (a)
```
RUN
2 5 2  6  3  5  3  6  4  5 4 6
```

(b)
```
1  1
2
1  1
2
1  1
2
```

(c)
```
GOOD BYE
GOOD BYE
GOOD BYE
```

(d)
```
1  0
2  1
3  3
4  6
5  10
```

21. (a) Interchange the statements in lines 30 and 40.

(b) Insert **35 NEXT X**

22. **7 9 11**

23. Interchange the line numbers **70** and **90**.

24. (a) In the line number 1 typing of **STEP** 1 is not necessary.

(b) Line 30 should be either **NEXT** or **NEXT Q**.

(c) **STOP** written in-stead of **STEP**.

(d) **STEP** value has to be negative.

(e) Line 30 should be either **NEXT** or **NEXT I**.

(f) Number missing after **TO**.

CHAPTER 9

The Conditional Statements

9.1 Relational Operators

We have already seen a very elementary example of relational operations in the previous chapters while we used **IF/THEN** statement.

In order to carry out what are known as conditional branching operations in BASIC, a mechanism is required to express conditions of equality and inequality. This mechanism is provided by the use of relational operators. When relational operators are used to compare two values expressed as numerics or strings, you must take care to ensure that similar type operands are used on both sides of the relational operator sign. That is, you cannot mix numeric and string constants or variables. Doing so would violate the grammatical construction of the language and would result in a syntax error.Table 9.1 lists the relational operators available in BASIC.

Table 9.1 Relational Operators

Symbol	Basic Operator	Example
=	Equality	NME$ = "BALA"
< >	Inequality	CODE$ < > "YES"
<	Less than	A < 5
>	Greater than	B > 9
< =	Less than or equal to	1/2 < = .5
> =	Greater than or equal to	STOCK > = 5

Relational operators can be used to control program execution flow by initiating branching based on certain conditions. In addition, they can be employed to cause a BASIC statement or sequences of BASIC statements to be executed when certain conditions occur.

In the short program segment that follows, a numeric value is read from the keyboard through the use of the BASIC INPUT statement and assigned to the variable X. Next, three conditional tests are conducted to see if the value entered is equal to, less than, or greater than 5. If the result of a comparison operation is "true", then the appropriate branch to the indicated line number in the program occurs. If results of the comparison are "false", then the next program line number is executed.

```
10 INPUT;X
20 IF X=5 THEN 500
30 IF X < THEN 1000
40 IF X > 5 THEN 1500
50 PRINT "EQUAL": STOP
60 PRINT "LESS THAN":STOP
70 PRINT "GREATER THAN" : STOP
```

```
Ok
RUN
? 5 EQUAL
Break in 50
Ok
```

When the program was executed with the **RUN** command, the value **5** was entered. This resulted in a branch to line **50** in the program where the string **"EQUAL"** was printed. The **STOP** statement on that line caused the message **"Break in 50"** to be generated,and the program terminated its execution. In the following example, the value of **X** is used as a decision variable regarding the value of the variable **P** in the program. If **X** is equal to **2**, then **P** will be set equal to **7**, otherwise **P** will be assigned the value **3**.

```
10 INPUT;X
20 PRINT
110 IF X=2 THEN P=7:ELSE P=3
120 PRINT "FOR X= ";X;"P= ";P
Ok
RUN
? 1
FOR X= 1 P= 3
Ok
RUN
? 2
FOR X= 2 P= 7
Ok
RUN
? 3
Ok
```

When arithmetic and relational operators are combined in one expression, the arithmetic operations are performed prior to the relational test. As an example, consider the following BASIC statement:

```
10 IF (A+B)^2 > C THEN 50
```

First, the values of A and B are added and then the combined value is squared. The result of the arithmetic operations is then compared to the value of C. If the square of A plus B is less than or equal to C, the branch to program line 50 occurs. Thus, if the expression is true (1), the branch occurs. If the expression is false (0), then the next sequential program statement is executed. For the expression to be false, the value of A plus B squared must be greater than C in this example.

9.2 Single Alternative : IF/THEN (or IF/GOTO)

In BASIC, the IF/THEN statement is used for a single alternative decision structure. The two general formats of the IF/THEN statement are as follows:

```
line #  IF condition {THEN or GOTO} transfer line #
line # IF condition THEN statements(s) {transfer line # or statements(s)}
```

The brackets in the first statement indicate that one of the enclosed words is to be chosen when writing the statements. In other words, the first format of the IF/THEN can be worded in either of two ways:

```
line #  IF condition THEN transfer line#
line #  IF condition GOTO transfer line#
```

The execution of the **IF/THEN** statement happens in following steps:

1. If the condition is true, the **THEN** or **GOTO** clause is executed. The program branches to the transfer line number and executes that statement (or the next executable statement).
2. If the condition is false, the **THEN** or **GOTO** clause is ignored and execution continues with the next executable line following the **IF/THEN** statement.

The format of the condition looks like this:

Format ***expression 1*** **relational symbol** ***expression 2***

The values of the expressions can be either numeric or character strings (both must be the of same type). The expressions can be constants, variable and/or arithmetic expressions. The condition compares the two expressions by means of relational operators as already defined in section 9.1.

Following are the examples of valid **IF/THEN** statements. Notice the various conditions that are possible and the types of statements that can be used.

```
IF A < 3 THEN STOP
```

stops program execution if the value of A is less than 3.

```
IF C = 5 AND D$ = "YES" THEN PRINT "THANK YOU"
```

displays **THANK YOU** if the values of **C** equals **5** and **D$** is **YES**.

```
IF X < A, THEN GOTO 30
```

branches execution to line **30 IF X < A**. If **X** is not less than **A**, the test fails and execution resumes on next line.

The flowchart of single alternative **IF/THEN** is shown in Fig. 9.1.While comparing string variable, the constant should be enclosed within double quotes.

Example

```
A$ = "hello"
```

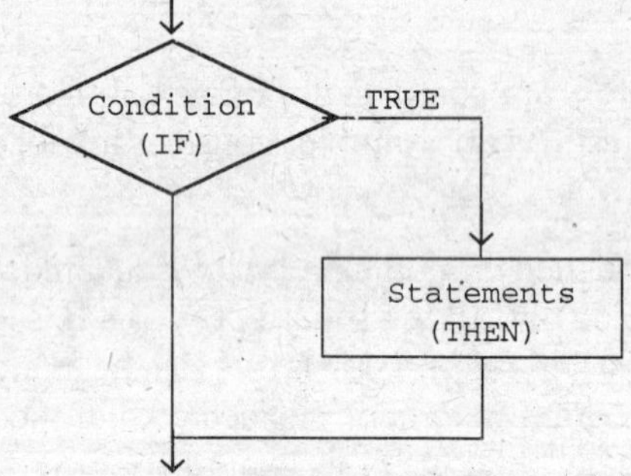

Fig. 9.1 Single Alternative Conditional Transfer (IF/THEN)

The following are some more valid examples of IF/THEN

(a) `IF A = 9 THEN 60`
(b) `IF A = X + Y THEN 10`
(c) `IF G$ = "NO" THEN 80`
(d) `IF X = A/B THEN 85`
(e) `IF A = B THEN PRINT "A = B"`
(f) `IF X > 5 * Y THEN LET N = N + 1`
(g) `IF C$ < > "CARRYONE" THEN END`
(h) `IF X = 9 THEN Y = X + 1`

(i) `IF N$ = "S" THEN PRINT "SUN"`
(j) `IF X = 3 * A ^ B THEN PRINT X$`
(k) `IF A > = 12 THEN 90`
(l) `IF A < = 9 + C THEN 65`

Example 9.1

Solving a quadratic equation of the form

ax² + bx + c = 0

where a,b and c are known and we wish to determine the value of x.

The roots of the quadratic equations can be written as

$$x_1 = [-b + \sqrt{(b^2 - 4ac)}]/2a$$

$$x_2 = [-b - \sqrt{(b^2 - 4ac)}]/2a$$

The above equation gives imaginary values if b^2-**4ac** is less than **0**.So let us assume that the values of the variables a,b and c are such that b^2 is always greater to **4ac** to make the solution easy.

Algorithm: Following steps will lead to definite solution.

1. Read numerical values for **a,b,c**. For this the user is to be guided to enter three values separated by commas.
2. Calculate the value for square root of b^2**-4ac**.
3. Calculate values for x_1 and x_2,using the above formulae.
4. Print the values for a,b,c, x_1 and x_2
5. End the program.

```
10 REM * PROGRAM TO CALCULATE THE ROOTS OF A QUADRATIC EQUATION *
20 PRINT "ENTER VALUES FOR A, B AND C SEPARATED BY COMMAS"
30 INPUT A,B,C
40 LET R =(B ^ 2 - 4 * A * C )^.5
50 LET X1 = (- B + R) / ( 2 * A )
60 LET X2 = (- B - R) / ( 2 * A )
70 PRINT
80 PRINT "A = "; A, "B = ";B, "C = "; C
90 PRINT "X1 = "; X1, "X2 = "; X2
100 PRINT
110 GOTO 20
120 END
```

(**Note**: The computer would give an error message if you try to take the square root of a negative number.)

Fig. 9.2 shows flowchart describing a program to solve the quadratic equation with **a,b,** and **c** entered as inputs;

Now run the program by pressing the F2 key after verifying the program entered by you through list command (or by pressing F1 key).The program sends the following message

```
ENTER VALUES FOR A, B AND C SEPARATED BY COMMA
?
```

Here you enter 2,6,4 as sample values for a,b,c respectively.And watch the screen to give the results as

```
A = 2 B = 6 C = 4
X1 = -1 X2 = -2
?
```

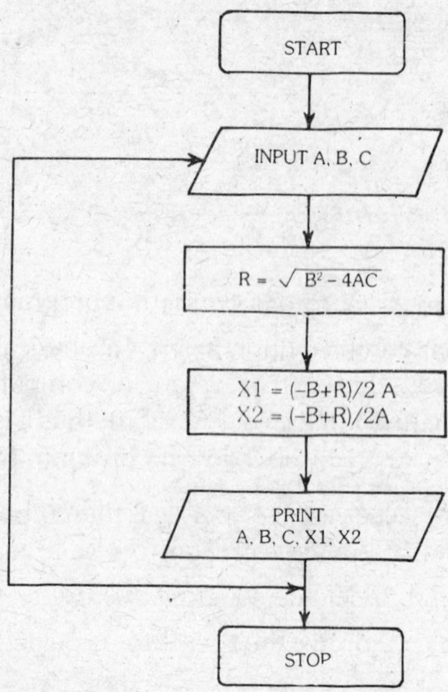

Fig. 9.2: Flow Chart for Example 9.1

Once again enter at the question mark prompt (?)

?1,0,1

and see the following message:

?1,0,1

Illegal function call in 40

Ok

This is because line 40 calculates the value of square root of **b^2-4ac** which in this case is negative and computer can not calculate the square root of a negative value.For this we must incorporate two lines shown as line numbers 80 and 90.Line number 80 finds out the negative effect if any in the desired expression and based on decision it directs the program to go further for calculating the values of the roots,else it asks the program to print the message.

NO REAL ROOTS

This message is printed by L.N. 90.The solution of the quadratic equation can be written in another way also as

$$X_1 = -b/2a + [(b/2a)^2 - c/a]^{1/2}$$

$$X_2 = -b/2a - [(b/2a)^2 - c/a]^{1/2}$$

*-In order for the solutions, X1 and X2 to be real,

$$(b/2a)^2 > c/a$$

9.3 Double Alternative : IF/THEN/ELSE

An extension of the **IF/THEN** statement is the **IF/THEN/ELSE** statement. Like the **IF/THEN** statement, it has two forms:

line # IF ***condition*** THEN GOTO ***transfer line*** #

ELSE ***transfer line # statements***

```
line # IF condition THEN statement (s)
ELSE transfer line # statements (s)
```

Examples

```
IF X = 9 THEN 100 ELSE STOP
```

instructs program to branch to line **100** if **X** equals **9**, but if **X** does not equal **9**. Without **ELSE** execution would drop to the next program line rather than STOP.

```
IF A$ = "YES" THEN 40 ELSE 50
```

sends execution to line 40 if **A$** equals **YES**, otherwise the program continues at line 50.

The entire **IF/THEN/ELSE** statement must appear on one physical line (a physical line ends with a carriage return). If a statement exceeds the width of screen, the computer causes the statements to "wrap around" to the next line without the use of the carriage return; thus it is still one physical line. A line can be upto 255 characters long. For example, the following program segment is invalid:

```
10 IF X > Y THEN Y = 0
20 ELSE X = 0
```

The statement should be written as follows:

```
10 IF X > Y THEN Y = 0 ELSE X = 0
```

The **IF/THEN/ELSE** statement is an example of the double alternative decision structure mentioned earlier in this unit. It is executed in this way:

1. If the condition is true, the **THEN** clause is executed and the **ELSE** clause is ignored.
2. If the condition is false, the **THEN** clause is ignored and the **ELSE** clause is executed.
3. The flowchart of double alternative **IF/THEN** statement is shown in Fig. 9.3.

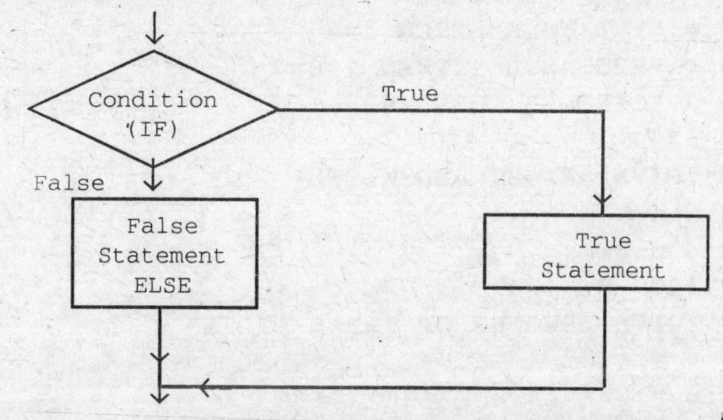

Fig. 9.3 Double Alternative Conditional Transfer (IF/THEN/ELSE)

The following are examples of the **IF/THEN/ELSE** statement:

```
70 IF X > 50 THEN PRINT "GOOD" ELSE PRINT "BAD"
80 IF A > B THEN C = A - B ELSE C = A + B
40 IF X > Y THEN BIG = X ELSE BIG = Y
```

9.4 Nested IF Statements

It is possible to nest two or more **IF/THEN** or **IF/THEN/ELSE** statements. This means that an **IF/THEN** or **IF/THEN/ELSE** statement can be placed within the **THEN** or **ELSE** clause of another **IF/THEN/ELSE** statement. The following is an example of an **IF/THEN/ELSE** statement nested within the **ELSE** clause of another **IF/THEN/ELSE** statement:

```
10 IF N > 0 THEN PRINT "POSITIVE" ELSE IF N < 0 THEN
PRINT "NEGATIVE" ELSE PRINT "ZERO"
```

Nesting statements in this manner can make a program difficult to follow. To avoid errors in logic, make sure that the nested **IF/THEN/ELSE** statements contain the same number of **ELSE** and **THEN** clauses; on execution, each **ELSE** is matched with the closed unmatched **THEN**. The following line illustrates this fact:

```
10 IF R = S THEN IF S = T THEN PRINT "R = T " ELSE " R < > T "
```

When **R** is not equal to **S**, this statement does not print "**R < > T**". The **ELSE** clause is matched to the second **THEN** clause. The statement could be written correctly as follows:

```
10  IF R=S THEN IF S=T THEN PRINT "R=T" ELSE PRINT "R < > T" ELSE PRINT
    "R < > T"
```

9.5 Combination of GOTO and IF/THEN

The use of **GOTO** and **IF THEN** is very important because of the way the statements allow complete programs to be constructed. It is always necessary to include some decisions in even the simplest of program and the reader should take time to understand fully the working of the program example given below. The purpose of this program is to calculate the area of a triangle, rectangle or circle (as selected by the user) from data supplied by the user.

Example 9.2 : Calculate area of given shape

```
10 PRINT "CALCULATE AREA OF GIVEN SHAPE"
110 PRINT
120 PRINT "TRIANGLE, RECTANGLE OR CIRCLE"
130 INPUT S$
140 IF S$ = "STOP" THEN 340
150 IF s$ = "TRIANGLE" THEN 190
160 IF S$ = "RECTANGLE" THEN 190
170 IF S$ = "CIRCLE" THEN 280
180 GO TO 120
190 PRINT "GIVE HEIGHT AND WIDTH"
200 INPUT H,W
210 LET Z = H *W
220 GO TO 310
230 PRINT "GIVE LENGTHS OF THREE SIDES"
240 INPUT A,B,C
250 LET X = 0.5 * (A + B + C)
260 LET Z = SQR (X * (X-A) * (X-B) * (X-C))
270 GO TO 310
280 PRINT "GIVE THE DIAMETER"
290 INPUT D
300 LET Z = 3.142 * D ^ 2/4
310 PRINT
320 PRINT "AREA OF "; S$ " IS"; Z ;"SQ. KM."
330 GO TO 110
340 STOP
```

Run the program by pressing F2 key and watch the screen for following to appear.

```
CALCULATE AREA OF GIVEN SHAPE
TRIANGLE, RECTANGLE OR CIRCLE
```

Type following after the PROMPT ?

```
?TRIANGLE
GIVE LENGTHS OF THREE SIDES
?7,9
AREA OF RECTANGLE IS 63
?0,-8
Redo from start
_
```

This message is due to our feeding the negative value.

```
?CIRCLE
GIVE THE DIAMETER
AREA OF CIRCLE IS 63.6255
TRIANGLE, RECTANGLE OR CIRCLE
?STOP
Break in 340
Ok
```

9.6 Computed GOTO Statement (ON/GOTO statement): Multiple Branching

The computed **GOTO** statement causes the branch to one of several specified line numbers, with the precise branch taken dependent on the value resulting from the evaluation of an expression contained in the statement. The format of the computed **GOTO** statement is shown below.

Format: **ON *exprnm* GOTO *line [line]. . .***

The value of the numeric expression exprnm can be a constant, variable, or expression. In any case its value must not exceed **255**.

The line to which **ON/GOTO** branches depends on the value of ***exprnm*** For example, if ***exprnm*** equals **1**, execution branches to the first linenum; if exprnm equals **2**, execution branches to the second linenum, and so on.

When exprnm is less than **1** or greater than the number of line listed, execution falls through the next statement. For example

```
ON X GOTO 100, 200, 300
```

branches to lines 100, 200, or 300 when the value of X is 1,2 or 3 respectively.

ON/GOTO Statement is executed in following manner

1. The expression is rounded to an integer value.
2. Depending upon the value of the expression, control passes to the corresponding line number.
   (a) If the value of the expressions is 1, control passes to the first line number listed.
   (b) If the value of the expression is 2, control passes to the second line number listed.
   (c) If the value of the expressions is n, control passes to the nth line number listed.

The following examples demonstrate the execution of the ON/GOTO statement.

Statement	Value of x	Execution
`10 ON X GOTO 30,50,70`	X = 1	Control passes to line **30**
	X = 2	Control passes to line **50**
	X = 3	Control passes to line **70**
`10 ON X-2 GOTO 100, 150`	X = 3	3-2=1, Control passes to line **100**
	X = 4	4-2=2, Control passes to line **150**
`20 ON X/3 GOTO 40, 60, 80`	X = 7	7/3 = 2.33, result rounded to 2, control passes to line **60**

Three additional rules apply to the **ON/GOTO** statement:

1. If the value of expression is zero, the rest of the **ON/GOTO** statement is ignored and control passes to the next statement in sequence.
2. If the value of the expression is greater than the number of transfer lines listed, control passes to the next statement in sequence.
3. If the value of the expression is negative, an error message is displayed and execution stops.

The following program segment illustrates the use of this program statement.

```
20 PRINT "ENTER DIRECTORY DESIRED"
30 INPUT "ENTER CHOICE (1,2, OR 3) ", CHOICE
40 ON CHOICE GOTO 100,110,120
100 PRINT TAB(5); "(1) TELEPHONE LIST"
110 PRINT TAB(5); "(2) ADDRESS LIST"
120 PRINT TAB(5); "(3) INCOME TAX "
```

Let us test the program by typing **RUN** command

```
RUN
ENTER DIRECTORY DESIRED
ENTER CHOICE (1,2 OR 3)2
(2) ADDRESS LIST
(3) INCOME TAX
```

We will have to improve the program to type only the name of desired directory with the help of **GOTO** statement after line numbers **100,110,120**.The revised program will look like

```
20 PRINT "ENTER DIRECTORY DESIRED"
30 INPUT "ENTER CHOICE (1,2, OR 3) ", CHOICE
40 ON CHOICE GOTO 100,110,120
100 PRINT TAB(5); "(1) TELEPHONE LIST"
105 GOTO 130
110 PRINT TAB(5); "(2) ADDRESS LIST"
115 GOTO 130
120 PRINT TAB(5); "(3) INCOME TAX "
130 END
```

Now if we enter 2 as our choice computer will list only 2nd list.

```
RUN
ENTER DIRECTORY DESIRED
ENTER CHOICE (1,2 OR 3)2
(2) ADDRESS LIST
```

In the preceding example, the statement in lines 20 through 40 cause headings of three program choices to be displayed. The display of program choice is normally called a menu, because the computer operator is provided with a number of items to select his or her action from. The **INPUT** statement in line 30 will first cause the prompt message **" ENTER CHOICE (1,2, or 3)"** to be displayed. Then the program will halt execution, awaiting a response from the keyboard. When a number is entered, it will be assigned to the variable named **CHOICE**. The computed **GOTO** statements in line **40** will cause a branch to one of the line numbers in the list depending on the value of the variable named **CHOICE**. If **CHOICE** is **1**, the program will branch to line number **100**. If **CHOICE** is **2**, the program will branch to line **110**.

Example 9.4: Depreciation computation

```
10 REM * COMPUTATION OF DEPRECIATION BY THREE DIFFERENT METHODS *
20 PRINT "THE VALUE OF ITEM IS RS.=";
30 INPUT V
40 PRINT "INPUT THE NUMBER OF DEPRECIATION YEARS =";
50 INPUT N
60 PRINT "ENTER 1 FOR STRAIGHT LINE METHOD"
70 PRINT "ENTER 2 FOR DOUBLE DECLINING BALANCE METHOD"
80 PRINT "ENTER 3 FOR SUM-OF THE YEARS METHOD"
90 INPUT I
100 PRINT
110 ON I GOTO 120 ,140,160
120 PRINT TAB(10) "STRAIGHT-LINE METHOD"
130 GOTO 170
140 PRINT TAB(10) "DOUBLE DECLINING BALANCE METHOD"
150 GOTO 170
160 PRINT TAB(10) "SUM-OF-THE-YEARS-DIGITS METHOD"
170 PRINT
180 PRINT "END OF YEAR", "DEPRECIATION", "CURRENT VALUE"
190 LET J=O
200 LET D1=V/N
210 LET F1=V/(N*(N+1)/2)
220 LET J=J+1
230 ON I GOTO 240, 290,350
240 REM STRAIGHT-LINE METHOD
250 LET V=V-D1
260 PRINT J,D1,V
270 IF J< N THEN 220
280 STOP
290 REM DOUBLE DECLINING BALANCE METHOD
300 LET D2=(2/N)*V
310 LET V=V-D2
320 PRINT J,D2,V
330 IF J < N THEN 220
340 STOP
350 REM SUM-OF-THE-YEARS-DIGITS METHOD
360 F2=N-J + 1
370 D3=F1*F2
```

```
380 V=V-D3
390 PRINT J,D3,V
400 IF J < N THEN 220
410 END
```

When run the program can be used to show following :

```
RUN
THE VALUE OF ITEM IS RS. =? 100
INPUT THE NUMBER OF DEPRICIATION YEARS =? 5
ENTER 1 FOR STRAIGHT LINE METHOD
ENTER 2 FOR DOBLE DECLINING BALANCE METHOD
ENTER 3 FOR SUM-OF THE YEARS METHOD
? 1
                     STRIGHT-LINE METHOD
END OF YEAR        DEPRECIATION      CURRENT VALUE
  1                 20                80
  2                 20                60
  3                 20                40
  4                 20                20
  5                 20                0
Break in 280
Ok
RUN
THE VALUE OF ITEM IS RS. =? 100
INPUT THE NUMBER OF DEPRICIATION YEARS =? 5
ENTER 1 FOR STRAIGHT LINE METHOD
ENTER 2 FOR DOBLE DECLINING BALANCE METHOD
ENTER 3 FOR SUM-OF THE YEARS METHOD
? 2
          DOUBLE DECLINNING BALANCE METHOD
END OF YEAR         DEPRECIATION         CURRENT VALUE
 1                   40                   60
 2                   24                   36
 3                   14.4                 21.6
 4                   9.639999             12.96
 5                   5.184                7.776
Break in 340
Ok

RUN
THE VALUE OF ITEM IS RS.=? 100
INPUT THE NUMBER OF DEPRICIATION YEARS =? 5
ENTER 1 FOR STRAGHT LINE METHOD
ENTER 2 FOR DOBLE DECLINING BALANCE METHOD
ENTER 3 FOR SUM-OF THE YEAR METHOD
? 3
SUM-OF-THE-YEARS-DIGITS METHOD
```

```
END OF YEAR          DEPRECIATION         CURRENT VALUE
 1                    33.33333             66.66667
 2                    26.66667             40.00001
 3                    20                   20.00001
 4                    13.33333             6.666675
 5                    6.666667             9.106232E-06
Ok
```

9.7 Menus

A menu is a displayed list of the functions that a program can perform. Just as a customer in a restaurant looks at the menu to choose a meal, so a menu displayed on the screen helps the program user to choose a desired function in the further portions of a program. The user makes a selection by entering a code, usually a simple number or letter, at the keyboard. Following program presents a simple example of a menu.

Example 9.5: Program for converting rupees into foreign currencies using on **GOTO**

```
10 REM * * * FOREIGN CURRENCY CONVERSIONS * * *
20 CLS
30 PRINT "MONEY EXCHANGE MENU"
40 PRINT
50 PRINT "ENTER AMOUNT IN RUPEES TO BE CONVERTED"
60 INPUT RUPEES
70 PRINT
80 PRINT "PLEASE ENTER ONE OF THE FOLLOWING NUMBERS:"
90 PRINT " 1 TO CONVERT TO POUNDS"
100 PRINT " 2 TO CONVERT TO LIRAS"
110 PRINT " 3 TO CONVERT TO FRANCS"
120 PRINT " 4 TO CONVERT TO DOLLARS "
130 PRINT
140 INPUT CODE
150 ON CODE GOTO 180,220,260,300
160 REM
170 REM * * * POUNDS * * *
180 RESULT = RUPEES * .022
190 GOTO 310
200 REM
210 REM * * * LIRA * * *
220 RESULT = RUPEES * 50
230 GOTO 310
240 REM
250 REM * * * FRANCS * * *
260 RESULT = RUPEES * .2
270 GOTO 310
280 REM
290 REM * * * DOLLARS * * *
300 RESULT = RUPEES * .03
310 PRINT "THE RESULT = "; RESULT
320 GOTO 80
999 END
```

```
RUN
MONEY EXCHANGE
ENTER AMOUNT IN RUPEES TO BE CONVERTED
?100
PLEASE ENTER ONE OF THE FOLLOWING NUMBERS:
1 TO CONVERT TO POUNDS
2 TO CONVERT TO MARKS
3 TO CONVERT TO FRANCS
4 TO CONVERT TO DOLLARS
?1
THE RESULT = 2.2
Ok
```

If you ask for conversion from 1000 Rupees to Marks type 100,and press your choice as 2

```
?2
THE RESULT = 5000
```

EXERCISE

1. Fill in the blanks
   (a) A statement that always alters the execution path when it is encountered is a(n) .... transfers statement.
   (b) A control statement that makes a decision based on the value of an expression is called a(n).......... transfer statement.
   (c) The expression on the **ON/GOTO** statement always is evaluated as a(n)......
   (d) The .... clause indicated that both conditions must be true for the **THEN/GOTO** clause to be executed.
2. Why is the **GOTO** statement an unconditional transfer statement?
3. Why is the **IF** statement a conditional transfer statement?
4. What is a menu?
5. Where are **RETURN** statements placed in programs?
6. What happens if the transfer line number in a **GOSUB** statement is a non executable statement?
7. Must the condition of the **IF/THEN** statement be evaluated only as true or false?
8. What is displayed when each of the following segments of code is run?

(1)
```
200 INPUT X
210 IF X < > 1 THEN PRINT "HERE" ELSE PRINT "THERE"
```
(a) **Assume the input is? 1**
(b) **Assume the input is? 2**

(2)
```
200 INPUT R$
210 IF R$ = "Y" THEN PRINT "HELLO"
220 LET R$ = "YES"
230 PRINT R$
```
(a) **Assume the input is? Y**
(b) **Assume the input is? N**

(3) Rewrite line 210 in exercise (2) so that the THEN clause is executed if the input is "Y" or "y".

9. Write the following code on a single line:

```
400 INPUT X
410 LET Y = X ^ 2
420 PRINT X ; Y
```

10. Correct following BASIC code.

```
500 IF TAG = 1 THEN LET TAG = TAG + 1
510 ELSE PRINT TAG
```

11. Correct following program segment

```
600 IF ANS$ = "y" THEN PRINT "START"
610 LET COUNT = COUNT + 1
620 PRINT "THE SALE PRICE IS"; PRICE
```

12. Choose one answer. A multiple alternative decision structure cannot be implemented by
    (a) an **ON/GOTO** statement
    (b) a sequence of **If** then structures.
    (c) several nested loops.
    (d) nested **If/Then/Else** structures.

13. What is displayed when the following program segment is run?

```
200 LET N = 3
210 ON N GOTO 220, 230, 240
220 PRINT "CASE 1"
230 PRINT "CASE 2"
240 PRINT "CASE 3"
```

14. Correct the code in exercise 13 so that it prints **CASE 2** and nothing else when **N = 2**

15. Choose the one attribute that does not apply to **IF/THEN** statements.
    (a) They can be used to implement single alternative decision structure.
    (b) They can be used in sequence to implement a **CASE** structure.
    (c) They must contain a line number after the keyword **THEN**.
    (d) They can be used to create both loop and decision structures.

16. Suppose, the value of a variable, K, is either 2, 3, or 4.Rewrite the following code using an **ON...GOTO** statement:

```
200 IF K > 2 THEN 230
210 PRINT "FIRST"
220 GOTO 270
230 IF K > 73 THEN 260
240 PRINT "SECOND"
250 GOTO 270
260 PRINT "THIRD"
270 PRINT "DONE"
```

17. Choose the one attribute that does not apply to the **ON/GOTO** statement
    (a) It can be used to implement some **If / Then / Else** structures.
    (b) It can contain variables in the list of line numbers.
    (c) It can always be replaced by a sequence of **IF/THEN** structures.
    (d) It can contain a numeric expression between **ON** and **GOTO**.

CHAPTER 10

Some Programming Applications

Problem 10.1

Device and run a computer program to input a temperature in degrees Fahrenheit, convert the temperature to degrees centigrade and output the result.

10.1.1 Problem Understanding

The four steps in the programming process are

- Define the problem,
- Design a solution,
- Write the program, and
- Submit the program to the computer, and debug, and test it.

Programs are best designed by the top-down approach, in which a large task is divided into smaller and smaller subtasks, moving from the general to the specific.

Program design can be documented by structure charts to show the results of the top-Down process, and by flowcharts to display the order and type of program steps to be performed.

10.1.2 Problem Analysis

In this case the input variable is the Temperature in degrees Fahrenheit: **F** and the output variable is the Temperature in degrees Celsius: **C**.

The formula for conversion between Fahrenheit and Celsius is

```
C = (5/9) (F - 32)
```

10.1.3 Program Design

It is obvious that first we have to ask the user to input the temperature in degrees Fahrenheit.Then above formula is to be coded in computer's language after which we have to ask the computer to print the program on screen of computer.We shall first draw up a flowchart for taking up above in sequential manner.

The pseudocode is as follows:

```
Set F = 95
Compute C = (5/9) * (F - 32)
Print C
```

The flowchart is shown in fig. 10.1

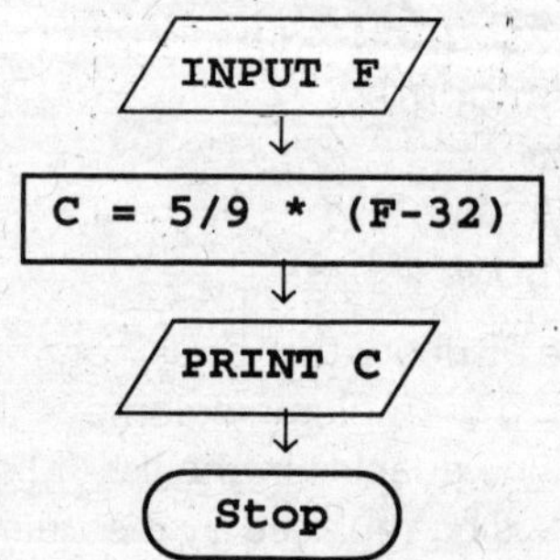

Fig. 10.1 Flow Chart for Temperature Conversion

10.1.4 Program Code

From flow chart one can easily code the program in proper.One way of writing the program could be as shown below:

```
NEW
10 INPUT F
20 LET C = ( F - 32 ) * 5 / 9
30 PRINT C
40 STOP
50 END
RUN
```

It is worth remembering that a program code may be written in a number of coding combinations.The best one is that which requires minimum program lines but without loss of any reductions in the desired output.

We are using two system commands **NEW** and **RUN** and observe that both of them are without line numbers.The command **NEW** clears the memory of any other program already entered in computer.

10.1.5 Executing the Program

Having written the program from the flowchart and given the program a dry-run the following is an example of a typical terminal session.

```
RUN
100 PROGRAM STOPPED AT 40
```

By this message computer informs user of line number that halted the program.Let us make our program more readable by inserting few remarks with the help of **REM** statement.

```
5 REM ** INPUT FAHRENHEIT ** 15 REM ** CONVERT TO CENTIGRADE **
25 REM ** OUTPUT RESULT **
```

Note here that we have given the intermediate line numbers so that statements are inserted in correct sequence.This also explains why we use to give line numbers in steps of 10.This is because later on if the programmer wants to insert a line later on he or she can choose an intermediate number.

Type above statements and see that they are actually inserted in the body of previous program segment.

```
LIST
5 REM ** INPUT FAHRENHEIT **
10 INPUT F
15 REM ** CONVERT TO CENTIGRADE **
20 LET C = (F - 32) * 5 / 9
25 REM ** OUTPUT RESULT **
30 PRINT C
40 STOP
50 END
RUN
PROGRAM STOP AT 40
```

Save the program for further use by name TEMP1.

10.1.6 Step by step wise Refinement

We will modify the previous program so that it will allow more than one temperature to be input.Clearly a loop will be introduced so that a section of the program can be used repeatedly. However, a method will have to be introduced to exit from the loop. In this example if a high temperature, say, 999 is input to stop the program running.

There will be no need to re-type the entire program because only a minor modification is necessary on the previous program.The previous program can be re-loaded into the memory of the computer:

```
OLD "TEMP1"
12 REM ** TEST FOR EXIT FROM LOOP **
13 IF F = 999 THEN STOP
32 INPUT F
35 GOTO 13
```

and by inserting four new lines 12,13,32 and 35 successfully edit the previous program.

```
LIST
5 REM ** INPUT FAHRENHEIT **
10 INPUT F
12 REM ** TEST FOR EXIT FROM LOOP **
13 IF F = 999 THEN STOP
15 REM ** CONVERT TO CENTIGRADE **
20 LET C = (F - 32) * 5/9
25 REM ** OUTPUT RESULTS **
30 PRINT C
32 INPUT F
35 GOTO 13
40 STOP
50 END
```

Upon inspecting the listing of the program it is learnt that program now contains two **STOP** statements.Clearly an edit is required by taking out line (40) by typing the line number only followed by **enter** to remove that line.

```
RUN
? 106
41.1111111111
? 212
100
? 32
0
? 999
PROGRAM STOP AT 13
```

Save this program by changing the filename to TEMP2 the computer has also retained the original program TEMP1.

Problem 10.2

Write a program to input the radii of circles and output their circumferences and areas. Terminate the routine by inputting a zero radius. Take the value of pie to be 3.14159 in the formula for circumference **C = 2** π **r** and area **A =** π **Rz**, where **R** is the radius of a circle.

Program

```
10 REM ** INPUT RADIUS **
20 INPUT R
30 REM ** TEST FOR EXIT FROM LOOP **
40 IF R = 0 THEN STOP
50 REM ** CALCULATE CIRCUMFERENCE
60 LET C = 2 * 3.14159 * R
```

```
70 REM ** CALCULATE AREA
80 LET A = 3.14159 * R ^ 2
90 REM ** OUTPUT RESULTS
100 PRINT C
110 PRINT A
115 INPUT R
120 GOTO 40
130 END
```

Dry Run

R	C	A
5	31.4159	78.53975
10	62.8318	314.159
15	94.2477	706.8578
20	125.6636	314.159

Notes:

- The accuracy to which a number is output from a calculation will vary between computers. The computer used to run this program gives an accuracy up to 13 significant figures, however, when calculating the results for **(C)** and **(A)** in the dry run 6 significant figures would have been more than adequate.
- However, in reality the accuracy to which data should be output must reflect the accuracy to which the original data could be measured. In the previous example if the radius **(R)** was measured to an accuracy of 1 decimal place, then the values for circumference **(C)** and area **(A)** should be output to 1 decimal place.
- A further point to note is that if a negative value for a radius **(R)** had been input to the computer the value for the circumference **(C)** would be negative, and area **(A)** positive. This is clearly an undesirable result and the reader should be aware that inputting bad data to the computer will produce erroneous results.

Problem 10.3: Design a program for averaging marks obtained in three subjects i.e. physics, chemistry, maths. The marks obtained are 96, 85 and 60 respectively.

10.3.1. Problem Analysis

The input variables are scores on the three tests: **P1 C1 M1**

The output variable is average score: **AVG**

The formula is **AVG = (P1 + C1 + M1)**

10.3.2 Program Design

The pseudocode is as follows:

Set first test score **(P1) = 96**
Set second test score **(C1) = 85**
Set third test score **(M2) = 5**
Compute average: **AVG = (P1 + C1 + M1)**
Print **AVG**

10.3.3 Program Code

```
5 REM PROGRAM to COMPUTE AVERAGE OF THREE TEST SCORES
```

```
10 REM
20 REM TEST SCORES INPUT BLOCK
30 LET P1 = 96
40 LET C1 = 85
50 LET M1 = 60
60 LET AVG = (P1 + C1 + M1) / 3
70 PRINT "FOR TEST SCORES OF : "
80 PRINT P1; C1; M1
90 PRINT "THE AVERAGE IS: "; AVG
99 END
RUN
FOR TEST SCORE OF :
95    83    72
THE AVERAGE IS : 83.33334
```

Problem 10.4: A wage Computing Program

The following sample program shall illustrate, how the program is written in its acceptable form after going throurh several refinements. The program determines the wages of an employee who works for a certain number of hours at a specific rate per hour. Deductions are made for Income Tax, HR (House rent), CGHS (Central Govt. Health scheme) and Provident Fund deductions . Here is the data needed for this program.

Hrs worked = 40

Rate = 10.50

House rent deduction = 50 /- per month.

CGHS deduction = Re 6.50 per month

PF Deduction = Re. 20.00 per month.

10.4.1 Design

(a) We shall use the **READ/DATA** statements to enter the number of hours worked, the rate per hour, and the deductions.

(b) Remarks are placed in strategic spots for help in understanding the program.

(c) Blank lines may be inserted only for clarity.

(d) Calculations:
Gross Pay = Hours x Rate
Total Deductions = House rent Deduction + CGHS + GPF Deduction
Net Pay = Gross Pay - Total Deductions.

(e) Following variables will be adopted
HR = House rent deduction.
CG = CGHS deduction
GF = General Provident Fund
H = HOURS
R = RATE
G = GROSS PAY
D = DEDUCTIONS
N = NET PAY

10.4.2 Coding

```
10 REM * READ / DATA STATEMENT *
20 READ H, R, HR , CG , GF
30 DATA 40, 10.50, 50, 6.5, 20
40 REM * GROSS PAY *
50 LET G H * R
60 REM * TOTAL DEDUCTIONS *
70 LET D HR + CG + GF
80 REM * NET PAY *
85 LET N G - D
90 REM PRINT STATEMENTS
100 PRINT
110 PRINT "HOURS"; H, "RATE";R
120 PRINT "GROSS PAY"; G
130 PRINT "HOUSE RENT" ; HR
140 PRINT "CGHS DED" ; CG
150 PRINT "GPF"; GF
160 PRINT "TOTAL DEDUCTIONS";D
170 PRINT "NET PAY"; N
200 END
RUN
HOURS 40    RATE 10.5
GROSS PAY 420
HOUSE RENT 50
CGHS DED 6.5
GPF 20
TOTAL DEDUCTIONS 76.5
NET PAY 343.5
```

Let us analyze how the program works

1. Statements 20 & 30 enter data into the computer.

   ```
   20 READ H, R, HR, CG, GF
   30 DATA 40, 10.50, 50, 6.5, 20
   ```

   Remember that all data elements and variables are separated by commas and not by semicolons.

2. Statement 50 calculates the gross pay.

   ```
   50 LET G = H * R
   ```

3. Statement 70 calculates the total deductions.

   ```
   70 LET D = HR + CG + GF
   ```

4. Statement 85 calculates the net pay.

   ```
   85 LET N = G - D
   ```

5. Statement 120 prints the gross pay.

   ```
   120 PRINT "GROSS PAY " ; G
   ```

   Since we want to print **GROSS PAY** in the output we have included these words in the qoutes to make them in a string.The computer will first print this string followed by the value of the variable **G** (Gross pay).Notice that one blank space was purposely left in the string so that the value of **G** is printed spaced apart in the output.

6. Statement 170 prints the net pay .

```
170 PRINT "NET PAY " ; N
```

10.4.3 First Refinement

Above program calculates an employee's earnings based on the number of hours worked and the hourly rate of pay. The program is to be modified for similar computations for three employees whose regular work week is 40 hours. They are paid double time and a half for overtime. Following data is to be used.

Emp.	Hrs	Rate	House Rent	CGHS Ded.	GPF Ded.
1	45	10.50	40	6.50	
2	35	13.70	45	6.50	20
3	40	15.00	50	6.50	20

(a) The **READ DATA** statements are used:

- To assign a special number to a variable that represents number of employees. This variable is used subsequently with a counter to terminate the loop.
- To input data (hours, rates, and deductions).

(b) **Calculations**: Following assignment statements shall be used.

1. Gross Pay (no overtime) = Regular Hours x Regular Rate
2. Gross Pay with overtime:
   - Overtime Hours = Regular Hours - 40
   - Overtime Rate = Regular Rate x 1.5
   - Overtime Pay = Overtime Hours x Overtime Rate
   - Gross Pay (with overtime) = 40 x Regular Rate + Overtime Pay
3. Net Pay:
   - Total Deductions House Rent + CGHS Ded. + GPF
   - Net Pay = Gross Pay - Total Deductions

When your program is executed the first few lines displayed should supply general information to the user, a welcome message. This might include a brief description of the program, special instructions, the name of the programmer, and so on. In general, the welcome message should ease the user into the program.

In addition to printing the results of your program, you should also display (or echo print) the input values. This leads to more readable output and reduces the possibility that the user will make an undetected error entering input.

(c) Let us define a few new variables :

```
K = COUNTER
N1 = NUMBER OF EMPLOYEES
H = REGULAR HOURS
R = REGULAR RATE
H1 = OVERTIME HOURS
R1 = OVERTIME RATE
V = OVERTIME
```

Coding

```
100 REM SET UP A CONUTER
```

```
105 LET K = 1
200 REM READ/DATA STATEMENTS
205 REM READ NO. OF EMPLOYEE
210 READ N1
215 DATA 3
220 REM READ HOURS, RATE, DEDUCTIONS
225 READ H, R, HR , CG , GF
230 DATA 45, 10.50, 40, 6.50, 15
235 DATA 35, 13.70, 45, 6.50, 20
240 DATA 40, 15.00, 50, 6.50, 20
300 REM CHECK FOR OVERTIME
305 IF H > 40 THEN 500
400 REM GROSS PAY -- NO OVERTIME
405 LET H1 = 0
410 LET R1 = 0
415 LET V = 0
420 LET G = H * R
425 GOTO 600
500 REM GROSS PAY —WITH OVERTIME
505 LET H1 = H - 40
510 LET R1 = R * 1.5
515 LET V = H1 * R1
520 LET G = 40 * R + V
600 REM NET PAY
605 LET D = HR + CG + GF
610 LET N = G - D
700 REM PRINT STATEMENTS
705 PRINT
710 PRINT "EMPLOYEE"; K, "HRS"; H, "RATE";R
715 PRINT "OVERTIME HOURS"; H1
720 PRINT "OVERTIME RATE"; R1
725 PRINT "OVERTIME PAY"; V
730 PRINT "GROSS PAY"; G
735 PRINT "HOUSE RENT" ; HR
740 PRINT "CGHS DED" ; CG
745 PRINT "GPF"; GF
750 PRINT "TOTAL DEDUCTIONS"
755 PRINT "NET PAY"; N
800 REM CHECK FOR LAST DATA ITEM
805 LET K = K + 1
810 IF K > N1 THEN 999
815 GOTO 225
999 END
```

You must have obeserved that each group of program has been given the line number out of a different century so as to identify the program groups, some of which are called subroutines.Let us analyse how above program works.

1. Following two statements enter the number of employees into the computer.

```
210 READ N1
215 DATA 3
```

2. Statement 810 compares the above variable with a counter.

```
810 IF K > N1 THEN 999
```

3. Statement 305 checks for overtime.

```
305 IF H > 40 THEN 500
```

4. If the above statement is true, routine 500 calculates the overtime.
5. Statement 510 finds the overtime rate.

```
510 LET R1 = R * 1.5
```

6. Statement 420 finds the gross pay without overtime and statement 520 with overtime.

```
420 LET G = H * R
520 LET G = 40 * R + V
```

7. Statement 815 transfers control back to the READ statement to read more data.

```
815 GO TO 225
```

10.4.4 Second Refinement

Let us enhance our program as follows: **A FOR/NEXT** loop terminates input rather than a counter. The index of the FOR statement represents the number of the employees.

(a) Use a **FOR/NEXT** loop to keep track of the employees.

(b) Use the **READ/DATA** statements to enter the hours, rates and deductions.

Remarks are introduced at the top of the program for defining the various variables.

```
1 REM E - INDEX (EMPLOYEE NUMBER)
2 REM H - REGULAR HOURS
3 REM R - REGULAR RATE
4 REM HR - HOUSE RENT
5 REM CG - CGHS DED
6 REM GF - GPF
7 REM H1 - OVERTIME HOURS
8 REM R1 - OVERTIME RATE
9 REM V - OVERTIME
10 REM G - GROSS PAY
11 REM D - DEDUCTIONS
12 REM N - NET PAY
100 REM SET UP A FOR/NEXT LOOP
105 FOR E = 1 TO 3
200 REM READ HOURS,RATES,DEDUCTIONS
205 READ H,R,HR,CG,GF
210 DATA 45, 10.50, 40, 6.50, 15
215 DATA 35, 13.70, 45, 6.50, 20
220 DATA 40, 15.00, 50, 6.50, 20
300 REM CHECK FOR OVERTIME
305 IF H > 40 THEN 500
400 REM GROSS PAY- NO OVERTIME
405 LET H1 =0
410 LET R1 =0
```

```
415 LET V =0
420 LET G =H * R
425 GOTO 600
500 REM GROSS PAY - WITH OVERTIME
505 LET H1 =H - 40
510 LET R1 =R * 1.5
515 LET V =H1 * R1
520 LET G =40 * R + V
600 REM NET PAY
605 LET D =HR + CG + GF
610 LET N =G - D
700 REM PRINT STATEMENTS
705 PRINT
710 PRINT "EMPLOYEE";E, "HRS"; H, "RATE"; R
715 PRINT "OVERTIME HOURS" ; H1
720 PRINT "OVERTIME RATE"; R1
725 PRINT "OVERTIME PAY" ; V
730 PRINT "GROSS PAY"; G
735 PRINT "HOUSE RENT"; HR
740 PRINT "CGHS DED";CG
745 PRINT "GPF"; GF
750 PRINT "TOTAL DEDUCTIONS"; D
755 PRINT "NET PAY"; N
800 REM TRANSFER TO BEGINNING OF LOOP
805 NEXT E
999 END
RUN
EMPLOYEE  1                   HRS        45     RATE  10.5
OVERTIME HOURS  5
OVERTIME RATE  15.75
OVERTIME PAY  78.75
GROSS PAY  498.75
HOUSE RENT  40
CGHS DED  6.5
GPF  15
TOTAL DEDUCTIONS 61.5
NET PAY 437.25
EMPLOYEE  2                   HRS        45     RATE  13.7
OVERTIME  HOURS  0
OVERTIME RATE  0
OVERTIME PAY  0
GROSS PAY 479.50
HOUSE RENT  45
CGHS DED  6.5
GPF  20
TOTAL DEDUCTIONS 71.5
NET PAY 408
EMPLOYEE  3                   HRS        39     RATE  12.34
```

```
OVERTIME HOURS  0
OVERTIME RATE  0
OVERTIME PAY  0
GROSS PAY  600
HOUSE RENT  50
CGHS DED  6.5
GPF  20
TOTAL DEDUCTIONS  76.5
NET PAY  523.5
```

Let us analyse the above

1. Statements 105 and 805 control the loop.

```
105 FOR E = 1 TO 3
805 NEXT E
```

2. Statement replaces following five statements of our just earlier version of the program.

```
105 LET K = 1
210 READ N1
215 DATA 3
805 LET K = K + 1
810 IF K > N1 THEN 999
```

3. Similarly statement No. 815 is replaced by statement **805 NEXT E.**

Now we shall rewrite the program so that it is divided into several subroutines.

Find the wages for three employees who are paid on the basis of a 39-hour week and who recive time-and-a-half for overtime. Deductions are made for income tax,union dues,and a registered pension plan.

(a) We shall device following four

 (1) One subroutine calculates the gross pay with overtims.This subroutine calls the subroutine that calculates the net pay.

 (2) A second subroutine calculates the gross pay with no overtime. This subroutine also calls the subroutine that calculates the net pay.

 (3) A third subroutine calculates the net pay. This subroutine call the subroutine that prints.

 (4) A fourth subroutine prints the information as shown below,using format free output.

(b) Use a **FOR/NEXT** loop to keep track of the employees with the index of the FOR statement denoting the number of the employee.

(c) Use the **READ/DATA** statements to enter the hours,rate, and deductions.

Problem:10.5

Write a program to prepare monthly pay bills for the employees of an maintenance organization having following categories of staff:

(1) Clerk (2) Eletrician (3) Fitter (4) Foreman (5) Wireman (6) Mason

The salary for each category includes basic pay,dearness allowance,houserent allowance (HRA) and overtime wages.Professional tax worth 2% of basic pay is deducted from all employees getting salary equal to or above Rs.1000/- per month.HRA is 15% of the basic pay.

10.5.1 Problem analysis

Data available:

(a) Name of employee

(b) Category

(c) Basic Pay

(d) Dearness allowance (15% of basic)

(e) Overtime worked (in days)

(f) Rate of overtime:overtime wage rate is as follows

Code	Trade	Daily rate (Rs.)	Basic pay	O.T.days	Dearness Allowance
1	Foreman	50	700	5	310
2	Electrician	30	400	10	275
3	Fitter	25	500	5	310
4	Wireman	25	350	0	250
5	Mason	20	350	0	250
6	Clerk	15	260	12	225

Total salary = Basic pay + Dearness allowance + House rent allowance + Overtime wage

Net pay = Total salary - Professional tax

10.5.2 Output Required

Name, Trade,Basic pay, Dearness allowance, Overtime wage, Total Salary, Net salary.

10.5.3 Conditions and constraints

HRA = 15% of basic pay

Professional tax = 2% of basic pay.

10.5.4 Coding: Let

N-Total employees

N$-Name of employee

T$-Trade (category)name **B**-Basic pay

D-Dearness allowance

T1-Overtime allowance

H-House rent allowance

W-Overtime wage

T2-Professional tax

S-Total salary

P-Net pay

R(1)-Daily wage rate for trade I

Observe above that since two T's were involved , they have been given the representation as **T1** and **T2**.

10.5.5 Algorithm

A flowchart is shown in figure 10.4.

Program

```
10 REM PAY ROLL CALCULATION
20 DIM R(8),N$(8),T$(10)
30 READ N
40 FOR = I 1 TO 6
50 READ R(I)
60 NEXT I
```

```
70 LET C = 1
80 READ N$,T$,B,D,T1
90 IF T$ = "FORMAN" THEN 150
100 IF T$ = "ELECTRICIAN" THEN 170
110 IF T$ = "FITTER" THEN 190
120 IF T$ = "WIREMAN" THEN 210
130 IF T$ = "MANSON"THEN 230
140 IF T$ = "CLERK" THEN 250
150 LET I = 1
160 GO TO 270
170 LET I = 2
180 GO TO 270
190 LET I = 3
200 GO TO 270
210 LET I = 4
220 GO TO 270
230 LET I = 5
240 GO TO 270
250 LET I = 6
260 REM * TOTAL SALARY*
270 H = 15 * B
280 W = T1 * R(1)
290 S = B + D + H + W
300 REM *PROFESSIONAL TAX*
310 IF S < THEN 340
320 T2 = B * .02
330 GO TO 360
340 T2 = 0
350 REM * NET PAY *
360 P = S - T2
370 LPRINT N$; TAB(0); T$; TAB(20); B; TAB(25)
380 LPRINT USING "0#####.##"; H; D; W;
390 LPRINT USING "######.##"
400 IF C = N THEN 500
410 C = C+1
420 GO TO 80
430 DATA 6, 50, 30, 25, 20, 15
440 DATA "SOLANKI", "FITTER", 500, 310, 5
450 DATA "SUNITI", "FOREMAN", 700, 310, 5
460 DATA "SANDEEP", "MASON", 350, 250, 0
470 DATA "JAIN", "CLERCK", 260, 225, 12
480 DATA "RAMDAS", "WIREMAN", 350, 250, 0
490 DATA "VIJAY", ELECTRICIAN", 400, 275, 10
500 END
```

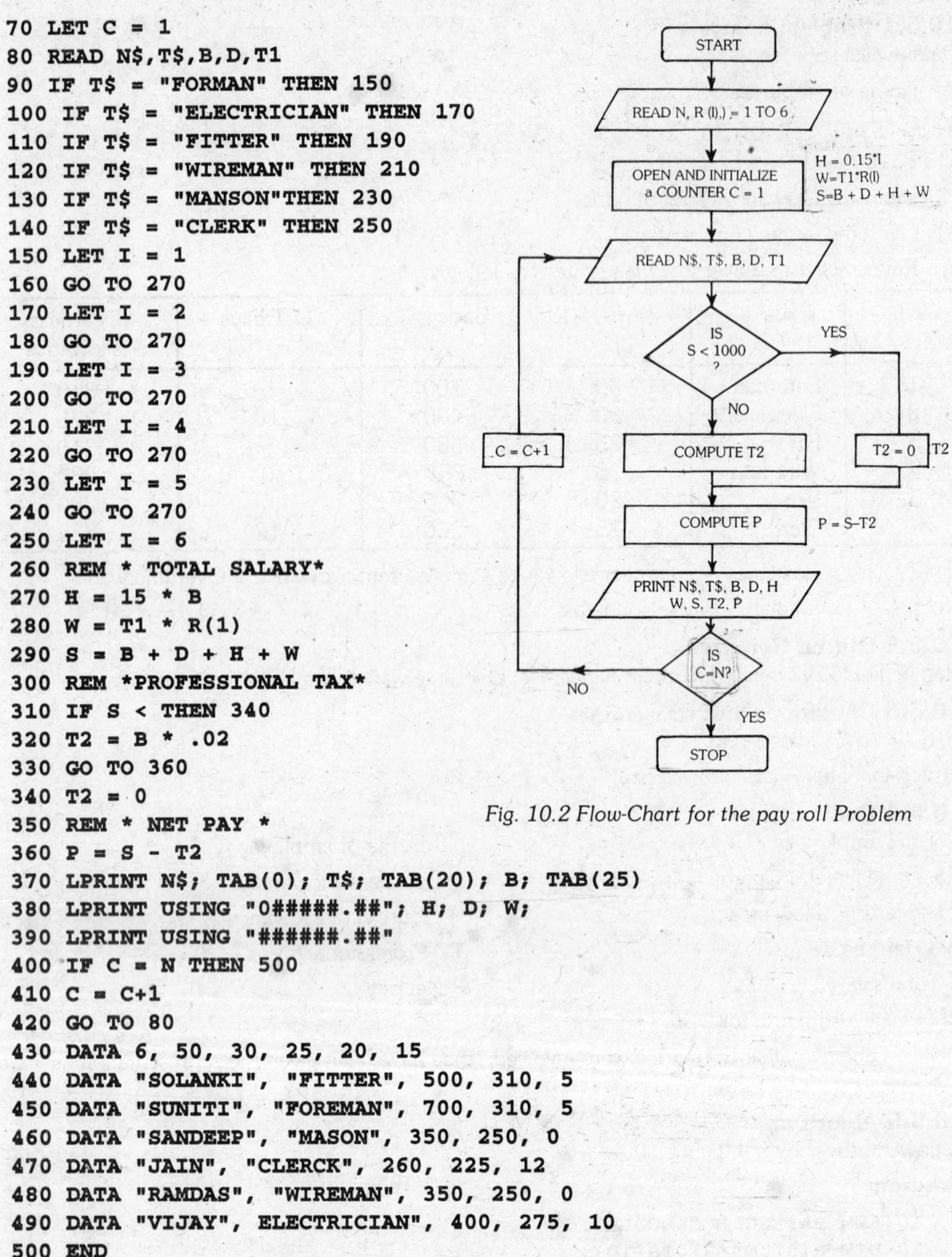

Fig. 10.2 Flow-Chart for the pay roll Problem

Problem 10.6 Evaluating an Exponential Series

A series consists of a number of terms,each term having a constant relationship to the next term.When devising computer programs for evaluating series,a procedure needs to be designed which allows the next term in the series to be calculated from the previous term.

For example,the exponential series may be evaluated as follows:

$$e^* = 1 + x + \frac{x^2}{2!} + \frac{x^3}{2!} + \ldots\ldots$$

where $2! = 1.2$

$3! = 1.2.3$

The steps in the repetitive process to calculate $\mathbf{e^x}$ to **n** terms are:

Step 1. Initialization ,set first term (T) to *x*, e^x to $1 + T$, and $I = 2$

Step 2. Calculate next term by multiplying previous term by x/I,and add this new term to the old value of $\mathbf{e^x}$.

Step 3. Repeat step 2a further $n-2$ times.

The BASIC routine to calculate e^x is shown below.

```
20 PRINT "NO OF TERMS FOR E^X ";
30 INPUT N
40 PRINT "VALUE OF X";
50 INPUT X
60 LET T = X
70 LET E = 1 + T
80 FOR I = 2 TO N
90 LET T = T * X / I
100 LET E = E + T
110 NEXT I
115 PRINT
120 PRINT "E^" ; X; " = "; E
125 PRINT "*****************"
130 END
```

Problem 10.7 Evaluation of Cos X

Write a BASIC program for evaluating cos x,given that:

$$\cos x = 1 - \frac{x^2}{2!} + \frac{x^4}{4!} - \frac{x^6}{6!} + \text{----}$$

The program is listed below.The value of **Cos 30** to 5 terms is calculated as 0.866025.

```
20 PRINT "NUMBER OF TERMS FOR COS X";
30 INPUT N
40 PRINT "VALUE OF X (DEGREES)";
50 INPUT X1
60 LET X = (X1*ATN(1)*4/180)^2
70 LET T = 1
80 LET C = 1
90 FOR I = 2 TO N*2 STEP 2
100 LET T = (-1)*T*X/((I-1)*I)
105 LET C = C+T
```

```
110 NEXT I
115 PRINT
120 PRINT "COS";X1;"=";C
125 PRINT "*****************"
130 END
```

Problem 10.7.1 Mortgage Calculations

The repayments required on a mortgage can be calculated from the following formula:

$$R = \frac{P_1(1+1)^n}{(1+1)^{n-1}}$$

where,

P = Principal (the amount borrowed)

n = Duration of mortgage

i = Interest rate per annum

R = Required annual repayment

Many organizations providing mortgages allow you to repay monthly.The monthly repayments are usually 1/12 of the annual repayments because they are regarded as simply advance payments of the annual premium.These monthly advance payments do not earn interest for themselves.

10.7.2 Requirements of the Program

In examining alternative mortage proposals you would want to change `P,n` and/or `i` as required.As successive changes were made, it would be useful to be reminded as to current values of these three variables.

This program is the type likely to be used by someone such as a broker in a working environment. As she or he is not likely to have any programming knowledge, the PRINT messages need be clear and the data is entered in the most natural way.Thus the variables to be revised are indicated by entering `I,P` or `N` rather than entering a numeric alternative such as 1,2 or 3.Although the program is slightly more complex as a result,this is regarded as a secondary consideration.

The input to the program is straightforward;the interest rate is entered as a percentage (i.e.12.5 not 125) as this is how it is commonly quoted.

10.7.3 Description of the Program

A listing of the program is given below with an example of the output.

```
30 DEF FNM(X) INT(X/.01 + .5)*.01
40 PRINT "ENTER INTEREST RATE IN % " ;
50 INPUT I
60 LET I = I / 100
70 PRINT "ENTER AMOUNT OF THE MORTGAGE " ;
80 INPUT P
90 PRINT "ENTER PERIOD OF LOAN (YRS) " ;
100 INPUT N
120 LET R = ( P * I * (1 + I) ^N) / ((( 1 + I) ^N) -1)
130 PRINT "MONTHLY REPAYMENTS " ; FNM ( R / 12)
140 PRINT
160 PRINT "ENTER I,P OR N TO REVISE"
165 PRINT "INTEREST,PRINCIPAL OR YEARS"
170 PRINT "EXISTING VALUES ARE"
```

```
180 PRINT "OR ENTER S TO STOP"
190 INPUT A$
200 IF A$ = "S" THEN 350
210 PRINT "ENTER REVISED VALUE";
220 INPUT X
230 IF A$ = "I" THEN 290
240 IF A$ = "P" THEN 310
250 IF A$ = "N" THEN 330
260 PRINT "REVISION ERROR:   " ; A$ ;"ENTERED"
270 PRINT
280 GOTO 160
290 LET I = X / 100
300 GOTO 120
310 LET P = X
320 GOTO 120
330 LET N = X
340 GOTO 120
350 END
```

Line 30 defines the function **FNM** which rounds to two decimal places thereby representing monetary amounts to the nearest paisa.Lines 40-100 request the starting values of **I,P** and **N**.The annual repayment is calculated in line 120 and printed as a monthly repayment in line 130.A blank line (line 140) is printed before looping and producing revised output.

Line 160 allows you to revise optionally the values of **I,P** or **N** and line 170 reminds you of the current values.The option you enter is identified by the program over lines 200-250.If an inappropriate character is entered, this character 'falls through' these lines and the error message (line 260) is printed.Otherwise the revised value entered in line 220 is assigned accordingly over lines 290 to 330.The program then loops back to line 120 to recalculate **R**.

```
ENTER INTEREST RATE AS A % ? 12.5
ENTER SIZE OF MORTAGE ? 10000
ENTER PERIOD OF LOAN (YRS) ? 25
MONTHLY REPAYMENTS = 109.95
ENTER I,P OR N TO REVISE INTEREST,PRINCIPAL OR YEARS
EXISTING VALUES ARE
.125            10000            25
OR ENTER S TO STOP
? P
ENTER REVISED VALUE ? 8000
MONTHLY REPAYMENTS = 87.[illegible]5
ENTER I,P OR N TO REVISE INTEREST,PRINCIPAL OR YEARS
EXISTING VALUES ARE
.125            8000             25
OR ENTER S TO STOP
? S
```

Example 10.8 Sun - Sign Evaluator

This program uses **VAL** statement about which we shall learn in the following unit 10.However this is very interesting program to indicate how one can create artificial intelligence in areas of interest other than mathematics by simple programming.

```
10 PRINT "TYPE YOUR NAME"
20 INPUT NME$
30 PRINT "PLEASE TYPE YOUR DATE OF BIRTH (e.g.24.03.93)"
40 INPUT BDAY$
50 D=VAL (LEFT$ (BDAY$,2))
60 M=VAL (MID$ (BDAY$,4,2))
70 IF M=1 THEN S=D
80 IF M=2 THEN S=D+31
90 IF M=3 THEN S=D+59
100 IF M=4 THEN S=D+90
110 IF M=5 THEN S=D+120
120 IF M=6 THEN S=D+151
130 IF M=7 THEN S=D+181
140 IF M=8 THEN S=D+212
150 IF M=9 THEN S=D+243
160 IF M=10 THEN S=D+273
170 IF M=11 THEN S=D+304
180 IF M=12 THEN S=D+334
190 IF S >=357 OR S<<=20 THEN S$="CAPRICORN" :GOTO 310<M=>
200 IF S <=50 THEN S$="AQUARIOUS":GOTO 310
210 IF S <=79 THEN S$="PISCES":GOTO 310
220 IF S <=110 THEN S$="ARIES":GOTO 310
230 IF S <=140 THEN S$="TAURUS":GOTO 310
240 IF S <=171 THEN S$="GEMINI":GOTO 310
250 IF S <=201 THEN S$="CANCER":GOTO 310
260 IF S <=232 THEN S$="LEO":GOTO 310
270 IF S <=265 THEN S$="VIRGO": GOTO 310
280 IF S <=295 THEN S$=LIBRA":GOTO 310
290 IF S <=326 THEN S$=SCORPIO": GOTO 310
300 IF S <=356 THEN S$="SAGITTARIUS"
310 CLS
320 PRINT "NAME = ";NME$
330 PRINT "DATE OF BIRTH = ";BDAY$
340 PRINT "YOUR SUNSIGN IS = ";S$
```

When the above program is run, following may be displayed.

```
RUN
NAME = V.K.JAIN
DATE OF BIRTH = 24.03.44
YOUR SUNSIGN IS = ARIES
```

CHAPTER 11

Arrays

11.1 Array

Array is defined as a collection of related data items. A single variable name is used to refer to the entire collection of items. BASIC permits us to deal with many related data items as a group by means of structure known as an array. The type of variable described in earlier chapters represented a single location in computer memory. For example, a variable **X** might represent the storage location of a numeric value, such as **786**. An array, by contrast, is used to store a series of values in adjacent storage locations. When two or more related data items need be entered, instead of giving each one a separate variable name, the programmer can give one variable name to the entire collection of data items. This capability is important when large quantities of data are needed in a program.

An array can be used to store integer, real, or string values, but the values in a given array must be of the same type, that is, if an array is given a numeric variable name, a string data item cannot be entered to it; only numeric values are allowed.

Single dimensional arrays are known as lists, two dimensional arrays as tables, and multidimensional arrays as matrix. BASIC only allows list and tables.

(a) Elements

Each individual data item within an array is called an element. An array consists of a group of consecutive storage locations, each containing a single value. The entire array is given one name; the programmer indicates an individual element in the array by referring to its position. For example, suppose that there are five test scores to be stored: 15,3,31,85,100. The scores could be put in an array called **TESTS**, which we might visualize like this:

Array Tests

15	03	31	85	100

(b) Subscripts

The array name **TESTS** now refers to all five storage locations containing the test scores. To gain access to a single test score within the array, a subscript is used. A subscript is a value enclosed in parentheses which identifies the position of a given element in the array. For example, the first element of array **TESTS** (containing the value 15) is referred to as **TESTS (1)**. The second test score is in **TEST (2)**, the third test score is in **TEST (3)**, and so on. Therefore, the following statements are true:

```
TESTS (1) = 15
TESTS (2) = 03
TESTS (3) = 31
TESTS (4) = 85
TESTS (5) = 100
```

The subscript enclosed in parentheses does not have to be an integer constant; it can be any legal numeric expression. When an array element subscript is an expression,the computer carries out the following steps:

- It evaluates the expression within the parentheses.
- It converts the result to an integer value, by truncation.
- It accesses the indicated element in the array.

(c) Subscripted Variable

Variables that refer to specific elements of arrays, such as **TEST (4)**, are called subscripted variables. A subscripted variable refers to one value in the array. It is possible to access a different value in the array by changing the subscript.

Example 11.1 A(I), A(2) or I = 2. —A(I) is subscripted variable.

The same rule that applies to naming simple variables also applies to naming arrays. It is possible to use the same name for both a simple variable and an array in a program, but this is not good programming practice because it makes the logic of the program difficult to follow.

11.2 The DIM Statement

When a program contains an array, the computer automatically sets aside eleven storage locations (0 through 10) for the elements in the array. The programmer does not have to fill all the reserved array storage spaces with values: it is illegal, however, to refer to an array element for which space has not been reserved. For example, if only eleven storage spaces have been set aside, twelve data items cannot be entered to the array.

The **DIM** (dimension) statement enables the programmer to override this standard array space reservation and to reserve space for an array of any desired size. A **DIM** statement is not required for an array of eleven or fewer elements, but it is good programming practice to specify **DIM** statements for all arrays to help document the array usage.

The general format of the **DIM** Statement is as follows:

```
DIM variable 1 (limit 1) [, variable 2   (limit 2),....]
```

The variables are the names of the arrays. Each limit is an integer constant that supplies the maximum subscript value possible for that particular array. For example, if space is needed to store **25** elements in an array **LIST$**, the following statement reserves the necessary storage locations:

```
10 DIM LIST$(24)
```

Although it may seem that this statement sets aside only **24** positions, remember that the array positions **0** though **24** are equal to **25** locations. For the sake of clarity and program logic, programmers often ignore the zero element. If we choose not to use the zero position, we dimension the array **LIST$** as follows:

```
10 DIM LIST$(25)
```

As indicated in the statement format, more than one array can be declared in a single **DIM** statement. For example, the following statement declares the variables **ITEM, BOOK** and **ACC$** as arrays:

```
10 ITEM(500), BOOK(25), ACC$(49)
```

ITEM can contain up to **51** elements, **BOOK** up to **26** elements, and **ACC$** up to **50** elements.

DIM statements must appear in a program before the first reference to the arrays they describe. A good practice is to place them at the beginning of the program. The following standard preparation symbol is generally used to flowchart the **DIM** statement:

Note: One variable can already have 10 subscripts (elements) even without a **DIM** Statement.

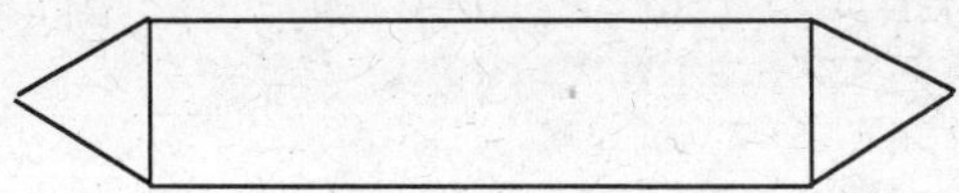

Fig. 11.1 The Preparation Symbol

11.3 One-Dimensional Arrays

All the arrays we have discussed so far in this chapter have been one dimensional arrays, that is, arrays with a single row of elements. One-dimensional arrays can be thought of as list of values. The following is a one-dimensional arrays named X:

25	35	23	18	07

11.4 Reading Data to an Array

A major advantage of using array is its ability to use a variable rather than a constant as a subscript. Because a single name such as **LIST(I)** can refer to any element in the array **LIST**, depending on the value of I, this name can be used in loop that varies the value of the subscript I. A **FOR/NEXT** loop can be an efficient method of reading data to an array if the exact number of items to be read is known in advance. The following program segment reads a list of five numbers into the array **LIST**:

```
10 FOR I = 1 TO 5
20 READ LIST(I)
30 NEXT I
40 DATA 81, 75, 60, 59, 99
```

The first time this loop is executed, the loop variable I equals 1. Therefore, when line 20 is executed, the computer reads the first number from the data list (which is 81) and stores it in **LIST(I)**. The second time through the loop,I equals 2.The second number is read to **LIST(2)**, the second location in the array.The loop processing continues until all five numbers have been read and stored.

An array also can be filled using an **INPUT** statement or an assignment statement within a loop. To initialize an array of ten elements to zero, for example, the following statements could be used:

```
50 FOR I = 1 TO 10
60 MARKS(I) = 0
70 NEXT I
```

It is possible to read data to several arrays within a single loop. In the following segment, each data line contains data for one element of each of three arrays:**NME$** for **NAME,ADD$** for address and **PIN** code.

Notice here that we have used first two arrays with string variable as array names,as they are to contain two strings as the element.Also note that we have used **NME$** as name for the array instead of **NAME$** because **NAME** is a reserved word and as such cannot be used in any other place in the statement.Alternatively we could have used **NAM$**.

Example 11.2 Making address list.

```
10 DIM NME$(5), ADD$(5), PIN(5)
20 FOR I = 1 TO 5
30 READ NME$(I), ADD$(I), PIN(I)
35 PRINT NME$(I),ADD$(I),PIN(I)
40 NEXT I
50 DATA "VIJAY", "MINTO ROAD", 110002
60 DATA "AJAY", "TAGORE ROAD", 110002
70 DATA "SANJAY","ASAF ALI ROAD", 110006
80 DATA "DHANAJAY", "MOTI BAGH", 110055
90 DATA "DIGVIJAY', "RK PURAM", 110056
99 END
```

When the exact number of items to be read to an array is unknown, a loop with a trailer value can be used. This method is demonstrated in the following segment, where the data contains a trailer value of -1. The programmer must ensure that the number of items read does not exceed the size of the array.

```
10 DIM X (5)
20 I = 1
30 INPUT X (I)
40 WHILE X (I) <> -1                    ( -1 is the trailer value )
50 I = I + 1
60 INPUT X (I)
70 WEND
99 END
```

When above program is run following may be the type of response:

```
RUN
?  4
?  5
?  -1
Ok
```

The above progarm has been terminated by computer due to the fact that the user is entering the trailer value,which is -1 due to statement in line 40.

11.5 Displaying the Contents of an Array.

The **FOR/NEXT** loop can be used to print the contents of the array **LISTS**, as shown in the following segment.

```
70 FOR I = 1 TO 5
80 PRINT LISTS (I);
90 NEXT I
RUN
81  75  60  59  99
```

As the loop control variable **I** varies from **1** to **5**, so does the value of the array subscript, and the computer prints elements 1 through 5 of the array **LISTS**.

The **DIM** statement can appear anywhere in a program, as long as it precedes the first reference to the array. As shown by the following example, the placement of a **DIM** statement after the reference to array will result in a "subscript out of range" message. Note that moving the **DIM** statement to a location before the reference to the array eliminates this error condition.

```
80 FOR I = 1 TO 40
90 X (I) = 0
```

```
95 NEXT I
100 DIM X (40)
110 END
Ok
RUN
Subscript out of range in 90
Ok
LIST
```

Corrected Program

```
70 DIM X (40)
80 FOR I = 1 TO 40
90 X (I) = 0
95 NEXT I
Ok
RUN
Ok
```

The **DIM** statement is non executable and, if you branch to that statement in a program, execution will resume at the next executable statement following the **DIM** statement. Several examples of the use of this statement are as following:

Example 11.3 Making a bill.

```
10 X = 0
20 PRINT "ITEM", "PRICE", "QUANTITY'
30 DIM ITEM$(3), PRICE(3), QNTY(3)
40 FOR I = 0 TO 3
50 READ ITEM$(I), PRICE(I), QNTY(I)
60 X = X + PRICE(I) * QNTY(I)
70 PRINT ITEM$(I), PRICE(I), QNTY(I)
80 NEXT I
90 DATA "LUX SOAP",4.40,200
91 DATA "DALDA 1 KG",36.50,5
92 DATA "OIL REFINED",46.00,5
93 DATA "BINACA",15.00,5
95 PRINT "TOTAL BILL = Rs"; X
RUN
ITEM           PRICE          QUANTITY
LUX SOAP        4.4            200
DALDA 1 KG      36.5           5
REFINED OIL     46             5
BINACA          15             5
TOTAL BILL =   Rs 1367.5
```

In the second example, one of the several methods of inputting data (i.e. **READ/DATA**) that can be used to **INPUT** string values to arrays is used. Here, a **READ** statement contained within a **FOR/NEXT** loop assigned the appropriate values to each element of the arrays **ITEM$, PRICE,** and **QNTY**. You could also use the assignment statement by **LET** command or use individual elements through an **INPUT** statements interactively. Note that after the counter that stores the value of each item (price times quantity) is incremented in line 60, the **PRINT** statement in line 70 is used to print data from the arrays.

This shows you that printing data from arrays is parallel to the mechanism used for filling arrays. You can print individual elements by using a **PRINT** statement or you can use that statement within a **FOR/NEXT** loop to print all or a portion of the elements within an array. This concept will be illustrated by several examples where you will initialize each element of an array to a value and then print out individual elements and selected portions of elements on the display.

Example 11.4 Typing squares of natural numbers.

```
10 DIM Q(10)
20 FOR I = 1 TO 10
30 Q (I) = I * I
50 NEXT I
70 FOR I = 6 TO 10
90 PRINT "SQUARE OF";I; " IS ";Q(I)
100 NEXT I
RUN
SQUARE OF     6 IS     36
SQUARE OF     7 IS     49
SQUARE OF     8 IS     64
SQUARE OF     9 IS     81
SQUARE OF     10 IS    100
Ok
```

Here the computer has remembered the matrix **Q(10)** by first reading in the data as **1,2,3,4** etc. by virtue of **FOR/NEXT** statement and then printed the squares of 6th to 10th element due to line **70** to **90**.

To obtain an understanding of some of the potential problems that can occur in array processing, several program segments that are designed to be non-operable will be created and executed.

(a) Inproper Dimensioning of the Array

Enter this program and see what happens

```
50   DIM X (15)
60   Z = 7
70   FOR I = Z TO Z + 10
80   X (I) = I
85   PRINT X (I) ;
90   NEXT I
Ok
RUN
7  8  9  10  11  12  13  14  15
Subscript out of range in 80
Ok
```

The computer has given this error message because the **FOR** statement needs 16th element, which does not exist in the array **X(I)** that is dimensioned to have only 15 elements.

When using variables to define the elements of arrays you wish to operate on, you should be careful to ensure that variables are used correctly. In the previous example, "the subscript out of range" error has occurred due to wrong selection of the value of constant **Z** as **10**.

Since numeric array elements are stored as single precision variables,each element will occupy four memory locations. The following example illustrates how easy it is to run out of memory from the dimensioning of just a few large arrays.This program uses **FRE** function to indicate the amount of free memory available with **BASIC** program.In this function **FRE** argument can be anything like **X** and is treated as a dummy variable value.

Example 11.5 Memory requirement.

```
5 PRINT FRE(X)
10 DIM A(2,2,2,2)                      (total (2+1)^4 =81 elements)
15 PRINT  FRE(X) 20 DIM B(5,5)         ( 6 x 6 = 36 elements )
25 PRINT FRE(X)
30 DIMX(49,49)                         (50x50=2500 elements)
35 PRINT FRE(X)
40 DIMQ(19,19,19)
45 PRINT FRE(X)
50DIM R(9,9,9,9)                       (10x10x10x10=1000 elements)
```

When above program is run, following is printed.

```
RUN
61826
61487
61332
51321
19308
Out of memory in 50
Ok
```

As indicated, arrays can rapidly reduce the amount of memory available for program computations. If you require the use of several large arrays in a program, you may wish to use the ERASE statement to eliminate from the program those arrays you have completed your operations on.

Example 11.6 Entering a series of numbers and finding their average.

```
10 DIM A(10)
20 S =0
30 FOR I = 1 TO 10
40 READ A(I)
50 SUM = SUM + A(I)
60 NEXT I
70 PRINT SUM/10
80 DATA 4.5, 3.75, 8.91, 6.23, 2.97
90 DATA 5.28, 135, 3.27, 5.33, 6.95
99 END
```

It prints the result as:

```
RUN
18.219
```

11.6 Deleting an Array: The ERASE statement

ERASE deletes an array from memory.

Format: `ERASE array name (,array name ....)`

Array is the array or list of arrays to be ERASE. For example:

```
ERASE D$
```

erases **D$** and all its array elements from memory.Similarly :

```
Erase A,B,C$
```

erases arrays **A,B** and **C$**.

Once an array is **ERASE**, it is as if that array never existed, and a new array with the same name can be created. For example:

```
10 DIM A (5)
20 ERASE A
30 DIM A (20)
```

Line 10 dimensions array **A** to have **5** elements. Line 20 ERASEs array **A**. Then line **30** creates a new array A with **20** elements. An array cannot usually be redimensioned in a running program unless it is first **ERASE**.

11.6.1 Re-dimensioning an Array

Suppose you had an array of 1001 elements in your program but it requires to store only the data contained in elements 0 through 200. If you wish to make available additional space for your program, you could first dimension a new array of 201 elements, transfer the values of the elements from the old array to the new and smaller array, and then erase the original array.

A program segment that illustrates this concept is listed below. Note that you merely have to list the array name in the **ERASE** statement.

```
10 DIM X(1000)                    (old array with 1001 elements)
.
.
100   DIM  Y (200)                (new array with 201 elements)
110 FOR I = 0 TO 200
120 Y(I) = X(I)                   (transfering elements from old to new)
130 NEXT I
140 ERASE X
.
.
```

Another use of the **ERASE** statement is in a program that used **INPUT** statements to enter data into one or more elements of arrays. Also, at the end of the program, it provides the operator with the option of requesting another program cycle, here, instead of constructing one or more loops to zero the array elements, you could **ERASE** the arrays and then branch back to the beginning of the program where your DIM statement could be located.

This concept is illustrated by the following program segment.

```
10 DIM X(30) , Y(40) , Y(40), Z(800)
.
.
.
150 PRINT "ANOTHER (C)YCLE OR (E)XIT"
160 A$ = INKEY$ : IF A$ = "E" THEN 199
165 IF A$ <>"C" THEN 150
170 ERASE X, Y, Z
170 GOTO 10
199 END
```

When above is run, the following message is exhibited:

```
RUN
ANOTHER (C)YCLE OR (E)XIT
```

Now if you type C then the same message is repeated,

```
ANOTHER (C)YCLE OR (E)XIT
```

If you type E then program is terminated displaying the prompt Ok.

11.7 OPTION BASE Statement

An OPTION BASE statement is provided so that PC BASIC can become compatible with other versions of BASIC that use a minimum value of 1 for array subscripts. The format of this statement is shown below.

Format: `OPTION BASE` *`value`*

Here, the default base is 0 and can be specified as such by the statement, or we can use the **OPTION BASE** statement to change the minimum value of array subscripts to 1. This statement must precede any **DIM** or array reference statement within a program. Since you may have a natural tendency to operate with subscript elements starting at 1, using the **OPTION BASE**, statement accordingly could eliminate storage allocation for array elements you do not intend to use in your program.

```
10 OPTION BASE
20 DIM X (30), Y (30), Z (30)
```

Thus, the preceding example would result in 12 storage locations being freed, since each element requires four memory locations. Without the **OPTION BASE** statement, one extra element requiring four memory locations of storage would have been reserved for each array.

11.8 Copying an Array in Reverse Order

Let us have a program to copy an array **A** comprising **N** elements into an array **B**, of the same size as **A**, in reverse order. For example, if **N** is **20**, **A(20)** will go into **B(1)**, **A (19)** into **B(2)**, etc. We shall assume that **N** is always a multiple of 5, and output array B in rows of 5 columns (positions 7,13,19, 25 and 31).

Example 11.7 Reversing the order of an array.

```
10 REM * REVERSING THE ORDER OF ARRAY *
20 INPUT N
30 DIM A (20), B (20)
40 FOR I = 1 TO N
50 READ A (I)
55 PRINT A(I)
60 NEXT I
65 PRINT
70 FOR I = 1 TO N STEP 5
80 LET K = 1
90 FOR J = I TO I + 4
100 LET B (J) = A(N + 1 - J)
110 PRINT B(J) ;
120 LET K = K + 1
130 NEXT J
140 PRINT
150 NEXT I
160  DATA  11,  12, 13, 14, 15, 16, 17, 18, 19, 20, 21, 22, 23, 24, 25,
```

```
26, 27, 28, 29, 30
    RUN
    ? 30
    30   29   28   27   26
    25   24   23   22   21
    20   19   18   17   16
    15   14   13   12   11
    Ok
```

First the given list is printed and then the re-ordered list is put in a matrix of 5 x 4 size. Now if you want only first 10 items to be re-ordered, type 10 and see.

```
RUN
? 10
11 12 13 14 15 16 17 18 19 20
20 19 18 17 16
15 14 13 12 11
Ok
```

11.9 Two-Dimensional Arrays (Tables)

All the arrays shown so far in this unit have been one-dimensional arrays; that is, arrays that store values in the form of a single list. A two-dimensional array, by contrast has both rows and columns, and are commonly known as tables also. The number of row is expressed by subscript **I** and column by **J** although not necessarily, but Array name is written as **X (I,J)** when the first subscript, which in this case is **I**, always indicates the number of rows and second subscript the number of columns in the array.

Assume that **I** = **4** and **J** = **3**, and that the array **X** contains the following (4 x 12) elements:

ARRAY X (I , J)

10	12	14
16	18	20
22	24	26
28	30	32

The following examples, based on this same array, show how the various forms of subscripts are used:

Example	Refers to
X(4,J)	**X(4,3)** - The element in the fourth row, third column of **X**, which is **32**.
X(J,I-2)	**X(3,2)** - The element in the third row, second column of **X**, which is **24**.
X(3,J)	**X(3,3)** - The element in third row, third column of **X**, which is **26**.

As with one-dimensional arrays, the computer automatically reserves space for a two-dimensional array. By default, it reserves room for 11 rows and 11 columns, so the space for a two -dimensional array is 11 x 11 = 121 elements. As mentioned earlier, the 0 subscripted element often is ignored.

The **DIM** statement must be used to set the dimensions of a two-dimensional array. The general format of such a **DIM** statement is as follows:

```
DIM variable 1 (limit, limit2) (,variable 2 (limit3,limit4),...)
```

where the variable is the array name and the limits are the highest possible values of the subscripts for each dimension. For example, the following statements reserves space for the two-dimensional character array **TABLE**, with up to 7 rows and 3 columns, for a total of 8 x 4 = 32 elements.

```
50 DIM TABLE (7,3)
```

11.10 Reading and Displaying Two-Dimensional Arrays

The loop control variable of the FOR statement is used as the array subscript in the single dimension arrays. as in the following example:

```
20 DIM X (10)
30 FOR I = 1 TO 10
40 READ X (I)
50 NEXT I
```

FOR/NEXT loops also can be used to read data to, and print information from a two-dimensional array. It may be helpful to think of a two-dimensional array as a group of one-dimensional arrays, with each row making up a single one-dimensional array. A single **FOR/NEXT** loop can read values to one row. This process must be repeated for as many rows as the array contains; therefore, the **FOR/NEXT** loop that reads a single row is nested within a second **FOR/NEXT** loop that controls the number of rows being accessed.

The arrays **X** of the previous example can be filled from the sales data table one row at a time, moving from left to right across the columns. The following segment shows the nested **FOR/NEXT** loops that do this:

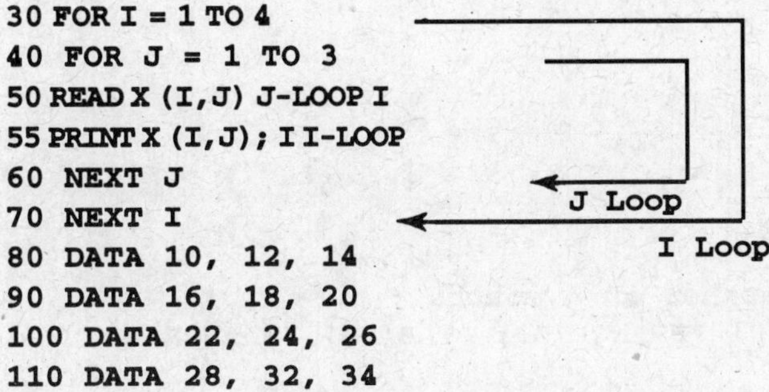

Each time line **50** is executed, one value is read to a single element of the array; the element is determined by the current values of **I** and **J**. The outer loop (loop **I**) controls the rows, and the inner loop **J** controls the columns. The **READ** statement is executed **I x J = 4 x 3 = 12** times, which is the number of elements in the array.

Each time the outer loop is executed once, the inner loop is executed three times, while **I = 1, J** becomes **1,2,** and finally **3** as the inner loop is executed. Therefore, on the first pass through the outer loop, line **50** reads values to **X(1,1), X(1,2)**, and **X (1,3)**, and the first row is filled:

J	=	**1**	**2**	**3**
X(I)	=	**10**	**12**	**14**
where **I**	=	**1**		

While I equals 2, J again varies from 1 to 3, and line 50 reads values to X (2,1), X (2,2), and X (2,3) to fill the second row:

J	=	**1**	**2**	**3**
X(I)	=	**10**	**12**	**14**
		16	**18**	**20**
where **I**	=	**2**		

After this **I** is incremented to **3** and then **4**, and the third and fourth rows are filled in the same manner.

To print the contents of the entire array, the programmer can substitute a **PRINT** statement for the **READ** statement in the nested **FOR/NEXT** loop. The following segment prints the contents of the array **X (I,J)**, one row at a time:

```
40 BLANK = 10
50 FOR I = 1 TO 10
60 FOR J = 1 TO 3
70 PRINT TAB(BLANK * J) ; X(I,J);
80 NEXT J
90 PRINT
100 NEXT I
```

The semicolon at the end of line 70 tells the computer to print the three values on the same line. After the inner loop is executed, the blank PRINT statement in line 90 causes a carriage return, so that the next row is printed on the next line. The following program shows how the tabular data of the sales results can be read to a two-dimensional array and printed in table form with appropriate headings.

Example 10.8: Making sales report using **ARRAYS** for **4** months in **3** different branches.

```
10  REM * * * T-SHIRT SALES REPORT * * *
20  DIM SALES (4,3)
30  REM
40  REM * * * READ THE DATA * * *
50  FOR I = 1 TO 4
60  FOR J = 1 TO 3
70  READ SALES (I,J)
80  NEXT J
90  NEXT I
100 REM
110 REM * * * Sales of 3 branches in 4 months * * *
120 PRINT  "MONTH #";  TAB(10) "BRANCH 1";  TAB(20) "BRANCH 2
    ";TAB(30)
    "BRANCH 3"
130 BLANK = 10
140 FOR I = 1 TO 4
150 PRINT I;
160 FOR J = 1 TO 3
170 PRINT TAB(BLANK * J ) ; SALES (I,J);
180 NEXT J
190 PRINT
195 NEXT I
200 PRINT
210 REM
220 REM * * * DATA STATEMENTS * * *
230 DATA 17,3,18,15,4,6,4,6,17,5,8,11
999 END
RUN
MONTH #  BRANCH 1     BRANCH 2     BRANCH 3
1   17    3     18
2   15    4     6
3   46          17
4   58          11
```

(a) Adding Rows of the Sales Report

Once data has been stored in an array, often it is necessary to manipulate certain array elements. For instance, the sales manager in charge of the promotional sale might want to know how much is the sale of each branch in 4 months.

Because the data for each month is contained in a row of the array, it is necessary to total the elements in one row of the array (the fourth row) to find the total sale done in the fourth month. The fourth row can be thought of as a one-dimensional array, so one loop is required to access all the elements in this row:

```
30 DAY4SALES = 0
40 FOR J = 1 TO 3
50 DAY4SALES = DAY4SALES + ITEM (4,J)
60 NEXT J
```

Notice that the first subscript of **ITEM (4,J)** restricts the computations to the element in row 4, whereas the column J, varies from 1 to 3.

(b) Adding Columns of the Report

To find the total number of **ITEM** sold by the third branch, for example, it is necessary to total the elements in the third column of the array. This time we can think of the column by itself as a one-dimensional array of four elements:

```
40 SALES3SHOP = 0
50 FOR I = 1 TO 4
60 SALE3SHOP = SALE3SHOP + ITEM (I,3)
70 NEXT I
```

In line 60, the second subscript (3) restricts the computations to the elements in the third column. The row, I, varies from 1 to 4.

(c) Totalling a Two-Dimensional Array

Consider the problem of finding the grand total of sales done during the entire four-month sale. The program must access all the elements of the array one a time and add them to the grand total. Remember that the nested **FOR/NEXT** loops were used to print or read values to a two-dimensional array. This same method can be used to total the elements of an array, by substituting an addition operation for the **READ** or **PRINT** statement:

```
50 TSHIRT =
60 FOR I = 1 TO 4
70 FOR J = 1 TO 3
80 TSHIRT = TSHIRT + ITEM (I,J)
90 NEXT J
100 NEXT I
```

This segment adds the elements in a row by row sequence. The same operation also can be performed in a column by column sequence:

```
50 TSHIRT = 0
60 FOR J = 1 TO 3
70 FOR I = 1 TO 4
80 TSHIRT = TSHIRT + ITEM (J, I)
90 NEXT I
100 NEXT J
```

The following program sums up individual columns and rows and prints the given array and the sum of the columns and rows both.

Example 11.9: Handling 2-D array: summing of rows and columns.

```
10  REM * PROGRAM TO SUM ROWS AND COLUMNS OF A 2-D ARRAY
20  REM
30  READ M,N
40  REM
50  REM READ ELEMENTS OF TABLE
70  FOR I = 1 TO M
80  FOR J=1 TO N
90  READ T(I,J)
100 NEXT J
110 NEXT I
130 REM PRINT TABLE
150 PRINT "GIVEN TABLE:"
160 PRINT
170 FOR I=1 TO M
180 FOR J=1 TO N
190 PRINT T(I,J);
200 NEXT J
210 PRINT
220 NEXT I
230 PRINT
250 REM SUM ACROSS EACH ROW
270 PRINT "SUM OF COLUMNS IN EACH ROW:"
280 PRINT
290 S1=0
300 FOR I=1 TO M
310 S(I)=0
320 FOR J=1 TO N
330 S(I)=S(I)+T(I,J)
340 NEXT J
350 PRINT "ROW ";I, "SUM = ";S(I)
360 S1= S1+S(I)
370 NEXT I
380 PRINT
390 PRINT "SUM OF ROW SUMS = ";S1
400 PRINT
420 REM SUM-DOWN EACH COLUMN
440 PRINT "SUM OF ROWS IN EACH COLUMN:"
450 PRINT
460 S1 = 0
470 FOR J=1 TO N
480 LET S(J) =0
490 FOR I=1 TO M
500 S(J) = S(J) + T(I,J)
510 NEXT I
```

```
520 PRINT "COLUMN"; J, "SUM = "; S(J)
530 LET S1=S1+S(J)
540 NEXT J
560 PRINT "SUM OF COLUMN SUMS = ";S1
580 DATA  5,6,5,6,0,-23,4,17,21,-8,15,5,5,-18,0,11,3,1,-  17,12,7,
590 DATA 13,2,13,-9,24,4,-27,-30,0,14,8,-10
600 END
```

When above program is run following is displayed.

```
RUN
GIVEN TABLE
5  6  0  -23  4  17
21  -8  15  5  5 -18
0  11  3  1  -17  12
7  0  13  2  13  -9
24  4  -27  -30  0  14
SUM OF COLUMNS IN EACH ROW:
ROW  1          SUM      =   9
ROW  2          SUM      =   20
ROW  3          SUM      =   10
ROW  4          SUM      =   26
ROW  5          SUM      = -15
SUM OF ROW SUMS          =   50
SUM OF ROWS IN EACH COLUMN:
COLUMN 1        SUM      =   57
COLUMN 2        SUM      =   13
COLUMN 3        SUM      =   4
COLUMN 4        SUM      = -45
COLUMN 5        SUM      =   5
COLUMN 6        SUM      =   16
SUM OF COLUMN SUMS       =  50
```

Example 11.10: Summing of diagonal elements.
Sum the elements on the diagonals of an **M** × **M** array. Allow for **M** to be odd (as well as even) when the central element must be added in only once. Test your program in one run with an odd and an even value for **M**. Output the array and the sum of the elements on the diagonals in each case.The program is listed below.

```
10 REM * SUM OF ELEMENTS PLACED IN DIAGONALS OF AN ARRAY *
20 DIM A (5,5)
30 INPUT M
40 IF M = 0 THEN 260
50 LET D = 0
60 FOR I = 1 TO M
70 FOR J = 1 TO M
80 READ A (I,J)
90 PRINT A (I,J) ;
100 NEXT J
110 PRINT
120 LET D = D + A (I,I) + A (I, M + 1 - I)
```

```
130 NEXT I
140 PRINT
150 IF M/2 = INT(M/2) THEN 180
160 LET N = INT(M/2) + 1
170 LET D = D - A(N,N)
180 PRINT "SUM OF ELEMENTS OF DIAGONALS = "; D
190 PRINT
200 PRINT
210 RESTORE
220 GOTO 30
230 DATA 10, 11, 12, 13, 14, 15, 16, 17, 18, 19
240 DATA 20, 21, 22, 23, 24, 25, 26, 27, 28, 29
250 DATA 30,31,32,33,34
260 END
```

11.11 Transposing the Arrays:

Occasionally, it is useful to transpose the rows and columns of an array.Transposition of elements of a two dimensional array can be done by converting rows into columns or columns into rows. For example, if **A** is

1	2
4	6
5	8

3 Rows and 2 columns Array (3,2)

the transpose of A is

1	4	5
2	6	8

2 Rows and 3 columns Array (2,3)

If the original array is **X (I,J)**,its transpose will be written as **X (J,I)**. Remember that here once again the first subscript **J** represents the number of rows.

11.12 Transposing the Matrix by Nested FOR/NEXT Loops

A **FOR/NEXT** loop may lie wholly within another **FOR/NEXT** loop, this facility is particularly useful for transposing arrays. For example, data is to be input into a two-dimensional array called A and output in the form of an array having columns converted into rows and vice versa.

Example 11.11: Transposing the elements of a two-dimensional array.

```
10 REM * TRASPOSING AN ARRAY *
20 DIM A(3,4)
30 PRINT "DATA ENTERED IN ARRAY IS: ";
40 FOR I = 1 TO 3
50 FOR J = 1 TO 4
60 READ A(I ,J)
70 PRINT A(I,J);
80 NEXT J
90 NEXT I
100 PRINT
```

```
110 PRINT
120 PRINT "THE DATA IS ARRANGED LIKE THIS DUE TO LINE 130 TO 180"
130 FOR I=1 TO 3
140 FOR J=1 TO 4
150 PRINT A(I,J);
160 NEXT J
170 PRINT
180 NEXT I
190 PRINT "TRASPOSED ARRAY IS ARRANGED LIKE THIS DUE TO LINES 200 TO 250"
200 FOR I = 1 TO 4
210 FOR J = 1 TO 3
220 PRINT A(J,I) ;
230 NEXT J
240 PRINT
250 NEXT I
260 DATA 1,2,3,4,5,6,7,8,9,10,11,12
```

The above program when run, will read an array of dimensions 3 x 4 and print the list of elements of old array. Then it transposes the array into a matrix of 4 x 3 dimensions and prints it in tabular (matrix) form.

```
RUN
1    2    3    4    5    6    7    8    9    10    11    12
THE DATA IS ARRANGED LIKE THIS DUE TO LINE 130 TO 180
1  2  3  4
5  6  7  8
9  10  11  12
TRASPOSED ARRAY IS ARRANGED LIKE THIS DUE TO LINES 200 TO 250
1    5    9
2    6    10
3    7    11
4    8    12
Ok
```

11.13 Sorting Arrays

Sorting data, that is, arranging it in some prescribed order, is one of the most common requirement of programming tasks.In case of an array containing numbers, the prescribed order would be either ascending (from smallest to largest) or descending (from largest to smallest); and for strings it would usually be alphabetical.In the sections to follow, we will discuss two popular sorting techniques: the Bubble Sort and Shell Sort.

11.14 Sorting Arrays-the Bubble Sort

Many Programming applications require data items stored in arrays to be sorted of ordered in some way. For example, name must be alphabetized, serial numbers must be arranged from lowest to highest, statisticals details must be arranged by a numeric value, and so on. There are various methods the programmer can use to sort data items. First we will examine only the bubble sort, as it is the easiest to understand.

The basic idea behind the bubble sort is to arrange the element of an array in ascending or descending order by making a series of comparisons of the adjacent values in the array. If two adjacent values are out of sequence, they are exchanged.

When arranging in array in ascending order, the bubble sort "bubbles" the smallest value to the top of the array. The values of two adjacent array elements are compared, and the elements are exchanged if the value of the first is larger than that of the second. Then the next pair of adjacent elements is compared and exchanged if necessary.

This sequence of comparisons (called a pass) is then repeated, starting from the beginning of the array. After each complete pass through the array, the element moved to the end of the array need not be included in the comparisons of the next pass, because it is now in its proper position. Successive passes are performed until no element requires switching over, indicating that the entire array is sorted.

As an illustration of this bubbling procedure, an array consisting of five integers is sorted into ascending order in Fig. 11.3. step by step.

75,	35,	48,	55,	12,	05,	63,	42
35,	48,	55,	12,	05,	63,	42,	75
35,	48,	12,	05,	55,	63,	42,	75
35,	12,	05,	48,	55,	63,	42,	75
12,	05,	35,	48,	55,	63,	42,	75
05,	12,	35,	48,	55,	42,	63,	75
05,	12,	35,	48,	42,	55,	63,	75
05,	12,	35,	42,	48,	55,	63,	75

Fig 11.2 : Bubble Sorting step by step

Notice that, after each pass is completed, the largest of the numbers compared in that pass becomes that last of those numbers. After the first pass through the array, some of the numbers are close to their proper positions, but the array is not yet completely ordered.In the second pass the largest value, 75 has been positioned successfully at the bottom of the array and therefore is not included in the comparisons in the following passes.

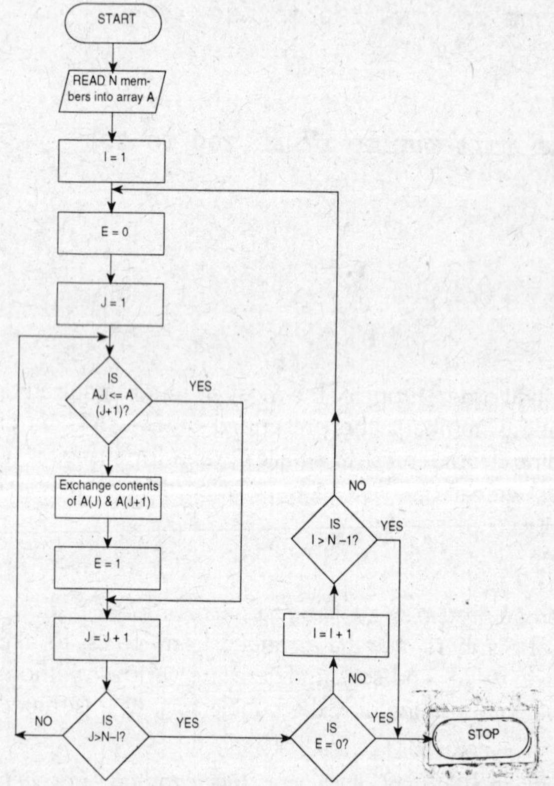

Fig. 11.3 Sorting a list of number into Ascending order

Example 11.12: Sorting an array by bubble sort method.

Following example sorts a list of N numbers, held in array A, into ascending numerical order. Choose the size of array which is just enough to hold the maximum number of numbers that may be input. The logic of the method is shown in Figure 11.1. This involves pushing the highest number to the end of the list by exchanging the higher number of each pair working through the list. That is, if element A(1) is greater than element A(2) then their contents are exchanged so that the higher value is in A(2); then the value in A(2) is compared with that in A(3) and exchanged if necessary.

The second pass through the list is shorter since at the end of the first pass A(N) contained the highest value in the list and does not need be compared again. If no exchange takes place during a pass (i.e. E = 0) then the list is the required sorted order and no further passes are necessary.

Output the list of numbers in its original order and after each pass of the sort so that you can see how this sorting method works. Use the following data, and create your own data, to provide a variety of different lists to be sorted.

```
10 REM * SORTING AN ARRAY *
20 INPUT N
30 DIM A(14)
40 FOR I = 1 TO N
50 READ A(I)
60 PRINT A(I) ;
70 NEXT I
80 PRINT
90 FOR I =1 TO N -1
100 E = 0
110 FOR J = 1 TO N-1
120 IF A(J) < = A(J +1) THEN 170
130 LET S = A(J)
140 A(J) = A(J+1) I                                    exchanging the values
150 A(J+1) = S
160 E = 1
170 NEXT J
180 IF E = 0 THEN 260
200 FOR K = 1 TO N
210 PRINT A(K);
220 NEXT K
230 PRINT
240 NEXT I
250 DATA -15, 45, 78,-97,45 ,59,37,1,-12, 0,99,-1,37,-0
260 END
RUN
?14
-15  45  78 -97  45  59  37   1 -12   0  99  -1  37   0
-15  45 -97  45  59  37   1 -12   0  78  -1  37   0  99
-15 -97  45  45  37   1 -12   0  59  -1  37   0  78  99
-97 -15  45  37   1 -12   0  45  -1  37   0  59  78  99
-97 -15  37   1 -12   0  45  -1  37   0  45  59  78  99
-97 -15   1 -12   0  37  -1  37   0  45  45  59  78  99
-97 -15 -12   0   1  -1  37   0  37  45  45  59  78  99
-97 -15 -12   0  -1   1   0  37  37  45  45  59  78  99
-97 -15 -12  -1   0   0   1  37  37  45  45  59  78  99
Ok
```

Example 11.13: Sorting a list of numbers in descending order by selection sort in which first element is compared with rest. After 1st pass, the smallest comes in top barying trust, second is compared with rush and so on.

Following example prints the given and sort both arrays.

```
10  REM * SORTING A LIST OF NUMBERS IN DESCENDING ORDER *
20 DIM K(25)
30 READ N
40 FOR I =1 TO N
50 READ K(I)
60 NEXT I
70 PRINT "GIVEN LIST OF NUMBERS"
90 FOR I= N TO 1 STEP -1
100 PRINT K(I);
110 NEXT I
120 PRINT
130 FOR I=1 TO N-1
140 FOR J=I+1 TO N
150 IF K(J)>=K(I) THEN 190
160 LET K1=K(I)
170 LET K(I)=K(J)
180 LET K(J)=K1
190 NEXT J
200 NEXT I
210 PRINT
220 PRINT "SORTED LIST OF NUMBERS"
240 FOR I=N TO 1 STEP -1
250 PRINT K(I);
260 NEXT I
270 DATA 21,23, 10, 15, 47, 68, 50, 45, 34, 23, 44, 304, 39, 501,389, 20
280 DATA 301, 399, 477, 720, 34 , 35, 36, 24, 25
290 END
```

When the above program is run, following will be displayed.

```
RUN
GIVEN LIST OF NUMBERS
23  10  15  47  68  50  45  34  23  44  304  39  501  389  20  301  399  477
720 34 35
SORTED LIST OF NUMBERS
720  501  477  399  389  304  301  68  50  47  45  44  39  35  34  34
23 23 20 15 10
```

Example 11.14: Alphabetical sorting of strings.
The program for a bubble sort is shown below. This program sorts the names of famous filmstars in ascending alphabetical order. The subroutine called at line **110** reads the names into an array **NAM$** and prints them. The subroutine starting at line **240** performs the bubble sort.

```
5 REM * ALPHABETICAL SORTING *
10 READ K
20 DIM N$(1000)
30 FOR I = 1 TO K
40 READ N$(I)
50 NEXT I
60 FOR I = 1 TO K - 1
70 FOR J = 1 TO K - I
```

```
80 LET A$ = N$(J)
90 LET B$ = N$(J + 1)
100 IF A$ < = B$ THEN 200
110 LET N$(J) = B$
120 LET N$(J + 1) = A$
200 NEXT J
210 NEXT I
220 FOR I = 1 TO K
230 PRINT N$(I),
240 NEXT I
300 DATA 20
400 DATA ZEBA, SARIKA, MADHURI, REKHA
410 DATA SADHNA, WAHIDA, JAYA, AMITA
420 DATA BABITA, DIMPLE, KIMI, SRIDEVI
430 DATA VYAJANTI, MALA, NUTAN, NILAM
440 DATA JUHI, SABANA, POOJA, ANITA
```

When the above program is run, following will be displayed.

```
RUN
AMITA    ANITA    BABITA    DIMPLE   JAYA
JUHI     KIMI     MADHURI   MALA     NILAM
NUTAN    POOJA    REKHA     SABANA   SADHNA
SARIKA   SRIDEVI  VYAJANTI  WAHIDA   ZEBA
```

11.15 Some Advantages of Using Arrays

1. Arrays can reduce the number of variable names needed in a program. We can use an array, rather than a number of simple variables, to store related data (as demonstrated in our previous examples).
2. Arrays can make for more efficient programs. Once data are entered into an array, they can be processed many times without having to be input again.

EXERCISE

PART 1

A1. State whether true or false ?

1. A subscript can consist of any legal numeric or character expression. True or false?
2. If an array is dimensioned as follows, it must contain 20 elements. True or false?
3. One array can be used to store more than one type of variable (string, real, and integer). True or false?
4. The Bubble sort is always slower than the Shell sort.
5. The Bubble sort cannot be used to sort a list of names.
6. Arrays of string data and arrays of numeric data can be declared in the same DIM statement.
7. One-and two-dimensional arrays can be declared in the DIM statement.
8. All elements of an array must be of either string type or numeric type.
9. The Bubble sort cannot be used to arrange numeric data in descending order.

B1 Fill in the blanks with appropriate words.

1. The .... statements provide an efficient method for manipulating arrays.
2. ...... are used with variables to identify a particular storage location within an array.

3. A(n) ...... array contains only one column.
4. A (n) ....stores values as a table consisting of rows and columns.
5. The first subscript of a two-dimensional array refers to the .... of the elements, and the second subscript refers to the ....
6. A(n) ...... consists of examining the elements of an array until the desired value of values are found.

EXERCISE
PART-II

1. Identify the errors, if any,in the program segments shown below.Make the necessary corrections.

(a)
```
10 DIM A(5)
20 FOR I=1 TO 10
30 READ A(I)
40 DATA 2, 4, 6, 8, 10, 12, 14,
16, 18, 20
50 NEXT I
...............
99 END
```

(b)
```
10 DIM B (10)
20 FOR K=1 TO 10
30 READ K(B)
40 DATA 2, 4, 6, 8, 10, 12, 14,
16, 18, 20
50 NEXT K
...............
99 END
```

(c)
```
10 DIM 45
20 FOR J=1 TO 45
30 READ A(J)
40 DATA -,-,-,.........(45 data
items)
50 NEXT J
...............
99 END
```

(d)
```
10 DIM R(15)
20 PRINT
30 FOR S=1 TO 5
40 PRINT "VALUE FOR R(S)";
50 INPUT R(S)
60 NEXT S
...............
99 END
```

(e) In this program segment,the data items are to be stored as follows:

Array A	3	6	9	12	15
Array B	9	18	27	36	45

```
10 DIM A(5),B(5)
20 FOR K=1 TO 5
30 READ A(K),B(K)
40 DATA 3, 6, 9, 12, 15, 9, 18,
27, 36, 45
50 NEXT K
.............
99 END
```

(f) In the program segment shown below,the data items are to be stored as follows:

Array C	2	4	6	8	10
Array D	12	14	16	18	20

```
10 DIM C(5),D(5)
20 FOR I=1 TO 5
30 READ C(I)
40 NEXT I
50 FOR J=1 TO 5
60 READ D(J)
70 NEXT J
80 DATA 2, 4, 6, 8, 10, 12, 14,
16, 18, 20
.............
999 END
```

2. What will be stored in each variable of the array(s) after executionof each of the following program segments?Show the name of the variable and its content.For example,if there are two arrays,you could show the contents in the following manner.

Array A		Array B	
A(1)	1	B(1)	10
A(2)	2	B(2)	20
A(3)	3	B(3)	30

(a)
```
10 DIM A(5)
20 FOR I=1 TO 5
30 READ A(I)
40 DATA 11,22,33,44,55
50 NEXT I
.............
99 END
```

(b)
```
10 DIM M(3),N(3)
20 FOR I=1 TO 3
30 READ M(I),N(I)
40 DATA 11,22,33,44,55,66
50 NEXT I
.............
99 END
```

(c)
```
10 DIM M(2),N(2)
20 FOR I=1 TO 2
30 READ M(I),N(I),C
40 DATA 11,33,55,22,44,66
50 NEXT I
.............
99 END
```

3. Is there anything wrong with each of the following programs? If there is no error,show the output;if there is an error,state what is wrong and make the necessary corrections.

(a)
```
10 DIM A(4)
20 PRINT
30 FOR I=1 TO 4
40 READ A(I)
50 DATA 5,10,15,20
60 PRINT A
70 NEXT I
99 END
```

(b)
```
10 DIM A(3),B(3),C(3)
20 PRINT
30 FOR I=1 TO 3
40 READ A(I),B(I),C(I)
50 DATA 1, 10, 100, 2, 20, 200,
3, 30, 300
60 PRINT A(I),B(I),C(I)
70 NEXT I
99 END
```

(c)
```
10 DIM A(3),B(4)
20 PRINT
30 FOR I=1 TO 4
40 READ A(I),B(I)
50 DATA 1,15,2,46,3,23,58
60 PRINT A(I),B(I)
70 NEXT I
99 END
```

4. Identify the errors,if any,in the program segments shown below.Make the necessary corrections.

(1)
```
10 DIM A(4,5)
20 FOR I=1 TO 5
30 FOR J=1 TO 4
40 READ A(I,J)
50 DATA -,-,-,.............
                 (20 items of data)
.............
100 NEXT J
110 NEXT I
999 END
```

(2)
```
10 DIM B(3,3)
20 FOR J=1 TO 3
30 FOR I=1 TO 3
40 READ B(J,I)
50 DATA -,-,-,........
                 (9 items of data)
.............
100 NEXT I
110 NEXT J
999 END
```

(3)
```
10 DIM C(3,2),D(3,2)
20 FOR J=1 TO 2
30 FOR I=1 TO 3
40 READ C(I,J),D(I,J)
50 DATA -,-,-,......
                 (6 items of data)
.............
100 NEXT I
110 NEXT J
999 END
```

(4)
```
10 DIM M(4),N(3,4)
20 FOR I=1 TO 3
```

```
30 FOR J=1 TO 4
40 READ M(I,J),N(I,J)
50 DATA -,-,-,.........
                    (24 items of data)
.............
100 NEXT J
110 NEXT I
999 END
```

(5)
```
10 DIM P(7,8),R(8,7)
20 FOR J=1 TO 7
30 FOR I=1 TO 7
40 READ P(I,J),R(I,J)
50 DATA -,-,-,.......
                    (98 items of data)
.............
100 NEXT I
110 NEXT J
999 END
```

(6) In the following program segment,the data items are to be stored in their respective arrays by rows.

```
A B
1 2 3 1 4 9
4 5 6 16 25 36
7 8 9 49 64 81
10 DIM A(3,3),B(3,3)
20 FOR I=1 TO 3
30 FOR J=1 TO 3
40 READ A(I,J),B(I,J)
50 DATA 1,2,3,4,5,6,7,8,9
60 DATA 1,4,9,16,25,36,49,64,81
-
100 NEXT J
110 NEXT I
999 END
```

5. Answer the following questions for each program shown below.

(1) How is the data read,by rows or by columns?

(2) What will be stored in the array(s) after execution of each program?You may show the contents in matrix form. For example,if there are two 2X3 arrays,you may display the contents in the following manner.

```
A B
1 2 3 10 20 30
4 5 6 40 50 60
```

(a)
```
10 DIM A(3,4)
20 FOR I=1 TO 3
30 FOR J=1 TO 4
40 READ A(I,J)
50 DATA 10,12,14,16,18,20
60 DATA 22,24,26,28,30,32
70 NEXT J
80 NEXT I
99 END
```

(b)
```
10 DIM M(2,3),N(2,3)
20 FOR I=1 TO 2
30 FOR J=1 TO 3
40 READ M(I,J)
50 NEXT J
60 NEXT I
70 FOR K=1 TO 2
90 READ N(K,L)
100 NEXT L
110 NEXT K
120 DATA 10,20,30,40,50,60
130 DATA 15,25,35,45,55,65
999 END
```

(c)
```
10 DIM M(2,3),N(2,3)
20 FOR I=1 TO 2
30 FOR J=1 TO 3
40 READ M(I,J),N(I,J)
50 DATA 10,20,30,40,50,60
60 DATA 15,,25,35,45,55,65
70 NEXT J
80 NEXT I
99 END
```

(d)
```
10 DIM M(2,3),N(2,3)
20 FOR J=1 TO 3
30 FOR I=1 TO 2
40 READ M(I,J),N(I,J)
50 DATA 10,20,30,40,50,60
60 DATA 15,25,35,45,55,65
70 NEXT I
80 NEXT J
99 END
```

(e) Notice that the data statements are the same in programs (c) and (d).Is there any change in the order of the data items in arrays **M** and **N** after execution of program (d) in comparision to the way the items were stored in program(c)? If the order has changed,state the reason.

6. The following questions ask for specific elements to be printed.Assume that the data has already been entered in a **4**X**4** array named A.

```
A
1 2 3 4
5 6 7 8
9 8 7 6
5 4 3 2
```

   (a) Write a **PRINT** statement that prints the last element of the array (fourth row,fourth column).

   (b) Write a **PRINT** statement that prints the first and last elements of the array widely spaced.

   (c) Write a program segment that prints the elements in the second row of the array closely spaced.(Hint:Use a **FOR/NEXT** loop for the columns and 2 as the subscript for the row.)

   (d) Write a program segment that prints the elements in the second column of the array one item per line. (Hint:Use a **FOR/NEXT** loop for the rows and 2 as the subscript for the column.)

   (e) Write a program segment that prints the elements in the principal diagonal of the array on one line closely spaced. The diagonal is shown below.

```
A
1 2 3 4
5 6 7 8
9 8 7 6
5 4 3 2
```

Notice that the diagonal falls on those elements whose row numbers and column numbers are the same-that is,where **I=J**.Thus, if **I=J**,the element is to be printed.Use nested **FOR/NEXT** loops that perform by rows.

```
RUN
1 6 7 2
```

7. What values are held in positions J(2) and J(5) in array J?

ARRAY J

125	135	230	890	355

8. Write a loop that adds the corresponding elements of arrays A and B, each containing ten elements, and stores the result in array C.

9. Write a **PRINT** statement that displays the value 899 from array J in Question 7.

10. What is the difference between a one-dimensional array and a two-dimensional array?

11. Given the statement 10 DIM (20,10),

    How many elements could this array contain?

12. In a sequential search of the following list, how many values will be examined before 236 is located?

```
12 44 103 177 236 586 978 1235
```

13. What is indicated when a Bubble sort makes an entire pass without making an exchange?

14. What is displayed when each of the following segments of code is executed?

(a)
```
10 DIM A (12)
20 LET A (2) = 10
30 FOR K = 1 TO 5
40 LET A (2*K+2) = K
50 PRINT A (2*K);
60 NEXT K
```

(b)
```
5 DIM N$ (5)
15 FOR J = 1 TO 5
25 READ N$ (J)
35 NEXT J
45 FOR J = 1 TO 5 STEP 2
55 PRINT N$ (J) ;
65 NEXT J
75 DATA P, R, R, D, N
```

15. Correct the syntax errors in the following statements:

(a) `200 DIMENSION D (6)`

(b) `200 DIM, GRADE $ (N +1)`

(c) `150 OPTION BASE 2`

16. Following code is supposed to find the average of the numbers read. It contains number of errors. Find and correct them.

```
200 DIM A (10)
```

```
210 LET SUM = 0
220 FOR K = 1 TO 10
230 READ XD (K)
240 LET SUM = SUM + X(K)
250 NEXT K
260 LET AVG = SUM / K
```

17. Write a program segment that will input 20 numbers and print them in reverse order.

18. State several reasons why arrays are important in programming.

19. How many storage locations are allocated by the statement

    150 DIM A(5,4)

    (a) the smallest subscript is **0**.

    (b) the smallest subscript is **1**.

20. A two-dimensional array **DOG** has two rows and four columns.

    ```
    5 10 15 20
    25 30 35 40
    ```

    (a) What are the values of **SUM (1,2)** and **SUM (23)**?

    (b) Which elements of **SUM** contain the numbers **15** and **25**?

21. What is displayed when the following segment of code is executed?

    ```
    200 DIM A (2,3)
    210 FOR I = 1 TO 2
    220 FOR J = 2 TO 3
    230 LET A (I,J) = 5 + J
    240 NEXT J
    250 NEXT I
    255 PRINT A (1,2); A(1,3); A(2,3)
    ```

22. Correct the syntax errors in the following statements.

    (a) `150 DIM A(12; 10)`

    (b) `250 LET B(X,Y) = "TOP"`

23. How many times is the prompt in the following code displayed?

    ```
    30 FOR I = 1 to 5
    31 FOR J = 1 TO 12
    32 PRINT "ENTER RAINFALL IN STATE";
    1; "IN MONTH"; J
    33 INPUT RAIN (I,J)
    34 NEXT J
    35 NEXT I
    ```

24. Write a segment of code that determines the smallest and largest elements of a two-dimensional array X (already input) with four rows and five columns.

ANSWERS
PART-I

A1. 1. F 2. F 3. F 4. F 5. F 6. T 7. T 8. T 9. F.

B1. 1. DIM
2. Subscript
3. One dimensional .
4. Two dimensional array.
5. Row, column.
6. Sequential search

ANSWERS
PART II

1. (a) There are not enough storage locations reserved for array A.Either increase the dimension of A to 10 or change the test value in the **FOR** statement to 5.In the second alternative,the data statement may remain unchanged since,on most computer systems,excess data is ignored.

```
10 DIM A(10)
```

or

—

```
20 FOR I=1 TO 5
```

(b) In line 30,the index and the name of the array are interchanged. The index should be the subscript of the array name.

```
30 READ B(K)
```

(c) The DIM statement must include the name of the array. Also,the number 45 must be enclosed within the parenthesis and must follow the name of the array.

```
10 DIM A(45)
```

(d) Nothing is wrong.

(e) The data items in the DATA statement are not listed in their proper order.Since they are being read as pairs,the first item of each pair must be assigned to an element of array A,the second item of each pair must be assigned to an element of array B.

```
30 READ A(K),B(K)
40     DATA 3, 9, 6, 18, 9, 27,
12, 36, 15, 45
```

```
array A B A B ............ A B
```

(f) Nothing is wrong.

2 (a) Array A

A(1) 11

A(2) 22

A(3) 33

A(4) 44

A(5) 55

(b) Array M Array N

M(1) 11 N(1) 22

M(2) 33 N(2) 44

M(3) 55 N(3) 66

(c) Array M Array N Variable C

M(1) 11 N(1) 33 C(55) (replaced by 66)

M(2) 22 N(2) 44 C (66)

Notice that the value 55,entered in the simple variable C,is lost,since it is replaced by the number 66.The other values are retained as each is stored in its own subscripted variable.

3. (a) In line **60**,the variable **A** in the **PRINT** statement must be a subscripted variable.

```
60 PRINT A(I)
```

(b) Nothing is wrong.

```
RUN
1  10  100
2  20  200
3  30  300
```

(c) There is insufficient data for the array **A**.Since the test value in the **FOR** statement is **4** and the data pattern for **A** is **1,2,3**, it appears that **A** should have one more value and that this value should be 4.This means that the **DIM** statement and the **DATA** statement should be changed.

```
10 DIM A(4),B(4)
50 DATA 1,15,2,46,3,23,4,58
```

4. (1) There is an insufficient number of storage locations reserved for the rows.Depending on the program,this may be corrected in one of two ways.

(a) Exchange the subscripts of the subscripted variable **A** in the **DIM** statement.

```
10 DIM A(5,4)
```

(b) Interchange the test values in the two FOR statements.

```
10 DIM A(4,5)
20 FOR I=1 TO 4
30 FOR J=1 TO 5
```

(2) Nothing is wrong.Notice that the subscripts of **B** are **B(J,I)**. In this case, **J** represents the number of the row,since **J** is the first subscript and the first subscript always indicates the number of the row. **I** represents the number of the column.The data is read in by rows because **J** (the row subscript) is the index of the outer loop.

(3) The program runs out of the data.There should be twelve items of data six values for array **C** and six values for array **D**.

50 data -,-,-,.......... (12 items of data)

(4) In the **DIM** statement,the array M must have storage locations reserved for the rows as well as for the columns. Because the row(I) loop has a test value of 3,the number of reserved locations for the rows must be at least 3.

```
10 DIM M(3,4),N(3,4)
```

(5) Nothing

(6) Since the **READ** statement lists two arrays (**A** and **B**) and since array **A** is coded before array **B**,the **DATA** statement must list the data items in pairs,so that the first member of each pair is sptored in array **A**,and the second member is stored in array **B**.

```
40 READ A(I,J),B(I,J)
50 DATA 1,1,2,4,3,9
60 DATA 4,16,5,25,6,36
70 DATA 7,49,8,64,9,81
```

5. (a) 1. The data items are read in by rows because the index of the outer loop is the first subscript of array **A**.The first subscript of a doubly subscripted variable represents the number of the row.

2. **A**

```
10   12   14   16
18   20   22   24
26   28   30   32
```

(b) 1. The data items are read in by rows.

2. **M N**

```
10 20 30 15 25 35
40 50 60 45 55 65
```

(c) 1. The data items are read in by rows.

2. **M N**

```
10 30 50 20 40 60
15 35 55 25 45 65
```

(d) 1. The data items are read in by columns since the index of the outer loop is the second subscript of arrays **M** and **N**.The second subscript of a doubly subscripted variable represents the number of the column.

2. **M N**

```
10 50 35 20 60 45
30 15 55 40 25 65
```

(e) The order of the data items in arrays **M** and **N** is changed after execution of program (d).This is because program (c) reads the data by rows, while program (d) reads the data by columns.

6. (a) **60 PRINT A(4,4)**

(b) `70 PRINT A(1,1),A(4,4)`

(c)
```
-
30 PRINT
40 FOR J=1 TO 4
50 PRINT A(2,J);
60 NEXT J
-
999 END
```

(d)
```
-
30 PRINT
40 FOR I=1 TO 4
50 PRINT A(I,2)
60 NEXT I
-
999 END
```

(e)
```
-
30 PRINT
40 FOR I=1 TO 4
50 FOR J=1 TO 4
60 IF I=J THEN 80
70 GO TO 90
80 PRINT A(I,J);
90 NEXT J
100 NEXT I
-
999 END
```

7. 135 and 355

8. **FOR I = 1 TO 10 C (I) = A (I) + B (I) NEXT**

9. **PRINT J (4)**

10. A one-dimensional array consists of only 1 row, whereas a two dimensional array consists of both rows and columns

11. 21 x 11 + 1 = 231

12. 5

13. 3

14. (a) 10 1 2 3 4

    (b) **PRN**

15. (a) **200 DIM D(6) (The command is DIM and not DIMENSION)**

    (b) **200 DIM GRADE$ (N + 1)** (No comma is needed)

    (c) **150 OPTION BASE 0 OR 150 OPTION BASE 1** (2 is not a valid argument for **OPTION** statement)

16. (1) **DATA** statement is not there containing **10** data elements.

    (2) Since in line the programmer has declared the dimensions of array by name A,therefore line **230** and **240** should contain array name as A only.

    (3) Line **260** should read

    260 LET AVG = SUM / 10

17.
```
200 DIM A (20)
210 REM
220 FOR K = 1 TO 20
230 INPUT A (K)
240 NEXT K
250 REM
260 FOR K = 20 TO 1 STEP -1
270 PRINT A (K);
280 NEXT K
```

18. Arrays can (in some situations) reduce the number of variables names needed, increase the efficiency of programs, and make for more general programs.

19. (a) 30 (6 x 5) (An array of size 5 x 4 will have 0 to 5 = 6 rows and 0 to 4 = 5 columns.)

    (b) 20 (5 x 4)

20. (a) **SUM (1,2) = 10, SUM (2,3) = 35**

    (b) **SUM (1,3) = 15, SUM (2,1) = 25**

21. 3 4 5

22. (a) **150 DIM A(12,10)** (comma to be used instead of semicolon.)

    (b) **250 LET B$ (X,Y) = "TOP"**

(Since we have a string on right hand side the array should also be string array.)

23. 60

24.
```
300 LET SMALL = X(1,1)
310 LET LARGE = X(1,1)
320 REM
330 FOR I = 1 TO 4
340 FOR J = 1 TO 5
350 IF X (I , J) < SMALL THAN LET
    SMALL = X (I , J)
360 IF X (I , J) > LARGE THAN LET
    LARGE = X (I , J),
370 NEXT J
380 NEXT I
```

Library and User Defined Functions

12.1 Functions and Their Types

Functions are the routines (i.e. a set of self-independent program lines which are designed for handling a task which may be needed a number of times in day to day computation. In most programs there are routines, often fairly standardized,that are self-contained or self-dependent in some way. These routines are quite often used more than once with in a program. It can be two types, built in or user defined. The build in can be accersed from the standard library of so called library functions. Library functions are the routines in the compiler of a programming language that form an integral part of language.

BASICA contains over 50 library functions in the areas of numeric functions,string functions,string-related function and I/O and miscellaneous functions. While some of the more commonly employed functions have already been covered, such as the **TAB** and **SPC** functions.

12.2 Argument of a Function:

User defined Functions have to be declared using the word **DEF**; they are normally placed at the end of the program well out of the way; and they are used to perform routines which may be needed more than once within a program.

Each of these functions, unless noted otherwise, is accessed by stating its name followed by whatever information must be supplied to the function, enclosing the information supplied in parentheses. The numeric quantity or string value passed to the function for use by its prewritten routine is known as its argument. Once you access the function and specify an argument, the desired operation will be conducted automatically.

Each function name is followed by the argument (an expression which may be either a number, numeric variable or arithmetic equation in brackets). The function operates on the argument, that is, the value of the expression is used in the standard routine represented by the function name. For example ,the SQR is a library function (available in BASIC) in following statement

```
100 LET S = SQR (B * B - 4 * A * C )
```

will evaluate the square root of the expression in brackets, i.e. $B^2 - 4AC$, and put the result in cell S.Here this expression inside the brackets is an argument of the function **SQR**. Which onturn is one value.

There may be restrictions regarding the values of the argument associated with a function. For example,

(i) it is not possible to take the square root of a negative number, therefore the argument used with SQR must not have a negative value.

(ii) Similarly the TAB function followed by a semicolon causes characters to be output in the column following the argument value; therefore, this value must correspond to a possible column position. A comma in place of the semicolon will have a different effect.

Library functions are used in a **LET** or **PRINT** statements of their own or in expressions of any complexity. These expressions may contain further library functions. The evaluation is, as usual, working from the innermost brackets outwards.

12.3 Mathematical (or numeric) functions:

Commonly used routines, such as those required for obtaining the integer part of a number (INT), the logarithm and antilogarithm of a number (LOG and EXP), and trigonometric functions (e.g. SIN) are available in BASIC. These are known as mathematical or numeric functions. The functions contained in the built-in library vary according to the implementation of a particular BASIC system.

All the BASIC mathematical functions and their operations are listed in Table 12.1.

Table 12.1 Numeric functions

Function	Operational Result
ABS	Returns the absolute value
CDBL	Converts the expression to a double-precision number
CINT	Converts the expression to an integer by rounding
CSNG	Converts the expression to an single-precision number
INT	Returns the largest integer that is less than or equal to value in the argument expression
FIX	Truncates the specified expression to an integer
SGN	Returns + 1 if expression is positive,-1 if negative, and 0 if its value is zero
EXP	Returns the base of the natural logarithm (e) raised to the specified power
LOG	Returns the natural logarithm of the specified number
RND	Returns a random number between ø & I
SQR	Returns the square root
SIN	Returns the sine of an angle expressed in radians
COS	Returns the cosine of a angle expressed in radians
TAN	Returns the tangent of an angle expressed in radians
ATN	Returns the arctangent in radians

Note: All the functions which end with $ is their name retrieve nonnumeric results and can be used as string variables.

Now let's see how easy it is to use functions. Suppose you want the square root of 2,4,6, 8 and 12. The arguments to be passed to the **SQR** functions are 2, 4, 6, 8, and 12. You can use a **FOR-NEXT** loop to control the passing of the arguments as follows.

Example 12.1 SQR Function

```
10 PRINT "NUMBER", "SQUARE ROOT"
20 FOR I = 2 TO 10 STEP 2
30 PRINT I , SQR (I)
40 NEXT I
RUN
NUMBER              SQUARE ROOT
  2                   1.414214
  4                   2
  6                   2.44949
  8                   2.828427
  10                  3.162278
```

If you require the square root of a variable within a program, your program statement might be:

```
100 X = SQR(Y)
```

Here, the variable X is set equal to the square root of the variable Y.

12.4 The ABS function

The ABS function returns the absolute value of a numeric expression. That is, the absolute value of a number is its value with its sign discarded; hence, the ABS function will first evaluate an expression and then discard its sign. The following example shows the use of this function.

```
5 LET X = 40
6 LET Y = -50
10 PRINT Y
20 PRINT ABS(Y)
30 PRINT (X+Y)
40 PRINT ABS(X+Y)
RUN
-50
 50
-10
 10
```

ABS is valuable when a positive value must always be the result of a math operation. **ABS** may act on a single element or a complex arithmetic operation.

12.5 DIV Function

This function gives the number of times that one number divides completely into another. If the numbers are not integers, they are converted to integers before the division.

Examples: Type

```
PRINT 17 DIV 6
```

This will print 2.

```
PRINT 20 DIV 2.9
```

This will print 12.

12.6 MOD Function

This function gives the remainder when one number is divided by another. If the numbers are not integers, they are converted to integers before the division.

Examples : Type

```
PRINT 17 MOD 6
```

This will print 5.

```
PRINT 19.3 MOD 4.3
```

will print 3, because 19 ÷ 4 = 4 remainder 3.But

```
PRINT 19.3 MOD 4.7
```

will print answer as 4,since 4.7 will get rounded off to 5.

12.7 The INT function

The INTeger function is used to round numbers down to their INTeger (whole number) value.

INT rounds numbers down to the next smallest value.Therefore, positive whole numbers remain the same regardless of their decimal value, and negative whole numbers are rounded down to the next smaller value. For example:

```
PRINT INT(-4.65)
```

displays -5, not -4.

Example 12.4

```
10 READ X
20 PRINT "INT FUNCTION CONVERTS ";X;"INTO "; INT (X)
30 GOTO 10
40 DATA 37.49, 2.511, .99, -3.15, 999.99, 12.51, 12.49
RUN
INT FUNCTION CONVERTS 37.49 INTO 37
INT FUNCTION CONVERTS 2.511 INTO 2
INT FUNCTION CONVERTS .99 INTO 0
INT FUNCTION CONVERTS -3.15 INTO -4
INT FUNCTION CONVERTS 999.99 INTO 999
INT FUNCTION CONVERTS 12.51 INTO 12
INT FUNCTION CONVERTS 12.49 INTO 12
```

12.8 Trignometric Functions:

BASIC uses four trignometric functions i.e **SIN, COS, TAN** and **ATN**. While the use of most of the functions listed in Table 12.1 should be apparent, some notes concerning the use of the trignometirc functions and description of the exponential and logarithm functions may be in order for those which are not familiar with their uses.

Each trignometric function, such as the **SIN, COS, TAN** and **ATN** functions, is used to calculate the trignometric value with the argument is expressed in radians. You can do this by multiplying degrees by **pi/180**, where **pi = 3.141593**. Since each trigonometric function is calculated in single precision, it is irrelevant to carry the value of pi to the any further degree of precision. The following example shows how you can generate a table of values of the sine and cosine of angle as the angle varies from 0 to 360 in increments of 30.

Example 12.6 Trignometric Functions

```
10 PRINT TAB(8); "A SHORT TABLE OF TRIGNOMETRIC";
20 PRINT " FUNCTIONS"
30 PRINT "ANGLE", SPC(2);"SIN",SPC(2); "COS",SPC(2);"TAN"
40 FOR I = 1 TO 54 STEP 1
50 PRINT "-";
60 NEXT I
70 PRINT
80 REM: FNA ROUNDS NUMBERS TO 6 DECIMAL PLACES
90 DEF FNA(X)=INT(1000000!*X+.5)/1000000!
100 FOR X = 0 TO 90 STEP 10
110 LET Y=3.14159*X/180
120 PRINT X,FNA(SIN(Y)),FNA(COS(Y)),FNA(TAN(Y))
130 NEXT X
140 END
RUN
A SHORT TABLE OF TRIGNOMETRIC FUNCTIONS
```

ANGLE	SIN	COS	TAN
0	0	1	0
10	.173648	.984808	.176327
20	.34202	.939693	.36397
30	.5	.866026	.57735
40	.642787	.766045	.839099
50	.766044	.642788	1.191752
60	.866025	.500001	1.732048
70	.939692	.342021	2.747469
80	.984808	.173649	5.671245
90	1	.000001	788898.2

In above pogram following items are noteworthy:

- COS 90 = 0 but computer has printed .000001 which is not zero but tending to be zero.This is due to the fact that we have used approximate value of pi (=3.14159).Similarly the value of TAN 60 is printed as .500001 and TAN 90 as 788898.2 which could have been .5 and infinity respectively.

  This and other slight variances are due to the fact that pi was entered rounded to six significant positions. The small magnitude of the error, while insignificant, does not do justice to any type of tabular output you may desire. You can avoid this problem by using a formatted PRINT statement and specifying the precision of accuracy you desire. Thus, specifying values of say five significant positions would result in a zero value being printed.
- In lines 90 to 120 the program uses a user-defined function FNA to calculate the values of trignometric functions. We shall learn about the user-defined functions in sections 12.17 onwards.
- At the same time the program uses INT function to round off the value of sin, cos and tan library functions.

12.9 Rounding Off Numbers:

Here is the formula that performs the rounding off function.

```
INT( N * 10^D +.5 ) / 10^D
```

N is the number to be rounded and **D** is the desired number of decimal places.Shown below are examples of rounding off the number **4.5678** to various decimal places-to the nearest tenth, hundredth, thousandth, and to the nearest whole number.

Example 12.8 Rounding off 4.5678 to the nearest tenth

Rounding off a number to the nearest tenth means that the rounded number has one digit to the right of the decimal point.(D = 1).

```
R = INT(N * 10^D +.5) / 10^D
  = INT(4.5678 * 10^1 + .5) / 10^1
  = INT(4.5678 * 10 + .5) / 10^1
  = INT(45.678 +.5 ) / 10^1
  = INT(46.178) / 10^1
  = 46 / 10^1
  = 46 / 10
  = 4.6
```

4.5678 has been rounded off to 4.6

Note: Output can also be rounded by the PRINT USING statement.

12.10 String Functions

String functions operate on strings and helps you in manipulating them. For example you can select left, right or mid letter out of a given string as illustrated below.Similarly you can play with words with following string functions.

(1) Concatenation : Joining of two strings addition:

You can add the contents of two string variables as shown below. This is the only mathematical operation that can be performed on string and is called concatentation.Type

```
10 A$ = "I LOVE COMPUTER SCIENCE"
20 B$ = "AND MATHS"
30 PRINT A$ + B$
RUN
I LOVE COMPUTER SCIENCE AND MATHS
```

If you need the space between quotation marks to leave a space between the words, put up a blank space inside the quotes.

displays the character p (in small case).Also use the following program for listing complete ASCII code:

```
FOR N = 1 TO 256
PRINT N;" = ";CHR($);
NEXT N
```

This will list all the numbers and corresponding ASCII code symbols.The ASCII code for number 7 is a beep sound,so whenever you type **PRINT CHR$(7)** the computer will produce a beeping sound.

Also try following

PRINT ASC(CHR$(112))to return the same value as in argument i.e **112** and **PRINT CHR$(ASC("A"))** to return A.

(8) VAL FUNCTION

Format VAL(var$)

VAL converts numbers written as strings into their numeric value. **VAL** has the effect of stripping off the quotes or dollar sign. var$ can be a string variable or string constant. When combinations of letters and numbers appear in var$, only the leading numbers are translated into a numeric value. If a letter comes first, **VAL** returns a numeric value of 0.

Examples :

```
PRINT VAL ("1520")
```

displays the number **1520**.

```
A = VAL(B$)
```

assigns A the numeric value of the numbers (if any) in B$. If B$ contains no numbers, or if a letter(s) comes first, A will be equal to zero. So, if you enter,

```
A = VAL (A420)
```

it will return a zero.

```
PRINT VAL ("19PQRS")
```

displays the numeric value 19.

```
PRINT VAL ("9ABC1520")
```

displays the numeric value 9. Because 1520 appears after the letters, it is not translated.

```
B$ = "HELLO"
A = VAL (B$)
```

assings **A** the numeric value of **0** because **B$** cotains no numbers.

(9) STR$ Function

Format STR$(v)

SRT$ converts a numeric value into a string. v is any number, numeric variable or numeric equation within the limits of the BASIC being used.

Example:

```
PRINT STR$(1994)
```

prints 1994

```
A$ = STR$(X)
```

assigns the value of **X** to **A$**.

The first character of the string **STR$** indicates the sign of the number. For negative numbers, the leading character is a "-". For positive numbers, it is a space.

Conversion of number to a string with **STR$** allows its manipulation using string modifiers, **LEFT$**, RIGHT$, MID$, INSTR, etc.

Example 12.10

```
10 REM "STR$" DEMO PROGRAM
20 A = 324
30 A$ = STR$(A)
40 PRINT "THE NUMBER " ; A; "IS CHANGED";
50 PRINT " TO THE STRING ";A$
RUN
THE NUMBER 324 IS CHANGED TO THE STRING 324.
```

(10) TIME and DATE$

These functions return the time and date known by the system. If the current time and date are entered during system start-up, the correct time and date are given (the internal clock in the computer keeps track).

12.11 User Defined Functions

BASIC provides you with the capability to avoid repeated programming steps to conduct the same computation. This is accomplished by the use of the **DEF FN** statement. This statement permits you to define your own functions.

There are four items in the statement which defines the function:

- The word **DEF**
- The name of the function, which consists of the letters **FN**, followed by the name
- The argument of the function which follows the name in brackets
- The formula, using the argument, for working out the function.

The **DEF FN** statement allows the user to **DEFINE** (create new functions which can then be used in the same manner as the library BASIC functions.

The format of this statement is

```
DEF FNvar(v1,v2,...) = equation
```

- **var** is a variable that names the function being defined.
- **v1**,**v2**,.... is a list of variabels to be evaluated by the defined function. The function's result is based on the value of the varibales **v1, v2**,...
- **equation** is the actual new function that is created by the **DEF FN** statement equation typically manipulates the variables **v1,v2**...

Once a function has been defined by **DEF FN**, that function can be used like any other BASIC function. To use a function defined by **DEF FN**, the format **FNvar(v1,v2...)** is used.

For example

```
DEF FNarea.(side) = side * side
```

defines a function to calculate the area of a square.

```
DEF FNround (number) = INT    (number*100 + 0.5)/100
```

defines a function to round a number to two decimal places.

```
DEF FNaverage(X,Y,Z)=(X+Y+Z)/3
```

defines a function to calculate the average of three numbers.

Three typical single-line function definitions are shown below.

```
10 DEF FNA (X) = X^3 + 2 * X^2 - 3 * X + 4
```

```
20 DEF FNC$ = "NAME AND ADDRESS:"
30 DEF FNR(A,B,C) = SQR (A^2 +B^+ 2 + C^2)
```

The first and third statements define the numeric **FNA** and **FNR**, and the second statement defines the string function **FNC$.** Notice that the second function does not contain an arguement. Also note that the third function makes use of the library function **SQR** in the function definition.

Having defined a function, we can use it with any variable, not just the one named in the definition.

It should be clear that the presence of a **DEF** statement serves only to define a function. In order to evalute the function it is necessary to refer to the function name elsewhere in the program, just as we would do with a library function. We will see how this is accomplished in the next section.

The following program segment illustrates the use of the **DEF FN** statement.

Example 12.11

```
10 DEF FNEQUATION (X,Y,Z) = X ^ 3+3 * Y^2+2 * Z + 27.5
20 LET A = FNEQUATION (1,2,3):                    PRINT A
30 LET B = FNEQUATION (4,5,6): PRINT B
RUN
 46.5
 178.5
Ok
```

In this example, line 10 defines the function **FNEQUATION**, which computes the expression $x^3 + 3y^2 + 2z + 27.5$. The function is called in line 20 with argument values 1, 2 and 3 that will replace the variables named **X, Y** and **Z** in the expression when it is evaluated. Similarly, line 30 calls the function for evaluation with **4, 5,** and 6 used to replace the variables named **X,Y** and **Z**. From this example, you see that the **DEF FN** statement only defines a function. To evaluate the function,you must refer to the function name elsewhere in the program by specifying the name of the function and providing the values of the arguments within a BASIC statement.

You can include one or more library functions within a **DEF FN** statement as illustrated by the next program segment.

```
10 DEF FNROOT (X,Y,Z) = SQR (X^3 + Y^2 + Z)
20 PRINT FNROOT (1,2,3)
RUN
2.828427
Ok
```

You can also define string operations as indicated by the next program segment.

```
10 N$ = "NAME "
20 A$ = "ADDRESS"
30 DEF FNONE$ (X$, Y$) = N$ + A$
40 PRINT FNONE$ (N$ , A$)
RUN
NAME ADDRESS
Ok
```

From the preceding examples, you may have noticed that the **DEF FN** statement precedes the reference of the function within a program. This is because you must define the function prior to calling it.

Example 12.12

```
10 INPUT "SIDE LENGTH OF SQUARE"; length
20 PRINT "AREA = ";FNarea(length)
30 END
40 DEF FNarea(side) = side*side
```

will provide with message as

```
Undefined user function
```

So change the line number 40 to line no. 5 and Run

```
SIDE LENGTH OF SQUARE? 10
AREA = 100
```

Example 12.13

```
DEF FNA(R) = R*R*3.141593
```

The formula to find the area of a circle (usually written πr^2), is defined as the function **FNA**. A is the variable which identifies the function.(R) matches the variable used in the equation . Each time `FNA(R)` is used, the value of `R` is calculated according to the equation. For example:

```
PRINT "THE AREA OF THE CIRCLE IS"; FNR(R)
```

(The value or variables R was assigned earlier in the program.)

Example 12.14

```
10 REM " DEF FN " TEST PROGRAM
20 INPUT "ENTER THE RADIUS OF A CIRCLE (IN INCHES)";R
30 DEF FNC(X) = 2*3.141593*X
40 PRINT "THE CIRCUMFERENCE OF A CIRCLES WITH A RADIUS OF"
50 PRINT R; "INCHES IS"; FNC(R); "INCHES"
RUN
ENTER THE RADIUS OF A CIRCLE (IN INCHES)? 4
THE CIRCUMFERENCE OF A CIRCLE WITH A RADIUS OF 4 INCHES IS 25.13272 INCHES
```

12.12 Use of DEF FN in Strings:

Some BASICs allow string functions to be defined with `DEF FN`. For example:

```
DEF FNA$(L$) = LEFT$ (L$,2)
```

defines a function that calculates the two left-most letters in the string `L$. FNA$(L$)` may now be used like any other BASIC function. For example"

```
PRINT FNA$("GODDESS")
```

displays `GOD`.

12.13 Use of DEF FN in Creating New Mathematical Functions

Example 12.15 Modulo Arithmetic

Let us create a Function to do MODular arithmetic. MOD is one of our math operators, but we'll use it to demonstrate the techniqe defined function.

```
10 CLS : PRINT
20 INPUT "ENTER X";X
30 INPUT "ENTER Y";Y
40 DEF FNC(X,Y) = INT(X-Y * INT (X/Y))
50 REM C = FUNCTION NAME X,Y = THE NUMBERS
60 PRINT X; "MOD" ; Y; "=" FNC(X,Y)
RUN.
ENTER X ? 17
ENTER Y ? 6
17 MOD 6 = 5
```

The variables X and Y used in defining the Function in Line 40 are really "dummy arguments". They only show the Computer how to perform the calculations. Change Line 40 to:

```
40 DEF FNC(A,B) = INT(A - B * INT(A / B))
```

and RUN. Same results? You. In fact, we could even use A and B elsewhere in the program; Line 40 won't effect their values at all.

Example 12.16 Rouding off numbers

The function for rounding a number can now be defined as a function as follows:

```
50 DEF FNR(A) = INT(A / F + 0.5) * F
```

This can be used subsequently in the same program to round a number to, say, the nearest 100 and to one decimal place as shown below;

Example 12.17

```
10 DEF FNR(A) = INT(A/F + 0.5) * F
20 READ B,C
30 DATA 650, 32.55, 649, 32.54, 651,32.56, 0,0
40 IF B = O THEN 190
100 REM ROUND B TO NEAREST 100
110 LET F = 100
120 LET B1 = FNR (B)
130 REM ROUND C TO 1 DECIMAL PLACE
140 LET F = 0.1
150 LET C1 = FNR(C)
160 PRINT "B =";B;"B1 = ";B1,:C = ";C;"C1 =";C1
170 PRINT
180 GOTO 60
190 END
```

12.14 Rules for Writing User-defined Functions:

1. User-defined functions may be numeric or string. if a type is specified in the function name, the value of the expression is forced to that type before it is returned to the calling statement. If a type is specified in the function name and the argument type does not match, a "Type Mismatch" error occurs.
2. A user-defined function may be defined more than in a program by repeating the **DEF FN** statement.
3. A **DEF FN** statement must be executed before the function it defines may be called. If a function is called before it has been defined, an "Undefined User Function" error occurs.
4. **DEF FN** is illegal in the direct mode.
5. A **DEF** statement can appear anywhere in a BASIC program. However, it is good programming pratice to group together all function definitions and place them near the beginning or the end of a program. This contributes to an orderly and legible program structure.

QUESTIONS

PART 1

1. What are library functions? What useful purpose do they serve?
2. What other names are sometimes used for library functions?
3. Name several of the more common library functions. State the purpose of each library function.
4. What is meant by an argument? Do all library functions require arguments?

5. How is a library function used in a BASIC program.
6. What happens if a negative value is supplied to a library function that requires a positive argument?
7. What is meant by truncation? Present an example illustrating truncation.
8. What is the purpose of the **INT** function? What happens when the INT function receives a positive argument? A negative argument?
9. What is the purpose of the **TAB** function? In which statement is it used?
10. Can a formula be used as a library function argument? Can a reference to another library function be used for this purpose?
11. What happens if a library function requiring an integer argument is supplied with an argument having a noninteger value?
12. Write a BASIC statement that corresponds to each of the following algebraic equation.
    (a) $z = Tant$
    (b) $w = \log_e (v)$
    (c) $y = a \exp \sin cx$
    (d) $x_1 = \frac{-b + \sqrt{b^2 - 4ac}}{2a}$
13. Write a BASIC statement for each of the following situations.
    (a) Determine the absolute value of the difference between the variables **U** and **V**. Assign this value to the variable **W**.
    (b) Determine the sign of x. If x is negative, go to statement 50; if a x equals zero, go to statement 20; and if x is positive , go to statement 170.
    (c) Determine the largest integer which algebraically does not exceed **z**, where **z** = **x**² + **y**². Assign this integer to the variable I.
    (d) In (c) above , if **x = 2.5** and **y = 6.3**, what value will be assigned to the variable I?
    (e) Print the values of **X$, X, Y$** and **Y** on one line. Let the string represented by **X$** begin in the 10th column, followed immediately by the value of **X**. Similarly, let **Y$** begin in the 46th column, followed immediately by **Y**.
14. Write a BASIC statement for each of the following situations.
    (a) Determine the sign of the quantity **(ab-cd)/ (f +g)**. Go to statement number 75 if the quantity is positive, to statement 260 if the quantity is zero, and to statement 135 if the quantity is negative.
    (b) Print the following on one line of the screen "X =" followed by the value of the variable **X, "Y =",** followed by the value of **Y;** and **"Z = "** followed by the value of Z. Begin printing in column 5,30 and 50.
    (c) Determine if the value of the variable N is even or odd, assuming that N has a positive integer value. (Hint: Compare the Value of N/2 with the truncated value of N/2).
    (d) In part (c) above, what will happen if N has a negative integer value.
15. What are the differences between a function and a subroutine?
16. Are functions and/or subroutines ever required in a BASIC program? What are the advantages in their use?
17. In what way can functions and subroutines be helpful in improving the organization of a BASIC program?
18. Summarize the rules for naming functions. How are numeric functions distinguished from string functions?
19. What is the purpose of the DEF statement? How is it written?
20. What are the rules that govern the use of arguments in a function? Can a function make use of variables that are not specified as arguments?
21. What is the difference between a function definition and a function reference? How is a function referenced?
22. What are dummy arguments? What correspondence must exist between a set of arguements in a function reference and the associated dummy arguments?

23. Can an argument consist of something other than a nonsubscripted variable (e.g, a constant, subscripted variable or formula)? Is this also true of a dummy argument?

25. Given that I = 6,what value does your computer assign to J in each of the following statements?

(a) `30 LET J = INT (I+3.3)`
(b) `40 LET J = INT (I-I)`
(c) `50 LET J = INT (I-12.99)`
(d) `60 LET J = INT (I-INT(I+1.54))`
(e) `70 LET J = INT (I+INT(I-4.85))`
(f) `80 LET J = INT (I-INT(I-8.63))`

ANSWERS

PART 1

12. (a) `10 LET Z = TAN (T)`
(b) `10 LET W = LOG (V)`
(c) `10 LET Y = A * EXP (B*X) * SIN (C*X)`
(d) `10 LET X1 = (-B + SQR (B^2-4 * A * C))/(2 * A)`

13. (a) `10 LET W = ABS (U -V)`
(b) `10 ON SGN (X) + 2 GO TO 50,20,170`
(c) `10 LET I = INT (X ^ 2 - Y ^ 2)`
(d) $X^2 - Y^2 = -33.44$, hence I = 34,
(e) `100 PRINT TAB (9); X$; X; TAB (45); Y$;`

QUESTIONS

PART II

1. What are in-built functions?What purpose do they serve?
2. What is the purpose of Fix statement and how does it differ from INT function?
3. Write the output

(a)
```
10 X = 2
20 PRINT INT(2^- X / 4)
```
(b)
```
10 X = 2
20 PRINT FIX (X^3 / 4 - 1.7)
```
(c)
```
10 X = 2
20 Y = 3
30 PRINT ABS (X-Y+X)/(X+Y)
```

4. Assuming
```
10 A$ = "CATCH"
20 B$ = "NOT
30 C$ = "HOLD"
40 D$ = ","
50 E$ = " "
```
find out, what shali be printed after following statemants?

(a) `60 PRINT A$ + D$ + B$ + C$`
(b) `70 PRINT A$ + E$ + B$ + D$ +C$`

5. If `Z$ = "CHARACTERISTIC".` Find out the value of the following :

(a) `LEFT$ (Z$, 4)`
(b) `LEFT $(Z$,9)`
(c) `RIGHT$(Z$, 3)`
(d) `MID$ (Z$,5,5)`
(e) `MID$(Z4, 4, 6)`
(d) `RIGHT$(Z$, 10)`

6. What shall be the output of following?

(a) `PRINT LEN ("ANGLE")`
(b) `PRINT LEN ("SHRI 420")`
(c)
```
10 A$ = "COMPUTERONICS"
20 PRINT LEFT$(A$,8);
30 PRINT RIGHT$ (A$,9); MID$
   (A$,4,7)
```
(d) `PRINT ASC("Z")`
(e) `PRINT CHR$(65)`
(f)
```
10 LET L$ = "LEFT "
15 LET R$ = "RIGHT"
20 PRINT "SEE ";L$;"OR "; R$
```
(g)
```
10 READ NAM$, DATE, YEAR
20 PRINT NAM$, DATE, YEAR
25 DATA "GITA",08,1992
```

7. Write a program to input the string "MOTHER INDIA" and print INDIA MOTHER.

ANSWERS

PART 2

2. (a) .0625
   (b) .3 (c) .2
4. (a) **CATCH, NOTHOLD**
   (b) **CATCH NOT,HOLD**
5. (a) **CHAR**
   (b) **CHARACTER**
   (c) **TIC**
   (d) **ACTER**
   (e) **RECTER**
   (f) **ACTERISTIC**
6. (a) **5**
   (b) **8**
   (c) **COMPUTER, UTERONICS.**
   (d) **90**
   (e) **A**
   (f) **SEE LEFT OF RIGHT**
   (g) **GITA 08 1991**
7.
```
10 READ A$,B$
20 DATA "ACADEMICS","INDIA"
30 PRINT B$ ; " ";A$
```
or we can have
```
10 PRINT "Input first word";A$
20 PRINT "Input second word";B$
30 PRINT B$ ; " " ; A$
```

QUESTIONS

PART 3

In the first four problems, perform all calculations by hand.

1 Find the value of B in each of the following program segments.The function on the function definition is the one that rounds off Rupees and paisa to the nearest PAISA.

```
10 DEF FNR(A) = INT( A * 10^D +.5)
                  / 10^D
20 LET D = 2
```

(a)
```
30 LET A = 13.485
40 LET B = FNR(A)
```
(b)
```
30 LET A = 14.163
40 LET B = FNR(A)*2
```
(c)
```
30 LET A = 14.163
40 LET B = FNR(A*2)
```
(d)
```
30 LET A = 16.398
40 LET B = SQR(FNR(A) + 32.60)
```

2. In the program shown below,find the net wages of an employee who has no overtime hours.The first user-defined function in the programs gives the value of W(wages not rounded).The second user-defined function rounds off the wages to the nearest cent.This gives the value of N.

```
10 DEF FNH(H1) = R * H1-D
20 DEF FNR(W1) = INT(W1 * 10^D2
   +.5) / 10 ^D2
30 LET D2 = 2
40 READ H,R,D
50 DATA 37,11,543,79.50
60 LET W = FNN(H)
70 LET N = FNR(W)
80 PRINT N
99 END
```

3. Suppose an employee's regular weekly hours are 39 hours and that the company offers time-and-half for overtime.The following function finds the employee's net wages,including overtime.

R * 39 + (H-39) * R * 1.5 -D

R denotes Rate per hour,**H** stands for Hours worked,and **D** means Deductions.

(a) **R * 39**-rate times regular hours gives regular pay.

(b) **H - 39**-hours worked minus regular hours gives overtime hours.

(c) **R * 1.5**-rate times 1.5 gives overtime rate.

(d) **(H-39) * R * 1.5**-Overtime hours times overtime rate gives overtime pay.

(e) **R * 39 + (H-39) * R * 1.5**-regular pay plus overtime pay gives gross wages.

(f) **R * 39 + (H-39)* R* 1.5 - D**-gross wages minus deductions gives net wages.

The following program uses that above formula as a user-defined functionto find the wages of an employee who has worked overtime.The wages are then rounded off to the nearest cent by the second user-defined function. Find the value of N.

```
10 DEF FNV(H1) = R*39 + (H1-39) *
   R * 1.5-D
20 DEF FNR(W1) = INT(W1 * 10^D2
   +.5) / 10^D2
30 LET D2 = 2
40 READ H,R,D
50 DATA 44,12.241,85
60 LET W = FNV(H)
70 LET N = FNR(W)
80 PRINT N
99 END
```

4. Find the value of Q in each of the statements shown below using the following function definition and the values given for A,B,and C.

```
10 DEF FNQ(A1,B1,C1) = B1^2-4 *
   A1 * C1
20 READ A,B,C
30 DATA 2,6,3
```

(a) `40 LET Q = FNQ(A,B,C)`
(b) `40 LET Q = FNQ(A,B,C)+10`
(c) `40 LET Q = FNQ(A,B + 1,C)`
(d) `40 LET Q = SQR(FNQ(A,B + 1,C))`

5. Fill in the missing lines for the following programs.

(a) Calculate the sales tax of an article.

(i) Sales Tax = Price X Rate

(ii) Complete line 10 with a DEF statement.

```
10 . . .
20 READ P,R
30 DATA 37,.05
40 LET T = FNT(P)
50 PRINT
60 PRINT P,T
99 END
RUN
37 1.85
```

(b) Calculate the amount of an investment by adding the yearly interest to the investment. Use Rs1000 as the initial investment for each of the rates, 17%,18% and19%.

(i) Amount = Investment + (Investment × Rate)

(ii) Complete line 60 with a function reference coded in a LET statement.

```
10 DEF FNA(R1) = I + (I*R1)
20 PRINT
30 LET I = 1000
40 LET R =.17
50 FOR N = 1 TO 3
60 . . .
70 PRINT A
80 LET R = R +.01
90 NEXT N
99 END
RUN
1170
1180
1190
```

(c) Calculate the squares of the numbers from 1 to 5 inclusive.

(i) Complete line 10 with a **DEF** statement.

(ii) Complete line 40 with a function reference coded in a **LET** statement.

```
10 . . .
20 PRINT
30 FOR N = 1 TO 5
40 . . .
50 PRINT N,S
60 NEXT N
99 END
RUN
1 1
2 4
3 9
4 16
5 25
```

(d) The following program uses a multiline user-defined function. It cubes a number if the number is less than or equal to 5, otherwise it squares the number; that is, if the number is greater than 5.

(i) Complete line 30 with a statement that squares the number.

(ii) Complete line 50 with a statement that cubes the number.

```
10 DEF FNB(A1)
20 IF A1 <= 5 THEN 50
30 . . .
40 GO TO 60
50
60 FNEND
70 LET A = 3
80 PRINT
90 PRINT A,FNB(A)
99 END
RUN
3 27
```

6. (a) What is a user-defined function?
   (b) State one of its advantages.
7. (a) What is the purpose of the DEF statement?
   (b) Where are DEF statements usually placed in a program?
   (c) Display and label a DEF statement.
8. (a) How are user-defined functions named?Give three examples of function names.
   (b) What restriction is placed on the name of a user-defined function if there are more than one such function in a program?
9. (a) State the difference between a function definition and a function reference.
   (b) Where may a function reference appear in a program?
10. (a) Where is a dummy argument coded in a program?What is its purpose?
    (b) Where is an actual argument coded in a program? What is its purpose?
11. (a) How can the argument in a function reference be expressed? Give four examples.
    (b) State one restriction placed on this argument in its relation to the dummy argument in a function definition.
    (c) How should the argument in a function definition be expressed?
12. What three rules must be observed when a computer system allows more than one argument in the function definition and in the function reference?

ANSWERS

PART-III

1. (a) **13.49**
   (b) **28.32**
   (c) **28.33**
   (d) **7**
2. **347.59**
3. **391.21**
4. (a) **12**
   (b) **22**
   (c) **25**
   (d) **5**
5. (a) `10 DEF FNT(P1) = P1 * R`
   (b) `60 LET A = FNA(R)`
   (c) `10 DEF FNS(N1) = N1^2`
       `40 LET S = FNS(N)`
   (d) `30 LET FNB = A1^2`
       `50 LET FNB = A1^3`

CHAPTER 13

Subroutines

13.1 Structured Programming

When computers were first developed, programming was extremely complex and programmers were happy just to get their programs to work. There was little concern about writing programs in a style that was easy for other people to understand. Gradually, however, programmers began to realize that working with such programs was very difficult, particularly when someone other than the original programmer had to alter an existing program.

Because of this problem, programmers began developing ways to make programs easier to understand and modify. These techniques, which have been developed over the past 20 years, are referred to as structured programming. Structured programming has two basic characteristics:

- The program logic is easy to follow, and
- The program is divided into smaller subprograms or modules, which in BASIC are referred to as subroutines. Subroutines are modules in BASIC, each designed to perform a specific task. A subroutine is a sequence of statements which typically is located after the main body to the program. It can be executed any number of times in a given program.

Many times in programming, you recognize that a sequence of statements that perform one or more functions require repeated usage. You can construct these statements as a subroutine and easily invoke their usage by branching to the statement where the subroutine starts. In addition, BASIC provides you with a mechanism to conveniently return program execution to the statement after the statement that invoked the subroutine or to any other program statement you may desire to resume program execution.

13.2 The GOSUB Statement

The GOSUB statement transfers the flow of program control from the calling program to subroutine. GOSUB is used to branch out a program's main stream and GOTO a SUBroutine. A subroutine can be called either from the main program or from another subroutine. The format of GOSUB statement is as follows:

```
line # GOSUB transfer line #
```

The transfer line number must be the first number of the subroutine. This is very important because the computer does not detect an error if it is instructed to branch to an incorrect line. It detects an error only if the transfer line number does not exist in the program.

The GOSUB statement causes an unconditional transfer to the specified line number. For example, the following statement causes a branch to the subroutine starting at 200.

```
50 GOSUB 200
```

Remember that

- A **RETURN** statement must be used at the end of a subroutine's execution to **RETURN** control from the subroutine to the main program.
- **GOSUB** can be used anywhere within a program.
- BASIC ignores any statements or data appearing on the same line after **GOSUB** line except for a statement separator (the colon).
- Although **GO** and **SUB** can be entered as two separate words, after a program is LISTed or SAVEd, **GO SUB** is changed to **GOSUB**.

13.3 The RETURN Statement

After a subroutine is executed, the **RETURN** statement causes program control to return to the line following the one that contained the **GOSUB** statement. The format of the **RETURN** statement is as follows:

line # RETURN line #

line (number) is optional and is used to **RETURN**.

Note that no transfer line number is needed in the **RETURN** statement. The computer automatically returns control to the statement immediately following the **GOSUB** statement that called the subroutine. If the line returned to is a non executable statement, such as a **REM** statement, the computer simply skips it. Each subroutine must contain a **RETURN** statement as its last line; otherwise the program cannot branch back to the point from which the subroutine was called.

BASIC ignores statements or data appearing on the same line on which **RETURN** statement is given.

13.4 Example of Subroutine Usage

The program prints a simple multiplication table. It contains a subroutine that prints a row of dashes to divide the multiplication table into sections to make it more readable. The subroutine is called from three places in the main program: line 40, line 60, and line 200. Each time this subroutine is called, program control transfers to line 1000.

In this program, the subroutine is very short, so it would be easy to repeat the statements each time they are needed instead of using a subroutine. If the subroutine were longer, however, it would be tedious and wasteful to type it three times. Using subroutines simplifies program logic by organizing specific tasks into neat, orderly subsections.

Example 13.1 : Multiplication Program Using a Subroutine

```
10 REM MULTIPLICATION TABLE
20 CLS
30 PRINT TAB(10); "MULTIPLICATION TABLE "
40 GOSUB 1000
50 PRINT TAB(5); "ONE", TAB(20); "TWO"; TAB(35) "THREE"
60 GOSUB 1000
100 REM
110 REM * * * PRINT TABLE * * *
120 OUTER = 1
130 INNER = 1
140 PRINT INNER; " *"; OUTER; "= "; OUTER * INNER; " ";
150 INNER = INNER + 1
160 IF INNER < 4 GOTO 140
170 PRINT
180 OUTER = OUTER +1
```

```
190 IF OUTER < 11 THEN GOTO 130
200 GOSUB 1000
220 END
1000 REM
1010 COUNT = 1
1020 PRINT "—";
1030 COUNT = COUNT + 1
1040 IF COUNT < THEN 1020
1100 PRINT
1110 RETURN
RUN
```

MULTIPLICATION TABLE

18th column	40th column	60th column
1 * 1 = 1	2 * 1 = 2	3 * 1 = 3
1 * 2 = 2	2 * 2 = 4	3 * 2 = 6
1 * 3 = 3	2 * 3 = 6	3 * 3 = 9
1 * 4 = 4	2 * 4 = 8	3 * 4 = 12
1 * 5 = 5	2 * 5 = 10	3 * 5 = 15
1 * 6 = 6	2 * 6 = 12	3 * 6 = 18
1 * 7 = 7	2 * 7 = 14	3 * 7 = 21
1 * 8 = 8	2 * 8 = 16	3 * 8 = 24
1 * 9 = 9	2 * 9 = 18	3 * 9 = 27
1 * 10 = 10	2 * 10 = 20	3 * 10 = 30

Example 13.2 Finding GREATEST COMMON DIVISOR of Three Numbers

```
10 REM FINDING GCD OF THREE GIVEN NUMBERS
20 PRINT "TYPE THE DESIRED THREE NUMBERS SEPARATED BY COMMAS WHEN ?
   APPEARS ON SCREEN"
30 INPUT X,Y,Z
40 A=X
50 B=Y
60 C=Z
70 GOSUB 160
80 X = G : Y = Z
90 GOSUB 160
100 RESTORE
110 PRINT "THE GCD OF ";A;B;C;"IS =" ; G
120 PRINT "TRY NEXT ?,IF YES,THEN PRESS Y OR N TO END THE PROGRAM"
130 INPUT E$
140 IF E$ ="Y" THEN 30
150 IF E$ ="N" THEN 270
160 REM EUCLID'S ALGORITHM TO FIND G.C.D.(X,Y) = G
170 Q = INT(X/Y)
180 R = X - Q * Y
190 REM Q IS QUOTIENT, R IS REMAINDER
200 IF R = 0 THEN 250
210 REM R NOT ZERO
```

```
220 X = Y
230 Y = R
240 GOTO 160
250 G = Y
260 RETURN
999 END
```

When above program is run,the following is displayed.

```
RUN
TYPE THE DESIRED THREE NUMBERS SEPARATED BY COMMAS WHEN ? APPEARS ON
SCREEN
? 24,36,84
THE GCD OF 24 36 84 IS = 12
"TRY NEXT ?,IF YES,THEN PRESS Y OR N TO END THE PROGRAM
? Y
? 13,56,14
THE GCD OF 13 56 14 IS = 1
"TRY NEXT ?,IF YES,THEN PRESS Y OR N TO END THE PROGRAM
? N
```

13.5 Advantages of Sub-Routines

Subroutines have the following advantages in program construction:

(a) The same subroutine can be used anywhere in the program without re-writing it.

(b) Subroutines can be written to perform specific tasks which are needed in a number of places in a program.

(c) The de-bugging of a program is faster since it is easier to trace through subroutines than it is through one large program.

(d) Altering parts of a program would be confined to inserting, deleting or amending subroutines.

(f) The documentation of a large program is much simplified by the documentation of individual subroutines.

13.6 The ON/GOSUB Statement

Because the GOSUB statement is an unconditional transfer statement, it always transfers program control to the subroutine starting at the indicated line number. Sometimes, however, it is necessary to branch to one of several subroutines depending on existing conditions. The **ON/GOSUB** statement is useful for this purpose. The format of the **ON/GOSUB** statement is as follows:

ON ***expression*** **GOSUB** ***transfer line*** **# 1 [*transfer lines* # 2,...]**

The **ON/GOSUB** is similar to the **ON/GOSUB** statement in that it uses an arithmetic expression to determine the line number to which program control will transfer. The transfer line numbers in the **ON/GOSUB** statement, however, are not within the main program. Each transfer line number indicates the beginning of a subroutine.

The execution of the **ON/GOSUB** statement proceeds as follows:

- The expression is evaluated as an integer, and is truncated if necessary.
- Control passes to the subroutine starting at the line number that corresponds to the value of the expression. If the value of the expression is n, control passes to the subroutine starting at the nth line number listed.

- After the specified subroutine is executed, control is transferred back to the line following the **ON/GOSUB** statement by the **RETURN** statement at the end of the subroutine.

If the expression in an **ON/GOSUB** statement is evaluated as a number larger than the number of transfer lines indicated, control is passed to the next executable statement.

The use of this statement is most beneficial if you wish to divide your program into segments and control the branch to the appropriate segment by the user. This can be accomplished by providing an initial menu and associating a value with the response to branch to the desired program segment that was written as a subroutine. Once the subroutine is completed, the **RETURN** statement will provide you with a mechanism to branch back to the line following the computed **ON/GOSUB** statement where you can provide the program operator with another segment by branching back to the menu. This concept is demonstrated, by the following program segment.

Example 13.3 Use of ON-GOSUB

```
100 CLS
110 LOCATE 10,15
120 PRINT "PROGRAM SECTION SELECTION"
130 PRINT
140 PRINT TAB(15) " (1) CONVERTIBLE BOND ANALYSIS"
150 PRINT TAB(15) " (2) INTEREST RATE ANALYSIS"
160 PRINT TAB(15) " (3) HOME MORTGAGE ANALYSIS"
170 PRINT TAB(15) " (4) RETIREMENT FUNDING ANALYSIS"
180 PRINT TAB(15) " (5) EXIT PROGRAM"
190 PRINT
200 LOCATE 18, 15
210 INPUT "ENTER SECTION DESIRED",X
220 ON X GOSUB 1000, 2000, 3000, 4000, 5000
230 GOTO 100
1000 REM Convertible bond analysis subroutine
........
........
........
1990 RETURN
5000 END
```

In this example, the section number desired is used as the mechanism to control which subroutine the program will branch to. Note that the entry of a number greater than 5 will cause line 230 to be executed, which will result in the initial menu being displayed again. In addition, each **RETURN** statement in the program will also cause line 230 to be executed, also causing the menu to be displayed again and allowing the operator to select another program section. If 5 is entered, a branch to line 5000 will occur. Here, an END statement is used to terminate the program. The initial menu displayed on the screen is indicated below.

Program Section Selection

(1) **CONVERTIBLE BOND ANALYSIS**
(2) **INTEREST RATE ANALYSIS**
(3) **HOME MORTGAGE ANALYSIS**
(4) **RETIREMENT FUNDING ANALYSIS**
(5) **EXIT PROGRAM**

Enter Section Desired

Line 220 calls the subroutine that starts at line 2000. The coding of the calling statement varies, depending on the computer being used.

After control is transferred to the subroutine, the statements in the subroutine are executed until a **RETURN** statement is reached. This transfers control back to the main program, specifically to the statement immediately after the **GOSUB** that referenced the subroutine. In the above program, this is statement **230**.

Execution continues in the main program until the **END** statements is encountered. This statement is required at the end of a main program to prevent execution from dropping through to the first subroutine. Some versions of BASIC allow a **STOP** statement. Experiment or check your manual to find out what your computer system requires.

13.7 Example on Sub-routine Usage

Example 13.4 A Main Program that Calls One Subroutine Once

```
10 REM THIS IS THE MAIN PROGRAM
20 LET A=5
30 LET B=3
40 REM CALL THE SUBROUTINE THAT ADDS
50 GOSUB 200
60 PRINT
70 PRINT "THE SUM IS:" ; S
80 END
.........
200 REM * THIS SUBROUTINE ADDS*
210 S = A+B
220 RETURN
RUN
THE SUM IS : 8
```

Example 13.5 A Main Program that Calls one Subroutine several times

```
10 REM THIS IS THE MAIN PROGRAM
20 LET A=5
30 LET B=3
40 REM CALL THE SUBROUTINE THAT ADDS
50 GOSUB 200
60 PRINT
70 PRINT "THE SUM IS:";S
80 LET A=15
90 LET B=13
100 GOSUB 200
110 PRINT "THE SUM IS:";S
120 LET A=25
130 LET B=23
140 GOSUB 200
150 PRINT "THE SUM IS:";S
160 END
200 REM THIS SUBROUTINE ADDS
210 LET S=A+B
```

```
220 RETURN
RUN
THE SUM IS: 8
THE SUM IS: 28
THE SUM IS: 48
```

In this program, subroutine 200 is called three times-in lines 50, 100, and 140. The RETURN statement transfers control to line 60, line 110, or line 150, depending on which GOSUB statement called the subroutine. Subroutine 200 means the subroutine that starts at line 200.

Example 13.6 A Subroutine that Returns More than One Value

```
10 REM THIS IS THE MAIN PROGRAM
20 A = 5
30 B = 3
40 REM CALL THE SUBROUTINE THAT PERFORMS SEVERAL CALCULATIONS
50 GOSUB 200
60 PRINT
70 PRINT "THE SUM IS: " ; S
80 PRINT "THE DIFFERENCE IS: " ; D
90 PRINT "THE PRODUCT IS: " ; P
100 END
200 REM THIS SUBROUTINE PERFORMS SEVERAL CALCULATIONS
210 LET S = A + B
220 LET D = A - B
230 LET P = A * B
240 RETURN
RUN
THE SUM IS: 8
THE DIFFERENCE IS: 2
THE PRODUCT IS: 15
```

Several calculations are performed in the subroutine before control is transferred back to line 60 in the main program.

Example 13.7 A Main Program that Calls More than One Subroutine

```
10 REM THIS IS THE MAIN PROGRAM
20 A = 5
30 B = 3
40 REM CALL THE SUBROUTINE THAT ADDS
50 GOSUB 200
60 PRINT
70 PRINT "THE SUM IS: " ; S
80 REM CALL THE SUBROUTINE THAT SUBTRACTS
90 GOSUB 300
100 PRINT "THE DIFFERENCE IS: " ; D
110 REM CALL THE SUBROUTINE THAT MULTIPLIES
120 GOSUB 400
130 PRINT "THE PRODUCT IS: " ; P
140 END
200 REM THIS SUBROUTINE ADDS
```

```
210 S = A + B
220 RETURN
300 REM THIS SUBROUTINE SUBTRACTS
310 D = A - B
320 RETURN
400 REM THIS SUBROUTINE MULTIPLIES
410 P = A * B
420 RETURN
RUN
THE SUM IS: 8
THE DIFFERENCE IS: 2
THE PRODUCT IS: 15
```

Line 50 calls subroutine 200; line 90 calls subroutine 300; and line 120 calls subroutine 400.After execution of one of the subroutines,control is transferred to the statement immediately following the **GOSUB** that referenced the subroutine.

Subroutines can also be rested i.e., in an subroutine another subroutine can also be called.

Example 13.8 A Subroutine that Calls Another Subroutine (Nested Subroutines)

```
10 REM THIS IS THE MAIN PROGRAM
20 A = 5
30 B = 3
40 REM CALL THE SUBROUTINE THAT CALCULATES
50 GOSUB 200
60 END
200 REM THIS SUBROUTINE ADDS, SUBTRACTS AND MULTIPLIES
210 PRINT
220 LET R=A+B
230 GOSUB 300
240 LET R=A-B
250 GOSUB 300
260 LET R=A*B
270 GOSUB 300
280 RETURN
300 REM THIS SUBROUTINE PRINTS
310 PRINT"THE RESULT IS:";R
320 RETURN
RUN
THE RESULT IS: 8
THE RESULT IS: 2
THE RESULT IS: 15
```

Line 50 in the main program calls subroutine **200** to perform various calculations. After each round of calculations,subroutine **300** is called to print the result. The **RETURN** statement in the second subroutine transfers control back to the first subroutine to line **240**, line **260**, or line **280**, depending on which **GOSUB** called the subroutine.Thus, in the first subroutine, calculations are performed and the PRINT subroutine is called until the **RETURN** statement is encountered. Control is then transferred to line 60 in the main program.

Example 13.9 A Subroutine with Multiple RETURNs

```
10 REM THIS IS THE MAIN PROGRAM
20 READ A,B
30 DATA 5,3
40 PRINT
50 FOR I=1 TO 3
60 READ C
70 DATA 1,2,3
80 REM CALL THE SUBROUTINE THAT CALCULATES
90 GOSUB 200
100 PRINT "THE RESULT IS:";R
110 NEXT I
120 END
200 REM THIS SUBROUTINE  ADDS, SUBTRACTS AND MULTIPLIES DEPENDING ON
201 REM THE VALUE OF THE CODE
210 ON C GO TO 220;240,260
220 LET R=A+B
230 RETURN
240 LET R=A-B
250 RETURN
260 LET R=A*B
270 RETURN
RUN
THE RESULT IS: 8
THE RESULT IS: 2
THE RESULT IS: 15
```

Line 60 reads in a code.A code of one denotes addition, a code of two means subtraction, and a code of three represents multiplication. Line 90 calls the subroutine,which performs an arithmetic operation depending on the value of C (the code). After each calculation, control returns to statement 100 in the main program.

EXERCISES

PART 1

1. Fill in the blanks with appropriate words.
   (a) Subprograms in BASIC are called ....
   (b) A(n) ...... statement causes an unconditional branch to a subroutine.
   (c) The .... statement causes control to be transferred from a subroutine back to the calling program.
   (d) The .... statement is used to prevent unnecessary execution of subroutines or other statements.
2. What is a subroutine?
3. State two advantages in the use of subroutines.
4. Explain how the GOSUB and RETURN statements work together.
5. How many times a given subroutine can be called in a program?
6. How many subroutines can be incorporated in a program?

EXERCISES
PART 2

1. Write a subroutine for the following main program to calculate the amount of cash a grocer has at the end of a day if he received Rs 431.00 and paid out Rs 16.50

   Balance = Receipts- Payments

```
10 REM THIS IS THE MAIN PROGRAM
20 READ R,P
30 DATA 431,16.50
40 GOSUB 200
50 PRINT
60 PRINT "RECEIPTS: ";R
70 PRINT "PAYMENTS: ";P
80 PRINT "BALANCE:" ;B
90 END
RUN
RECEIPTS: 431
PAYMENTS: 16.5
BALANCE: 414.5
```

2. Modify the program in Problem 1 so that there are two subroutines;the first one is called by the main program,the second one is called by the first subroutine.

   (a) The first subroutine calculates the balance.

   (b) The second subroutine formats the headings and amounts starting from Tabs 3, 16 and 29.

```
10 REM THIS IS THE MAIN PROGRAM
20 READ R,P
30 DATA 431,16.50
40 GOSUB 200
50 END
```

3. What is the output of each of the following programs?

   (a)

```
10 PRINT
20 LET P=0
30 LET N=0
40 FOR I=1 TO 6
50 READ A
60 DATA 5,-2,9,-4,3,-6
70 GOSUB 200
80 NEXT I
90 PRINT P,N
100 END
200 IF A << 0 THEN 230
210 LET P=P+A
220 RETURN
230 LET N=N+A
240 RETURN
```

   (b)

```
10 DIM P(4),R(4)
20 PRINT
30 FOR I=1 TO 4
40 READ P(I)
50 DATA 4,3,1,2
60 PRINT
70 NEXT I
80 GOSUB 200
90 END
200 PRINT
210 FOR J=1 TO 4
220 LET P(J)=P(J)*2
230 PRINT P(J);
240 NEXT J
250 RETURN
```

   (c)

```
10 DIM R(3,4)
20 PRINT
30 FOR I=1 TO 3
40 FOR J=1 TO 4
50 READ R(I,J)
60 DATA 3,2,0,1
70 DATA 1,0,2,3
80 DATA 2,4,1,0
90 GOSUB 200
100 NEXT J
110 PRINT
120 NEXT I
130 GOSUB 300
140 PRINT
150 PRINT S
160 END
200 PRINT R (I, J);
210 RETURN
300 LET S=0
310 FOR L=1 TO 4
320 LET S=S+R(1,L)
330 NEXT L
340 RETURN
```

4. What is wrong with each of the following programs?

   (a)

```
10 LET A=B
20 LET B=4
30 GOSUB 200
```

```
40 LET S=A+B
50 PRINT S
60 END
200 PRINT
210 PRINT A,B
```

(b)
```
10 LET S=0
20 LET A=8
30 LET B=4
40 GOSUB 200
50 END
200 LET S=A+B
210 PRINT
220 PRINT A,B,S
230 LET A=A^2
240 GOSUB 30
250 RETURN
```

(c) This program is to find the square of A after its initial value has been added to B.

```
10 LET S=0
20 LET A=8
30 LET B=4
40 GOSUB 200
50 END
200 LET S=A+B
210 PRINT
220 PRINT A,B,S
230 RETURN
240 LET A=A^2
250 RETURN
```

(d)
```
10 LET S=0
20 LET A=8
30 GOSUB 200
40 END
200 LET S=S+A
210 PRINT
220 PRINT A,S
230 LET A=A+1
240 IF S<< 20 THEN 10
250 RETURN
```

5. Write the output of following program segments

(a)
```
200 GOSUB 400
210 GOSUB 500
220 RPINT "ONE"
230 STOP
400 REM
410 PRINT "TWO"
420 RETURN
500 REM
510 PRINT "THREE"
520 RETURN
```

(b)
```
200 LET N = 2
210 ON N GOSUB 400 300
220 GOTO 999
300 PRINT "IS FUN"
310 RETURN
400 PRINT "BASIC";
410 RETURN
999 PRINT "?"
```

ANSWERS
PART 2

1.
```
200 REM THIS SUBROUTINE
    CALCULATES THE BALANCE
210 LET B=R-P
220 RETURN
```

2.
```
200 REM THIS SUBROUTINE
    CALCULATES THE BALANCE
210 LET B=R-P
220 GOSUB 300
230 RETURN
300 REM THIS SUBROUTINE PRINTS
310 PRINT
320 PRINT TAB(3); "RECEIPTS";
    TAB(16); "PAYMENTS";
    TAB(29); "BALANCE"
330 PRINT
340 PRINT TAB(4); "$";TAB(5);R;
TAB(17);"$"; TAB (18); P; TAB(29);
"$";
TAB(30);B
350 RETURN
```

CHAPTER 14

Sequential Files

14.1 Data File Types

To enter data into our programs thus far, we have used **LET, INPUT**, and **READ** statements. There is another way of using data files. A data file is a collection of related groups of data (the file records) stored on magnetic tape or disk separately from the program that uses it.

Using data files offers several significant advantages over other forms of input

- Data files can be used by more than one program.
- Data files can store the output of a program for future review or as input for another program.
- Data files can be created or modified by a program.

BASICA supports two types of files: sequential files and random-access files. Sequential files, as the name implies, contain data that can only be accessed or written sequentially. You can have sequential files on cassette or disk; hence, all versions of BASICA support sequential operations on cassette, while disk and advanced BASIC support sequential operations on both cassette, and diskette.

For example, to print the 20th record in a file, we must first "file through" the 19 that precedes it. We cannot access it directly as we can with a random file.

14.2 Creating a Sequential File

To some extent, a sequential file resembles a series of **DATA** statements. Each record in a file is terminated by a carriage return, and the items within it (its fields) are separated by commas. Moreover, to read a certain file record (or **DATA** statement), we must first read all those that precede it. However, whereas **DATA** statements are created by simply typing them at the keyboard, data files are set up by a program (or program segment) written exclusively for this purpose.

The PROGRAM to create a sequential file must contain:

- An **OPEN** statement that names the file, declares its mode as **OUTPUT**, and assigns a file number to it.
- A **PRINT#** (or **WRITE#**) statement that writes (transmits) the desired data to the file.
- A **CLOSE** statement that disassociates the file from the file number and from mode,both set up when it was opened.

14.3 OPEN Statement

The OPEN statement must be used prior to any I/O statements in a program because it establishes a path to the file that will be used by subsequent file reference statements. The format of this statement for sequential file operations is:

Format `OPEN filename [FOR mode1] AS[#] filenum`

Where filename is the name which user may like to give the concerned file for identification purpose.

In general, file names may consist of two parts separated by a period, as name.extension where name is one to eight characters long (in some dialects only six characters are permitted), and the period and extension are optional. If the extension does appear, it may be one, two, or three characters long (see table 14.1). (Extensions are sometimes included to identify the type of file, for example, DAT for a data file, **BAS** for a BASIC file, and so on.)

Table 14.1 Some Valid and Invalid File Names

Valid	Invalid	Reason
PAYROLL	INCOME 90	(Blank not permitted)
PAYROLL	DAT INVENTORYDAT	(Name is too long)
GRADES 9A	COURSE.BASICA	(Extension is too long)

Note:

1. If you want to write a file to a disk drive other than the current one, in the OPEN statement, precede the file's name by the drive letter and a colon (:) For example, "**B:INVLIST**"refers to a file named **INVLIST** which will be created (or canbe found) on the B (right-hand) drive .
2. If a file is opened for OUTPUT and a file of that name already exists on the disk, all data in the existing file will be lost. As we shall see, this is sometimes useful when modifying a file, but it may have catastrophic results if done accidentally.
3. Data files, like variables and subroutines, should be listed as a matter of good practice in the header comments of the program module in which they are used. Both the file name and the variables used to represent the items within a record (itsm fields) should be listed and described.

   OUTPUT to specify sequential output mode

   INPUT to specify sequential input mode

   APPEND to specify sequential output mode

Where output will be added to the end of the file; if the file does not exist, the file will be created and data will be treated as in the **OUTPUT** mode

The file number (filenum) must be less than or equal to 3 if you are in disk or advanced BASIC. If the **/F** option was in the BASIC command, the file number must be less than or equal to 15 and cannot exceed the number used in the **/F** option. When working with tree structured directories under BASIC release 2.0 or above, you can include a path to the file in the file specification. Some examples of the use of this statement and the operational result are as follows.

Example 14.1

Following statement permits output to the file named **HISTORY** with the extension **DAT** in the current directory on the diskette in drive B, using file number 3.

```
100  OPEN  "B:HISTORY.DAT"  FOR  OUTPUT  AS  #3
```

Following statement permits input from the file named JAN with the extension **DAT** in the current directory on the diskette in the current drive using file number 2.

```
200 OPEN "JAN.DAT" FOR INPUT AS #2
```

Following statement permits output to the file named **DATA** in the directory called **SALE** in drive C, using file number 1.

```
300  OPEN  "C:\SALE\DATA" FOR OUTPUT AS #1
```

Following statement permits the adding of data to the file named **FEB** with the extension **DAT** in the current directory on the current drive, using file number 1.

```
400   OPEN   "FEB.DAT"   FOR APPEND AS #1
```

Remember that A # in front of file is optional.

Since you may wish to control the operational mode of data flow within your program, an alternate format of this statement is provided in BASIC. This format is:

Format `OPEN mode2, [#] filenumber  file spec[LEN  reclen]`

Where mode2 is a string expression whose first character indicates the I/O operation as follows:

O specifies sequential output mode

I specifies sequential input mode

If a record length (reclen) is not specified, BASIC will use a default record length of 128 bytes. Two examples of this statement and their operational result follow.

Example 14.2

Following statement permits input from the file named **JAN** with extension **DAT** on the diskette in drive B, using file number 2.

```
100   OPEN   "I", #2, "B:JAN.DAT"
```

Following statement permits output to the file named **DATA** in the directory called **SALES** on drive C, using file number 1

```
200   OPEN   "O", #1, "C:\SALES\DATA"
```

To see how you can use this second format of the **OPEN** statement to control data flow within a program, consider the following program segment.

```
10 IF x < 5 THEN A$ "O" ELSE A$ "I"
20 OPEN A$, #1, "JAN.DAT"
```

In the preceding example, when **X** is less than **5**, the file **JAN** with the extension **DAT** will be opened for output. Note that this will destroy any existing data on the file if the file already exists. If **X** is not less than **5**, the file will be opened for input. When you open a file for input, which does not exist, a "File not found" error will result.

When you process sequential files, you must execute an **OPEN** statement prior to using any of the following statements or the INPUT functions: **PRINT#, WRITE#, PRINT# USING, INPUT#, LINE INPUT#**,and **INPUT$.**

14.4 File Numbers : IF Option

I/O operations performed in BASIC require a file number. This is a unique number that will be associated with the actual file you wish to read data from or write data onto. The file number provides a physical path between subsequent file I/O statements and the file you wish to access. This path is established by the **OPEN** statement. The file number can be a number, variable, or expression. Its value must be equal to or greater than 1 and less than or equal to the maximum number of files permitted to be open at one time in the version of BASIC you are using. Advanced BASIC permits a maximum of three **OPEN** files in the default mode. You can increase the maximum number of **OPEN** files permitted in advanced BASIC by invoking what is known as the F option in the BASIC command. The format of this optional parameter is:

```
/ F : files
```

where **1 <= files <= 15.**

When you bring up advanced BASIC, you would use the **<B>F** option at that time to specify the number of **OPEN** files your program requires that exceed three since, when omitted, the number of files the program can have **OPEN** at one time defaults to that value. If you require five files, your BASIC command would be following:

```
BASICA  / F : 5
```

Since each sequential file requires 188 bytes of memories and random access files require a minimum of 316 bytes, you should insure that you do not specify more files in the BASIC command than necessary. Otherwise, you will remove memory from use by the program that is reserved for files you are not using.

14.5 CLOSE Statement

Once you have concluded your file operations, you may wish to terminate the path between your program and a particular file or files. You can use the **CLOSE** statement to conclude I/O to a device or file. The format of this statement is:

Format `CLOSE[ [#] FILENUM [, [#] FILENUM]. . .]`

When used without specifying any file numbers, this statement will close all devices and files that were previously opened. If you specify one or more file numbers, only those specified will be closed. Examples of the use of this statement and the operational result follow.

```
100  CLOSE
```

Above statement causes all open devices and files to be closed

```
200 CLOSE  #1,#3,#5
```

Above statement causes the files and devices associated with file numbers 1, 3, and 5 to be closed

```
300  CLOSE  #2, #4
```

Above statement causes the files and devices associated with file numbers 2 and 4 to be closed

Once the **CLOSE** statement is executed, the association between a particular file or device and its file number will terminate. If the device or file was opened for sequential output, the contents of the information in the file buffer will be written to the file or device prior to the termination of the association.

Since the execution of the **END** statement or the BASIC commands **NEW, RESET**, or **SYSTEM** will cause all open files and devices to be automatically closed, a logical question is why would you use this statement in place of the **END** statement or a command that performs the same function?

First, the **CLOSE** statement performs the function within a program. You can place a program reaching an **END** statement or the operator keying in a BASIC command.

Second, suppose you require access to a large number of files within your program. Since the default value of the number of files that can be opened at any one time in disk or BASICA is three, what happens if you require access to four or more files? You could use the /F option in the disk or advanced BASIC command to permit up to 15 files to be at any instant in time.

Since each sequential file uses a buffer of 128 bytes, you may either run out of program memory as you open additional files or you could reach the maximum number of 15 files permitted to be opened. In such situations, the **CLOSE** statement allows you to terminate the path between one or more file numbers and specified devices or files after you performed operations on each file. This allows you to reuse the file number to **OPEN** another device or file or you can reopen the previously **CLOSED** device or file if you require access to it later in the program.

Thus, the **CLOSE** statement permits you to conserve program memory and to access an almost infinite number of files from program, although you can only have 15 such files opened at one time.

The following program segment illustrates the use of the CLOSE statement.

```
100 OPEN "JAN.DAT" FOR INPUT AS #1
110 OPEN "FEB.DAT" FOR INPUT AS #2
120 OPEN "MAR.DAT" FOR INPUT AS #3
.
.
500 CLOSE #1, #2, #3
510 OPEN "APR.DAT" FOR INPUT AS #1
520 OPEN "MAY.DAT" FOR INPUT AS #2
530 OPEN "JUN.DAT" FOR INPUT AS #3
```

In the preceding example, due to memory limitations you may wish only three data files opened at time. Thus, after you close file numbers 1 through 3, you can reopen them to three new files and continue processing.

Now, let's examine the format and utilization of each of the statements and functions requiring the **OPEN** statement to write data onto and read data several programs that demonstrate sequential processing.

Example 14.3

```
10 REM Opening & Closing SEQUENTIAL FILE
20 OPEN "DATA" FOR OUTPUT AS #1
30 INPUT "ENTER YOUR NAME ";N$
40 INPUT "ENTER YOUR AGE ";A
50 PRINT # 1,N$
60 PRINT # 1,A
70 CLOSE
80 OPEN "DATA" FOR INPUT AS #1
90 INPUT #1, A$, B
100 PRINT "YOU ARE ";A$; "AND ARE "; B;" YEARS OLD"
110 CLOSE
RUN
ENTER YOUR NAME? VIJAY KAPOOR
ENTER YOU AGE? 45
YOU ARE VIJAY KAPOOR AND ARE 45 YEARS OLD
```

Example 14.4

This program segment creates a file called CRICKET containing a list of names input by user.

```
200 OPEN "CRICKET" FOR OUTPUT AS #1
210 REM
220 LET NM$ "AAA"
230 WHILE NM$ < > "ZZZ"
240 INPUT "ENTER CRICKETER'S NAME (OR 'ZZZ' WHEN  DONE) "; NM$
250 PRINT #1, NM$
260 WEND
270 REM
280 CLOSE #1
```

In this program segment, the **OPEN** statement (line 200) assigns the number 1 to a file that will be referenced as CRICKET, and prepares it for **OUTPUT** (to be created). Then, statement 220 initializes NM$ and ensures that the **WHILE/WEND** loop will be executed at least once. Within this loop, each name is input from the user, and then written to the file by the **PRINT#** statement (line 250). After entering the final name, the user types the sentinel value, **ZZZ**, which is also written to the file as in end-of-file indicator. (It will be a sentinel record for other programs using the file CRICKET as input data.) Finally, the file is closed by statement 280.

Suppose the data entered by the user is:

```
ENTER CRICKETER'S NAME (OR 'ZZZ' WHEN DONE) GAVASKAR
ENTER CRICKETER'S NAME (OR 'ZZZ' WHEN DONE) KAPIL DEV
ENTER CRICKETER'S NAME (OR 'ZZZ' WHEN DONE) RAVI SHASTRI
ENTER CRICKETER'S NAME (OR 'ZZZ' WHEN DONE) ZZZ
```

Then, after execution of this program segment, the file CRICKETERS is stored on disk, and can be pictured as:

```
GAVASKAR <CR> KAPIL-DEV <CR> RAVI-SHASTRI ZZZ <CR> <EOF> ZZZ
```

where <CR> is a carriage return symbol and <EOF> is an end-of- file symbol placed there by the computer.

14.6 PRINT# Statement

The PRINT # statement provides you with the capability to write data sequentially onto a file. The format of this statement is

Format `PRINT #filenum, list of expressions`

where filenum is the file number that was used when the file was opened for data output and list of expressions is a list of string and / or numeric expressions that will be written onto the file.

The **PRINT#** statement functions the same as a **PRINT** statement, with the exception that data is written to a file instead of being displayed on the screen. When you use the **PRINT #** statement to write data to a file you must be careful in your selection of delimiters used to separate each expression in the list of expressions contained in the statement.This is because different delimiters result in a different amount of blanks inserted between print fields. You can see this from the following example in which you will use the normal **PRINT** statement, since it will provide a screen display of the image of data written to a file using the **PRINT#** statement.

```
100 READ X,Y,Z
110 DATA 1,3,5
120 PRINT X,Y,Z
130 PRINT X;Y;Z
RUN
1             3             5
1  3  5
Ok
```

In the preceding example, note that the commas used as delimiters between variables result in extra blanks being inserted between print fields. Since the same image of the data displayed on the screen with a PRINT statement is written to a file using a PRINT # statement, the blanks between print fields will be written to the file. Thus, the PRINT # statement does not compress data on the file.

To reduce the amount of required file space necessary to store data, you should use semicolons as delimiters when you have numeric expressions in your list. Since there is always at least one blank space between numeric expressions written to a file using semicolons as a separator, that space will serve to distinguish each numeric expression as distinct entity when you input them from the file to the computer with an appropriate INPUT statement. Since the data written to sequential files is in sequential order, note that the following statements

```
100 PRINT #1, X
110 PRINT #1, Y
120 PRINT #1, Z
```

Perform the same function as the statement.

```
100 PRINT #1, X, Y, Z
```

Thus, in sequential file operations, you must be careful to ensure that the program stores data in the same format that you will use for the retrieval of data.

When strings are written to a file, you may use semicolons to separate them from other string expressions in the list of expressions as well as to conserve file space when the data is written onto a file. Further more, you must insert the appropriate delimiter into the file; otherwise, two separate strings would be written to the file as one interconnected string. Thus, the following program segment.

```
10 OPEN  "MAILLIST.DAT" FOR OUTPUT AS #1
20 NAMEL$ "DIVYA"
30 NAMEF$ "BHATNAGAR"
40 PRINT #1 NAMEL$; NAMEF$
```

Would result in the interconnected string **DIVYABHATNAGAR** being written to the file. If you later attempt to read this record, you would have no way to read the data as two separate strings that represent a last and first field. You can correct this situation by one of several methods that can be used to insert the appropriate delimiter into a file. The most obvious method to add the required delimiters is by inserting them into the **PRINT#** statement as indicated.

```
40 PRINT #1 NAMEL$ ; "," ; NAMEF$
```

The execution of this statement would cause the following data image to be written to the file.

```
DIVYA,BHATNAGAR
```

This results in two distinct fields separated by a comma. The information in the record now can be read back into the computer as two distinct strings, each representing one field of information.

A second method that can be used to generate a required delimiter between strings is obtained by concatenation of each odd numbered string in a sequence of strings with a string representing a delimiter. This is illustrated below.

```
35 DELIMIT$ ","
40 PRINT NAMEL$ + DELIMIT$; NAMEF$
```

In line 40, the concatenation of the comma to the first string will result in the comma serving as a separator that will distinguish two separate strings for later input. Now that you can add the appropriate delimiter, a logical question is what you do when one string naturally contains an embedded comma? For example, suppose you wish to write the string **ANAME$** to a file where

```
ANAME$ "DIVYA,BHATNAGAR"
```

Note that you cannot use NAME$, since it is a reserved word. The statement

```
PRINT #1, ANAME$
```

Would write the following data image to the file:

```
DIVYA,BHATNAGAR
```

When you attempt later to read the record from the file, your string variable used in an **INPUT#** statement will only read information from the record until the delimiter is reached. This will result in the string "DIVYA" being extracted from the record instead of both the last and first names as well as the comma used in the string. To write the string to the file so that it will be read back as one string, requires you to surround the string with double quotation marks.

You can use the **CHR$** function that converts an ASCII code to its character equivalent. Here, you would use the value 34 which would result in the one character string of a double quotation mark being written to the file each time a **CHR$(34)** function is encountered in the statement. Your previous statement would then be rewritten as follows:

```
PRINT #1 CHR$(34); ANAME$; CHR$(34)
```

The execution of this statement would cause the following data image to be written onto the file:

```
"DIVYA,BHATNAGAR"
```

Since the information contained in a pair of double quotation signs is treated as one string, this will solve your problem of unintentionally reading only a portion of a string previously written to a file.

Strings processing can be a very valuable tool in storing information in an efficient manner. By concatenation of each field with a string variable containing a comma and then concatenating the result to the previous field, you can construct one string of variable length containing a last name, first name, middle initial, address, and so on, with each field separated from the next field by a comma.

Once you read a string, you could develop a short subroutine that could easily break each part of the resulting stored sting into its various components stating for a comma. Each character that is not a comma would be concatenated with the null string until a comma encountered. Then, the appropriate string variable would be assigned the value of the concatenated string, that string would be set to null value, and the search would resume for a second comma or the end of the string. By storing each data record on a file as one string, you can optimize your storage capacity.

When you mix both strings and numerics in a PRINT# statement, you must also insert appropriate delimiters into the **PRINT#** statement or you may obtain an error when you attempt to retrieve the stored data. To illustrate this point, consider the following example.

```
100  A$ "BHAT DIVYA"
110 YOB 1983
120 PRINT #1 A$; YOB Year of birth)
```

After executing these statements, the data would be stored sequentially as one string as indicated below.

```
BHAT DIVYA 1983
```

If you later attempt to retrieve the stored information using the statement

```
INPUT #1, A$, YOB
```

the entire string "**BHAT DIVYA 1983**" would be assigned to **A$** and an "Input Past end" error would occur, since there would be no data on the file to assign to **YOB**. If you used a literal comma as a string delimiter in the **PRINT#** Statement as follows

```
120 PRINT #1, A$; A$; ","; YOB
```

The data would have to be written to the file as

```
BHAT DIVYA, 1983
```

Then, the **INPUT#** statement would correctly assign **BHAT DIVYA** to **A$** and **1983** to **YOB**.

14.7 WRITE# Statement

Another mechanism that provides you with the capability to write data onto a sequential file is obtained by the use of the WRITE# statement. The format of this statement is indicated below.

Format `WRITE# filenum, list of expressions`

The format and the operational result of the **WRITE#** statement are similar to the **PRINT#** statement;

however, several important differences result from the execution of these two statements. First, the **WRITE#** statement will automatically insert commas between items as they are written onto a sequential file as well as delimiting strings with quotation marks. Thus, whereas it is necessary to put explicit delimiters in the list of expressions when using the **PRINT#** statement, you can avoid this requirement by using the **WRITE#** statement. The **PRINT#** statement functions like all **PRINT**-related statements by placing a blank character in front of positive numbers as they are written to a file. This services as an automatic separator between items written to a file, printed or placed on the screen using one of the appropriate **PRINT** statements. Since the **WRITE#** statement automatically inserts commas between items, no blank character is required in front of a positive number. After all items in the list of expressions are written , a carriage return/line feed sequence will be generated onto the file. The following use of the **WRITE#** statement.

```
10 NAMEL$ "DIVYA"
20 NAMEF$ "BHATNAGAR"
30 YOB 1983
40 WRITE #1 NAMEL$, NAMEF$, YOB,
```

would write the following image to the file.

```
"DIVYA","BHATNAGAR",1983
```

Now, consider the following example.

```
100 READ A,B,C, D$
110 DATA 1,3,5, IMAGE
120 WRITE #1 A,B,C, D$
```

The execution of this programme segment preceded by the appropriate **OPEN** statement would write the following image to the file —

```
1,3,5,"IMAGE"
```

In developing programs in BASIC that use sequential files, you will normally prefer the **WRITE#** statement over the **PRINT#** statement. This is because it is easier to use the **WRITE#**statement to write data to a sequential file that a subsequent INPUT# statement can read.

14.8 PRINT# USING Statement

The **PRINT# USING** statement permits you to write to a file using a specified format. The **PRINT#USING** statement functions similarly to the **PRINT USING** and **LPRINT USING** statements, with the only difference among the three statement being that the **PRINT USING** statement causes data to be printed in a specified format, while the **PRINT USING** statement causes data to be printed in a specified format, while the **PRINT#USING** statement writes the data image specified by the format of the statement onto a file. The format of the **PRINT#USING** statement is indicated below:

Format `PRINT #`*`filenum`*`,USING` *`var$; list of expressions`*

The string variable following the keyword USING contains the formatting characters that define the field and format of strings or numbers that will be written onto the file.

One of the primary uses of the PRINT# USING statement is to generate reports onto a diskette instead of a printer. If the system you are working on does not have a printer or perhaps does not have a better quality printer, you can generate the report onto a file. A file "dump" program would then read the file and dump its image onto the printer, producing a hard copy of the report. Even you have a printer, it is considerably faster to write data to a file than to a printer. Thus, you may wish to execute a program without tying up your printer for a long period of time. Some examples using this statement are as follows:

```
100 A 3.71
110 B 4.978
120 PRINT#1, USING "#.## #.####"; A,B
```

The resulting image

```
3.71 4.9780
```

being written onto the file opened with file number 1.Changing line number 120 to

```
120  PRINT#1, USING ".## #.####" ; A,B
```

results in the print image

```
%3.71 4.9780
```

being written onto the file. The percent sign (%) in front of the first number indicates that the number to be printed is larger than the specified numeric field.

14.9 INPUT# Statement

The INPUT# statement provides you with the capability to read data items previously written to a sequential file. As data items are read, they will be assigned to program variables, permitting you to use those data items within your program. The format of this statement is:

Format `INPUT# filenum, var[,var]. . .`

The file number in the statement must be the number previously used when the file was opened for input. Unlike the conventional BASIC **INPUT** statement, no prompt message will be generated, nor will a question mark be printed when the **INPUT#** statement is executed.

When an **INPUT#** statement is executed, a type comparison is performed between the names of the variables in the statement and the type of data on the record to be read. If they do not match, a "Type mismatch" error will result. This is illustrated by the following example where it is assumed each record on the file contains three fields providing quantity-on-hand, cost, and an item description. The first two fields are numeric, while the third field is a string. Suppose our **INPUT#** statement used to read information from the file is as follows:

```
100 INPUT#1, QTY, COST, ITEM
```

Since the third variable was entered as a numeric type, a "Type mismatch" error would occur. You can correct this by modifying your statement changing **ITEM** to **ITEM$**. Thus,

```
100 INPUT#1, QTY, COST, ITEM$
```

would have three variable names that match the type of data in the file.

If you are reading numeric values from the file, all leading spaces, carriage return, and line feed characters will be ignored. The first character encountered that is not a space, carriage return, or line feed is assumed by BASIC to be the start of a number. Each number of the file is considered to be terminated when a space, carriage return, line feed, or comma is encountered.

When a string variable is specified in the **INPUT#** statement, BASIC will scan the record for a string. Again leading spaces, commas, carriage returns, and line feeds will be ignored. The first character encountered that is not a space, comma, carriage return, or line feed will be assumed to be the start of the string. When the first character of the string is a quotation mark ("), BASIC will assign all characters on the record between this quotation mark and a second quotation mark to the string variable in the **INPUT#** statement. This "quoted" string may not include a quotation mark within the string, since it would cause BASIC to misinterpret where the string ends.

When the first character in the string is not a quotation mark, the string is an "unquoted" string.

Unquoted strings are terminated when a comma. carriage return, or line feed is encountered as data is read from a file record.. For both "quoted" and "unquoted" strings, the maximum string length that can be read is 255 characters. The examples in Table 10-1 illustrate the resulting values of variables used in an **INPUT#** statement based on the indicated record information stored on the file.

The sequential file actually read by the **INPUT#** statement will depend on the file specification used in OPEN# statement that contains the matching file number used in the INPUT# statement. Although you will normally specify the diskette (A: or B:) or fixed disk (C: or D:) in the OPEN statement, you could specify the Key board (KYBD:). Such a specification would result in the INPUT# statement reading data directly from the keyboard. Since the communications adapter is treated similarly to other devices, you can use the INPUT# statement to read a sequential data stream from that device.

Table 14.2 INPUT# Statement Variables

INPUT # Statement	Record Information	Variable Assignments
100 INPUT # A,B	105.7 2089	A 105.7 B 2089
100 INPUT # A,B	105.7,2089	A 105.7 B 2089
100 INPUT # 1,N$, X$,X	BAJAJ,GITA,25	N$ "BAJAJ" X$ "GITA" X 25
100 INPUT # 1,N$, X	BAJAJ,GITA",25	N$ "BAJAJ,GITA" X 25
100 INPUT # 1,N$,X	"BAJAJ,GITA" 25	N$ "BAJAJ,GITA" X 25

14.10 INPUT$ Function

The **INPUT$** Function provides you with the capability to read a string of specified length from a file or from the keyboard. The format of this function is :

Format **INPUT$(exprnm[,[#]filenum])**

The numeric expression in the format defines the number of characters that will be returned when the function is invoked. The following example illustrates the use of the **INPUT$** function.

```
100 OPEN "KYBD:" FOR INPUT AS #1
110 X$ INPUT$(30, #1)
120 PRINT X$
```

The file name has been given as KYBD to indicate that this file is concerned with inputting the data from keyboard.Now suppose you want to enter INPUT$ STATEMENT IS VALUABLE STATEMENT, see that computer provides only first thirty characters.

```
RUN
INPUT$ STATEMENT IS VALUABLE S
Ok
```

When the **INPUT#** function is executed, no characters will be displayed on the screen. If you wish to display the characters you entered, you should follow this function call by a **PRINT** statement as indicated in the previous example.

In line 110, 30 characters are read from the keyboard and assigned to the string variable **X$**. The **PRINT** statement in line 120 echoes the characters previously input to the screen. When the **INPUT$** function requests data from the keyboard, no prompt message nor a prompt question mark (?) is generated. Therefore, it is good programming practice to prefix this statement with a **PRINT** statement that prompts the user for the required data.

The **INPUT$** statement will read all characters upto the specified length of the string requested to include special control characters, with the exception of the Ctrl + Break, which will interrupt program execution. This ability to read strings regardless of their content makes this function valuable for reading ASCII codes that could otherwise be interpreted by the BASIC Editor as a request to perform a specific functions. Thus you could use this function to enter a backspace character from the keyboard into your program. When the INPUT$ function requests data from the keyboard, the function call will be automatically completed when the required number of characters are entered, alleviating the necessity of pressing the Enter key to terminate input.

The following examples illustrate the use of this function and its operational result.

Function	Operational result
`10 X$ INPUT$(50, #1)`	Reads a string of 50 characters and assigns them to the string variable X$.
`10 Y$ INPUT$(30,#2)`	Reads a string of 30 characters from file number 2 and assigns them to the string variable Y$

In the next example you will use the **INPUT$** function to read 1 character from the keyboard. This is similar to the **INKEY$** variable, with the exception that program execution will be suspended while the **INPUT$** function awaits a key to be pressed. In comparison, the **INKEY$** variable will read the keyboard state at the time the variable is encountered. Thus:

```
100 open "KYBD:" FOR INPUT AS #1
110 X$ INPUT$ (1,#1)
120 IF X$ "E" THEN END ELSE 500
500 REM program continues
is the equivalent of
100 X$ INKEY$
110 IF X$ "E" THEN END
120 IF X$ " " THEN 100 ELSE 500
500 REM program continues
```

14.11 EOF Function

The EOF function provides you with the capability to test for an end-of-file condition. The format of this function is:

Format *varnm EOF (filenum)*

The EOF function returns one of two values depending on whether or not the end-of-file mark has been reached on the specified file. A - 1 (true) will be returned if the end-of-file mark is reached, while a 0 (zero) will be returned if the end-of-file mark has not been reached. Since attempting to read past the end- of-file will cause an error, you should prefix each file INPUT statement in program with an end-of-file test. Thus, your file dump program should be modified as indicated below.

```
100 OPEN "REPORT.DAT" FOR INPUT AS #1
105 IF EOF(1) THEN 140
110 LINE INPUT #1 ,X$
120 PRINT X$
130 GOTO 105
140 CLOSE #1
```

There are two additional functions that can be used in sequential file operations- the **LOC** functions and **LOF** functions.

14.12 LOC Function

The LOC function returns the number of physical records that were read from or written onto a file since it was opened. The format of this function is:

Format `varnm LOC (filenum)`

The number of physical records on a file is a function of the format you employ to record data on the file. In the following example, the numbers 1 to 512 were records first on the file named "JUNK.BAS, which resulted in 19 records of information, since a semicolon(;) was used after the variable 1 in line 105. In the next example, we removed the semicolon, which resulted in space being placed between the numbers. Here, the number of physical records required to record the same data increased to 27.

```
100 OPEN "B: JUNK.BAS" FOR OUTPUT AS #1
105 FOR I 1 to 512 : PRINT #1 ,I;: NEXT I
106 PRINT "RECORD# " ; LOC(1)
140 CLOSE #1
RUN
RECORD# 19
Ok
105 FOR I 1 TO 512 : PRINT#1, I : NEXT I
RUN
RECORD#= 27
Ok
```

Since sequential files can be opened in only one mode at a time, you cannot easily update or delete information on such files. To change a piece of information previously written onto such a file requires you to read the file until you locate the information you wish to update or delete and close the file. After you reopen the file, you will read information from the old file onto a new file until you reach the point where you wish to update or delete a record. If you wish to update the record, you will **INPUT** the changes from the keyboard and skip the information on the old file, writing the new information and all remaining information from the old file onto the new file.

14.13 LOF Function

The LOF function returns the actual number of bytes allocated to a file. The format of this function is:

Format `varnm (filenum)`

You can use this function to determine the number of sectors on the diskette that a file occupies as shown by the following program segment.

```
100 OPEN "B: JUNK.BAS" FOR OUTPUT AS #1
105 FOR I 1 TO 512: PRINT #1, I: NEXT I
106 PRINT "RECORD#=";LOC(1)
107 X LOF (1)
108 S X / 128
110 PRINT "FILE OCCUPIES ";S;"  SECTORS"
140 CLOSE #1
RUN
RECORD# 27
FILE OCCUPIES 27 SECTORS
Ok
```

14.14 Sequential File Processing

Now that file I/O statements and functions relevant to sequential files have been reviewed, let's use these statements and functions to construct a series of programs that use such files.

In each of the following examples, certain file-related processing steps will be used to create a sequential file which could access the data on that file. As a minimum, you should consider the following steps to ensure correct sequential file processing.

- Prior to writing data onto a file in output or append operations, ensure that the file is opened.
- Write data onto a file using the **PRINT#, Write#,** or **PRINT# USING** statements. Remember that the **PRINT# USING** statements do not automatically write field delimiters onto the file.

  If the file, you are writing onto, previously existed and was not opened in the APPEND mode, existing data on that file will be destroyed.
- To access data on a file created by your program or opened by the program for output, you must close the file and reopen it for input.
- Read data from sequential files using the **INPUT#** or **LINE INPUT#** statements.

Example 14.5

Following program creates a file called CLASS containing records of the form student name, test score

```
150   REM STUDENT  "CLASS" FILE
190   OPEN "CLASS" FOR OUTPUT AS #1
210   CLS
220   PRINT " ENTER NAMES OF STUDENTS AND TEST MARKS FOR EACH"
240   PRINT
250   PRINT TAB(5); " ENTER STUDENT NAMES AND MARKS"
260   PRINT TAB(5); " ENTER ZZZ, 0 WHEN DONE"
270   PRINT
280   LET STD$ "AAA"
290   REM
300   WHILE STD$ < > ZZZ"
310   INPUT "NAME, MARKS = . . . . .  ",STD$,  MARKS
320   PRINT #1, STD$; ","; MARKS
330   WEND
340   REM
350   CLOSE #1
360   END
```

The PRINT # statement writes the same information to a file that the corresponding PRINT statement would display on the screen. For example, suppose the input on a run of this program is

```
NAME, MARKS = . . . . . JAYA, 76
NAME, MARKS = . . . . . MANOHAR, 63
NAME, MARKS = . . . . . SUSHMA, 84
NAME, MARKS = . . . . . ZZZ, 0
```

When run, the file **CLASS** would contain the following data:

```
JAYA, 76<CR> MANOHAR, 63<CR> SUSHMA, 84<CR> ZZZ,<CR>0<CR> <EOF>
```

NB: **PRINT#** even places blanks before and after every positive number in the file, just as PRINT would do on the screen.)

Example 14.7

By typing program segment, we create a file called **DUMP** which is identical to **CLASS** except for a record deleted at the request of the user.

14.15. Sequential File Maintenance

The process of making changes in an existing sequential file, we need to adopt a group of processes

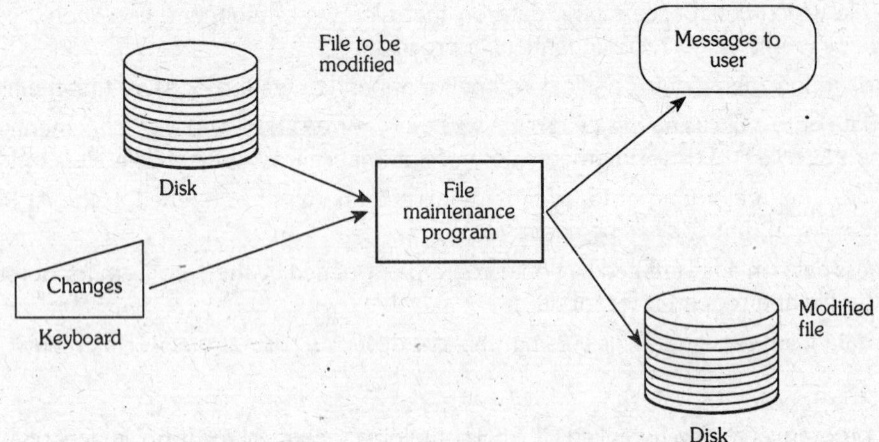

Fig. 14.1 A system flow-chart of file maintenance process

known collectively as file maintenance. These include data file. We will also discuss the operation of merging two data files.

(1) Deleting, Adding and Modifying Records

Sequential files cannot be modified quickly. If any change is made,the entire file must be rewritten. Every record in it must be read (and modified if so desired), temporarily stored somewhere else, and, after all records have been processed, written back to the given file.

One general procedure to accomplish this uses a second file, called a scratch file, to temporarily store the contents of the given file. The process proceeds as follows:

1. Open the given file for **INPUT** and the scratch file for **OUTPUT**.
2. Input data concerning the change from the user.
3. Read records from the given file and write them to the scratch file until you reach the one to be modified.
4. Make the change: write a new or modified record to the scratch file, or in the case of a deletion, do not write the specified record to the scratch file.
5. Read the rest of records from the given file and write them to the scratch file.
6. Close both files.
7. Transfer all data from the scratch file to the given file.

The file maintenance process can be illustrated graphically using a system flowchart (fig. 14.1) that shows the flow of data within the computer system for a particular application. For example, a rectangular shape represents the computer itself and a cylindrical shape represents a disk.

The next few examples illustrate the maintenance process. In all of these, we shall create a file "CLASS" with records of the form student name, test score arranged in alphabetical order and program terminated by "ZZZ", o.

14.16 Deleting a Sequential File

In this program segment, a file named DUMP is created which is identical to the file CLASS except for a record deleted at the request of the user.

Example 14.5 Deleting a Record from a Sequential File

```
200 OPEN "CLASS" FOR INPUT AS #1
210 OPEN "DUMP" FOR OUTPUT AS #2
230 INPUT "NAME OF STUDENT TO BE DELETED" ; NM$
240 LET STD$ "AAA"
250 REM
260 WHILE STD$ << >> "ZZZ"
270 INPUT #1, STD$, MARKS
280 IF STD$ << >> NM$ THEN WRITE #2, STD$, MARKS
290 WEND
300  REM
310 CLOSE #1, #2
```

The `WHILE/WEND` loop reads all records in this program segment, one at a time, from the file `CLASS` and writes each of these, except for the specified one, onto DUMP. At the end of execution, `DUMP` is identical to `CLASS`, except for the deleted record. For example suppose `CLASS` contains and the user inputs the name MANOHAR for deletion. Then, after execution, **DUMP** would contain

```
"JAYA", 76<CR> "MANOHAR", 63<CR> "SUSHMA", 84<CR> "ZZZ", 0<CR> <EOF>
```

and the user inputs the name MANOHAR for deletion. Then after execution, DUMP would contain:

```
"JAYA", 76<CR> "SUSHMA", 84<CR> "ZZZ", 0<CR> <EOF>
```

The file `CLASS` will not change during the execution of the program segment in example 14.5. To restore `CLASS` as the name of the updated (modified) file, we could execute the following program segment:

```
320 REM
330 OPEN "CLASS" FOR OUTPUT AS #1
340 OPEN "DUMP" FOR INPUT AS #2
350 LET STD$ "AAA"
360 REM
370 WHILE STD$ << >> "ZZZ"
380 INPUT #2, STD$, MARKS
390 WRITE #1, STD$, MARKS
400 WEND
410 REM
420 CLOSE #1, #2
```

This code copies the file `DUMP` onto the file `CLASS`, (Remember: when `CLASS` is opened for `OUTPUT` in line 330, its contents are erased.)

However, this copying proces is a very in efficient one. A much better way, available in most BASIC dialects, is to simply rename the scratch file as `CLASS`. To do this in Microsoft BASIC, we use the pair of statements:

```
320 KILL "CLASS"
330 NAME "DUMP"  AS "CLASS"
```

The `KILL` statement erases the file `CLASS` (which has to be done before the renaming) and the NAME statement renames `DUMP`. (Both files must be closed prior to execution of these statements). After the renaming, only one file, `CLASS`, will appear in the disk directory.

14.17 Inserting a Record

To insert a record specified by the user into the **CLASS** file at the appropriate place (retaining alphabetical order) you have to write a program something similar to following program.

Example 14.6 Inserting a record in a sequential file

```
200 OPEN "CLASS" FOR INPUT AS #1
210 OPEN "DUMP" FOR OUTPUT AS #2
220 REM
230 INPUT "NEW STUDENT AND MARKS" ;NM$, SC
240 REM
250 WHILE NM$ < > STD$
260 INPUT #1, STD$, MARKS
270 IF NM$ < STD$ THEN WRITE #2, NM$; SC
280 WRITE  #2, STD$, MARKS
290 WEND
300 REM
310 WHILE STD$ < > "ZZZ"
320 INPUT #1, STD$; MARKS
330 WRITE #2, STD$; MARKS
340 WEND
350 REM
360 CLOSE #1, #2
370 KILL "CLASS"
380 NAME "DUMP" AS "CLASS"
```

The first **WHILE/WEND** loop in lines 250-290 reads records from the **CLASS** file and writes them onto the dump file until the input name (**NM$**) precedes (in alphabetical order) the current record name (**STD$**). At this point, the new record is written to the scratch file, as well as the current record, and the loop is exited. The second **WHILE/WEND** loop in lines **310-340** reads the rest of the record from **CLASS** and writes them to **DUMP**. Finally, statements **370** and **380** rename the updated file as **CLASS**.

If prior to execution of this program segment, **CLASS** contained

"JAYA", 76<CR> "SUSHMA", 84<CR> "ZZZ", 0<CR> <EOF>

and the user inputs the name **PREM** and the score 81, then after execution, **CLASS** would contain the data

"JAYA", 76<CR> "PREM", 81<CR> "SUSHMA", 84<CR> "ZZZ" 0<CR> <EOF>

14.18 Modifying or Upgrading a Record

Example 14.7 Modifying or Upgrading a record in Sequential File

This program segment modifies a specified record in **CLASS** in the way indicated by the user.

```
200 OPEN  "CLASS" FOR INPUT AS #1
210 OPEN  "DUMP" FOR OUTPUT AS #2
220 REM
230 INPUT "ENTER NAME OF STUDNT=—— ", NM$
240 INPUT "NEW  TEST MARKS—— ", SC
250 LET STD$ "AAA"
260 REM
270 WHILE STD$ < > "ZZZ"
280 INPUT #1, STD$, MARKS
```

```
290 IF STD$ NM$ THEN WRITE #2, NM$, SC ELSE WRITE #2, STD$,MARKS
330 REM END IF
310 WEND
320 REM
330 KILL "CLASS"
340 NAME "DUMP" AS "CLASS"
```

Here, the **WHILE/WEND** loop copies all records from **CLASS** onto scratch except for the one to be modified. It is replaced (due to the **IF/THEN/ELSE** statement) by the one containing input data. Thus, if prior to execution, **CLASS** contains

```
"JAYA", 76<CR> "PREM", 81<CR> "SUSHMA", 84<CR> "ZZZ", 0<CR> <EOF>
```

and the user enters the name **SMITA** and the score 56, then after execution, the **CLASS** file will contain

```
"JAYA", 76<CR> "PREM", 81<CR> "SUSHMA", 56<CR> "ZZZ", 0<CR> <EOF>
```

EXERCISES

PART- I

1. State whether True of False
   (1) A file can be used by more than one program.
   (2) A file can store a program's output for future use.
   (3) A file name cannot contain any blanks.
   (4) To read a given record in a sequential file, we must first read all those that precede it.
   (5) If a file is opened for **OUTPUT**, and a file of that name already exists on the disk, then an error message is displayed.
   (6) To be read by an **INPUT#** statement, data items in a file must be separated by commas or carriage returns.
   (7) A **PRINT#** statement writes the same characters to a sequential file as the corresponding **PRINT** statement would have displayed on the screen.
   (8) When a file is opened for **INPUT**, data can be written from the program to the file.
   (9) If a sequential file is created and then read in the same program, it must be closed and reopened between these operations.
   (10) If any change is made to a sequential file, the entire file must be rewritten.
   (11) A file cannot be renamed with the name of another file that already exists
   (12) In order to delete a record from a file, we use the Kill statement.
   (13) Before two files can be merged, both must be opened for INPUT.
2. Correct the syntax errors in each statement.
   (a) **20 OPEN "FILE1" AS #1 FOR OUTPUT**
   (b) **25 WRITE #2 A, B, C**
   (c) **30 KILL FILE3**
3. Correct the syntax errors in each statement.
   (a) **200 NAME "MASTER" FOR "UP DATE"**
   (b) **250 INPUT #1, COST; PROFIT**
   (c) **300 PRINT #3 A$; ","; B**
4. The following program segment is supposed to create and display (on the screen) a file containing the integers from 1 to 100, but is not run properly. Correct the errors.

```
100  OPEN "WRONG" FOR INPUT AS #1
110  FOR K 1 TO 100
120  PRINT #1, K
130  NEXT K
140  FOR K 1 TO 100
```

```
150  INPUT #1, K
160  PRINT #2, K
170  NEXT K
180  CLOSE #1
```

5. Which of the following is not a valid file name?
   (a) **PARTS.DAT**
   (b) **PARTSDAT**
   (c) **PARTS DAT**
   (d) **PARTS**

6. Find the syntax errors in the following statements:
   (a) `20 OPEN "SALES" AS #1 FOR OUTPUT`
   (b) `25 PRINT #2 A; ","; B$; ","; COST`
   (c) `INPUT #3, S: T; P`

7. The following program segment is supposed to create and display a file of numbers. Correct the errors in it.

```
200  OPEN "PAYFILE"FOR INPUT AS #1
210  FOR K 1 TO 6
220  READ N
230  PRINT #2, N
240  NEXT K
250  FOR K 1 TO 6
260  WRITE #1, N
270  PRINT N
280  NEXT K
290  CLOSE #1
300  DATA 6,9, 36, 48, 100
```

8. A series of **DATA** statements is sometimes called an internal file. In what ways is an internal file similar to and in what ways is it different from, an external sequential data file?

9. Assume that a file **PAYROLL** exists with records of the form employee number (NUM), name (**NM$**),rate of pay (**RATE**) and a sentinel record of **0, "ZZZ",0.** Write a program segment that
   (a) renames this file as **PAY**.
   (b) deletes a records with employee number 138.
   (c) adds the record **167,"M.JAYANT", 9.35**
   (d) changes the rate of pay of employee **456** to **7.89**

ANSWERS

1. (1) T (2) T (3) T (4) T (5) F (6) F (7) T (8) F (9) T (10) T (11) F (12) F (13) T
   (a) 20 OPEN "FILE1" FOR OUTPUT AS #1
   (b) 25 WRITE #2, A, B, C
   (c) 30 KILL "FILE3"
2. (a) 20 OPEN "FILE1" FOR OUTPUT AS #1
   (b) 25 PRINT #1, A, B, C
   (c) 30 CLOSE # 1
3. Change:
   200 OPEN "WRONG" FOR OUTPUT AS #1
   260 PRINT K
   Insert: **233 CLOSE #1**
   236 OPEN "WRONG" FOR INPUT AS #1
4.

```
100 OPEN "PAYFILE"FOR INPUT AS #1
110 FOR K = 1 TO 100
120 PRINT #1, K
130 NEXT K
140 CLOSE
150 OPEN "WRONG"FOR INPUT AS #1
160 FOR I = 1 TO 100
170 INPUT #1, K
180 PRINT K
190 NEXT I
200 CLOSE #1
```

5. (c) is not valid.
6. (a) `20 OPEN "SALES" FOR OUTPUT AS #1`
   (b) `25 PRINT #2, A; ","; B$; ","; COST`
   (c) `30 INPUT #3, S, T, P`

7. Change the following lines:

```
200  OPEN "PAYFILE" FOR OUTPUT
     AS #1
230  PRINT #1, N
260  INPUT #1, N
```

Insert the following lines:

```
243   CLOSE #1
246   OPEN "PAYBILL" FOR INPUT
      AS #1
```

8. The similarities are that records must be accessed sequentially, records are separated by carriage returns; items in records are separated by commas. The differences are that **DATA** statements are part of the program; data in them must be known at the time the program is written. Sequential files can store the output of a program; and can be used by several different programs.

9. (a)
```
200 NAME "PAYROLL" AS "PAY"
```
(b)
```
300 OPEN "PAYROLL" FOR INPUT
    AS #1
310 OPEN "DUMP" FOR OUTPUT
    AS #2
320 REM
330 LET NUM 1
340 WHILE NUM < > 0
350 INPUT #1, NUM, NM$, RATE
360 IF NUM < > 138 THEN
    WRITE #2, NUM, NM$, RATE
370 WEND
```
(c)
```
400 OPEN "PAYROLL" FOR INPUT
    AS #1
410 OPEN "DUMP" FOR OUTPUT
    AS #2
420 REM
430 LET NUM 1
440 WHILE NUM < > 0
450 INPUT #1, NUM, NM$, RATE
455 IF NUM=0 THEN WRITE
    #2, 167, "M.JAYANT",9.35
460 WRITE #2, NUM, NM$, RATE
470 WEND
```
(d)
```
600 OPEN "PAYROLL" FOR INPUT
    AS #1
610 OPEN "DUMP" FOR OUTPUT
    AS #2
620 REM
630 LET NUM=1
640 WHILE NUM < > 0
650 INPUT #1, NUM, NM$, RATE
660 IF NUM=456 THEN LET
    RATE = 7.89
670 WRITE #2, NUM, NM$, RATE
680 WEND
```

System Commands

15.1 System Command

It is an instruction to the computer to do something to the program. It is not preceded by a line number and does not become part of the program.LIST is an example of system command.

A BASIC command is commonly referred to as a system command, since it is recognized by BASIC as a request to perform a pre-defined operation built into that system on the entire program. Thus, commands are normally entered in direct mode without a line number; however, in BASICA, most commands can be entered in either direct or indirect mode. In comparison, a BASIC language statement is an instruction within a BASIC program that will be interpreted by that BASIC language interpreter to perform an operation within the program. Thus, commands can be thought of as initiating operations at the system level, while statements initiate operations at the program language level.

15.2 The command AUTO

AUTO provides new line numbers AUTOmatically when writing BASIC programs.

Format `AUTO linenum, inc`

After typing **AUTO**, a new BASIC line number is supplied each time the ENTER key is pressed. New program lines continue to appear until the BREAK key is pressed.

In above format linenum is optional and indicates the first line numberAUTO should supply. **AUTO 100**, for example, begins numbering with line **100. AUTO 24** begins with line **24. 10** is the default value for linenum. Using a period (.) instead of a number starts line numbering at the most recently used program line.

Examples

AUTO 5 produces the line numbers **5, 15, 25, 35...**

AUTO 100 produces the line numbers **100, 110, 120...**

AUTO 3 produces the line numbers **3, 13, 23, 33...**

In above format inc is the increment, or spacing, between line numbers. BASIC programs typically use an increment of **10**, as in **10, 20, 30**. The default value of inc is **10**. inc may be set to any positive integer. If inc is used without a linenum (as in **AUTO**, **10**), linenum defaults to zero (line number 0).

Examples

AUTO 100, 100 produces the line numbers **100, 200, 300...**

AUTO 8, 8 produces the line numbers **8, 16, 24, 32...**

AUTO ,10 produces the line numbers **0, 10, 20, 30...**

If either linenum or inc is omitted, the values from the last **AUTO** command are assumed.

Exercise 15.1

Type the **AUTO** command and press **ENTER**. The line number **10** is displayed After the number **10**, type this line:

```
10 REM A TEST FOR 'AUTO'
```

Pressing the ENTER key produces line number 20. Add the following:

```
20 REM LINE 20
```

Press ENTER again. Line number 30 appears. Press BREAK to exit the **AUTO** command, then **LIST** the program

If a BASIC program is in memory and AUTO issues a line number which already exists, an asterisk appears warning that this existing line will be erased if you proceed. Type:

```
AUTO 10
10*
```

Press ENTER to skip that line number, Line 10 remains unaltered and the next line number is displayed. Press BREAK to leave the **AUTO** command mode.

15.3 The command LOAD

The command **LOAD** is used to **LOAD** a program into memory from a disk drive or other storage device.

Format `LOAD filename, R`

where filename is the name of the program to be LOADed. See Appendix B for information on file names. R is an optional parameter that RUNs the program after it is loaded. R causes LOAD to act like RUN with the filename option.

Specifying the **.BAS** extension when LOADing BASIC programs is optional.

Examples

```
LOAD "MUSIC"
```

loads the program **MUSIC.BAS** into memory.

```
LOAD "A:DINGDONG.BAS"
```

loads the program **DINGDONG** from disk drive A:

```
LOAD "CHEM", R
```

loads and RUNs the program named CHEM.

Exercise 15.2

Type this program and save it as **LOAD.BAS**

```
10 REM "LOAD" DEMONSTRATION PROGRAM
20 PRINT "PROGRAM LOADED"
```

After saving, type **NEW** to erase it from memory and therefore from screen. Verify its erasure by typing **LIST**. Then type:

```
LOAD "LOAD"  R

Run

PROGRAM LOADED
```

Command structure	Operational result
LOAD "STAT"	Loads the program file named STAT from the default drive.
LOAD "C:\SALES\ANALYSIS"	Loads the program the named ANALYSIS in the SALES directory on drive C
LOAD "B:SALES.BAS,R	Loads and runs the program file named SALES with extension BAS on the diskette in drive B
100 LOAD "A: SALES.BAS,R	Loads and runs the program file named SALES with extension BAS from the diskette in drive A
200 LOAD "C:\SALES\DATA"	Loads but does not run the program file named DATA on the fixed disk under the directory named SALES

15.4. The command SAVE

The command SAVE records, or SAVEs, programs from memory to disk or to another storage device.

Format `SAVE filename, option`

where **`filename`** is a string variable or string constant enclosed in quotes which specifies the names under which the program is to be SAVEd. **`option`** defines the way the program is SAVEd.

,A	SAVEs the program in ASCII format (using the same characters displayed on the screen).
,P	SAVEs the program in a special Protected format. A program SAVEd with ,P can only be RUN. Any attempt to LIST, EDIT or add lines triggers an error message. Since a program SAVEd with this option cannot be unprotected, an unprotected copy should also be kept.
,B	SAVEs the program in a compressed Binary format. If option is omitted, programs are SAVEd to disk in a special abbreviated (tokenized) format which can be read by LOAD.

Examples

```
SAVE "ADDNUM"
```

SAVEs the program in memory as **`ADDNUM.BAS`**. (BASIC automatically adds a **`.BAS`** file extension to BASIC programs.)

```
SAVE "HANGMAN",A
```

SAVEs the program **`HANGMAN.BAS`** in ASCII format. This makes it possible to send the program over a telephone line, or to edit it with a word processing program.

Exercise 15.3

```
10 REM * SAVE DEMO PROGRAM *
20 PRINT " SAVE "
30 LIST
```

SAVE the program using the **`,P`** option. Type:

```
SAVE "PRO2" ,P
```

LOAD the program back into memory with LOAD "PRO2". Typing LIST, EDIT or trying to add new lines will produce an Illegal function call error.

Command structure	Operational result
SAVE "A:STAT	Saves program under name STAT in tokenized format on diskette in drive A
SAVE "A:STAT,A	Saves program under name STAT in ASCII format on diskette in drive A
SAVE "A:STAT,P	Saves program under name STAT in protected format on diskette in drive A
SAVE "C:\SALES\EST"	Saves program under name EST in the directory named SALES on the fixed disk drive C

15.5. The command RUN

The command RUN instructs BASIC to execute the program .

Format `RUN linenum`

where linenum is an optional program line number which specifies where program execution is to begin. If omitted, program execution begins with the first line.

Exercise 15.4

```
10 REM 'RUN' PROGRAM
20 PRINT "EXECUTION STARTED AT LINE 10"
30 PRINT
40 PRINT "EXECUTION ENDED AT LINE 40"
RUN
EXECUTION STARTED AT LINE 10
EXECUTION ENDED AT LINE 40
```

Type RUN 40 to force BASIC to start executing the program at line 40.

```
RUN 40
RUN
EXECUTION ENDED AT LINE 40
```

Another Format: `RUN filename, R`

where **filename** is the name of a BASIC program on disk. When RUN is used in this format, that program is loaded and is immediately executed. If the **,R** option is exercised, BASIC keeps all current data files **OPEN** for access by the new program; otherwise all data files will be closed. RUN can be used as a statement to "chain" programs together. When a program encounters **RUN**, all variables are reset to null, or 0, and all files closed (unless the ,R option is used). If **RUN** does not specify another filename, the current program is re-**RUN**. If **RUN** specifies a filename, then that program is loaded and executed. For example:

```
100 RUN "PRO1"
```

loads a new program named **PRO1** from disk and RUNs it.

Exercise 15.5

```
10 REM USING 'RUN' AS A STATEMENT
20 PRINT "HELLO"
30 RUN
```

```
RUN
HELLO
HELLO etc.
```

Press **BREAK** to regain control of the computer.

15.6. The command EDIT

EDIT is a command that activates a special BASIC feature which permits EDITing individual program lines.

Format `EDIT linenum`

where linenum is the number of the line to be edited A period can be substituted for linenum to specify the "current" line.

Examples

```
EDIT 50
```

displays line 50 of the program, puts the cursor on that line and places BASIC in the EDIT mode. The IBM EDIT combines the abilities of both a "line editor" and a "screen editor". Once EDIT mode has been entered, special keys are used to do the actual EDITing. Most of these keys are on the keypad.

15.7 The command CLS

The command **CLS** clears the Screen before printing the results or having the graphics display.ASCII code 12 can also be used.After **CLS** the cursor is placed on the first row and first column and program remains undisturbed.

Format `CLS`

Exercise 15.6

```
10 FOR X = 1 TO 15
20 PRINT "WATCH THAT SCREEN WILL BE CLEARED AFTER PRINTING THIS 15 TIMES";
30 NEXT X
40 CLS
```

You can do the same thing by changing line 40 with following

```
40 PRINT CHR$(12)
```

15.8 The command CONT

CONT command is used to restart, or CONTinue, program execution after it has been "broken" by a **STOP** statement or by pressing the BREAK key.Unlike the RUN command, which restarts execution at the beginning of the program, **CONT** resumes execution at the line following the BREAK. Also, program variables and data are not reset to zero by **CONT**.

Format `CONT`

CONT has no application as a program statement since it is only used when the program has been STOPped due to **STOP** statement.

Exercise 15.7

```
15 REM "CONT" PROGRAM
25 PRINT "ENTER THE `CONT' COMMAND"
35 STOP
45 PRINT "PROGRAM CONTINUED"
RUN
ENTER THE 'CONT' COMMAND
Break in 30
```

```
Ok
CONT
PROGRAM CONTINUED
```

If the program is edited after it is STOPped (or BREAK is pressed), **CONT** cannot make the program continue.

IBM BASICs allow **CONT** to CONTinue a program, after an END statement is encountered, but additional BASIC statements must appear after the END statement.

15.9 The command LIST

LIST is used to display one or more program lines.

Format: **LIST linenum, filename**

where **linenum** is the specific line number (or range of line numbers) to be displayed. The current line number can be abbreviated as a period, as in LIST . If a range of line numbers is desired to be listed,this can be accomplished by specifying the lowest number first, followed by a hyphen (-), then the highest number. To display line numbers 20 through 40, use LIST 20-40. If linenum is omitted, the entire program is LISTed.

filename is optional. When specified, the LIST output (normally displayed on the monitor) can be sent to a disk file, the printer, or out to the communications port. For example:

```
LIST, "LPT1:"
```

sends the program listing to a printer attached to LPT1.

To abort a LIST in progress, press BREAK key.For suspending, or "freezing," a LISTing, press [Ctrl] [Num Lock]

Examples

LIST displays all program lines.

NB: Though LIST is a command, it may appear as a program statement. It is very useful as the last program line for development and/or debugging. When used as a statement, the program is first LISTed and then stops.

Command structure	Operational result
LIST	Lists the entire program in memory on the screen
LIST 10	Lists line 10 in memory on the screen
LIST 20-60	Lists line 20 through line 60 on the screen
LIST 10-	Lists line 10 through the last line in memory on the screen
LIST -50	Lists all lines from the beginning of the program through line 50 on the screen
LIST .-100	Lists all lines from the current line through line 100 on the screen
LIST 500-.	Lists all lines from line 500 through the current line on the screen
LIST 50,"LPT1:"	Lists line 50 on the printer
LIST 50-500,"LPT1:	Lists lines 50 through 500 on the printer LIST -500,"LPT1:" Lists all lines from the beginning of the program in memory through line 500 on the printer.
LIST,10-300," A:JOB1.BAS"	Lists lines 10 through 300 from the program in memory to a file named JOB1 with the extension BAS on the diskette in the A drive.

LIST, "LIST.DAT" sends a copy of the program in memory to disk and stores it under a file named LIST.DAT. LIST.DAT is in standard ASCII format so it can be further edited with a word processor or sent over a modem to another computer. The comma is required every time a program LISTing is sent to a filename.

15.10 The command DELETE

The command DELETE is used to "erase" specified program lines.

Format `DELETE linenum`

where **`linenum`** is the specific line number or range of line numbers to be removed from the program. The current line number can be abbreviated as a period (**`DELETE.`**). If a range of line numbers is to be DELETEd, the lowest number is listed first, followed by a hyphen and the highest number. To **`DELETE`** line numbers 30 to 50 (inclusive), use:

```
DELETE 30-50
```

Exercise 15.8

```
10 PRINT "LINE 10"
20 PRINT "LINE 20"
30 PRINT "LINE 30"
40 PRINT "LINE 40"
50 PRINT "LINE 50"
60 PRINT "LINE 60"
```

RUN the program to ensure that all lines are properly entered.

```
LINE 10
LINE 20
LINE 30
LINE 40
LINE 50
LINE 60
```

Type **`DELETE 40`** then **`RUN`** and **`LIST`** the program. This eliminates line **`40`**.

Type **`DELETE 20-30`**, then **`RUN`** the program. Lines **`20`** and **`30`** will vanish.

Command structure	**Operational result**
DELETE 30 or 30	Deletes line 30
DELETE 20-50	Deletes lines 20 to 50
DELETE -50	Deletes all line numbers up to and including line 50
DELETE .-50	Deletes all line numbers from the current line up to and including line 50
DELETE 20-.	Deletes all line numbers from 20 up to and including current line

NB: A program line can always be DELETEd by simply typing its line number, then pressing the ENTER key. To eliminate all program lines in one operation, enter NEW.

15.11. The command KILL

KILL removes access to a file or program from a diskette by removing its name from the disk directory. For all practical purposes, the file has been "KILLed." Once killed, a program may be "unKILLed" only by extraordinary means, and even then, recovery is not a certainty.

Format: `KILL filename`

where **filename** is the name of any BASIC, Binary or Data file on disk. It can be a string variable or a constant enclosed in quotes. If a specific drive number or DOS path is needed, it should be specified with the filename. KILL can be used either inside a program or in the command mode.

Example

```
KILL "PRO3.BAS"
```

Removes the file **PRO3.BAS** from the active drive. Note that the complete file name including file extension (**.BAS** in this case) must be specified.

The wildcard characters (? and *) can be used with **KILL** to remove groups of files with similar names. The question mark (?) is a wildcard used to replace a single character in filename. The asterisk (*) wildcard replaces a group of characters in filename.

15.12 The command NEW

The command NEW erases the BASIC program stored in memory and resets all variable values to zero or null. NEW is used before entering a NEW program to ensure that existing program has been deleted.

Format **NEW**

Exercise 15.9

```
10 REM * ENTERING NEW PROGRAM *
20 PRINT " GITA"
RUN
GITA
```

LIST the program to be sure, it has been entered as shown. Check the remaining memory space with the FRE(0) function.

Type **NEW** to erase the Program from memory. LIST to make sure it's gone.Type:

```
FRE (0)
```

To confirm that the available memory size has increased (due to the absence of the program in memory).

15.13. The command SYSTEM

Format **SYSTEM**

When BASIC executes a program line containing the SYSTEM command, or when SYSTEM is typed at the command level, the computer exits BASIC and returns to PC DOS. For example:

```
100 IF X = 5 THEN SYSTEM
```

returns to DOS if the value of X is 5.

CHAPTER 16

Programming Design and Problem Solving

16.1 Characteristics of a Good Program

The following are the main characteristics of a good and efficient computer program

(1) Correctness and performance

(2) Robustness

(3) User Friendly interface

(4) Documentation

(5) Adaptability

(6) Maintainability

(7) Portability

(8) Cost effectiveness.

(1) Correctness and Performance

Does the program (or system of programs) do what you want it to do? And does it respond fast enough? An accounting system may do exactly what you want it to do but may take an annoying amount of time to do it.

(2) Robustness

A robust program is one that produces meaningful output for any set of input data, regardless of how incorrect or implausible it is. Robustness is a very desirable property because it allows the program to maintain control, produce meaningful messages, and, if possible, keep on going. To write a robust program you should carefully check before you perform any potentially "dangerous" operations that could result in a run-time error. The occurrence of a run time error is usually an indication of a poorly written program.

(3) User Friendly Interface

Another important measure of a program is the quality of its user interface. Most users will treat your program as a "black box" that accepts some input and produces some output. They could not care less about what goes on inside and how we determine the results.

Their evaluation of the program will be based strictly on the interface between the program and the user, and how "friendly" it is.In case of Input whether

- Is it easy to prepare and submit?
- Is it easy to proof-read and verify?
- Will the machine accept it in the existing form or do
- I have to change it manually (e.g., units)?
- Are there defaults for things I choose to omit?

- Does the program tell you what input it is waiting for?
- Does the program have a "help mode" if the user is confused and does not know what to do? This feature is otherwise called as `User's Friendliness`. Some of the things which go into making a system easy to use are
- Does the user always know where she/he is within the system?
- Does the program handle data entry errors well?
- Is it easy to enter data using a minimum of keystrokes?

(4) Easy Documentation

Every program (software system) should have a user's guide. The purpose of this written documentation is to guide the user to a full understanding of the program and how to use it correctly.If a program is easy to read and understand, it is easier to find and correct errors. The program should be easy to test. If a program is not easy to test, it probably will not be tested. Consequently, no one including the programmer will have any confidence in the program.

(5) Adaptability

The user's actual needs will change from time to time. Therefore, a good program should be easy to change.

Users' needs are not static. They change frequently in response to such things as new laws, new ideas, new products, or new computer facilities. The ease with which such changes can be made is a measure of the program's adaptability. This aspect of program quality depends not only on program clarity, but also on modularity and program structure. Adaptability comes naturally from a well-structured, modular design because changes are localized to one or a few specific modules. The effects of the changes will not propagate to other program units.

(6) Maintainability

Program maintenance is the process of fixing program errors which arise during normal program use and during its improvement. Ideally, the program proves so useful that users like to continue it and request for various modifications. Hopefully, the program is easy to change.

(7) Portability

This means writing a program in a particular language and its particular version which can run on a particular operating system. If you are writing a program for BASICA or GW-BASIC it may not run on BBC MICRO, as BBC MICRO does not have the same facilities as are available in BASICA. The same thing happens with an updated version of the BASIC. Turbo-BASIC or Q-BASIC program cannot be adopted on the compiler of BASICA.

(8) Cost Effectiveness

This is the last but main criterion for which any of the features but the first one can be sacrificed. It is one of the key measures of program quality. Cost effectiveness is the ability to produce correct answers for the lowest possible cost. However, we must remember that costs must be measured over the life of the program and must include both the machine costs and the people costs of producing these programs.

(9) Other Tips on Good Styling

(a) Punctuation and formatting

Some care must be given to the matter of punctuation, particularly the use of the semicolon. The following rules apply.

(b) The END statement

Special rules apply to STOP and END. In BASICA it is not necessary to write END statement. However it is good practice to add END at the end of program either as a statement or as a direct command.

(c) The Layout

The layout of the program text should be designed for easy reading. Each constant definition, each variable declaration and each statement should be on a separate line. The symbols within each line should be well spaced out.

(d) Indentation

The use of indentation is closely related to the sequencing of groups of statements within a program. Whereas sequencing affects the order in which a group of operations is carried out, indentation illustrates the subordinate nature of individual statements within a group. The advantages of indentation are fairly obvious.

(e) Comments

Comments should always be included within a BASIC program with the help of REM statement. If written properly, such comments can provide a useful overview of the general program logic. They can also delineate major segments of a program, identify certain key items within the program and provide other useful information about the program. Comments of this type can be of great use to a programmer as well as to other persons trying to read and understand a program, since programmers sometimes forget the details of their own programs over a period of time. This is especially true of long, complicated programs. Frequently, the comments that are placed within a program need not be extensive; a few well-placed comments can shed a great deal of light on an otherwise obscure program.

It must be emphasized that these stylistic features are intended solely for the benefit of the human reader. The layout of the program text is of no concern to the compiler (except that consecutive words and numbers must be spaced apart, just as in ordinary English).Comments, also are entirely ignored by the compiler. Finally, any significance suggested to the human reader by remarks like WD WORKING-DAYS is quite lost on the compiler (which understands no English).

(f) Generation of legible output

Another important characteristic of a well-written program is its ability to generate clear, legible output. Two factors contribute to this legibility:

The first is labeling of the output data.

The second is the appearance of some of the input data along with the output, so that each set of input data (if there is more than one) can be clearly identified. The manner in which this is accomplished depends upon the environment in which the BASIC program will be executed.

16.2 Program Design

(1) Selection of Algorithm

There can be several alternative ways and approaches in solving of a problem.A selection of a particular method largely depends upon the accuracy and skill needed.There are several ways of calculating the anticipated population of a city or a nation but selection of proper mathematical estimation method depends upon the accuracy and social pattern of a particular occupancy.Wisdom plays a great role in deciding an algorithm of problem solving.

(2) Program Simplicity and Clarity

A program must be very simple and clear so that it could be easily understood not only by the person designing it but it should be in a format clearly understandable by all persons handling it.Complex logic and tricky coding may be avoided.Large expressions can be broken into parts.Most of the programs may have to be preserved and should therefore be documented in such a manner that it contains all information like name and purpose of the program, subroutines, functions, author's name, date of generation and programming,memory and time limitations.

Due to limitations of character in naming variables,it is very difficult to name the quantities,which are self-explanatory and representative.Therefore all such variables and symbols should be explained clearly using REM statements.Similarly all important sections of the program,loops and subroutines should begin with explanatory remarks indicating their purpose or function.These remarks are very helpful in understanding the program at a later date.

(3) Blank Spaces and Line

Blank spaces may be used to improve the appearance and legibility of program and its output or data input.This can be easily visualized from the following two examples which are exactly identical except for the introduction of few blank spaces in the later program.

```
LET A = B*C^3 LET A = B * C ^ 3
FOR I=1 TO 25 STEP 1 FOR I = 1 TO 25 STEP 1
PRINT X,Y,Z PRINT X,Y,Z
```

Blank spaces can help in editing of the wrong statements and it may help in debugging also. However, it may be noted that there should not be any gap between TAB and its argument.It is peculiar with BASIC that it is the only TAB function which calls for its argument written immediately after it.Rest all function's argument may have gaps in between.

(4) Selection of Mathematical Operators

Arithmetical expressions are constituted using arithmetical operators:addition, subtraction, multiplication,division and exponentiation. In all computers, addition and subtraction are basic hardware operations.

In some machines,multiplication and division are carried out by machine language routines,while in others these operations may be included in the set of hardware operations.Multiplications is normally more efficient and consumes less computer time than the operation of division. Exponentiation is performed by machine language routines and hence more time is taken up by the exponentiation operation.Thus,note that arithmetical operations are performed at different speeds. Computing speed decreases as we move from left to right in using operators **+, -, ***, / and ^.

As addition is faster than multiplication,addition may be substituted for multiplication in cases where smaller number of operations are involved. For example, the expression 3*B may be replaced by **B+B+B**. But if the expressions are not made up of integer quantities, inaccuracy may be introduced because of the way real (floating point) arithmetic is performed in the machine.Therefore round off or truncation error may also occur. For instance,**3.0*B** is more accurate than **B+B+B**.Thus,each problem should be judged according to the given situation.

The operation of multiplication is faster than that of division, Therefore, wherever possible, division should be replaced by multiplication. Consider the statements

```
30 FOR M = 1 TO 500
40 B(N) = A(M)/2.0
50 NEXT M
```

It will be more efficient if we write these statements as:

```
30 FOR M = 1 TO 500
40 B(N) = 0.5*A(M)
50 NEXT M
```

In statement 40,we have undertaken multiplication by 0.5 in place of division operation by 2.

Exponentiation is the slowest of all the operations.It may be replaced by multiplication whenever possible. For instance, **X^2** is less efficient than **X*X**. This is because exponentiation is performed by library subprograms.Repeated multiplication saves both time and computer memory spaces.

Integer quantities should be used as exponents (powers) as far as possible. This is because when integers are used as exponents, the operation is performed by repeated multiplications. When floating point quantities are employed as powers, a special library routine is invoked to perform operations. For example, evaluation of the expression N^8.0 is performed more slowly than the expression N^8.

(5) Generality of the Program

Several times,some expressions in a program are to be evaluated again and again. Such expressions should be calculated at a place, stored as a variable,and then should be used wherever needed.Consider the statements:

```
30 LET A = (B + C) + D
40 LET E = (B + C + D) / F
50 LET G = EXP(3.0*(B + C) ^ 7)
```

Here the expression **B + C** occurs in all the three statements. So, introduce a variable **X** in all the statements.The above statements can be coded as:

```
60 LET X = B + C
70 LET A = X + D
80 LET E = (X + D) / F
90 LET G = EXP (3.0 * X)^7
```

This saves time (though more memory is needed) when calculations are to be done repeatedly.

(6) Interdependence

When a program is prepared,care should be taken to minimize its dependence on a particular value of a parameter. For example, consider the following program:

```
10 LET A =4
20 LET B = 5
30 LET C = SQR(A ^ 2 + B ^ 2)
```

This program has been written to compute the value of hypotenuse of a right-angled triangle having arms of length 4 and 5 units.The same set of statements cannot be used for any other values of **A** and **B**. A more general form could be

```
10 READ A,B
20 LET C = SQR(A ^ 2 + B ^ 2)
```

Without changing any statement,it is possible to compute C for various values of A and B.

(7) Versatility of Program

Another important place where generality is desirable is the **FOR / NEXT** Statement.The program

```
15 LET S = 0
20 FOR I = 1 TO 10 STEP 1
30 LET S = S + 1
40 NEXT I
```

adds numbers 1,2 and 10.Suppose more numbers are to be added or only odd numbers to be added,this program has to be modified.The following generality can accomplish all these tasks.

```
15 LET S = 0
20 INPUT L,M,N
30 FOR I = L TO M STEP N
40 LET S = S + 1
50 NEXT I
```

By changing the values of **L,M** and **N**, we can accomplish various tasks. For example,

(a) for **L = 1,M = 25** and **N = 1**,

the program adds all the numbers from **1** to **25**;

(b) for **L = 1,M = 100** and **N = 2**,

the program adds all the odd numbers upto 100,and

(c) for **L = 2,M = 100** and **N = 2**,

it adds all even numbers upto and including 100.

(8) Minimization Techniques with Subscripted Variables

(1) Sizing of Arrays

When handling subscripted variables,it is always useful to denote the size of the arrays by variables rather than constants.Then the array variables can be used to handle any size without much modifications.

(2) Subscripted variables are very useful in a ranging and processing data and thus play an important role in computer programming. But their use involves more memory storage and machine time. While using subscripts, the following cares which result in improved efficiency of the program must be taken:

Consider the evaluation of following term in a program:

```
A(7)^2 + A(7)/B + COS(A(7))
```

Here the subscripted variable A(7) is being used three times. If we replace A(7) by a simple variable X as X A(7) then above expression can be rewritten as:

```
X^2 + X/B + COS(X)
```

Here, the subscripted variable needs evaluation only once. This reduces the execution time.

Similarly, the statement such as:

```
40 FOR J = 1 TO 500
50 FOR K = 1 TO 500
60 LET A(K) = A(K) * B(J)
```

should be coded as

```
40 FOR J = 1 TO 500
50 LET R = B(J)
60 FOR K = 1 TO 500
70 LET A(K) = A(K)*R
```

More the number of values a subscript assumes,the less efficient is the program,as the computer has to search for more values of subscripted variables. For instance, use of **X(20,40)** in a program will require more machine time than **X(800)**. So, whenever possible, programmer should try to use simple variables in place of one dimensional arrays,and one-dimensional arrays in place of two-dimensional arrays.

(9) Minimizing GOTO Statements

The use of unconditional **GOTO** statement should be avoided in a program.This is because tracing the flow of a program execution and debugging (finding an error in the program) becomes more difficult. However, for multiple branching,**ON-GOTO** Statement may be employed.For instance,the purpose achieved by the statements

```
105 IF J = 1 THEN 15
110 IF J = 2 THEN 16
120 IF J = 3 THEN 17
130 IF J = 4 THEN 18
```

may also be achieved more efficiently,by·the statement which saves computer memory as well.

```
140 ON J GOTO 15,16,17,18
```

The **GOTO** statements are a major source of difficulty in understanding the logic of a program. Although in many cases, it is difficult to avoid the use of **GOTO** Statements, it is good to minimize their number.

(a) Consider the following sample program:

```
20 Read P,Q,R,S
30 GOTO 80
40 LET Z = X * Y
50 GOTO 100
60 LET Y = R - S
70 GOTO 40
80 LET X = P + Q
90 GOTO 60
100 PRINT Z
105 DATA , , ,
110 END
```

Here **GOTO** statements have been unnecessarily used.In fact following seven statements shall be sufficient.

```
20 READ P,Q,R,S
30 LET X = P + Q
40 LET Y = R - S
50 LET Z = X * Y
60 PRINT Z
65 DATA
70 END
```

(b) The **GOTO** statements are normally used with **IF / THEN** statements .The program:

```
150 IF X > 500 THEN 170
160 GOTO 190
170 LET T = 0.15 * X
180 GOTO 200
190 LET T = 0
200 LET N = X - T
```

can be modified as:

```
150 IF X < 500 THEN 180
160 LET T = 0
170 GOTO 190
180 LET T = 0.15 * X
190 LET N = X - T
```

Here we have reduced the number of GO TO statements from 2 to 1.

(10) Use of FOR / NEXT Statement

The **FOR/NEXT** loops inevitably occur practically in almost every program.They involve an indexed variable whose value is adjusted and tested every time the **FOR/NEXT** loop is executed.This consumes computer time. Therefore, **FOR/NEXT** loops should be introduced only when calculations are to be repeated several times. For instance, calculation of the sum of **A(1), A(2), A(3)** as

```
40 LET S = A(1) + A(2) + A(3)
```

is faster than calculating the sum as

```
50 LET S = 0
60 FOR K = 1 TO 3
70 LET S = S + A(K)
80 NEXT K
```

This is because the value of k is compared with 3,every time the statement **FOR/NEXT** in line 60 is executed,while in the case of the statement 40,no checking of value is involved.In the second case;therefore it will need more computer memory and time.

Computer takes up more time in execution of a program if there are more of **FOR/NEXT** loops, due to time involved in checking.Thus,it is preferable to reduce the number of loop executions as far as possible. For instance, changing the statements:

```
70 FOR I= 1 TO 500
80 LET A(I) 0
  90 NEXT I
  to
70 FOR I= 1 TO 500 STEP 2
80 LET A(I) 0
90 LET A(I+1) = 0.0
100 NEXT I
```

reduces the number of loop executions by a factor of 2. However, additional computing is involved due to the subscripted variable A(I+1) in statement 90.Still it leads to saving in computer time as the loop increments and tests are more complex.Also more storage space is needed for the extra line 90.

Many **FOR/TO** statements may be combined to achieve the same purpose in a program. For example, the following statements:

```
90 FOR I = 1 TO 500
100 LET M(I) = 1
110 NEXT I
120 FOR J = 1 TO 500
130 LET N(J) = 1
140 NEXT J
```

may be combined as below so that only one **FOR-NEXT** loop is required.It saves in both i.e. computer time involved and in booking memory locations:

```
90 FOR I= 1 TO 500
100 LET M(I) = N(I) = 1
110 NEXT I
```

Let us see the following program

```
110 FOR J = 1 TO N
120 LET X(J) = EXP(2*C5) + SQR(J)
130 NEXT J
```

Here **2*C5** will be calculated for all values of j from **1** to **N.** If we rewrite the above statement as:

```
110 LET Y = EXP(2*C 5)
120 FOR J = 1 TO n
130 LET X(J) = Y + SQR(J)
140 NEXT J
```

the program will be executed much faster.

(11) Output Formation

This portion of programming should be given utmost care.There is no use of writing an efficient program if its output results are difficult in interpretation. A poorly designed output not only takes long time in printing but may render itself very difficult in reading and sometimes may lead to wrong conclusions.The format of output should always be defined in the program.

(12) Structuring the Program

It is the method of preparation of a program in such a manner that each of its sections consist of an independent set of small modules which are self contained.Each module is designed as a single entry single exit block of coding, although due to this the program may become little lengthy in typing, but they help the programmer in reading, debugging and testing.Thus, these programs use,minimum number of GOTO statements.

(13) Program Efficiency

A program which requires least memory locations and takes minimum time in execution is called most efficient program.Since the length of a program is very much concerned with utilizing two major resources of a computer system,namely memory and computer time,every possible efforts should be made to synthesize the program in such a manner that it takes least time in writing and execution as well as in booking memory locations.However,the prime concern of a programmer should be the correctness and accuracy of results rather than the efficiency of program.Therefore,as a general rule the programmer should tend to optimize in its requirement of resource utilization. Syntax error could be then found out by debugging facilities.

The following steps should be adopted to minimize the memory requirement.

1. Selection of algorithm in such a manner that needs fewer steps but this should not be done at the cost of accuracy.
2. Minimize the number of variables required.
3. When a variable is not required any more in the program, reuse it rather than selecting another variable.
4. Minimize the use of string variables.
5. Do not store heading lines in memory; use them in **PRINT** statements directly as string constants.
6. When you use array variables,declare their sizes exactly in **DIM** statements.
7. Do not read anything which can be calculated inside the program.
8. Do not break large expressions into small bits using new variables (unless it is essential)
9. Wherever possible, use self-replacement statements.

(14) Selection of Proper Algorithm

An algorithm is a procedure to solve a problem which is translated into a programming language. Proper choice of an algorithm, in the beginning before coding it into a program, is very important.It saves in coding effort and makes the program more efficient. Let us consider the evaluation of the polynomial

```
Y = PX3 + QX2 + RX + S
```

which may be expressed in the form of a statement as

```
330 LET Y= P*X*X*X+ Q*X*X + R*X + S
```

Here the computer has to do six multiplications and three additions. We may rewrite the polynomial formula as:

```
Y = X(PX2 + QX + R) + S
  = X(X(PX+Q)+R) + S
```

This may be programmed as:

```
330 LET Y = X*(X*(P*X+Q)+R)+S
```

Now there are only three multiplications and three additions present.Therefore, this statement is more efficient.

Let us consider the evaluation of

$$A = \ln(B^2) - \ln(C^2)$$

Normally the beginner will write the program like

```
300 LET A=LOG(B*B)-LOG (C*C)
```

But an efficient way to do this computation is by writing:

$$A = \ln(B^2 / C^2)$$

$$\ln(B / C)^2$$

$$2\ln(B / C)$$

with the corresponding BASIC code as

```
300 A 2 * LOG(B / C)
```

(15) Execution Time

Any programmer should strive for as much time saving as is possible, because time is the costliest resource. Time saving becomes more important when a program is to be used repeatedly. Some methods have been already discussed earlier. However following resources must be adopted for minimizing the execution time, apart from whatever can be deduced by common sense and intelligent applications of tricks.

(a) We have already seen that computing speed decreases as we go from operations **+, -, /, *, ^,**. Therefore one should try to replace slow operators by fast operators as far as possible. Few examples will make the issue more clear:

(a) Replace **X^3** by **X*X*X**

(b) Replace **3*Y** by **Y*Y*Y**

(c) Replace **N/5** by **0.2 N**

Exponentiation can be reduced to series of multiplication as is clear from following:

Slower Program

```
10 INPUT Z
20 Z2 Z^2
30 Z3 Z^3
40 PRINT Z, Z2, Z3
50 END
```

Modified Program

```
10 INPUT Z
20 Z2 Z * Z
30 Z3 Z2 * Z
40 PRINT Z, Z2, Z3
50 END
```

Above programs calculate the square and cube of the given numbers.Although both the programs are correct, the modified program is more efficient.Exponentiation takes more time since it is performed by library subprograms.Repeated multiplication saves both in time and in memory allocations.

16.3 Program Errors

When a program is compiled or executed, it may produce a variety of errors. Errors do occur in almost all programs, no matter how experienced is the programmer. The beginning programmer may become discouraged because of bugs, but this should not be the case. Debugging should be considered to be a part of programming. In general, bugs can be divided into two categories. The first type is detected during compilation while the second is detected during or after execution. If the rules of syntax are violated, then the program will not compile. On the other hand even if the program is syntactically perfect, there can be a logical error.

The three types of errors that can occur in a program are

(a) syntax error,

(b) run-time errors, and

(c) logic errors.

16.3.1 Syntax Errors

Syntax errors occur when there is a violation in any of the rules of language formation. Errors caused by misunderstanding or misinterpreting the syntax and type rules of the programming language are trivial. Mistakes may arise due to applying rules of one higher language to another. A student who has learnt PASCAL and FORTRAN first and now learning BASIC may tend to apply rules of these two languages into the statements being written in BASIC.

A person habitual of PASCAL may tend to write the assignment statement **MARK : 5** instead of **MARK 5** and **WRITELN** instead of **PRINT**. These errors are usually easy to correct because the compiler will point out where an error has occurred. These error messages are produced by the BASIC interpreter or compiler while it is attempting to translate a BASIC program into machine language. Any grammatical mistake will cause problems when the translation is performed. The compiler will attempt to produce a message indicating where and what the mistake is.

16.3.2 Run-time Errors

A run-time error is an error which is detected during the execution of the program. It is defined as an error occurring in the program that causes abnormal program behavior during execution.These errors are usually easy to find and correct. For example, when the computer tries to execute this statement

```
AVERAGE = TOTAL / COUNT
AVERAGE = SUM DIV NUMBER
```

with the value of zero in variable **COUNT** or **NUMBER**, a run-time error occurs. The computer will simply halt because it will not know what to do when requested to divide by zero.

This fact will not be apparent until the program is actually executed, and that is why it is termed a run-time error.

Some of the most common run-time errors include:

1. Taking square-root of a negative number
2. Division by zero
3. Subscript out of order.

16.3.3 Logic Errors

A logic error is an error which causes the computer to do something other than what was intended. These errors must be found and corrected by the programmer. Sometimes this can be a time consuming and difficult job. Moreover, computer does not help in sorting out such errors anyway.

Once it is recognized that an error exists, there are two steps involved in debugging. First, the error (bug) has to be pinpointed. Then it has to be corrected.

16.4 Debugging

Debugging is the process of checking the correctness of the Debugging either manually or through means provided with the compiler program for error checking as already discussed.

It's unusual for complex programs to run to completion on the first attempt. In fact, the time spent in DEBUGGING and testing often equals or exceeds the time spent in program coding. To reduce the number of errors, the programmer should carefully check the coding for accuracy before entering it into the computer. This DESK-CHECKING process should include an examination of program logic and program completeness. Furthermore, typical input data should be manually traced through the program processing paths to identify possible errors. After desk-checking, an attempt is made to convert the source program into object program form. Compiler programs and interpreters contain error-diagnostic features, which detect (and print messages about) mistakes caused by the incorrect application of the language used to prepare the source program.

When changes have been made in response to detected errors, a new compilation can be ordered. This process may continue until all detected syntax errors have been remedied.

16.5 Testing

The purpose of testing is to determine whether the results are correct. The testing procedure involves using the program to process input test data that will produce known results. The items developed for testing should include:

- Typical data, which will test the generally used program paths.
- Unusual but valid data, which will test the program paths used to handle exceptions.
- Incorrect, incomplete, or inappropriate data, which will test the program error-handling capabilities.

A testing procedure that is often followed is to separately test different portions of a program. this helps to isolate detected errors to a particular program segment. The use of a modular programming approach, of course, eases this procedure. Another technique that is often used is to entrust much of the testing to someone other than the programmer who wrote the code. A fresh outlook is often helpful and errors that are missed by a programmer who is "too familiar" with the code may be easily picked up by someone else.

EXERCISES

1. What is meant by top-down programming? Discuss its advantages.

   How does it differ from top-down programming?
2. Name at least one other characteristic of structured programming
3. Discuss the necessity for placing comments within a basic program? How extensive should these comments be?
4. How many types of errors can occur in a program? What is meant by a syntactical error?
5. What is meant by a logical error? How do syntactical errors and logical errors differ from one another?
6. State some of the common syntactical and logical errors with arbitrary examples. State what are diagnostic messages.

TEST YOUR KNOWLEDGE

1. The goals of structured programming include reducing and associated with program development while increasing
2. Top-down design involves breaking a problem into subproblems that can be written as separate each performing a particular task.

ANSWERS

1. Time; costs; producitvity.
2. Modules,